What Twenty-Eight of the World's Foremost E-Learning Leaders and Thinkers Say about *Adding Some TEC-VARIETY*

"As online learning continues to evolve, we hear a great deal about the access it allows and the flexibility it provides. But as Bonk and Khoo so clearly demonstrate, it also affords endless opportunities to engage and inspire learners of all ages and abilities. Using a well-researched theoretical framework, they have captured more than 100 easy-to-replicate virtual learning activities, guaranteed to enrich any technology-enhanced learning environment. This powerful and practical resource is a must-read for educators in any setting, looking to expand their repertoire of evidence-based, student-focused teaching tools and strategies."

—Susan C. Aldridge, PhD, President
Drexel University Online

"The arrival of the digital era offers vast opportunities and challenges to higher education institutions in facing a new culture of teaching and learning. This book by Drs. Curtis Bonk and Elaine Khoo bring new insights on how we can maneuver through the complexities of online teaching and learning. TEC-VARIETY tackles motivation and retention grounded in psychology research. This is one of the few books that has scholarly rigor and is interesting and engaging reading. It is a must for academics, scholars, and course developers."

—Grace Javier Alfonso, PhD, Chancellor
University of the Philippines, Open University

*"What a grand book! This is going to be a highly valuable resource for countless instructors and designers in online learning. **Adding TEC-VARIETY** is unique in that it combines the theoretical and pedagogical foundations of effective learning with 100 easy-to-implement activities that promote the engagement of online students in deep learning. These strategies can instantly breathe life into courses that fail to tap the enthusiasm and imagination of students. **TEC-VARIETY** has become a handbook for my design of engagement in online classes."*

—Ray Schroeder, Associate Vice Chancellor for Online Learning and
Founding Director of the Center for Online Learning, Research and Service (COLRS)
University of Illinois Springfield

"This is the best way forward for those of us teaching online, Bonk and Khoo have provided a wealth of activities to ensure that the interactions online really do enhance the experience. Increasingly as the world splits into big and small data—MOOCs and apps, this book can help us ensure that better learning and teaching can follow. The work shows the journey that we have taken over several years to improve the experience and learning outcomes for the distance and online learner. It suggests great strategies (100 actually!) based in solid theoretical foundations with loads of practical suggestions. I particularly enjoyed Chapter 14 with strategies about how you might work with colleagues to encourage them to try some of the ideas."

—Professor John Hedberg, PhD, Millennium Innovations Professor of ICT
and Education, School of Education, Macquarie University, Australia

"Whilst some educators are still pondering whether to move towards the 'new' world of on-line, Bonk and Khoo have captured 2 decades of e-experience into one highly usable guide. They offer us immense joy for the online world—a principles-based approach to motivation and engagement offering variety but also ways for us to make thoughtful choices in the service of full engagement for learners. You can search for whatever your latest pedagogical challenge demands—feedback, surprise, tension, involvement . . . name your own adjective . . . and find a solution! Don't go online without it!"

—Professor Gilly Salmon, Pro Vice Chancellor Learning Transformations
Swinburne University of Technology, Melbourne, and author of *E-moderating and E-tivities*

"No more excuses for boring online courses! The TEC-VARIETY framework is the ulti-mate approach to combining theory and practice in online and blended learning. Not only do Bonk and Khoo present a solid theoretical framework on which online and blended learning rests, they couple that with fun, practical exercises far beyond "read and discuss" courses. The result? A highly dynamic place of motivation and engagement. This is a must read for anyone who works online."

—Rena M. Palloff, PhD, Faculty, Fielding Graduate University and Owner/Lead Consultant,
Crossroads West, and author of numerous books about online and virtual learning,
most recently, the 2nd edition of *Lessons from the Virtual Classroom*

"Curt Bonk and Elaine Khoo provide a welcome, much-needed resource for online teaching and learning, offering an amazing array of ideas and activities to transform online content delivery into a motivating and exciting way to learn. This toolbox of great yet very practical and tested ideas will spark the imagination of online teachers in ways to engage learners with the curriculum. It will also deepen our understanding of the potential of online educa-tion. Learning and curiosity about our world is our most basic human characteristic, and with this book Bonk and Khoo introduce educators to activities that can encourage and motivate innovative thinking and doing in online learning environments. Imagine having access to a 100+ activities that we can use or customize for our online classes: that's an apple for the teacher with a cherry on top!"

—Linda Harasim, PhD, Professor, School of Communication,
Simon Fraser University, and author of five books about collaborative technologies and online
learning, most recently, *Learning Theory and Online Technologies*

"Back in 1987, Chickering and Gamson articulated seven principles of good teaching. Then came the web, online learning, MOOCs, and myriad directions in support of student success. With clarity and verve, Bonk and Khoo combine memorable acronym with moti-vational principles that move us into meaningful action. Reflect on the stories, examples, and ideas herein; raise awareness and engagement; and become motivated to recraft and perfect the art of online instruction. Awesome book!"

—Ann Hill Duin, PhD, Professor of Writing Studies, University of Minnesota,
and author of several books in higher education and information
technology, most recently, *Cultivating Change in the Academy*

"Professors Bonk and Khoo answer the dreams of all faculty development departments. Their **Adding Some TEC-VARIETY** is the perfect primer for incoming faculty and a page-turning reminder to the old-timers that this "new-fangled" online methodology is not only here to stay but it works."

—Robert F. Bromber, PhD, Head, Education Technology Branch, Marine Corps University

"How to engage and motivate online learners has long been the enduring problem that frustrates online instructors and scares away many would-be online instructors. Bonk and Khoo form a dynamic duo leveraging over three decades of research to deliver a rare book that offers substantial theoretical insights into the problem while also giving clear practical guidance on how to apply those insights. This is a book that deserves a special place on your digital bookshelf, worth turning to again and again for examples and inspiration as you plan your next online adventure in learning."

—Michael Wesch, Associate Professor of Anthropology
Kansas State University

"e-Learning has been around more than two decades and now it is part of mainstream instruction. It is time to be concerned with the emotional aspects of online learners for their deep and impactful learning. With this book, Curt Bonk and Elaine Khoo, who have each been investigating e-learning for a long time, do exactly that. They have taken many years to thoroughly review the research literature and lead us on a wonderful journey through countless innovative instructional practices that they have seen or experimented with. Get this book—it contains extensive methods of how instructors can promote quality learning with some TEC-VARIETY."

—Okhwa Lee, Professor, Dept. of Education, Director, Educational Research Institute
Chungbuk National University, South Korea

"Bonk and Khoo wrote an excellent book, providing many interesting learning activities for online tutors, teachers, developers, etc. It is not necessary anymore to be extremely creative to find the right online pedagogic activity for your students. You just need this book and your classes will instantly become more fun. I'm definitely going to use it with my students!"

—Theo J. Bastiaens, PhD, Professor of Educational Technology
Fernuniversität in Hagen, Germany and Open Universiteit, Netherlands

"Bonk and Khoo suggest that we all need to "renew our passport" to prepare for innovative and exciting online learning adventures. Their new book, **TEC-VARIETY**, provides a roadmap for online and blended learning excursions. Using 10 themes and then charting 10 pathways to learning for each, the authors offer a unique framework that online instructors will find invaluable. One of the most useful part of the book is the final section detailing the Web tools mentioned in each chapter. Thirty years ago when we started using computers, they did little without additional hundreds of dollars invested in software. Today our digital devices can literally transport us around the world with minimal cost."

—Margaret Riel, Director, Center for Collaborative Action Research
Pepperdine University

"One of the most common complaints I hear from organizations that offer online education is that many—sometimes most—learners do not finish online courses and those who do often are not very engaged by the experience. It would be hard to underestimate the impact **Adding Some TEC-VARIETY** could have for these organizations and, more importantly, their learners. Curt Bonk and Elaine Khoo have created a highly practical, highly actionable resource for anyone serious about creating truly successful online learning experiences."

—Jeff Cobb, Host of Mission to Learn, and author of
Leading the Learning Revolution and *10 Ways to Be a Better Learner*

*"**TEC-VARIETY** is the kind of book that every teacher would need to have as a guide for their online teaching and learning. Through years of research and experiences we know that student retention is a major problem in distance and online learning, and motivating students plays a significant role in the learning process. This book by Prof. Curt J. Bonk and Dr. Elaine Khoo is a repository of ideas on motivating your learners online and how to engage them in learning. In it, you have over 100 ideas organized systematically within the TEC-VARIETY framework. I even found the CTRL-D (indicating cost, time, risks, learner-centeredness indices, and duration for each activity) as given by the author as guide at the end of each activity highly useful. If you are looking for practical tips to improve student retention, here is the 'Library of Congress' for you to choose from!"*

—Sanjaya Mishra, Director, Commonwealth Educational Media Centre for Asia
New Delhi, India and editor of *Interactive Multimedia in Education and Training* and *Cases on Global E-learning Practices*

"With the rising demand for online courses more and more instructors are being asked to teach online, often with little or no preparation. To them, as well as to more experienced instructors, Bonk and Khoo's book is a godsend. The authors set out the TEC-VARIETY framework to guide instructors on how to enhance online courses in 10 areas including student boosting student curiosity, engagement, and motivation. For each of these 10 areas they provide 10 online activities to support them. What sets this book apart from other similar ones is that Bonk and Khoo provide a solid research base to justify the activities. I'm recommending the book to all of my faculty who teach or intend to teach online!"

—Ron Owston, PhD, Dean, Faculty of Education, University Professor,
and Founding Director of the Institute for Research on Learning Technologies (IRLT)
York University, Toronto, Ontario, Canada

"Bonk and Khoo articulate that we are in the 'Learning Century' and explain that learning now resides within everyone's reach. They highlight how important it is for instructors and designers to understand theory to better meet the needs of adult learners. In practice, this means that educators must also take into account the wider sociocultural, developmental, and ecological factors influencing learner actions. Using a theory to practice approach, this book offers great tools for educators and designers who want to motivate and actively engage learners in the online environment in this new learning age."

—Simone C.O. Conceição, PhD, Professor, Department of Administrative Leadership,
School of Education, University of Wisconsin-Milwaukee School of Education,
and author of five books on online teaching and learning, most recently,
Motivating and Retaining Online Students: Research-Based Strategies That Work

*"In my job as an officer, I meet young cadets who are eager to learn for their future occupation. My job is to keep them motivated to do just that and this is why I enthusiastically embrace the contents of this book. It is easy to understand, use, and access. **Adding Some TEC-VARIETY** and the 100+ activities described are a perfect tool for those who want to make a difference in their online teaching. So, what are you waiting for? Go and discover the benefits of TEC-VARIETY. And that´s an order!"*

—Major Thomas Lyck is the Head Teacher of War Studies
at The Swedish Armed Forces School of Logistics, Skoevde, Sweden

"WOW! After getting an advance copy of **TEC-VARIETY**, I immediately emailed Curt Bonk to see if I could share it with my online course design team. The book is already a "go-to" resource for fresh course development ideas."

—Rovy Branon, PhD, Associate Dean and Chief Technology Officer
University of Wisconsin-Extension's Continuing Education,
Outreach and E-Learning Division

"Are you usually suspicious of books full of activities, tips and tricks? Do you find their lack of context and depth annoying? Me too, which is why I was so happily absorbed (but not surprised) by Curt Bonk and Elaine Khoo's most recent offering. Yes, this is a book chocka-block with ideas and practical tips for engaging learners in online learning, and for keeping them engaged. But it is more. This collection of useful approaches is grounded in learning theory and research, weathered by experience, and brought sharply into focus with clear examples, each with estimates of risk, time, cost, learner-centricity, and duration. The TEC-VARIETY categories ring true, and every reader, especially those with experience in online learning, will locate gaps in their own practice. For example, Bonk and Khoo treated me to a useful collection of fresh ideas for building curiosity and for creating helpful tension or dissipating counterproductive tension—things I've largely neglected in my own courses. I plan to keep extra copies of this book available for colleagues who think online learning is confined to correspondence school methodologies, and I'll either give them a copy or smack them over the head with one, depending on their redemption quotient."

—Richard Schwier, Professor and Head, Educational Technology and Design,
Department of Curriculum Studies, University of Saskatchewan,
and author of several educational technology books, most recently,
Connections: Virtual Learning Communities

"Every teacher would benefit from this book and should keep it next to their computer and close by wherever they go. **Adding Some TEC-VARIETY** provides easy to understand principles and teacher-friendly activities that students will love. If you believe in holistic education and would like to see your students engaged and happy, this book is for you."

—Dr. Nellie Deutsch, eLearning Professional Development Specialist,
online teacher at WizIQ, faculty member of Atlantic University,
Masters of Arts in Transpersonal and Leadership Studies, Toronto, Canada

"Curt Bonk and Elaine Khoo are most impressive with this latest handbook on motivating participants in online learning. **Adding Some TEC-VARIETY** is engagingly readable, in-for-matively research based, and highly practical with its 100 suggestions for what to do not only on Monday, but conceivably for an entire online course. Perhaps most significantly, this book is free and open and available for online instructors and practitioners to share. It is clear, the world is truly open!"

—Vance Stevens, Webheads in Action and HCT/CERT, Al Ain, UAE

"This book provides a wealth of ideas and strategies for establishing the three Rs (relevance, rigor, and relationships) for online learning."

—Norm Vaughan, Professor, Department of Education & Schooling,
Mount Royal University, Calgary, Alberta and author of *Blended Learning in Higher Education* and *Teaching in Blended Learning Environments*

"There is no reason for online students to not be engaged in your class. In **TEC-VARIETY**, Curt Bonk and Elaine Khoo demonstrate 100+ practical ways to motivate your students. A strongly motivated student can overcome a plethora of learning obstacles. Spend some time with this book and you can help your students love the subject matter as much as you do and clear up all their muddiest points. If you can't engage your students with just a handful of the 100+ practical ideas in this book, you might consider retirement."

—Al Lind, Vice President for Innovation and eLearning,
Council on Postsecondary Education, Kentucky Virtual Campus

"Finally there is a publication that every online educator needs to read! In **Adding Some TEC-VARIETY**, Bonk and Khoo have hit a home run by putting theory into action with principles we all need to teach with. From the introductory chapters focused on motivation and retention, to the fantastic principles with practical approaches anyone can put into action, online instructors and trainers need to have this book in their tool box."

—Aaron H. Doering, PhD, Associate Professor,
Learning Technologies, Co-Director, LT Media Lab, Bonnie Westby-Huebner Endowed Chair
of Education and Technology, Institute on the Environment Fellow,
College of Education + Human Development, University of Minnesota,
and book author, most recently, of *The New Landscape of Mobile Learning*

Bonk and Khoo deliver by laying out a solid, well-researched foundation for online learning that includes their signature TEC-VARIETY framework and by detailing over 100 practical and effective activities. This book can help refresh and motivate seasoned online instructors as well as inspire novice instructors to provide engaging online instruction for their students. Every instructor in my online program is going to get a copy of this!

—Joan Kang Shin, PhD, Professor of Practice and Director of TESOL Professional Training,
Department of Education, University of Maryland, Baltimore County,
and author of *Our World* for National Geographic Learning and Cengage

"Curt and Elaine know online learning and pinpoint exactly what will foster student success in computer-mediated instruction. Adding Some TEC-VARIETY is a must-read for anyone teaching a Web-enhanced, blended, or online course, and a required resource for all online learning administrators. As an online instructor myself, I cannot wait to try the volume of relevant, action-oriented activities in my own courses to enhance student achievement."

—Jarl Jonas, Program Director, Business Development, Blackboard,
and Adjunct Instructor, Excelsior College

"Engaging and motivating online learners is a challenge for everyone. Here is a book that you can use for yourself for the students you are teaching about online teaching, and learners learning online. There is even a chapter for administrators and organisational leaders; please set them their 'homework'! All of this is freely available as chapters and also beautifully printed as a book, if you want to buy it. Thank you Curtis and Elaine."

— Niki Davis, PhD, Professor of E-learning and Director of the College of Education
e-Learning Lab, University of Canterbury, New Zealand;
Editor-in-Chief, Journal of Open, Flexible, and Distance Learning

ADDING SOME
TEC-VARIETY

100+ Activities for Motivating and Retaining Learners Online

Curtis J. Bonk
Elaine Khoo

First published in 2014 by Open World Books, Bloomington, Indiana, USA
(additional information and resources available at http://OpenWorldBooks.com).

Paperback and Kindle versions of this book are available from Amazon and other distributors.
A special hardcover version of the book is available only by contacting the first author.

PDF of entire e-book as well as all 15 individual chapters available for free downloading from the book homepage at http://tec-variety.com.

Cover design: Alex Bonk

Front cover image
Copyright: Joachim Wendler
Shutterstock.com

Adding Some TEC-VARIETY: 100+ Activities for Motivating and Retaining Learners Online
Authored by Curtis J. Bonk, Authored by Elaine Khoo
ISBN-13: 978-1496162724
ISBN-10: 1496162722
LCCN: 2014904769

To the memory of Kim Foreman—educational technology professor, big sister, online learning experimenter, colleague, blogger, poet, friend, and Christian missionary.

—cjb

To the millions of online learners around the world, brave enough to take on this online learning beast; you blaze the path for our understanding of what it takes to succeed.

—ek

Kim Foreman (front row, fourth from left, above; and third from left, below) and friends celebrate student graduation from a bible school program, National University of Rwanda.

CONTENTS

Acknowledgments

Many people influenced the development of the TEC-VARIETY framework, and ultimately, the production of this book. We thank each person who has attended our workshops or presentations on TEC-VARIETY during the past decade and later used the framework and gave us feedback on it. With your timely and insightful ideas, we have continued to refine and improve it. Millions of thanks to each of you!

There are many kindred spirits leading our path to completion of this book. In particular, we thank Vanessa Dennen from Florida State University who originally outlined aspects of this book project. Her 2006 book chapter with Bonk on online motivational strategies proved extremely helpful to us in detailing many of the activities of this book. Thanks so much, Vanessa. Visions you had for this book more than a decade ago are finally coming to fruition. If this book makes an impact anywhere in the world, it will do so as a result of your creative approach to instruction, high octane energy, and extremely agile mind. Vanessa as well as our colleagues, Drs. Debra East, Xiaojing Liu, and YaTing Teng, gave us extensive feedback on the initial draft of this book. Their timely comments and insightful suggestions definitely enhanced the final product and sped up the production process.

As she had done with previous book projects with Bonk, Donna Jane Askay provided invaluable editing support. Donna is not the typical editor. She immerses herself in her book projects and learns the material so well that she can challenge the authors to raise their game. She definitely did that with us. When our editor tells us she is inspired after reading our chapters, we know we are on to something. It also gives us timely momentum in the homestretch. Suffice it to say, we were delighted that Donna found time to participate in this project. We were also appreciative of the timely indexing services of Audrey Dorsch and the book design skills of Robyn Taylor Barbon.

William Tyler Bryan-Askay did a marvelous job proofreading this big book in a timely fashion. Seth White was his usual highly reliable, efficient, and conscientious self on many project pieces from inception of this book project till the very end. And we would be remiss not to mention the highly creative and responsive talents of Alex Bonk on the cover design and introductory chapter graphics. Thanks for the book publishing insights and suggestions, Alex! You are the best son anyone could ask for.

We also thank Ke Zhang from Wayne State University. Her previous collaboration with Bonk on the R2D2 model resulted in a book, *Empowering Online Learning: 100+ Activities for Reading, Reflecting, Displaying, and Doing* with Jossey-Bass in 2008. This earlier book served as a guidepost for the construction and formatting of the entire TEC-VARIETY book. It provided the starter text that every writer dreams to have. Thanks, Ke. We deeply appreciate your sage insights into trends in the field, ever-abundant enthusiasm, heartwarming encouragement, and unique charm.

There are several others still to recognize. We appreciate Jay Cross and Jeff Cobb for their advice and examples on self-publishing. We also express thanks to Travis Craine and others at Amazon CreateSpace for their timely and informative advice and for answering our questions over more than two years. We deeply appreciate Rose Benedict for retrieving many of the research and theory articles referenced in this book. People like

Tom Reynolds from National University, Tom Reeves from the University of Georgia, Okhwa Lee from Chungbuk National University in Korea, Mimi Lee from the University of Houston, and Grace Lin from the University of Hawaii, served as sounding boards for some of the ideas expressed in this book. Their frank feedback, encouragement, and friendship provided the energy and sense of optimism for many of the activities and variations we detail.

In addition, many other people around the planet offered us inspiration, candid feedback, encouragement, ideas, suggestions, advice, and a host of useful Web resources. Such individuals include our wonderful colleagues and students at Indiana University and the University of Waikato, as well as many others who are far too numerous to list individually here. Thank you all. We think of each of you daily. We hope that you can use some of the ideas expressed here to find immense success online as well as support the successes of others in the Web of Learning.

In closing, Curt Bonk would like to thank Professor John Stephenson for being the first to ask him to speak on online motivation back in March 2005 at Middlesex University in London. That talk eventually evolved into plans for this book. He also thanks his family members and friends for supporting him while he was writing this book.

Elaine Khoo sends deep gratitude to JC, then JH, Nat, and Dan, who are her inspirations between the sunrises and sunsets.

About the Authors

Using decades of combined experience in online and blended learning environments, Curt Bonk and Elaine Khoo designed a book that they felt was grounded in both practice and theory. Too many technology books and resources side with one or the other but seldom both. In terms of the former, counting the activity variations and extensions, there are hundreds of interactive and engaging online learning activities outlined in this book. Suffice it to say, this book is meant to be highly practical. At the same time, each principle or component of TEC-VARIETY is based on decades of research in various fields of psychology, education, business, computer science, and cognitive science. In particular, the fields of human motivation as well as human learning and cognition have contributed an enormous pool of research findings from which Bonk and Khoo have dipped into to develop and refine their framework.

Bonk and Khoo have also conducted dozens of their own studies in online and blended learning as well as emerging technologies for learning, Bonk since the mid-1980s and Khoo since the late 1990s. This work spans the gamut of educational sectors including K–12 schools, higher education, military and corporate training, and a diverse array of informal and nontraditional settings. Throughout this work, the authors have been especially interested in the design of effective support structures for creating, delivering, and evaluating the highest quality online teaching and learning.

Curt Bonk is a former corporate controller and CPA who, after becoming sufficiently bored with such work, received his master's and PhD degrees in educational psychology from the University of Wisconsin. Curt Bonk is now professor of Instructional Systems Technology at Indiana University and president of CourseShare. Drawing on his background as a corporate controller, CPA, educational psychologist, and instructional technologist, Bonk offers unique insights into the intersection of business, education, psychology, and technology. He has received the CyberStar Award from the Indiana Information Technology Association, the Most Outstanding Achievement Award from the US Distance Learning Association, and the Most Innovative Teaching in a Distance Education Program Award from the State of Indiana. In 2003, Curt founded SurveyShare, which he sold in 2010. In early 2012, 2013, and 2014, Bonk was listed in *Education Next* and *Education Week* among the top contributors to the public debate about education from more than 20,000 university-based academics. In 2014, he also was named the recipient of the Mildred B. and Charles A. Wedemeyer Award for Outstanding Practitioner in Distance Education. A well-known authority on emerging technologies for learning, Bonk reflects on his speaking experiences around the world in his popular blog, *TravelinEdMan*. He has coauthored several widely used technology books, including *The World Is Open: How Web Technology Is Revolutionizing Education* (2009), *Empowering Online Learning: 100+ Activities for Reading, Reflecting, Displaying, and Doing* (2008), *The Handbook of Blended Learning* (2006), and *Electronic Collaborators* (1998). He can be contacted at cjbonk@indiana.edu or curt@worldisopen.com, or via his homepage at http://mypage.iu.edu/~cjbonk/.

Elaine Khoo is a research fellow at the Wilf Malcolm Institute of Education (WMIER) based in the Faculty of Education at The University of Waikato, Hamilton, New Zealand. Her master's in psychology with an emphasis in cognitive science is from Vanderbilt University and her doctorate is in education from the University of Waikato. Elaine Khoo's research interests include teaching and learning in environments supported by information and communication technology (ICT). She is also interested in online learning settings with a particular concern for how to build and sustain online learning communities as well as participatory learning cultures and collaborative research contexts. One of her key aspirations in life is encouraging teachers and learners to see the potential of different ICTs and how they can realistically adopt them to transform their teaching and learning practices. Khoo has been involved with a number of externally funded research projects associated with online learning, Web 2.0 tools, and ICTs in K–12 as well as higher education classrooms. She has recently completed two projects investigating networked science inquiry in secondary classrooms and exploring the educational affordances of iPads among preschoolers. At present, Dr. Khoo is heading a newly funded project examining the notion of software literacy, including how it develops and affects university teaching and learning as well as overall student experiences. Dr. Khoo can be contacted at ekhoo@waikato.ac.nz or via her homepage at http://education.waikato.ac.nz/about/faculty-staff/?user=ekhoo.

PREFACE TO TEC-VARIETY

Ki te kahore he whakakitenga ka ngaro te iwi.
Translation: Without foresight or vision the people will be lost.

—Kingi Tawhiao Potatau te Wherwhero, demonstrating the urgency
of unification and strong Maori leadership

The Web of Learning

Many ideas and events led to the development of the TEC-VARIETY framework and the 100+ activities for motivating and retaining online learners described in this book. Much of it has its roots in the mid-1980s, long before most educators had ever heard of online learning.

At the time, Bonk was, in fact, a deeply bored accountant working in a high-technology company. In his spare time, he enrolled in paper-based correspondence and television courses as well as outreach and extension courses to qualify for graduate school in educational psychology at the University of Wisconsin. During these courses, he learned much content knowledge in education as well as psychology. Perhaps more important, Bonk gained an appreciation for the multiple modes of educational delivery as well as the varied ways in which learners could access courses, and then change or improve their lives. When online learning began taking off a little over a decade later, he coordinated several national research projects on the state of e-learning and blended learning in both higher education and corporate training in the United States. His research soon entered into K–12 and military training settings and then expanded globally.

In each project, many benefits and challenges regarding online learning were documented. For instance, as with centuries of correspondence and face-to-face (F2F) courses, most online courses initially relied on text alone. There was often a cookie-cutter or one-size-fits-all mentality of the right way to do things and often a favored instructional design model that would win the day. Such is the history of the instructional design field. As was soon apparent, however, prescriptive forms of instruction belonged to the previous world of scant learning resources and limited selections; they were not applicable to an open learning world housing vast resources, choices, and opportunities to learn.

Fast-forward to the age of the Web 2.0 in the second decade of the twenty-first century. We live in a world rich with golden nuggets of free and open learning content as well as technologies for interacting and collaborating about this content. Not too surprisingly, relying on prescriptions and preset paths can lead to boredom and protests. There might also be contempt for instructors who are unwilling to allow individuals to learn as they do in more informal settings where they might rely on Twitter feeds, text messages, online news and reports, mobile applications, Facebook postings, and shared online video. Today's learners also want instruction to be highly connected to their occupations and interests. This yearning for relevant and meaningful learning will not subside anytime soon.

With the growing zest for interactive, collaborative, dynamic, and relevant instruction, there is something significant happening in learning environments today across every educational level and sector. Simply put, the creation of learning materials is no longer the sole province of the instructor, instructional designer, or some other educational expert. In this new age of learning, everyone can contribute something to the palette of course materials and resources. The Web 2.0 tilts the balance of power in the classroom toward those doing the learning. They no longer have to passively consume or browse through available contents. Now, they can add to them. As Brown and Adler (2008) contend, learners' minds are now on fire as they discover and create new information and then reveal it to others.

To emphasize the learning possibilities of the Web, at times we often refer to the Web as "the Web of Learning." This Web of Learning brings a rich tapestry of learning possibilities to each connected citizen of this planet (Bonk, 2009c). The Web of Learning metaphor reminds those teaching and learning online of the thousands or perhaps millions of interconnected learning-related uses of online resources and technologies. In effect, it expands the confines of traditional classroom learning by empowering learners to draw from informal learning and active social networks. Online instructors can bring in experts to their classes for real-time discussions as well as asynchronous ones. In addition to experts, learners from remote parts of the world can collaborate or interact with global peers and mentors. Curiosity is piqued. Feedback is enhanced. There is an authentic audience to interact with that extends beyond the instructor or online course system. The motivational level of learners can be elevated several degrees.

Learning now resides within everyone's reach. It comes along with us when we attend a musical or art exhibit. When in such a setting, mobile devices can call up pertinent information that is contextually based, thereby filling in the gaps in one's knowledge and accelerating personal growth within a field of study. Today, resources laid down by others along our learning trail can be quickly accessed and explored. These learning markers might come in the form of comments and ratings on news articles, suggested links in Facebook status updates, tweets in Twitter to still other resources, or trackbacks embedded in blog postings. Without a doubt, this is a new learning age. We are in the "Learning Century."

Despite the plethora of ways to learn today, most online courses remain caught up in old expectations of how a course is conducted. There are captured lectures to watch and articles or e-books to read prior to unit quizzes and summative examinations. Such courses remain firmly rooted in a text-centered past. A joke often heard at the dawn of online learning was that some institutions and organizations were giving certificates and degrees in electronic page turning. Suffice it to say, in the age of the Web 2.0, such an approach is definitely not a laughing matter. It is no small wonder why students spurn such dreary classes in favor of those that are more in keeping with the times.

Intentions

Each day, and at times, each moment of that day, educators come face-to-face with the vast technological changes of the past decade. They listen to podcasts. They Skype to communicate with distant friends and relatives. They text message their spouses and children about dinner plans or the movies. Some might have a personal blog or one that they use for class activities. Others use a wiki to organize class content or to set the agenda for a meeting. To get ready for such a meeting, they might turn to Google Docs or Wikispaces to gather and share initial ideas. The technology list and possibilities for putting them into use are only limited by one's imagination and willingness to try them out.

The TEC-VARIETY framework purposely takes into account these current technology trends and attempts to stimulate their use in pedagogically effective ways. As such, it rests at the intersection of such exciting educational affordances brought about by emerging learning technologies, intrinsic as well as extrinsic motivation-related theories, and the rapidly shifting perspectives on teaching and learning philosophies and approaches.

For online educators who are frustrated with never-ending waves of technology and the lack of training on how to effectively use them in their courses, we hope that the TEC-VARIETY framework can offer a ray of sunshine and a new beginning for online educators worldwide. As part of that hope, such educators might find activities and strategies that they can make use of to nurture engagement and success online. These strategies can breathe life into current classes and programs that are failing to engage their learners. They tap into learners' inner resources and desires to learn and grow toward a better future. At the same time, they can invite the global sharing of ideas and knowledge as part of a worldwide community or family of learners.

Since the dawn of Web-based instruction, most educators have grown accustomed to ceaseless calls to change their educational practices and reform their schools, institutions, or training programs. They have probably read countless reports about the need for learning to be situated and constructed by the learner. Active learning is a repeated mantra that is heard whether one is peeking in to observe a teacher in a K–12 classroom, walking down a cavernous hallway of some large higher education institution, sitting in the back rows of a military or corporate training summit or institute, or attending a grantees meeting of an educational foundation or government agency.

The proponents of new learning theories (e.g., social constructivism, situated cognition, connectivism, and so on) are well intended. However, educators in the trenches of teaching and learning need memorable, practical, and easier ways to implement active learning ideas. This book showcases a timely and extremely usable framework for nearly any application of technology in teaching or training. However, it is particularly suitable for fully online and blended learning courses and programs. We want online educators and trainers to apply it immediately in their instructional practices. We also want them to discuss and debate with other instructors as they work with it, and compare it to any other framework or theory on which they are presently relying.

Just how can theory help inform our use of technology? More specifically, how might theories of human motivation become applied in online and blended learning environments? For one, there is a growing realization that human motivation is not simply about understanding learner drives and internal feeling states but must also take into account the wider sociocultural, developmental, and ecological factors influencing learner actions. The learning context or environment is as critical an aspect for continuing performance as one's personal volition or passion to learn. Of course, personal passions and goals are vital to learning, but influential too is the learning environment or path that is laid out to help in that success. The TEC-VARIETY framework considers all of these factors—the individual motivational state of the learner or sets of learners you are working with as well as the technology tools and resources, the pedagogical practices or activities, and various other contextual variables.

In this digital era, educators are faced with a host of difficult questions to which the general public wants answers. Some of these questions are economic in nature as the costs of traditional education skyrocket. There is much sentiment that online learning can save both time and money. Many educators and politicians note that open educational resources such as the freely available course contents from MIT, Berkeley, and Harvard might save learners tens of thousands of dollars in their educational pursuits. Unfortunately, there will be scant savings if learners become bored online and drop out of a class or a program entirely.

In response, we hope that the 15 chapters of this book will enlighten online educators and learners across the planet about the prospect of online learning. After reading part or all of this book, educators will come to realize that in a short decade or two, we have moved from a few highly limited alternatives for delivering education to hundreds of new instructional formats, many of which were totally unimaginable just a year or two back. Where correspondence and television courses as well as books on tape once were the only nontraditional educational options, today you will discover virtual, open, collaborative, massive, and mobile learning formats that can reach learners anywhere and anytime.

We fully realize that there may be dozens or even hundreds of other frameworks available to take advantage of emerging theory and technology. Perhaps TEC-VARIETY can be one of the beacons which online educators can use to help signal some safe and exciting learning passages. The motivational principles detailed in this book can assist online educators to appropriately harness the many affordances of the Web. When that happens, their students can participate in engaging teaching-learning interactions that lead not only to some short-term learning successes but also to more positive views of themselves as learners and a genuine love for this process we call learning.

During the evolution of Web-based forms of learning, you may come across new tools, resources, and materials. If there is a particular technology, Web resource, or learning activity that you believe would enhance this book or would open our eyes to unique learning opportunities found in the Web of Learning, please do not hesitate to share it with us. Perhaps you were able to expand on or modify one or more of the activities suggested in this book in ways that suited your own teaching styles, content, audiences, and contexts. Or maybe you discovered powerful new approaches for implementing one or more of our activities. We encourage those who created new adaptations of the activities to share their ideas and success stories with us as well as any setbacks and challenges.

We are looking forward to such sharing as we grow and learn from them as part of a community of worldwide scholars and practitioners who use a little bit of TEC-VARIETY each day. To facilitate this flow of information, we intend to continually update the TEC-VARIETY book website (http://tec-variety.com) with new pedagogical activities and ideas, technology tools, reviews, and announcements as well as stories of best practices. You can find a free PDF of the entire book at the TEC-VARIETY website that anyone is most welcome to download, use, copy, and share with others. Information on ordering paper and digital versions of the book from Amazon CreateSpace can also be found there. Feel free to contact the first author at Curt@worldisopen.com or cjbonk@indiana.edu and the second author at ekhoo@waikato.ac.nz with such ideas and suggestions. We hope to hear from you.

Curtis J. Bonk   *Elaine Khoo*
Indiana University   *University of Waikato*
Bloomington, Indiana, USA   *Hamilton, New Zealand*

CHAPTER ONE

INTRODUCING TEC-VARIETY

Do you want to know who you are? Don't ask. Act!
Action will delineate and define you.

—Thomas Jefferson

Background

There comes a moment when you just know the time is ripe to push into an area. Today that area happens to be motivation and retention in online learning. Some might argue that the need for such a book was already apparent more than a decade ago. Online learning exploded in the late 1990s, especially for those in adult sectors like higher education, corporate training, and the military (Allen & Seaman, 2004, 2007, 2010b, 2014). The K–12 sector, in contrast, heated up much more recently (Picciano & Seaman, 2008; Watson, Murin, Vashaw, Gemin, & Rapp, and colleagues at Evergreen Education Group, 2010; Watson, 2007). Research conducted at the turn of the century, including that by Bonk, revealed enormous online drop-out rates. In higher education settings, it was not unusual to hear about the loss of 20 to 30 percent of enrolled students (Bonk, 2002a). That percentage would often double in the world of corporate and military training (Bonk, 2002b; Frankola, 2001a). These data were troubling. What was happening to cause so many individuals to give up their quest to learn online? And what could be done about it?

The common refrain was that there was little engagement within online courses. Students would complete assigned tasks similar to those given in a correspondence or television course and wait for feedback or comments from the instructor. For many, there were technical barriers and problems that surfaced even before they could enter the online course. Once they surmounted such challenges, they had to figure out what was expected and when. The directions for all this were often sketchy and assumed a level of online technology prowess that few had.

Overcoming such issues was not particularly easy. Making matters worse, all that your technology access got you was a stamp on your ticket to the online learning club. Then it came time for completing your assigned tasks and submitting them. Unlike traditional classrooms, there were often no peers to run ideas by, remind each other of upcoming tasks, or discuss and debate ideas with. Given that online learning was so new for everyone involved, there were limited examples of prior work and minimal job aids for completing tasks. Compounding such problems, most online content was severely lacking in quality.

For those who persisted with their online learning quests, there were few learning enticements in those early online learning days. Online courses typically provided limited goals or products to strive toward. When there was a goal, there was a highly constrained or unclear audience for learners' work. Who would be providing feedback on students' final products? Too often, little such feedback came. There was much irony here given that, unlike in F2F settings, students working in online or blended courses expected feedback on everything they posted to the Web. This was somewhat of a revelation for those accustomed to teaching in traditional, walled classrooms. Those with experience teaching correspondence courses or with tutoring students might not have been so shell-shocked. But most were not adequately prepared for this brave new online learning world.

Suffice it to say, without feedback or comparison points, online students were uncertain of their learning progress. They were in a state of learning limbo. As Stanford psychologist Albert Bandura (1986, 1997) might say, there was scant opportunity to develop students' self-efficacy as online learners. Part of the problem was that there were few benchmarks to which to compare their performance. And when there was a target, they were often told that they were lacking in some skill or competency and could not pass on to the next level. Such gated learning communities with limited forms of feedback were especially prevalent in military and government training settings (Bonk, Olson, Wisher, & Orvis, 2002).

Given this situation, it was no small wonder that there were quite hearty student dropout numbers and plenty of other problems in those early years. Of course, these were just a few of the barriers and challenges facing online learners. Further fuel for the online retention travesty was the general lack of instructor and student training for such environments. Add to that poorly designed courses, insufficient or inept strategic planning, and constantly changing demands and expectations, and much could and did go wrong in those early online courses. Still, the hype bandwagon kept playing the all-too-familiar songs, such as "if you build it, they will come" and "if you do not jump in now, it will be too late."

The Read, Reflect, Display, and Do (R2D2) Model

In partial response to this situation, in 2005, Bonk and Professor Ke Zhang at Wayne State University designed an easy-to-apply and highly practical framework for addressing more diverse learner needs (Bonk & Zhang, 2006). It is called the Read, Reflect, Display, and Do (R2D2) model (see Figure 1.1). The R2D2 model was published in a book titled *Empowering Online Learning: 100+ Activities for Reading, Reflecting, Displaying, and Doing* (Bonk & Zhang, 2008). In the book, there are 25 activities for each of the four quadrants of the model, or 100 activities in total. As explained in *Empowering Online Learning*, some might think of the R2D2 model as a knowledge acquisition and use cycle as well as a problem-solving wheel.

FIGURE 1.1: R2D2 COMPONENTS.

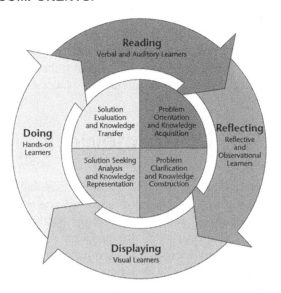

The first phase of the model emphasizes reading, listening, and text-based activities. That initial phase or component helps to focus instruction on acquiring knowledge through various mechanisms including online readings, podcasts, and Web-streamed lectures. Next, in the second phase, the R2D2 model highlights the observational side of learning. In this component, the online instructor targets reflection on content and self-checking or reviewing learners' understanding of, for example, blogging, online practice tests, and shared online video reflections. Third, the model highlights visual forms of learning including timelines, concept maps, flowcharts, and videos. Here, the learner is required to create visual representations of her learning and put it on display for the instructor or others to review and comment on. Alternatively, a learner might use or review the visual content or depictions created by others. Finally, the fourth phase of R2D2 is intended to encourage practice or hands-on experimentation with the learned content. In this phase, learners operationalize the content by solving cases, completing various problems in a simulation, or posting a report or video summary. As these activities take place, course content and activities become more enriching and personally meaningful for learners.

As with any educational model, there are many caveats and guidelines. For instance, the four phases can proceed in any order. In addition, those using R2D2 should keep in mind that many activities take place in two or more phases of the model. In the end, the instructor and others involved in the design, delivery, and implementation of the course can decide on how, when, and where R2D2 might prove beneficial for their context. They might even employ it as a means to design or prepare instruction.

Rather than an instructional design model per se, R2D2 is a means to make sense of the learning and instruction possibilities of the Web. It is a simple four-part model of what is now possible online, and is also intended to help with addressing diverse learners and offering more variety, flexibility, choice, and learning empowerment. Some may, in fact, use it as a learning style model. Others could use it to fashion courses from a problem-solving point of view.

Whatever the perspective, R2D2 can help teachers think about their online instructional practices. It is just one model. But it is a starting point for online teaching and learning considerations. And it can be a means of reducing the tension and stress of teaching online. Given the never-ending parade of emerging technologies for learning, both experienced and novice online instructors face great difficulties deciding which tools, activities, and resources can enhance their online and blended courses. R2D2 can help.

The TEC-VARIETY Framework

A second guide to assist those new to online learning or seeking additional support is an acronym called the TEC-VARIETY framework. As indicated by the title, this book will present many stories, examples, and ideas regarding how this easy-to-remember mnemonic aid can enhance online instruction. In some ways, the TEC-VARIETY framework builds on the R2D2 model. For instance, it also synthesizes the varied ways for enhancing Web pedagogy into a few principles or ideas that, when combined, can powerfully boost the chances for online learning success. However, instead of four aspects of learning— reading, reflecting, displaying, and doing—this framework addresses different aspects of learner motivation. In fact, as noted below, each letter of TEC-VARIETY stands for one or more motivational principles.

1. **T**one/Climate: Psychological Safety, Comfort, Sense of Belonging
2. **E**ncouragement: Feedback, Responsiveness, Praise, Supports
3. **C**uriosity: Surprise, Intrigue, Unknowns
4. **V**ariety: Novelty, Fun, Fantasy
5. **A**utonomy: Choice, Control, Flexibility, Opportunities
6. **R**elevance: Meaningful, Authentic, Interesting
7. **I**nteractivity: Collaborative, Team-Based, Community
8. **E**ngagement: Effort, Involvement, Investment
9. **T**ension: Challenge, Dissonance, Controversy
10. **Y**ielding Products: Goal Driven, Purposeful Vision, Ownership

The TEC-VARIETY framework represents our combined three decades of research, teaching, and general exploration in Web-based learning environments. Since the start of this millennium, each of us had thought deeply about ways to elevate the quality of online learning. From time to time, we shared our insights and ideas with each other. Initially, we were concerned about issues related to effective online moderating and facilitating. Khoo, in fact, closely studied online moderation for a number of years as part of her dissertation research. As the two of us discussed, reflected on, and wrote about effective pedagogy, we found among online educators and those considering teaching online a general lack of understanding about how to motivate their students and raise their level of engagement. This concern extended to Web-enhanced or supplemented courses, not just fully online ones. In fact, the following quotation from an instructor whom Khoo interviewed epitomizes some of those issues. He described how his online teaching pedagogy eventually evolved from "shovelware" into a more refined practice: "We're all new at the game and we all evolve in how we go about teaching because when we did start we were very much 'shovelware' sort of people. We almost transcribed our on-campus lectures and put them up there on the computer for people to sit and read our lectures but as time has gone by, we've found that that isn't very effective."

The transition for this instructor, however, did not happen overnight. The evolution required a constant examination and reflection of his teaching beliefs and practices coupled with a degree of risk taking and experimentation to take advantage of the Web's capabilities to enhance his students' learning. Only once this had occurred could this instructor begin to recraft and perfect his art at online instruction—an important point which we will revisit several times in the remaining chapters of this book.

It was also clear from our own experiences and from the prevailing literature that motivation has a direct bearing on student satisfaction and ultimately on learner retention in online and blended courses. Of course, we realized that motivation was a major concern not only for instructors but for administrators faced with decisions about whether to offer particular classes, degrees, or programs online. Students, too, wanted to be assured that they were not being sent to some type of learning purgatory or detention camp when enrolling in such courses. Although technology-rich learning environments initially intrigued them, many had heard horror stories about online courses and programs.

With that in mind, we spent a couple of years collecting, reading, and categorizing articles related to student motivation. For over a decade, Bonk has presented ideas related to online motivation and retention to many audiences, from K–12 to higher education to corporate and military training and beyond. During this time, he has accumulated a suite of online learning examples for an assortment of motivational principles from audience members, colleagues, and his own personal explorations. Gradually, these principles became formulated in the "TEC-VARIETY" mnemonic or framework.

We hope that, like R2D2, TEC-VARIETY can be a catalyst for discussing, developing, and delivering online courses or course components. Each time we share the TEC-VARIETY framework, audience feedback indicates extensive interest. They soon discover that when the ten principles are combined, the results can be extremely powerful. People who have applied the framework have not only told us that it works, but they have sent us hundreds of engaging examples of how they are using it.

In addition to such anecdotal evidence, our own research in corporate and military training as well as K–12 schools and higher education environments indicates that each of the 10 principles plays a key role in online learning success. As you will discover in the ensuing chapters, our research and that of many others highlights the importance of moving from traditional instructional formats with teacher telling or lecture-based practices and requisite textbooks to an environment where there is much more learner discussion and reflection on content. Success occurs when learners feel that they know each other well. It also happens when there are choices and at least some degree of flexibility in learning, when students take ownership over their learning, and when galleries of learner projects and products are on display for others to discuss and debate. Such environments are more hands-on, collaborative, and active (Kim & Bonk, 2006). TEC-VARIETY can guide and facilitate such educational transformations.

Each framework, R2D2 and TEC-VARIETY, can play a role in enhancing your online courses and activities. Their respective use will depend on your course content and context, the cultural backgrounds of the participants, student and instructor familiarity with online learning, and any known learning preferences. As indicated, we firmly believe that motivation provides the core structure for online learning success. When instructors can capture student interest in the specific learning activity, or, better yet, the overall course or program, then the road to success is more swiftly and energetically traveled. Besides a desire to learn, students need to feel curiosity and excitement about the course contents as well as some sense of tension and challenge along the way. They need to experience a sense of empowerment and control over their learning destinies, enhanced by the social presence of their instructors and fellow students. Such individuals help lay the markers and signposts along the trail of learner success.

Book Content and Organization

As in the R2D2 book, a set of instructional options facing online instructors and support personnel has been detailed for each activity in this book. These options include the degree of risk, time, and cost; all are rated from low to high. We also note the degree of learner-centeredness of each task. Most online instructors we encounter in our respective travels claim to be seeking activities that contain minimal risk, are user-friendly and inexpensive, and do not chew up a ton of time. Although low-risk, low-cost, and low-time activities can pique instructors' interests, in actuality, many are quite willing to experiment at the outer edges of the risk and time continua. Some might even have funding to pay for websites or tools that charge a fee. Our detailed information about such variables is intended to help with task selection as well as professional reflection on your teaching. We hope that it also helps to nudge many of you reading this book to try out ideas you had not considered previously and then share them with your colleagues.

In the coming chapters, we will often mention an educational setting where we have seen an activity used. That does not preclude its use in another area or environment. In fact, it is crucial to point out that an online activity deemed applicable to a particular discipline, educational group, or age level can often find substantive use within another educational population or environment. With appropriate modifications and guidelines, nearly all of the 100 strategies outlined in this book can be applied to any population of learners.

The format of this book is intended to help the reader make sense of the powerful learning opportunities in this Web of Learning. As with the R2D2 book, in this particular book, you will find the following:

- Details on 100 easy-to-implement online instructional activities.

- Ideas for varying and extending each activity, amounting to a wealth of ideas for creating highly motivational online learning courses and environments.

- Caveats and practical guidance for each activity as well as recommendations for the TEC-VARIETY framework as a whole. Such advice should prove beneficial to online instructors, instructional designers, courseware designers, course management developers and vendors, training managers and administrators, and many others.

- Ideas, anecdotes, and examples to which online instructors and their students can personally relate.

- An assembly of Web-based learning tools and resources that are potentially useful in a range of learning situations, educational sectors, and fields or disciplines, in addition to ideas for how to thoughtfully integrate them.

This book is divided into three parts. At the beginning of the first section, the Preface describes the background information for this book. Here in Chapter One, we introduce the TEC-VARIETY framework and explain the journey that led to it. We also delineate the purpose and scope of this book. The second chapter lays out the theory, research, and practice related to online attrition and retention. In the third chapter, key motivational concepts and principles are detailed from the standpoint of four perspectives on human learning—namely, behaviorism, cognitivism, constructivism, and sociocultural theory. We also delve more deeply into the associated psychological principles of the framework. Given that research on human motivation extends back for more than a century, we will focus on that which is most pertinent to online learning environments. As such, Chapter Three will concentrate on principles such as feedback, psychological safety, control, dissonance, fantasy, engagement, goal setting, and interactivity. The first few chapters along with the Preface, therefore, will form the core or base for the online motivation-related applications documented in much of the rest of the book.

The TEC-VARIETY framework has 10 main principles. Each principle will have its own featured chapter; that is, Chapters Four to Thirteen will each contain 10 activities, forming the second key section of this book. To help the reader, Table 1.1 is an overview of the 10 main principles of the framework and the corresponding instructional activities for each principle detailed in this book.

In the third section, Chapter Fourteen offers an assortment of ideas for how to work with resistant and less experienced online instructors, those who are new to online learning and instruction, and those who are more experienced but have not yet attempted a blended or fully online course. As noted in that chapter, such ideas should be bound into a systemic professional development program or initiative, not simply treated as one-off solutions. Finally, Chapter Fifteen recaps the journey within the book and the components of the TEC-VARIETY framework while suggesting how the framework

TABLE 1.1: 100+ ACTIVITIES FOR TEC-VARIETY.

TONE/CLIMATE	ENCOURAGEMENT	CURIOSITY	VARIETY	AUTONOMY
1. Personal Introductions	11. Critical Friends	21. Online Events in the News	31. Online Séance or Roundtable	41. Cool Resource Provider
2. Video Introductions	12. Student Polling and Voting	22. Live Science, Creative Expression, or Artistic Invention	32. Virtual World Role Plays	42. Technology Tool Demonstrator
3. Goals and Expectations	13. Online Suggestion Box	23. Live Scientific Discovery or Invention	33. Mobile and Social Networking Content Games and Apps	43. Starter-Wrapper Technique
4. Personal Commitments	14. Minute and Muddiest Point Papers	24. Just-in-Time Syllabus	34. Educational Music Videos	44. Shotgun Questioning
5. Eight Nouns	15. Comments and Annotations	25. Just-in-Time Teaching	35. Database Problems and Search Competitions	45. Hot Seat Questioning
6. Two Truths and One Lie	16. Screencasted Supports and Directions	26. What's My Line Guest Games	36. Task and Activity Randomizer	46. Open Exploration Weeks
7. Accomplishment Hunts	17. Embedded Reviews and System Scored Practice Tests	27. A Day in the Life of a Scientist, Scholar, or Celebrity	37. Time-Constrained Presentations	47. Open Educational Resources Explorations
8. Course Fan Pages	18. Asynchronous Expert Feedback and Mentoring	28. Cultural or Contextual Blogs and Resources	38. Virtual Community Brainstorming	48. Pick and Choose Options
9. Favorite Websites	19. Synchronous and Mobile Mentoring	29. Extreme Learning	39. Extreme Teaching and Online Mentoring	49. Open Syllabus Course Portal with Options
10. Online Cafés	20. Learner-Self-Interaction and Self-Feedback Forms	30. Quests and Probes on the Web	40. Exploring Dynamic Web Content	50. Open Teaching and MOOCs

	RELEVANCE		INTERACTIVE		ENGAGEMENT		TENSION		YIELDING PRODUCTS
51.	Multimedia Case Vignettes and Decision Making	61.	Scholar, Scientist, or Innovator Role Play	71.	Interactive Maps and Databases	81.	Debating Controversial Online News, Blogs, and Other Media	91.	Cartoon and Animated Movie Productions
52.	Job Connection and Strategic Planning Papers	62.	Interactive Learner Questioning and Discussion	72.	Interactive Multimedia Glossaries	82.	Structured Controversy	92.	Student Documentaries
53.	Wiki Editing Projects (including Wikipedia)	63.	Jigsaw the Online Content	73.	Talking Dictionaries and Lang. Translation	83.	Structured Role Debates (e.g., Court Forums)	93.	Course Video Summaries and Movie Festivals
54.	Language Learning Conversations and Mentoring	64.	Flipping the Class	74.	Interactive Timelines	84.	Online Study Group Challenges	94.	Book Trailers
55.	Online Current News Feeds and Streaming Data	65.	Product Brainstorming and Co-Creation	75.	Exploring Animations, Simulations, and Pop-Up Media	85.	Timed Disclosures and Issue Voting	95.	Online Book Reviews
56.	Cross-Cultural Web Conferencing and Interactions	66.	Collaborative Mindmapping and Idea Visualization	76.	Virtual Tools and Scientific Instruments	86.	Argument and Debate Mapping	96.	Content Databases and Learning Portals
57.	Instructor Online Video Demos	67.	Collaborative Video Annotations	77.	Microblogging Course Discussions	87.	Challenge-Based Videoconferencing	97.	Oral History Interviews
58.	Video Study Guides, Tutorials, and Microlectures	68.	Video Discussion and Questioning	78.	Online Subject-Specific Picture Galleries	88.	Digital Media Competitions	98.	Grammar Check, Peer Check
59.	Pubcasts and Researcher Interviews	69.	Word Cloud Interactions	79.	Interactive Online Exhibits (e.g., Art and Bones)	89.	"Best of" Nominations (e.g., Quotes)	99.	Recording Accomplishments (e.g., I Done It)
60.	Oral History or Situational Research	70.	Backchannel Conference and Course Participation	80.	Three-Level Questioning	90.	Online Games, Puzzles, and Quizzes	100.	Poster Sessions and Gallery Tours

might find even more extensive use in the future. In this final chapter, we summarize the 100+ activities and assorted ideas from the previous chapters into one table showing the degree of time, risk, and cost for each activity. We also discuss ways to integrate various principles of the framework to create more effective and engaging fully online and blended learning courses.

Using the two recap tables, the reader can quickly find needed information applicable to one or more component of the TEC-VARIETY framework. When combined, Chapters Four through Thirteen contain the 100+ advertised activities of this book. If it is the start of your online class and you are in need of an icebreaker, there are 10 sample ones in Chapter Four. On the other hand, if you are reaching the end of a unit or the course, you might find the product-based ideas of Chapter Thirteen more to your liking. And if you simply desire a change of pace, then the ideas and activities of Chapter Seven on variety may have just what you seek. In whatever ways you plan to use this book, it is vital to be thoughtful in your integration and exploitation of Web technology.

As indicated, there are more than 100 different activities in this one book. To help the reader review and understand as many of these as possible, a description and purpose is included for each activity. Also detailed are the skills and objectives, advice and ideas, and various instructional considerations related to the degree of time, risk, cost, and learner-centeredness of each activity. We also offer a variation for each activity. Such variations raise the pool of instructional ideas in this book from 100 to at least 200. And when the ideas from both the R2D2 book and this one are combined, juxtaposed against one another, and intermingled in ways heretofore not seen, there are seemingly countless ideas for online instructors to consider.

What should become apparent is that this book simultaneously provides an overarching lens related to motivation with technology as well as a series of specific approaches for effective instruction. You will find a macro framework in addition to dozens of more micro-level ideas that can be implemented each time you journey online. This book should provide you with a convenient and purposeful toolkit to boost your confidence as an online instructor or instructional designer. It should also offer needed information for managers and directors of learning organizations and enrichment for the casual observer who is simply interested in online learning. As TEC-VARIETY becomes part of your instructional blood, it may even have an impact on your instructional decisions in traditional F2F instructional settings. Once the framework is internalized, you might be better equipped to address diverse learner needs and personalize their learning environment in novel and exciting ways. We hope so and we look forward to hearing about your results.

As a resource for more personalized and engaging learning, we hope that you will make journeys back to sections of this book as needed. When you do, you will come across several key learning resources intended to help you best use this book. First, embedded in Chapter One is a table listing the 100 activities in this book according to the main 10 motivational principles of the TEC-VARIETY framework. In addition, a similar table in the final chapter recaps these activities according to indices of time, risk, and cost as well as learner-centeredness. There is also a list of Web resources which are sorted by chapter to help with your search. These Web resources and references at the back of the book can be used to further explore most topics mentioned in the book. To expedite your explorations, both the book references and Web links can be found at the book's website, http://tec-variety.com. Of course, we welcome and appreciate any suggestions you may have for enhancing the site.

Goals and Uses of this Book

This book can be employed in a variety of settings and situations. Some might use it in a master's course in educational technology such as online learning leadership, instructional design, technology and motivation, distance learning, and e-learning. Others could use it with pre-service or in-service teachers in one or more technology applications or methods courses. Students in such courses will begin to grasp the range of learning opportunities on the Web as well as grapple with how they could personally employ various technology tools and Web resources.

Those in corporate, government, and military settings may see this book as a means to create, review, and modify online course content and activities. They might set up institutes, workshops, and summits around some of the ideas from this book and others in the field. Many individuals we have encountered in such adult-based learning situations are in the midst of a significant overhaul of their online content due to concerns about learner completion rates, sustainability, cost-effectiveness, and the impact of their training programs. We believe that the TEC-VARIETY framework speaks directly to each of those concerns.

As noted with the R2D2 book, this book offers one view or perspective on how to design effective online and blended learning environments. There are countless others. Neither R2D2 nor TEC-VARIETY is intended as an instructional design model. Still, each provides a mechanism for reflecting on the quality of online courses and course contents as well as a guide for designing new ones. TEC-VARIETY is a tool to assist those pondering teaching online for the very first time. It can also help the more seasoned online instructor seeking to verify her online teaching practices and perhaps push beyond them. The audience of the book, therefore, includes instructors, tutors, trainers, instructional designers, administrators, and anyone wanting to know about effective forms of Web-based instruction.

Caveats Regarding the Web Resources, Tools, and Activities Listed

Many aspects of this book are purposefully intended to help the reader understand and then find resources that can assist in motivating and retaining online learners. We cover a wide gamut of Web resources, technologies, and disciplines. As already mentioned, at the end of the book, we recap the Web resources mentioned along the way. We must caution the reader, however, that we did not select a particular technology tool or resource to promote or advocate personally, nor do we offer any guidelines or recommendations for deciding between them. Nevertheless, in each chapter, we include references to the prevailing literature related to many of the techniques and tools suggested.

Keep in mind that there are undoubtedly dozens of other highly useful tools that you may have heard about or already use in your classes. This is not a technology book nor is it a book devoted solely to instructional methods; instead, it is a text addressing the intersection of technology, pedagogy, and learning. As such, it is filled with options and opportunities to ignite the interest of experienced and novice instructors and that of their students. Given the range of options, we recommend that you test out or experiment with a particular website or tool before incorporating it into a learning experience in your classes.

You should also keep in mind that during the coming years, many of the tools and resources that are documented in this book will be replaced or discarded, or will have morphed into some larger system. Websites and associated URLs may change or disappear in the blink of an eye and then reemerge a week or month later in a more robust or useful format. New ownership often results in name changes or new locations for a popular technology or resource. If you cannot find something that we mention and it sounds interesting, keep searching or perhaps write to one of us.

What should become obvious as you scan through this book is that the 100+ activities outlined in it are often real examples that we have personally encountered or seen in use by others. A few of them may remain future goals and visions for our own classes, but all are possible today. We must also remind the reader that although we have attempted most of the tasks and activities described in this book, there are dozens of different ways to use each one. Our examples, therefore, are not prescriptions or the only ways to use them some of these ideas. Instead, you should flexibly apply these activities according to your specific learning situation or context.

We realize that some of these ideas will not work in every educational sector or course level. Ignore or put a red "X" by activities that will not work for you. Concentrate on those that might find success in your learning environment or situation. And for any activities you are not sure about, use your creative juices and imagination to enhance, extend, and transform them. When you do that, the 100+ ideas of this book explode to tens of thousands. We provide the kernels or skeletons for many instructional ideas. As you review each one, you should reflect on how to add some meat to those bones and get those kernels popping.

You should also realize that there are thousands of other ideas that did not make it into this book. Given that the field is changing so rapidly, it is impossible for a single book to point to all the opportunities educators have today. Need more ideas? Explore the R2D2 book as well as other online learning books. Be patient. If there is something that you really want to do online in your classes or programs, eventually you will be able to do it.

We hope you enjoy the rest of the book.

CHAPTER TWO

ONLINE LEARNING ATTRITION AND RETENTION

Theory to Practice

> I didn't fail the test, I just found 100 ways to do it wrong.
>
> —Benjamin Franklin

Background

We remember growing up in the 1970s and 1980s when the norm was to try to get into college or university after high school so you could find a good job and eventually attain a productive and well-respected career. Competition to get the best grades was fierce. Many of our friends wanted to attend the most prestigious universities. "Correspondence courses" (as distance learning was called back then) were viewed as the poor cousin to the more traditional campus-based courses. Fueling such attitudes, the correspondence courses offered were often clerical, administrative, or semivocational in nature.

This situation did not deter the millions of correspondence learners brave enough to give it a go, including Bonk, who enrolled in a couple of television and correspondence courses in the mid-1980s prior to entering graduate school. Bonk formed a personal bond with his designated course instructor, Dr. Robert Clasen of the University of Wisconsin, and as a result, he fairly quickly completed each of these courses. A few months later, Professor Clasen hired him to help with a new television course on critical thinking shortly after he arrived at the University of Wisconsin for graduate school.

Near the end of that decade, Khoo's good friend, Jamie, took up the challenge of learning through correspondence after she and Khoo had completed high school. Not being academically inclined, Jamie signed up for a clerical course via correspondence. Within a few weeks, she was sent her first few packages of manuals, instructions, and assignments via the postal service. She would complete her assigned tasks, mail them back, and get the next lot of assignments. This went on for about 10 months. Early enthusiasm with the course and materials eventually turned to despair.

Her lament? Jamie felt that she was mostly on her own throughout this course. Unlike Bonk's experience, there was no one to support or help her when she had questions. She received written feedback every couple of months upon submitting her work. In between, she was basically in isolation. And as the material became more difficult, Jamie's anxieties increased. Soon she quit. The process was just too hard. Jamie's story is typical of the early distance learning scenario. Of course, there were many highly visible success stories like Bonk's who, coincidentally, would likely not have authored this book had he not had access to such distance learning courses. Nevertheless, a majority of folks found it too frustrating to sustain the motivation to chug on alone in such courses.

Fast-forward to the twenty-first century. Today's distance educators have a multitude of choices when it comes to selecting from available communicative technological tools to enhance their teaching or training practices and support their students' learning. Unlike Jamie's learning options, technology resources have expanded to include podcasted lectures, mobile flashcards, expert blog posts, wiki-based multimedia course glossaries, YouTube video lectures and expert demonstrations, course announcements and reminders in Twitter, and other vast information networks contributed by people around the planet (e.g., Wikipedia). With these new means to foster learner interaction, collaboration, engagement, and personal study, schools, universities, and corporate training departments worldwide have embraced the culture and fervor surrounding Web-based distance learning. There is now wide recognition and elevated status accorded to online courses and programs in a range of academic disciplines that are either offered entirely online or use different forms of blended learning to supplement current F2F programs.

Consider current statistics. We increasingly hear reports on how the number of students and corporate employees attracted to the potential of open, flexible, and distance learning options continues to accelerate. By 2011, the worldwide expenditures for e-learning services and products amounted to over $35.6 billion. Equally astounding, it was forecasted to grow at a 7.6 percent five year compound annual growth rate, thereby reaching nearly $51.5 billion by 2016. Double-digit five year growth forecasts (from 2011 to 2016) for online learning are estimated for the top two fastest growing markets, namely, Asia (at 17.3 percent), and Eastern Europe (at 16.9 percent). The US market alone was expected to hit $27.2 billion by 2016 (Ambient Insight, 2012).

Online student numbers rose significantly since the start of the century. As of August 2012, there were more than 30 million online higher education students worldwide who took one or more of their classes online. Over half were in the United States (Ambient Insight, 2013). Forty percent of these students view online learning components as essential to their learning experience (Blackboard K–12, 2011). In 2011, over 320,000 primary and secondary school students in the United States were found to attend a virtual school. The fastest growing sector of online learning, in fact, was the PreK–12 market which has been growing at a rate of nearly 17 percent. In fact, it has been projected that a whopping 17 million K–12 students in the United States will be taking at least one online course by 2015 (Ambient Insight, 2011).

A national survey from the Sloan Consortium on online learning in 2010 indicated that there were 5.6 million college students enrolled in at least one online course in the fall of 2009 (Allen & Seaman, 2010b). This figure increased to over 7 million by 2013 (Allen & Seaman, 2014). The 2014 report from Allen and Seaman revealed that more than one-third of all college and university students were taking at least one online course. Perhaps most impressive was the 12.7 percent growth rate for online enrollments from 2008 to 2013 which far exceeded the paltry 3.1 percent enrollment growth rate for higher education overall.

Such news keeps coming. Late in the summer of 2011, a massive open online course (MOOC) offered by two of the world's leading artificial intelligent researchers from Stanford University drew more than 100,000 students (Markoff, 2011). In early 2012, MOOC providers like Coursera, edX, and Udacity sprang forth to offer these new types of online courses. By August of that year, Coursera enrolled more than a million learners from nearly 200 countries. Students in a single MOOC can come from hundreds of countries (Koller, Ng, Do, & Chen, 2013). Such figures signal that the radical growth of online learning is likely to increase dramatically in the coming decades.

Commonly cited reasons for enrolling in Web-based learning include the flexibility of learning across time, distance, and space. Another factor typically mentioned is an opportunity for empowerment and autonomy with the wide array of learning options and choices at one's fingertips. With online learning, students enjoy enhanced personalization and a sense of control or ability to take charge of what they need to learn. Other reasons include a personal desire to explore knowledge and ideas, the ability to network globally with peers and exchange ideas with like-minded others, and a chance to satisfy one's curiosity. At the K–12 level, the reasons range widely from needing remedial courses to wanting to take advanced coursework, to needing classwork while on an extended stay in the hospital, to being homeschooled, whether by choice or because of pregnancy, bullying, or other issues (Bonk, 2009a).

A Chink in the Online Learning Armor

In tandem with the development of new communicative technologies in the distance learning arena come concerns for effective instructional design and pedagogies to ensure that students are effectively learning the content. During the past two decades, online learning researchers and educators around the world have voiced loud concerns about innumerable problems in online pedagogy. In Australia alone, there are dozens of books and research reports from established online learning pioneers like John Hedberg, Gilly Salmon, Jan Herrington, Catherine McLoughlin, and Ron Oliver who are highly critical and cautious about the state of online pedagogy.

A major concern, not just in Australia but around the planet, is with the lackluster and disconcerting news of low online learner completion rates. We are confronted with headlines screaming, "Online and Incomplete" (Jaschik, 2011), "Online Learning Facing 80% Attrition Rates" (Flood, 2002), "Preventing Online Dropouts: Does Anything Work?" (Parry, 2010), and "100 Pounds of Potatoes in a 25-Pound Sack: Stress, Frustration, and Learning in the Virtual Classroom" (Mello, 2002). Such reports reveal a chink in the online learning armor, echoing the same story of frustrated and bored distance learners living Jamie's experience all over again. Unfortunately, many educators become so enamored by every new wave of learning technology that each is adopted in superficial ways akin to "gift wrapping" old wine in new bottles (Fischer, 2003). A report in early 2014, however, found that four in ten academic leaders in higher education settings in the United States felt that it was more difficult to retain online learning students than F2F students (Allen & Seaman, 2014; Kolowich, 2014).

Such concerns are not without merit. Online learners, in fact, are reported to have higher noncompletion, withdrawal, or drop-out rates (i.e., attrition) compared to their counterparts taking F2F campus-based courses (Park, 2007; Phipps & Merisotis, 2000). A survey by Jaggars and Xu (2010) among two-year community college students found that students enrolled in purely online courses fare worse than their contemporaries enrolled in hybrid and F2F courses on campus. The noncompletion rate for these fully online students was estimated to be 10–15 percent higher than the rate among students in hybrid and F2F contexts (Xu & Jaggars, 2011). Similarly, Cellilo (n.d.) reported dropout figures amounting to 30 percent in online classes compared to the 10–15 percent drop-out rates experienced in traditional classes.

The numbers are often even worse in the corporate world. In the early years of Web-based instruction, drop-out rates in the online training world ranged dramatically from about 10–20 percent (Frankola, 2001b) to well over 50 percent and perhaps as high as 80 percent (Bonk, 2002; Flood, 2002; Ganzel, 2001).

Fast-forward a decade and the retention news is even more depressing; at least for the latest distance learning phenomena—MOOCs (Kolowich, 2014). Drop-out rates for MOOCs often exceed 90 percent. In fact, MOOC completion rates of a mere 5 percent are not uncommon (Koller et al., 2013). As an example, in a course on bioelectricity at Duke University in the fall of 2012, nearly 13,000 people signed up but only 350 participants, or less than 3 percent, completed it (Rivard, 2013). Although the course introduction video was viewed 8,000 times, most of those enrolled did not watch more than one or two instructor lectures and even fewer took the course quizzes. Such numbers are not atypical.

A key question, then, is how to get those enrolled in MOOCs, or any type of online course, to stay beyond the first week or two. A decade ago, a study at the U.K. Open University (Simpson, 2004) revealed that only the more confident distance students completed assignments at any stage of their study. Such research suggests that it is critical to extensively support novice online learners in the early stages of such a course. As part of that support, MOOC participants, and perhaps all online learners, need to feel connected or part of a learning community where their questions and concerns can be addressed. Hence, there are often local meet-up or study groups that get together or interact in physical or online settings to discuss their course progression. Given the projected increases in the use of MOOCs in higher education as well as other educational sectors, such types of support groups will increase in the coming years.

Online student retention (the number of students following through a course or program; also called "persisters") is a highly distressing issue for institutions, administrators, and educators all over world. In fact, it has been cited as one of the greatest weaknesses in online education (Berge & Huang, 2004; Herbert, 2006; Jun, 2005). Chief among the factors contributing to attrition is lack of student motivation (Bonk, 2002; Cocea, 2007; Wolcott & Burnham, 1991), conflicts of time (Hiltz & Goldman, 2005), and lack of interaction or support from the instructor (Carr, 2000; Hara & Kling, 2000; Moore & Kearsley, 1996). In addition, the survey by Xu and Jaggars (2011) touched on reasons such as lack of both faculty and peer support and interaction, sense of isolation, time constraints, technical difficulties, and a general lack of structure as common reasons for dropping out of online courses.

Naturally, educational institutions and corporations must justify their investments in online learning programs to their stakeholders. Decisions about the degree to which they utilize the Web for fully online and blended forms of instruction affects wider issues such as organizational planning, training, and assessment (Bonk, 2002; Tyler-Smith, 2006). Never before have considerations about effective approaches to engaging students in online courses been more urgent. Issues such as access to education, learning outcomes, and the perceived value and credibility of online courses, programs, and qualifications all hang precariously on the extent to which institutions and organizations are capable of retaining their students (Cocea, 2007; Tyler-Smith, 2006). We turn now to research in online student attrition and retention to gain an understanding of some of the factors influencing a student's decision to leave or to complete an online course or program.

Understanding Online Student Attrition

In the latter part of the previous century, several popular models of student attrition and retention in formal educational programs were conceived. Vincent Tinto, whom some consider the godfather of student retention issues in higher education, has a model that has been widely cited and used (Tinto, 1975). The results from Tinto's longitudinal study of on-campus student retention rates led him to surmise that the likelihood of a student choosing to persist with or discontinue formal study is based on the degree to which she is able to integrate into the academic system of the institution. The components of such a system include intellectual development as typically exhibited by grade performance and learner portfolios as well as the social interaction system composed of the course lecturers, guest experts, and peers. The combination of academic and social integration factors was revolutionary for that time and became the basis from which later models were designed and adapted.

David Kember (1989) expanded on Tinto's model to consider unique learner characteristics typical in distance education arenas. Such characteristics include the fact the students in these courses are likely to be mature adults studying part-time who are simultaneously juggling family and work responsibilities. Elements of Kember's model include Learner characteristics, Learner Goal commitment (intrinsically versus extrinsically motivated), the Academic environment, and the Social/Work environment. Cost/benefit analyses also play a role in retention in his model. Kember pointed out that these elements need to be integrated and often change during the students' academic career. From his perspective, students then weigh together all these factors when making the decision to complete or drop out of a course or program.

Building on these ideas, recent models of online student attrition attempt to construct a more comprehensive understanding of the factors influencing a student's decision to drop out of online courses. Alfred Rovai (2003), for instance, proposed a composite model to explain student drop-out containing two distinct stages. In the first stage, he considers two factors that are apparent prior to admission: (1) learner characteristics including age and gender; and (2) learner skills such as computer literacy and reading and writing ability. In the second stage, Rovai includes two after-admission factors, namely: (1) external factors such as finances, time constraints, and work commitments; and (2) internal factors such as academic integration, social integration, and self-esteem. Noteworthy in Rovai's model is that the two-stage process helps administrators, educators, and even learners themselves unpack, identify, and act upon factors likely to hinder their progress through the adoption of appropriate intervention strategies. As apparent in Table 2.1, we employ his dual-stage idea in our synthesis of the common strategies applied in mitigating student attrition.

Based on Rovai's work, Berge and Huang (2004) developed a dynamic and context-sensitive model to illustrate the importance of individual and institutional perspectives in the online attrition process. They incorporated three variables: (1) personal variables (e.g., demographic and prior educational experience), (2) institutional variables (i.e., bureaucratic variables, academic variables, and social variables), and (3) circumstantial variables (i.e., social interaction) in their model. The model from Berge and Huang is advantageous in its flexibility in allowing different weightings to be allocated to each of the key variables as priorities for planning and implementing changes for the different stakeholders involved (e.g., students, educators, and administrators). This model, therefore, allows for timely interventions to be quickly put in place to enhance retention.

Building on the need to concretize the range of individual, institutional, and circumstantial (external) factors affecting a student's decision to persist with online learning, Jun (2005) conceptualized a holistic model of five general areas accounting for most of the causes of online student attrition. These five areas are (1) individual background, (2) motivation, (3) academic integration, (4) social integration, and (5) technological issues.

It is clear that these models highlight a range of individual, institutional, and circumstantial factors that have an impact on a student's decision to persist in online distance education contexts. Given the complex nature of online retention, we decided to survey a wide body of literature with the intention to identify the varied reasons and explanations offered for learner attrition. These factors are synthesized and illustrated in Table 2.1. They are categorized into three factors: (1) Individual, (2) Course-Related, and (3) Technological. As can be seen in Table 2.1, the bulk of the factors affecting retention in online courses are related to individual factors involving learners' assumptions, motivation, skills, background experiences, and personal circumstances that impede their participation in online courses. Next, we combed the literature looking for strategies

TABLE 2.1: A SURVEY OF FACTORS AFFECTING ONLINE LEARNER ATTRITION.

Individual Factors *(Learner circumstances, learning skills, coping skills)*	Course-Related Factors *(Course design and communication factors, faculty responsiveness, peer interaction, learning preference)*	Technological Factors *(Course-related technical issues, systems, and design)*
1. Lack of self-management skills.	1. Lack of course structure.	1. Limited training available; no help or support systems.
2. Underprepared for challenges in distance learning or perceive distance learning courses to be easy.	2. Incompetent instructor.	2. Technical difficulties, including access, slowness, password problems, navigational issues, etc.
3. First year online students are especially affected by: • lack of self-directed learning strategies. • poor time management skills. • poor independent learning skills.	3. Availability of academic support; approachability of staff. Access and friendliness of administrative system and staff. General lack of support.	3. Poorly designed courses (i.e., suitability of program design, content, delivery, assessment strategies).
4. Lack of time or time conflicts between family or work commitments.	4. Ease of content.	4. Must download software client to run.
5. Financial strain.	5. Lack of interaction between students and between students and instructor.	5. System favors those with technology backgrounds or programming (i.e., HTML) skills.
6. Low language literacy ability (reading and writing).	6. Isolation, lack of sense of belonging in an academic community.	6. Using complex, unfamiliar, or new technology.
7. Learning difficulty.	7. Lack of learner choice/learning preference.	
8. Impact of previous educational encounters.	8. Lack of personal and immediate feedback on coursework.	
9. Low level of motivation (insufficient self-motivation, inadequate self-directed learning skill).		
10. Low commitment to study.		
11. Poor incentives to learn.		
12. Lack of social/family support.		
13. Low computer literacy skills (slow typing skills, difficulty using the Course Management System, or CMS).		
14. Lack of confidence with using computers (lack of computer literacy).		

TABLE 2.2: A SURVEY OF STRATEGIES TO MITIGATE ONLINE LEARNER ATTRITION.

	Prior to Admission	**After Admission** *(during period of study)*
Institutional	1. Providing learner orientation to distance learning (induction into online course/precourse training or online tutorial/preenrollment advice).	1. Assign "learning guides" especially for first-time online learners as liaison between students and other available resources.
	2. Implement policies in support of ongoing high-quality online courses and programs; develop a culture that says online learning is as important as classroom learning.	2. Provide online access to a variety of student support (e.g., academic advisement, social, personal, technical) services (where possible, available on a 24/7 basis and not just limited to normal working hours).
	3. Offer short courses rather than long ones.	3. Hold managers accountable for corporate trainee access to and completion of online training courses.
	4. Select qualified online instructors.	4. Provide formal rewards and recognitions for trainee completion of online courses.
	5. Provide training for those who support online learners (general staff).	5. Keep online class size small.
	6. Provide pedagogical and instructor training prior to teaching first online course.	6. Provide faculty support services.
	7. Provide student advice about the choices they have to make in their programs of study and future career goals (to establish expectations about distance learning and to provide a road map to completion and achievement of personal goals).	
	8. Post all course syllabi, coursework, assignments, and learning outcomes on the Web for prospective students to gauge the workload prior to signing up for a course.	
Instructional (Pedagogical)	1. Train instructional designers and lecturers in the pedagogy of online teaching.	1. Adjust the suitability and level of content to learner needs; include graded activities that start learners with simpler tasks to gain confidence from early course success, then lead them to more challenging endeavors.
	2. Improve online tutoring/academic services.	2. Simplify or limit course content navigation options to prevent cognitive overload; make graphics easy and simple to understand.
	3. Personalize learning content by referring to learner profiles.	3. Use active learning and learner-centered strategies.
	4. Put in place supplemental tutoring services.	4. Improve the learning process to include more interactions and foster collegiality; emphasize the importance of teacher presence in the class.

Prior to Admission	After Admission *(during period of study)*
5. Initiate contact with students via phone calls.	5. Have proactive contact; pace and prompt learners; track learner performance to ensure they do not fall by the wayside.
	6. Begin courses with icebreakers.
	7. Set high expectations for student success.
	8. Post your own introduction and encourage student introductory posts as well.
	9. Assign online students peer mentors.
	10. Set clear course expectations.
	11. Make classes fun, interesting, and rewarding.
	12. Make classes relevant for learners— "What's in it for me?"
	13. Provide timely feedback and encourage feedback from learners.
	14. Incorporate a variety of synchronous and asynchronous instruction to reinforce the learning of new material or assignments.
	15. Give encouragement and praise; applaud when students do well.
	16. Provide flexible, convenient scheduling, and frequent instructor contact.
	17. Have additional activities and extra-credit assignments for fun and creative touches.
	18. Require learner commitment and participation in the course.
	19. Provide timely intervention for learners.
	20. Facilitate informal online chats to build relationships.
	21. Align pedagogical goals with teaching activities and appropriate assessment strategies so that students understand the big picture in the course.
	22. Provide prompt and reliable responses to student queries.
	23. Use group-based projects to develop a learning community.
	24. Build in activities that empower students to become lifelong learners.

Technological	1. Improve technical infrastructure and design; ensure technology is robust and working.
	2. Enhance online support services (technical support) for instructors and students.
	3. Embed personalized support or help systems.

recommended by students, educators, practitioners, and corporate trainers for addressing learner attrition.

Table 2.2 showcases the strategies commonly cited. The table is divided into two broad sections to illustrate strategies that can be adopted (1) prior to enrollment in an online course or program, and (2) once a student has been admitted into an online study program. Under these two headings, the strategies are further organized according to those undertaken at the Institutional, Instructor (i.e., Pedagogical), and Technological levels.

The message from the recommendations highlighted in the preceding table is clear. The bulk of the strategies emphasize what most good instructors already know across any effective teaching-learning or training context—that is, high interaction levels and support from educators (and peers), timely feedback, meaningful learning experiences, and active learning strategies all enhance learner engagement and, ultimately, retention. As J. Olin Campbell (1997) from Brigham Young University aptly put it, "it's not the delivery method that makes the difference—it's the learning strategies employed with the delivery method, and the implementation of those strategies, that matter most" (p. 3).

Such guidelines raise the urgency for educators to understand the learner and the learning process, including the factors that facilitate students' motivation and internal drive to excel and those that inhibit, or worse, debilitate it. These strategies are not merely random ideas pulled out of a hat. For more than a century, psychologists interested in human learning, cognition, and motivation have referred to many of these very principles. They are, in fact, grounded in a well-established body of theory and conceptual understanding of how people learn.

Retention Wrap-Up

In this chapter, we detailed the explosive trends and demands for online learning courses and services. There is little doubt that online learning will have an impact on all of us in significant ways in the future no matter our age levels, occupations, or interests. We also discussed how different institutions and organizations are grappling with the realities of high online learner attrition. In response, we surveyed a wide array of guidelines and report recommendations intended to enhance online learner retention. Many of these retention-related suggestions are summarized in the two tables included in this chapter. Those who implement some of them as part of a long-range strategic plan or vision for online learning should see a positive effect in terms of reduced course attrition and withdrawal rates. Naturally, that is a big ticket item for many institutions and organizations.

We now turn to Chapter Three, which outlines four key perspectives on human learning and then considers how each, in turn, explains the role of motivation in learning online. We also discuss the rationale for adopting different motivational strategies, including a few of those mentioned in this chapter, and their placement in our TEC-VARIETY framework which we will further detail in the 10 chapters that follow after that. The overall intention is to help educators, trainers, and instructional designers to create more motivationally effective and engaging learning environments.

We want to note that although many ideas in this chapter pertain to what school, university, and corporate administrators might put in place to increase retention in online courses, the majority of the ideas in the remaining chapters are directly focused on motivational strategies and activities at the course or instructor level, especially Chapters Four through Thirteen. Administrators and decision makers seeking content pertinent to their needs might read the next chapter on online motivation. They might also scan through Chapter Fourteen on how to motivate and support novice online instructors as well as those who might be deemed more hesitant or even resistant to the idea; in particular, they might review the 10 specific online instructor support ideas listed near the end. Finally, the table reviewing the 100+ activities in Chapter Fifteen should prove valuable no matter your role or responsibilities in online learning.

CHAPTER THREE

ONLINE MOTIVATION FROM FOUR PERSPECTIVES

> Give me a dozen healthy infants, well-formed, and my own
> specified world to bring them up in and I'll guarantee to take any
> one at random and train him to become any type of specialist I might
> select—doctor, lawyer, artist, merchant-chief, and, yes, even beggarman
> and thief, regardless of his talents, penchants, tendencies, abilities,
> vocations, and race of his ancestors. I am going beyond my facts and
> I admit it, but so have the advocates of the contrary and they have
> been doing it for many thousands of years.
>
> —John B. Watson, *Behaviorism*, 1930, p. 82

Motivation: An Introduction

Former US Secretary of Education Terrel Bell hit the nail on the head when he mentioned, "There are three things to remember about education. The first is motivation. The second one is motivation. The third one is (you guessed it) motivation" (Ames, 1990). Bell echoes the sentiments of many others who view motivation as the essence of education (Bransford, Brown, & Cocking, 2000; Dennen & Bonk, 2007). Consider the following quotation from an online instructor we interviewed:

> Getting the kids hooked in for the graduate courses . . . I'm constantly racking my brain as to how to get them more involved and get more interaction going. . . . Because it seems to me as though they are not necessarily engaging. I don't know whether the re-

> sources aren't catchy enough or whether there's nothing I can do, whether it's actually them in the sense of they just haven't got the time or they just don't see it worthwhile. I tear my hair out. I don't know what to do to change it and I don't have the time to change it which is probably part of it as well (Laura, novice online lecturer).

Laura's comments typify some of the challenges faced by online lecturers. How do they motivate their learners to engage productively in Web-based learning environments? In Web-based contexts, understanding what motivates learners to study online and to continue to completion can give us clues as to how to best design and structure online courses to engage learners and encourage them to run the race to the end. Enhanced knowledge of learner motivation can give us greater insight into why some learners are more likely to be more successful than others along the way.

We begin by offering several perspectives on the term "motivation." Atkinson (1964) defined it as "the immediate influences on the direction, vigor, and persistence of action." Wlodkowski (1999, p. 8) expanded on this definition when he said motivation is "the natural human capacity to direct energy in the pursuit of a goal. . . . [W]e are purposeful, we constantly learn and when we do we are usually motivated to learn, we are directing our energy through the processes of attention, concentration and imagination, to name only a few, to make sense of our world." Fundamental in these definitions and viewpoints is the idea that human beings are purposeful in their actions and intents; that is, they focus their energies and interests in the process of striving toward a desired goal.

Educational theorists have typically considered the issue of human motivation from the standpoint of the current thinking on how humans learn. As a basis for our recap of several pertinent learning theories in this chapter as well as in the introductory sections of the next 10, we spent several years accessing and reading many special reports, monographs, and education books related to motivation in education (e.g., Ames & Ames, 1989; Brophy, 2010; Deci & Ryan, 1985; Lambert & McCombs, 1998; McCombs & Pope, 1994; Raffini, 1996; Reeve, 1996; Schunk, Pintrich, & Meece, 2008; Stipek, 1998). We uncover many of these motivational ideas through the following brief overview of four major theoretical eras: (1) behaviorism, (2) cognitivism, (3) constructivism, and (4) sociocultural theory.

Learning Theory #1: Behaviorism
Learner Motivation Through Carrots and Sticks

Behaviorists generally believe in scientific and objective measures of behavior to provide plausible explanations of learning. Such objectivistic theories were prominent throughout the first half of the twentieth century and still permeate educational settings today. Take the recent emergence of course management systems to offer online courses in a prestructured manner. Such highly structured or "canned" approaches are also apparent in MOOCs, which often rely on the instructor's preset delivery of content and later student regurgitation of it in computer-scored objective tests.

Unfortunately, internal aspects of human motivation were often ignored back in the 1920s, 1930s, and 1940s when behaviorism rose in prominence (Svinicki, 1999). The human mind was considered a "black box" that was too subjective and not to be trusted for scientific scrutiny. Experiments from this era were often conducted using water- or food-deprived animals, such as pigeons, dogs, mice, and cats. Among the best-known studies are Ivan Pavlov's training of dogs to salivate in response to the sound of a bell. You can watch a video today on YouTube of Pavlov and his dogs and another of Edward Thorndike's cats learning to escape from puzzle boxes, which showcase the concepts of trial and error and reinforcement.

A central aspect of behaviorism is that animals (including humans) learn by associating a stimulus to a response (or paired responses) that is promoted through external manipulation. In effect, human behavior can be reinforced or extinguished. It is malleable through rewards or punishments, hence the notion of carrots and sticks.

From this view, in an online or F2F classroom setting, the instructor is the dispenser of rewards and punishments while learners are mere passive respondents. Important in this idea of external manipulation is that external stimuli can affect student motivation to learn. For example, extrinsic motivational factors such as online scaffolds and guides, praise from tutors and instructors, and offering certificates on the way to master's degrees are deemed important to online learners (Singh, Singh, & Singh, 2012).

Encouragement and Feedback Principle. Based on work by Skinner (1938), the role of feedback in enhancing student motivation is particularly underscored. Providing feedback has been shown to enhance student performance and self-efficacy in learning (Wang & Wu, 2007). Timely feedback is widely recommended as part of an online lecturer's pedagogical repertoire and is consistently mentioned as a vital principle of effective teaching and learning in general (Butler, 2003; Chickering & Gamson, 1987). An example of providing learners with ongoing personalized feedback and assessment to enhance their motivation for learning is seen in the assessment of large undergraduate classes in Japan. This system allows students in basic computing courses to sit for a number of short online tests throughout the course to assess their ongoing performance, obtain feedback on their progress, and receive recommended resources and teaching materials suited to their improvement level (Koike, Ishikawa, Akama, Chiba, & Miura, 2005).

Similarly, among the latest developments in this area of computerized learning programs is the creation of Knewton. As an adaptive learning platform, Knewton can be integrated into online or hybrid courses to provide customized, personalized, and immediate feedback. In effect, it adapts the learning materials according to students' learning curves (Fischman, 2011). Based on behavioristic notions of feedback and corrective learning behavior, Knewton assesses what students are learning and how they best learn (that is, their learning styles). It also tracks their performance and progress, involves parents in students' learning, recommends a range of learning resources (videos, animations, interactive games, quizzes, and so forth) that are staged according to progressive levels of difficulty. Drawing from a networked database of learner progress, it can even recommend and pair students with partners of a similar learning style or profile to supplement their learning. Such forms of personalized learner feedback are currently growing and they not only free up teachers to focus on helping learners develop their higher-order thinking skills, but also give them the opportunity to customize their teaching strategies.

Based on the theoretical and empirical ideas emerging from this era, behavioristic ideas related to shaping, feedback, and support underpin the second aspect of the TEC-VARIETY framework. Although considered antiquated by many psychologists and educators today, behaviorist elements still exist in countless education, training, and clinical settings. Educational strategies embracing behaviorist ideas were pervasive in first-generation online learning programs through their use of clear objectives and learning outcomes, clear presentation of content and multimedia materials, and the incorporation of online testing to assess the individual learner's achievement and provide rapid and individualized feedback.

As we see, the behaviorist tradition often reduced ideas of human motivation and learning to that of external stimulation and fairly rigid quantitative measures. Fortunately, the next wave of views of human learning and motivation recognized the centrality of the human mind and sought out qualitative measures for understanding human motivation and learning. At that time, researchers began to investigate increasingly intrinsic aspects of human motivation.

Learning Theory #2: Cognitivism
Learner Motivation Through Intentional Goals, Beliefs, and Expectations

In the 1970s and 1980s, cognitivism shifted the prevailing emphasis on external or environmental conditions toward a focus on the internal or mental processes occurring between a stimulus and response (Schunk, 2008). Simply put, the black box was opened up. With the rise of the computer and computing technologies, human learning or information processing became analogous to computer processing that could address more complex forms of learning (thinking, memory, problem solving, language, concept formation, information processing) (Ertmer & Newby, 1993). Learning in the era of cognitive psychology was viewed as a process of knowledge acquisition where the teacher transmitted information and assisted learners to develop more efficient processing strategies to organize information in a meaningful way. From this viewpoint, learners are active seekers and processors of information, able to attend to, code, select, transform, rehearse, store, and retrieve information. Along the way, they develop the appropriate metacognitive skills, including self-planning, self-regulation, and summarization. With such skills, the learner can assert greater control over his own learning (Schunk, 2008).

Cognitive psychology research inspired a host of experimentations with distance learning. Although such research initially took place with satellite technology, television, and interactive videoconferencing, its impact is now apparent in fully online learning and blended learning courses and programs. The initial goal of such research was to begin incorporating strategies that would enable learners to process the material more efficiently. A cognitive approach leveraged the processing and multimedia capabilities of the computer to present information in different modes, be they textual, verbal, or visual (i.e., multimedia), and to allow learners to explore such material according to their personal needs (i.e., hypermedia). This approach also encouraged information encoding through the use of concept maps as well as analogies and acronyms. Similarly, online notecards, outlining tools, job aids, and question prompts could augment or support learners' limited working memory capabilities when reading or writing (Bonk, Medury, & Reynolds, 1994).

Research in cognitive psychology lends insight into how to adapt learning materials to suit a variety of learning styles or perspectives. It also influences how instructors utilize intrinsic and extrinsic motivational strategies to encourage learners to learn, giving learners opportunities to reflect on their learning and to monitor their own progress through self-check questions and exercises with feedback. When effectively implemented, such approaches help learners develop the requisite metacognitive strategies that can drastically improve their learning approach and outcomes (Mayer, 2003).

At the height of the cognitive psychology movement, much headway was made in terms of motivational theory development (Brophy, 2010; Svinicki, 1999). Key motivational theories derived at that time included attribution theory (Weiner, 1980), self-efficacy (Bandura, 1989), goal orientation theory (Ames, 1992; Dweck, 1986), and self-determination theory (SDT) (Deci, Vallerand, Pelletier, & Ryan, 1991).

Attribution theory focuses on explanations for motivation based on individuals' beliefs regarding the causes of their success or failure. Learners may attribute their success or failure on a task to themselves (e.g., their own ability) or to external situational factors (e.g., luck). Teachers can take appropriate measures to focus students' attention on factors that they have control over instead of uncontrollable external forces.

Self-efficacy is the belief or judgment of your ability to perform a task at a certain level to achieve particular goals. Learners with a high self-efficacy for learning believe in their ability to initiate successfully, cope with, and complete their learning task. Self-efficacy determines the level of effort and the degree of perseverance a learner is willing to invest when faced with setbacks (Bandura, 1986). Bandura's notion of self-efficacy and self-regulation has been successfully applied in the design of motivationally engaging online learning environments to encourage personalization, adaptivity, effective tutoring, and collaborative learning among students (Cocea & Weibelzahl, 2006).

Goal orientation theory examines individuals' cognitive motives and their relationship to intrinsic motivation. It highlights learners' behavior as determined by the type of goals they hold, such as learning goals or performance goals. When focused on learning goals, on the one hand, students are motivated to learn for intrinsic reasons, such as to enhance their knowledge, skills, and attitudes. Students with performance goals, on the other hand, are motivated by the need to demonstrate their competency and capability especially in competition with their peers. Performance-oriented goals tend to lead to more shallow and less diverse learning strategies.

Self-determination theory (SDT), however, describes motivation as being intrinsic or extrinsic in nature (Deci et al., 1991). Intrinsically motivated individuals are driven by an interest or enjoyment of a task, whereas extrinsically motivated individuals are driven by external rewards such as grades, punishment, coercion, and money. SDT emphasizes that individuals need to be self-determining or to have some degree of control in determining behavior. Importantly, it advocates that individuals' natural and intrinsic tendency to grow and develop can be fostered through supportive learning contexts that encourage learner autonomy, competence, and relatedness (Ryan & Deci, 2000).

Autonomous individuals exhibit higher levels of control and tend to experience a sense of freedom and choice over their actions.

Autonomy Principle. Studies that have explored how to facilitate learner intrinsic motivation support the need for autonomy, competence, and relatedness (Pink, 2009). For instance, a study by Hartnett, St. George, and Dron (2011) revealed how situational factors can disrupt online learner autonomy and competence, thereby having an adverse impact on learners' levels of intrinsic motivation and collaborative effort in a blended learning context. Without sufficient intrinsic motivation, online learners will fail to elaborate on their arguments or problem solutions in group discussions (Xie & Ke, 2010). Not too surprisingly, Xie, DeBacker, and Ferguson (2006) have found that learners' intrinsic motivation was significantly related to their participation rates, and thus to the overall learning process. In fact, intrinsically motivated learners exhibited two to three times the participation rate of those who were extrinsically motivated.

Recently, other cognitivist principles such as learner academic locus of control (internal as opposed to external attribution of outcomes) and metacognitive self-regulation skills (such as the ability to self-evaluate, organize, monitor, review, and seek information) have been explored (Lee, Choi, & Kim (2012). Youngju Lee and her Korean colleagues compared differences between online students who persisted with their studies and those who dropped out. They found that students' perceptions of academic locus of control and metacognitive self-regulation for learning were the most important factors influencing their decisions to drop out. They recommend that online educators assess these two factors prior to students embarking on an online program, so that customized support and lessons can be tailored to students' learning needs.

Curiosity Principle. Applications of SDT in educational settings to promote learners' intrinsic motivation have been extended to include learner-centered elements in the design of F2F as well as online courses. Such elements include enthusiasm, challenge, curiosity, choice, engagement, control, novelty, fun, fantasy, relevance, collaboration, and project tasks (Deci et al., 1991; Kawachi, 2002; Lepper & Hodell, 1989). Not too surprisingly, each element is aligned with the TEC-VARIETY framework.

As will be discussed in Chapter Six, researchers interested in the psychology of gaming, such as Thomas Malone (1981), have explored the intrinsic motivational properties of computer games. In particular, Malone was interested in how these games fostered a sense of fun, fantasy, challenge, and curiosity. Gaming principles related to learner Curiosity (surprise, intrigue) and Autonomy (choice, control) underpin the third and fifth components in the TEC-VARIETY framework.

Learning Theory #3: Constructivism
Learner Motivation Through Active and
Social Construction of Meaning

Although cognitivism is progressive in bringing the need for students' control of their own learning to the forefront, it is still a highly individualistic concept of learning and knowing. In the 1980s and into the 1990s, constructivism enjoyed increasing popularity. It championed a view of learners as actively involved in creating meaning from their experiences, instead of being spoon-fed knowledge through instruction (Ertmer & Newby, 1993). Decades prior to wider acceptance, proponents of constructivism had already included such notables as John Dewey, David Ausubel, Jerome Bruner, and Jean Piaget.

Constructivist views deem learning to occur best in problem-based settings where learners are required to use their prior knowledge and experiences to explore, inquire, interpret, reflect upon, judge, and construct understandings for themselves. Constructivist teaching approaches shift the focus from the teacher to the learner. In this approach, the teacher becomes the coach or the guide at the side who helps learners acquire knowledge on their own schedule. Specific constructivist-advocated teaching strategies include many active learning principles such as situating tasks in real-world contexts, goal-based learning attuned to learner interests, and guiding and coaching a novice toward expert performance as in a cognitive apprenticeship (Collins, Brown, & Newmann, 1989).

In terms of specific principles, an instructor wedded to constructivism might rely on the presentation of multiple perspectives by using collaborative learning to develop and share alternative views. She might also require social negotiation as found in debates, controversial discussions, and evidence giving. And she might utilize authentic examples and offer opportunities for reflective awareness on solutions, thereby fostering the development of self-regulatory skills (Jonassen, 1994).

Tension Principle. Motivational theories that embrace constructivist ideas are based on the need for learners to have "consistent, accurate and useful understandings of the world" (Svinicki, 1999, p. 20). For example, Jean Piaget (1926) and his followers found that tension or controversy can move learners into a state of disequilibrium, thereby motivating them to find out more information in order to return to a state of equilibrium. Such principles are embedded in the ninth principle of the TEC-VARIETY model related to arousing motivation through tension and conflict.

Variety Principle. A study by Leslie Miller and her colleagues (2011) at Rice University tested the extent to which Web-based forensic games were useful in engaging secondary science students to consider science, technology, engineering, and mathematics (STEM) careers. The games were designed to be ill-structured situations where students had to role-play and solve a real-life scientific problem. This process appealed to students and challenged them to engage with new science ideas in a novel manner. It also tapped into their personal fantasies and provided a fun and relevant context for them to engage with science content. At the end of the study, not only did students' content knowledge increase but, more important, the role-play exercise elevated their motivation to take up future science careers. This gaming task relates to the curiosity and variety principles of the TEC-VARIETY framework.

Setting the Tone/Climate Principle. In the current age of much learner choice and autonomy, humanistic ideas from decades past have begun to flourish once again. Humanistic psychologists view learners as seeking to better themselves through their learning experiences. Learner-centered ideas that place the learner at the core of the education process are central to humanistic psychology doctrine. Without a doubt, such views have recently risen in prominence. We should not forget, however, that giving learners the autonomy, choice, and control over what they are learning and how best to learn was derived decades ago from the work of famed humanistic psychologists, such as Carl Rogers (1983) and Abraham Maslow (1987).

Both Rogers and Maslow spoke of the need to have a psychologically safe environment for learning. According to Rogers, the learning environment should be filled with respect, genuine forms of learning, and choice or freedom to learn. This has been a challenge for online learning environments, particularly those involving only asynchronous forms of communication which are often presumed to be cold and impersonal. Such environments lack the usual communicative cues we take for granted in F2F learning environments. The lack of social presence and verbal cues from the instructor as well as from peers in the course is often blamed for the acute sense of isolation and disconnectedness that online learners experience.

Research conducted during the past couple of decades has shown that it is possible to reduce the traditional social and psychological distance perceived by participants in online courses. The use of teacher "immediacy behaviors" is pivotal, however. Teacher immediacy behaviors can be verbal or nonverbal. Verbal immediacy relates to the increase in the psychological closeness between teachers and students. It is displayed in the use of student names, humor, encouraging student feedback, finding out how students are, and sharing personal experiences. In contrast, nonverbal immediacy includes cues communicated through smiling, eye contact, body movements, and vocal expressiveness (Hutchins, 2003).

In online environments, the teacher's verbal immediacy behavior is particularly essential for setting the tone and climate conducive to enhancing student participation, satisfaction, and overall learning. Ben Arbaugh's study (2001) of student satisfaction in an online MBA course found that lecturer immediacy behavior was a positive predictor of student satisfaction. Hutchins (2003) added that a sense of immediacy can also be related to course design or how a teacher arranges the course components in support of learners' internal learning processes. For example, embedding help systems, online tutorials, and computer-scored exams can lend a sense of immediacy in feedback and support.

The TEC-VARIETY framework reflects these important principles, specifically that of setting appropriate tone or climate in the class (first principle), adding a variety of interesting tasks (fourth principle), and using tension or challenge (ninth principle) to facilitate learner interaction and exploration of course materials.

Learning Theory #4: Sociocultural Views Learner Motivation Through Considerations of the Cultural Milieu

In the 1990s, there was an obvious shift in education and psychology toward acknowledging the role of social and contextual processes in how we learn. Some have argued that our cognitive processes are inherently cultural and thus inseparable from the specific situations in which we live (Rogoff, 2003). Most prominent among sociocultural theorists is Russian psychologist Lev Vygotsky (1978). Vygotsky recognized that scaffolded instruction by more knowledgeable others at the edges of a learner's zone of proximal development is pivotal to understanding human learning and development. Today, technology tools can foster new forms of such scaffolded support with word processors, grammar checkers, concept mapping tools, online think sheets, and referenceware like Wikipedia. People learn through their participation in commonly valued activities of a particular group where cultural tools such as language and artifacts help mediate learner understanding and meaning making in a highly collaborative learning process (Lave & Wenger, 1991). The sociocultural orientation is manifested through popular learning approaches and instructional ideas that have arisen since the late 1980s including situated cognition (Brown, Collins & Duguid, 1989), problem-based learning (Savery & Duffy, 1996), communities of practice (Wenger, 1998), and various ecological perspectives on learning (Barab & Roth, 2006).

Current online learning programs provide learners assorted means of electronic access and interaction with the learning materials. They also encourage fellow learners and tutors to emphasize strategies such as collaborative learning and the negotiation of ideas. Perhaps most salient and striking is the change in the role of the lecturer from an expert to that of a colearner or learning concierge and curator. As this change occurs, students become increasingly responsible for their own learning.

Interaction Principle. The role of interaction with instructors and expert guests as well as with peers is underscored by the sociocultural approach. Various types of interactions are necessary to promote a supportive community of inquiry or learning community in online learning contexts. For example, Karen Swan emphasized learner interaction with the course content, the lecturer, and with peers (Swan, 2001). Other online learning researchers like Liam Rourke and his colleagues (Rourke, Anderson, Garrison, & Archer, 1999) have explored affective, interactive, and cohesive interactions. Still others have highlighted intellectual, social, and emotional interaction (Khoo & Forret, 2011).

Studies have revealed that interaction and socialization have a direct impact on online learner motivation (Xie & Ke, 2010). Specifically, interaction and socialization foster learners' intrinsic motivation and engagement in a course (Shroff, Vogel, Coombes, & Lee, 2007). They also influence student satisfaction and their perception of learning (Swan, 2001) including those of students in online MBA courses (Arbaugh, 2000).

So crucial is the notion of interaction in traditional and online learning environments that it is frequently cited as a key feature in principles of effective teaching practices (e.g., Chickering & Gamson, 1987). Besides learner-learner and learner-content interactions, learner-expert interactions are also vital in designing environments rich with authentic and problem-based learning (Grabinger & Dunlap, 1995).

Relevancy Principle *(also Curiosity, Interactivity, Engagement, Tension, Yielding Products).* Perhaps the most widely researched teaching strategy of this recent sociocultural learning era is that of making learning relevant, authentic, and meaningful to students. Researchers such as Herrington, Reeves, and Oliver (2006) have advanced current ideas on authentic learning in Web-based learning contexts to spur students to undertake deeper and more meaningful approaches to learning. Authentic learning tasks are typically ill-structured and complex. They also tend to utilize different forms of collaboration, involve creating a group product, embedding opportunities for reflection, and encouraging the exploration of a diversity of ideas and solutions. In such contexts, learners are empowered to choose what they need to learn, why they need to learn it, and how and in what order that learning will take place.

Current studies also underscore the importance of using relevant and authentic tasks among self-directed online learners as a way of fostering their intrinsic motivation to learn (Kim, 2009). Online corporate trainees tend to prefer the goal-driven aspects of product- and case-based learning approaches as well as opportunities for role play and debates (Bonk, Kim, & Lee, 2004). Similarly, students enrolled in professional programs want their learning related to real-life practice (Kember, Ho, & Hong, 2008). At the community college level, authentic tasks have been shown to reduce attrition rates (Aragon & Johnson, 2008).

The notion of relevancy is pivotal in many contemporary pedagogical frameworks that recognize learner-centered principles such as authenticity, collaboration, and active engagement (Toporski & Foley, 2004). Having a purpose or mission as well as a variety of challenging and fun topics is also vital (Butler, 2003).

Relevancy is also a cornerstone in the ARCS model developed by John Keller (1987, 2010) of Florida State University. The ARCS model can help online educators and trainers plan and design motivationally engaging courses and programs. In the ARCS model, four dimensions of motivation—attention, relevance, confidence, and satisfaction—contribute to students' interest, effort, and performance in a course. Gaining students' attention through resources that increase their curiosity or sense of inquiry is foundational for learning. This model is renowned for its systematic design and application of the ARCS dimensions across a variety of educational contexts (Cocea & Weibelzahl, 2006; Keller, 1999; Keller & Suzuki, 2004; Kember et al., 2008; Song & Keller, 2001). Kim and Frick's study (2011), for instance, highlighted the relevancy element in the ARCS model. More specifically, their study found that in addition to age and competence with technology, the best predictor of student motivation to initiate self-directed e-learning was the relevancy of the course to students' personal learning goals.

In sum, active and social collaborative strategies emphasizing the use of relevant and meaningful tasks (sixth principle), interactivity (seventh principle), engagement (eighth principle), and yielding products (tenth principle) underpin the entire TEC-VARIETY framework.

Tone/Climate and Variety Principle. A further contribution from the sociocultural era is the incorporation of ideas centered on "culture" in education. Social psychologists and anthropologists have long indicated the need to understand the virtues and unique aspects of how groups form, be it according to culture, ethnicity, or gender. Understanding group formation and growth is increasingly vital for online educators as social media proliferates and Web contexts continue to attract a rich and diverse range of learners across varied geographical locations, languages, cultures, gender, ages, and socioeconomic backgrounds (Hartnett, Bhattacharya, & Dron, 2007).

Considerations of culture in the design of online learning environments have largely been ignored until recently. However, as online learning becomes increasingly global, it is critical for online lecturers to be culturally sensitive in their tasks and examples. In order to ensure the success of all learners, effective online educators acknowledge the cultural capital and contribution that each student brings into the learning context. For instance, some students may come from collectivist-oriented cultures where one would quickly identify with a particular group's culture and goals, whereas others will undoubtedly come from more individualistic and competitive cultures and maintain goals geared toward personal success (Clem, 2005).

Along these same lines, Wlodkowski (1999) highlighted how strategies adopted by educators may, in fact, contribute to a lack of intrinsic motivation among some students. As an example, course icebreaker activities typically require students to share aspects of their personal experiences, beliefs, or feelings with others in the course. Although some students enjoy such interactions, those from cultures unfamiliar with such self-disclosure may be distressed by it. Wlodkowski cited how such experiences can be disconcerting for Asian Americans, Latinos, and Native Americans who typically confine such expressions to family members. Such tasks, in fact, can alienate some students from the rest of the class. Suffice it to say, such studies across countries and cultures raise important considerations for online educators to account for student diversity and their cultural contexts when adopting learning and motivational strategies to ensure the success of all students in the course.

Recognition of learner cultural diversity is acknowledged in our TEC-VARIETY framework, specifically that of setting appropriate tone or climate to foster a sense of belonging in the class (first principle) and using a variety of culturally relevant and inclusive strategies (fourth principle).

Trends and Takeaways

Current trends in motivational research highlight the dynamic, complex, and multi-dimensional nature of the factors influencing human motivation and action in online learning contexts (Hartnett et al., 2011). The evolution of motivational models (including our TEC-VARIETY framework) portrays a shift from individual cognitive and affective processes to current views of a more dynamic and embedded relationship between the individual and her social context. Wlodkowski reminds educators not to focus only on one particular motivational technique or strategy as a panacea for facilitating intrinsic motivation but rather to consider a combination of strategies and how to combine them meaningfully in a way that their mutual influence might bring about maximum effect in a class.

And that is a key intent of the TEC-VARIETY framework. There are 10 principles that educators can put to work either singly or using two or more together. The more integrated and coordinated the elements in the instructional design, the more likely they are to sustain learner intrinsic motivation. Our friend Tom Reeves (2006) from the University of Georgia expanded this idea of integration to include aligning course components such as goals, tasks, student and instructor roles, course design, content, the available technology, and the instructor's own assessment practices. When thoughtfully blended together, these components develop students' capacities across the cognitive, affective, conative (i.e., striving, volition, desire, and so on), and psychomotor realms.

TABLE 3.1: THEORETICAL UNDERPINNINGS OF THE TEC-VARIETY FRAMEWORK.

Principles / Learning Theories	Tone/climate: Psychological Safety, Comfort, Sense of Belonging	Encouragement: Feedback, Responsiveness, Praise, Supports	Curiosity: Surprise, Intrigue, Unknowns	Variety: Novelty, Fun, Fantasy	Autonomy: Choice, Control, Flexibility, Opportunity	Relevance: Meaningful, Authentic, Interesting	Interactivity: Collaborative, Team-Based, Community	Engagement: Effort, Involvement, Investment	Tension: Challenge, Dissonance, Controversy	Yielding Products: Goal Driven, Purposeful Vision, Ownership
Behaviorism		✓								✓
Cognitivism			✓		✓	✓	✓	✓	✓	✓
Constructivism	✓			✓	✓	✓	✓		✓	✓
Sociocultural	✓	✓	✓	✓	✓	✓	✓	✓	✓	✓

In this chapter, we visited four different theoretical perspectives and their underlying assumptions of how people learn and are motivated to take action to achieve their learning goals. While discussing these four psychological accounts of learning that have arisen in succeeding order during the past century, we highlighted studies that provided evidence for the viability of the 10 principles of our TEC-VARIETY framework. To help visualize the connection between learning theory and aspects of the TEC-VARIETY framework, see Table 3.1 which is intended to help instructors locate each principle in our framework in relation to the theoretical underpinning it serves (a check mark indicates that a theory supports a particular principle).

We encourage educators to gauge the usefulness of each motivational component found in TEC-VARIETY and consider how well it fits with their typical instructional strategies, course goals, content, types of learners, and overall teaching philosophy. Consider for a moment your own beliefs about how people learn. Then reflect on the extent to which you are comfortable in taking risks in using new technologies and teaching strategies. Perhaps this chapter will help you begin to think about which motivational principles may be lacking in your own courses. We hope that you continue to reflect on your pedagogical practices when perusing and selecting from among the 100+ activities put forward in the following 10 chapters of this book in accordance with the TEC-VARIETY framework.

The TEC-VARIETY framework is intended to be a helpful mnemonic for 10 key motivational principles for online learning success. It is a toolkit or online teaching guide. It can also be a framework that offers theory-to-practice-driven personal reflections at the end of a task, module, or course. TEC-VARIETY and the repertoire of practical ideas in the 100+ activities that follow in the following 10 chapters can empower you to adapt your instruction for higher levels of student motivation and engagement. If successful, you will enhance the quality of your class interactions, facilitate lifelong learning ambitions in your students, and help mitigate against student attrition.

It is now time to read on through the next 10 chapters and, we hope, to add a bit of TEC-VARIETY to your own courses.

CHAPTER FOUR

PRINCIPLE #1 TONE/CLIMATE

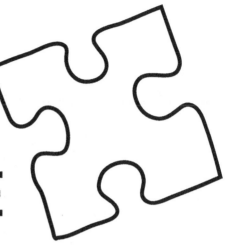

(Includes Psychological Safety, Comfort, and Sense of Belonging)

> I never teach my pupils; I only attempt to provide
> the conditions in which they can learn.
>
> —Albert Einstein

Perhaps the most obvious place to begin a framework related to online motivation and retention as well as to start a course is to introduce ideas related to the tone or atmosphere of the class. How an instructor welcomes learners into a course is perhaps tantamount to success. As noted in Chapter Three, those adhering to principles from Abraham Maslow, Carl Rogers, and other humanistic psychologists start with a focus on establishing a psychologically safe climate for learning. From this humanistic perspective, learners must be comfortable with the course, the instructor, and themselves as online learners. In addition, such learners must feel that their ideas are respected and encouraged. Establishing a welcoming environment allows the student to settle in and adjust to this relatively new form of instructional delivery.

Ideas from Carl Rogers have been influential in education for decades. His *Freedom to Learn* (1969) and *Freedom to Learn for the 1980s* (1983) are considered classic texts by many espousing learner-centered instructional approaches and opportunities for students to construct and share personal ideas and innovations. For Rogers, at the core of education, learning should be open and active, involve genuine tasks, respect students' backgrounds and ideas, and embed student-driven activities where and when possible. These principles should hold no matter what the age group or discipline.

What becomes apparent from reading Rogers' *Freedom to Learn* books is that there should be invitations for learners to make decisions and take responsibility for their own learning. In collaborative settings, there is a unique sharing of ideas and perspectives among the students. In effect, for Rogers, the more that learners are free and open to experiences, the more likely that they will be creative and participate in productive ways in the world at large.

When people feel valued and understood, there is a sense of safety to explore and a freedom to continue to grow. Such a perspective would resonate with those who incorporate aspects of Web 2.0 technology in their instruction. For instance, an instructor could be considered a Rogerian if he relied on student reflection blogs, Twitter feeds, and podcast shows. Such a humanistic and learner-centered approach is also apparent in collaborative document building using Wikispaces or Google Docs, as well as in social networking activities using systems like Facebook or LinkedIn. From a pedagogical perspective, an instructor could be a Rogerian if she relies on product- and problem-based learning and emphasizes the construction of knowledge and learning participation in the classroom. With such technologies and activities, students take ownership over the learning process. There is a freedom to express ideas, create new products, share inventions, and, in general, make significant learning contributions in the classroom, be they physical or virtual.

Instructors, no matter the situation, can create climates that are learner-centered and invitational in nature. Such environments are filled with a sense of meaning, individualization, belongingness, and encouragement. There are challenges but also supports to meet those challenges. Challenges do not mean roadblocks.

The initial sense of understanding or empathy expressed by an instructor can create strong bonds with students. These interpersonal connections can nurture student support early on in the course when some of them may feel lost or confused by the structure of the course and assigned tasks (Salmon, 2011). Opening activities can foster mutual knowledge among those enrolled as well as a set of expectations that the course will be highly engaging and interactive. Students will realize that an active learning approach will be utilized and that their productive participation is required.

While that is the optimistic side of education, opening moments in the course can also isolate students as well as disrespect them in some way. When that happens, there is scant motivation to participate in the course. Think about some new organization or conference in the physical world. When you arrive and no one is there to greet you, or you feel uncomfortable with the surroundings, you are unlikely to be an active participant, at least not immediately. The same is true if you do not know the mission or purpose of the institution, organization, or event. However, if social icebreakers or meet-and-greet activities took place before the start of the event or at the very beginning, you would likely feel greater dedication, commitment, and willingness to pursue difficult tasks later on.

Activities that set a positive tone such as social icebreakers help learners and instructors become acquainted with each other. This mutual knowledge can facilitate later small-group activities and hasten the effective functioning of online teams. Opening social activities like scavenger hunts of online course resources can also help to familiarize learners with the content that they will encounter in the course, as well as with the very tools that they will need to effectively access that content. There is far less stress in experimenting with passwords, access issues, and tool features at the start of a course than later on in the semester or term when one or more assignments are coming due.

When used effectively in an online or blended course, these early class activities help overcome emotional, social, or cultural discomfort and establish "swift trust" (Meyerson, Weick, & Kramer, 1996), a social glue that binds the online class participants together during the duration of the course to successfully complete the course's learning activities and goals. Feelings of trust, rapport building, and a sense of camaraderie are typically assumed to be quite difficult to establish in online courses compared to F2F courses due to the separation of distance, space, and time. A study by Meyerson et al. (1996) indicated that online instructors can shortcut this process by putting in place building blocks for establishing swift trust.

The first week of an online course is especially crucial for developing trust via instructor actions such as initiating early communication with students and developing a positive tone and social climate through activities, such as those exemplified in this chapter. Online courses where swift trust had been achieved early in the semester were deemed to be more successful than those that had not (Coppola, Hiltz, & Rotter, 2004). Online lecturers who downgrade the importance of setting a psychologically safe class tone and swift trust do so at their own peril, leaving their students vulnerable to a higher likelihood of feeling isolated and uncared for (Jarvenpaa & Leidner, 1998).

Once established, that sense of trust is sustained through frequent and predictable communication with the instructor as well as regular feedback from him. There are also opportunities to provide feedback back to the instructor. Such a course is designed for high levels of interactivity and trust building. Many of the activities in this chapter as well as the nine that follow are meant to help in that regard.

Technologies for Principle #1: Tone/Climate

When it comes to establishing a certain tone and climate, there are many technology tools from which to select. For instance, a public wiki for a course or training event allows the world to peek in and contribute to it. Such a tool helps students realize that their learning in this particular course will be global in nature. At the same time, a private class wiki can also foster an awareness that students can contribute to the learning of their peers in this class while assuring class members that their ideas will not be read, commented on, or pirated by those outside their course. Polling students as to their preferences—public or private—would best determine the route chosen.

An instructor might also welcome students to her course with a short online video offering a brief course overview and an explanation of her teaching philosophy. That same instructor might refer newly enrolled as well as potential students to a class website or instructor blog. Students might also become acclimated to the class by watching Web-streamed lectures of the instructor or listening to one or more of her podcasted lectures from previous semesters.

Instructors relying on several methods to create a warm climate for learning might think about creating an online template or job aid for navigating all of them. Many online instructors post their course syllabi to the Web with links to course readings, videos, and other online resources. Posting a syllabus to the Web is akin to having an online welcome mat for potential students as well as recent graduates or course alumni. For those currently enrolled in the course, it is a sign that the course materials will be open, online, and free to explore at will. The tone of the class will be one of learner self-exploration and discovery.

Most of the activities described in this chapter do not involve cutting-edge or expensive technologies. Many simply utilize computer conference systems and their online discussion forums, which have existed for decades. In such forums, students and instructors can make introductions, form relationships, share personal and professional information, and generally learn more about each other. Such social icebreakers, while not necessarily heavy when it comes to course content, set the stage for many later course activities. Bonk, in fact, had 30 percent of his students drop his first fully online course back in 1997. After he added a few social icebreakers, the percentage of students failing to complete his online courses dropped to zero the next time he offered that same course online.

Ten Online Activities in Principle #1: Tone/Climate

In this chapter, we detail 10 learning activities that correspond with the first principle of the TEC-VARIETY model, namely "Tone" or "Climate." Attached to this principle are concepts such as psychological safety, comfort, and sense of belonging. There is extensive overlap within the 10 principles of our framework. As a result, with minor tweaking, many of the activities in this book could be relocated as prime examples for one of the other nine principles. In fact, many of the activities listed in this chapter relating to the Tone or Climate principle address other principles, such as encouragement, curiosity, or autonomy, in direct or indirect ways.

As was noted in Chapter One, the scales provided for each of the 100 activities—related to the risk, time, cost, and degree of learner-centeredness—are highly subjective but reflect our extensive online experiences and backgrounds. The reader should be aware that each rating is dependent on many factors including the content area, degree of learner familiarity with the Internet, and the age of the learners. You should also keep in mind that these risk, time, and cost indices, in this chapter as well as the following nine, are in regards to the instructor, trainer, moderator, tutor, or course developer, not the learner or learning participants. And what is deemed high risk to one instructor or trainer might be extremely comfortable for another. Keep this in mind as you explore the following 10 activities for establishing a safe tone and climate.

Activity 1. Personal Introductions

Description and Purpose of Activity. Introductions are a universal instructional technique across all forms of instructional delivery, content areas, and age groups. They break the ice on opening day of a class or training activity.

Many online educators would prefer to create a discussion thread for learners to make explicit introductions. Instructors or trainers could structure the introduction activity by asking for specific items or characteristics. For instance, ask learners to list their professional interests, goals in signing up for the course, and jobs that they have held in the past; in addition you could ask about personal matters such as hobbies and interests outside of school, favorite places to visit or vacation, or salient personality traits. We have found that the most interesting and useful posts are those that combine the personal as well as the professional. Again, be sensitive to student cultural issues when asking for these types of personal information.

As with many other activities in this chapter, the purpose of this technique is for the creation of socially shared knowledge and opportunities that might foster intersubjectivity among course participants (Rogoff, 1990). It is from social interaction and dialogue that many solutions are often found in education and training settings (Brown & Duguid, 2000). What may seem unimportant or inconsequential at first is often central to student learning. In addition, the personal introduction threads provide a space that students can revisit throughout the course; especially when they are matched with others for small-group activities.

Skills and Objectives. These include course interactivity, feedback, social interaction, sharing, appreciation of multiple perspectives, course diversity, community building, and mutual knowledge.

Advice and Ideas. Once again, the instructor should be one of the course participants who posts a personal introduction. In fact, he should be among the initial responders. Being the first to post establishes expectations for later course participation. There might also be instructional guides related to how much to post and the number of peers to whom learners need to provide feedback or comments. If someone has posted something really interesting or connected to a topic covered later in the class, highlight it. The instructor might also highlight commonalities across participant posts.

Variations and Extensions. To help reduce tension about the course, students could be assigned a partner (e.g., a Web buddy, e-mail pal, or critical friend) for the semester, with whom they would share their introductory information. Partners could ask a few clarifying questions or seek additional information. After a few exchanges, ask team members to share what they have learned about each other in a discussion forum, allowing students to add to any information that their partner reveals about them.

Another extension of this task would be for the instructor to create an online hangman game or crossword puzzle using information about the students in the course. A third variation would be to have separate discussion threads for personal introductions and professional introductions. Fourth, the students might initially vote on what areas or topics they want to include in their respective introductions. Such student decision making would set the stage for later learner-centered activities and autonomy.

Key Instructional Considerations

Risk index: Low
Time index: Medium
Cost index: Low
Learner-centered index: High
Duration of the learning activity: 1–2 weeks

Activity 2. Video Introductions

Description and Purpose of Activity. One activity that we have seen students and instructors use more and more is video introductions. There are many reasons why instructors are increasingly relying on them. First, there is the growing recognition of the need for social presence on the part of online instructors across all educational sectors. The communicative cues that can be embedded in a short instructor video of one to three minutes helps to personalize a seemingly "cold" Web-based environment and can set the stage for later learning in the course. Students can quickly understand the scope, purpose, and history of the course and associated course topics.

There are many other reasons for the surge in video introductions within online and blended courses. Enhanced bandwidth, lowered storage costs, and a vast array of emerging technologies for recording, categorizing, and storing shared online video has made such activities an efficient and effective aspect of online courses. In the past, the costs of video production and storage were too exorbitant for most online training and education, except perhaps for military or corporate training environments. And when video materials were produced, few learners had the requisite bandwidth to watch them.

Recording a video introduction serves many purposes. First, it lowers the tension among students signing up for the course by personalizing the course. Second, it advertises the course and program. Third, it can help boost the reputations of the instructor and program. Fourth, it can be replayed as many times as a student feels is warranted. Fifth, it can be reused in later semesters or versions of the course. It might also find use in similar courses by other instructors.

Skills and Objectives. These include observational skills, course planning, visual learning, and learner motivation and engagement. A key goal here is for lecturers to introduce the course in a personalized and engaging fashion to students (using audio and visual cues). Such an approach helps to familiarize students with the course content and resources so as to reduce personal hesitancy to enroll.

Advice and Ideas. Watch video introductions from other courses and instructors before creating your own. Take notes on them. Maybe talk to colleagues in your department or in your organization about what you ought to include. Check out your production studios and other available resources. Then script it out. Next, practice the introduction or have dry runs through the content before you go to production. We realize that it feels strange to see and hear a recording of yourself. Until you become comfortable with the technology and recording process, you will tend to be overly critical of yourself. Relax, this feeling is natural and the situation will get better over time. In addition, consider how props, jokes, and interesting stories or examples might pull potential students into the course.

To create the video, you might be able to use the technical support services of your organization or institution. Find out what resources are available. Some instructors use a common audio screen and lecture capture tool such as Panopto to record themselves from the convenience of their desktop. Alternatively, you can sign up for a free screen capturing service like Screencast-O-Matic, Jing, or Screenr and use an internal camera and microphone on your laptop computer. Hit the record button and stop when done. Then post a link to the video file that was created. It is that simple.

There is much you can do with the video introduction once you have created it. As with most course content and resources, instructors can create a reflection activity on their video introductions. For instance, you could begin a discussion thread related to the introduction. Alternatively, online instructors might build question and answer (Q&A) sessions around their introductory videos. Such Q&A activities can help personalize the information in the course introduction. At the end of the semester, be sure to solicit student feedback on the videos you used in the course and take suggestions on how they could be improved.

Some instructors create a video at the beginning of a new course topic or module to give students an overview of what they will be learning. They may also include a video related to each of the course assessment activities as a means to walk students through the requirements. However, instructors also need to keep in mind that there could be students with auditory disabilities. If that is the case, they will need to create a transcript of the video or closed-captioning in order to be ADA compliant. Along these same lines, visually impaired students will need an auditory file or the ability to access the text in a braille reader.

Variations and Extensions. One option or extension to this task is to have the learners create their own video productions. In our own classes, many students have voluntarily created and shared their personal introductions after viewing the instructor's introduction. A student video introduction is yet another means to personalize the course and grant students more power and control over their own learning.

Khoo was involved in a research project where intermediate-level science students (11 to 12 years old) recorded videos discussing their assumptions about what it meant to be a scientist at the beginning of the unit. This was followed by a second recording after the unit was completed. Being able to revisit their initial ideas and misconceptions on video proved an amazing learning experience for students in terms of seeing how far they had shifted in their thinking by the end of the unit. It also provided a valuable multimodal learning experience that was especially appealing to the more visually oriented learners.

A second option is to have students watch video introductions from instructors at other institutions or organizations and compare the content with that from their own instructor. Such an approach offers a different interpretation of the importance of the course or field of study. Perhaps key historical insights or milestones will be offered in those other introductions. Another possibility would be to have students watch the various introductions and provide a short summary, integration paper, or presentation across these videos to gain a more macro perspective of the course or entire field.

Key Instructional Considerations

Risk index: Medium
Time index: Medium to High
Cost index: Medium
Learner-centered index: Low to Medium
Duration of the learning activity: 1–2 weeks

Activity 3. Goals and Expectations

Description and Purpose of Activity. Each online course or training situation has a set of goals and learning outcomes established by the instructor or designer of the course. However, learners have their own goals and expectations. In this activity, students share their expectations for the class, including why they enrolled in it and what they intend to get out of the course or module (Dennen & Bonk, 2008). To emphasize the importance of this task, it might be the very first item to which students respond in a course discussion forum. After opening the "Course Goals and Expectations" thread, students would post a few of their goals and expectations for the course as well as comment on those of their peers.

There are many benefits to be gained from this one simple strategy. For instance, other students can read what their peers are expecting from the course and compare these to their own goals and expectations. There might be some commonalities across most of them in terms of their intentions for taking the class. And a few students with unusual requests may understand that the instructor might not be able to meet all of them. Another benefit is that fellow students in the course could offer each other tips or suggestions on how to meet some of their goals. In addition, this is a goal-oriented activity, meaning that it can shape the behavior of students toward the goals that they each have personally established. Posted goals give them something to strive for and feel a sense of personal pride or accomplishment when achieved.

Instructors gain an important perspective from reading through and commenting on students' goals and expectations. They can mention that they will get to a topic or issue of interest at some later point in the semester, thereby lowering any students' felt anxiety levels about the personal benefits of the course or inner tension that their needs may not be met in this course. At the same time, the instructor could alter or shift aspects of the course if she senses that there is an area with sufficient student interest that was not being addressed. Allowing for some degree of student choice and negotiation of the course's goals to meet student personal or professional needs is another way for instructors to effectively support and respect the many and varied student learning perspectives (Duffy & Jonassen, 1992).

Skills and Objectives. These include idea generation, reflection, goal setting, comparison and contrast, analysis, community building, and basic terms or factual knowledge. A key aspect of this activity is sharing what students know and plan to learn in the course.

Advice and Ideas. As with the eight nouns activity (Activity 5), direct modeling from the instructor will help students understand the "goals and expectations" task. Consequently, we recommend that the instructor and any teaching assistants be among the first to complete this task. In addition, the instructor could post interesting comments mentioned by students in previous semesters, with permission, of course.

The instructor can use the information that is posted to the course expectations thread in myriad ways. At the very least, she should read these posts and adjust ensuing classes appropriately. This is especially important for instructors hoping to build a learning community in their classes. A positive online class atmosphere can be promoted when negotiating and steering the class toward common learning goals. More specifically, such an environment is salient when encouraging students to work hard toward their goals and gently reminding them when they are off track. It is also useful when pointing out how the different tasks and activities will lead to achievement of the chief course goals listed at the onset of the course. Finally, instructors can use this information when drawing student attention to how the achievement of mutual class goals can result in reaching their individual learning goals and vice versa. Such techniques can foster a positive tone and feeling of mutual collaboration and respect for one another.

As part of this effort, the instructor could send a course announcement or an e-mail message that discusses or highlights some of the student goals and expectations, pulling out common themes as well as subtle differences. During this process, the instructor should respond to as many student postings as possible.

There are innumerable benefits from acquiring this information early in the course. Keep in mind that any listing of course goals or expectations is an indirect reflection of student prior knowledge of a topic. Students will indicate terms, principles, theories, and subject areas wherein they have preexisting knowledge or abilities, which enables the instructor to create conceptual anchors and tasks to incorporate that knowledge.

Some final advice relates to the reality of teaching and learning. Although this activity is highly learner-centered, students must realize that not every item in their lists can be fully addressed. Still, instructors and trainers must use their best judgment as to where and when an idea from a student could be implemented or even alter the course in some valuable manner.

Variations and Extensions. Many course tasks often spin off this one early course activity. For instance, we sometimes ask our students to post their goals and expectations in teams or in accordance with their career interests or occupational pursuits. Student goals and expectations in a counseling psychology course, for instance, may depend on whether they plan to enter school counseling, health care or government settings, or private practice. Once completed, they might be required to summarize the expectations for their respective group or theme area to compare it with other groups or career discussion threads. The instructor could also end the course or semester with a reflection paper task where students are asked to compare their initial goals and expectations to what they learned in the course.

To build a sense of community, ask students to name one or more people who posted certain goals and expectations. They could also build on the goals and expectations of students who took the course previously. Alternatively, instructors can summarize student goals and expectations in a list for students to rank or vote on so that they can have a more active voice in the class or indicate some of their learning priorities. Suffice it to say, this is one activity that can be operationalized in dozens of different and highly intriguing ways.

Key Instructional Considerations

Risk index: Medium
Time index: Low
Cost index: Low
Learner-centered index: High
Duration of the learning activity: 1 week

Activity 4. Personal Commitments

Description and Purpose of Activity. Similar to the goals and expectations activity, this activity simply asks students to post their commitments to the course. For instance, a student may say that he is committed to reading a certain technical report or book listed in the syllabus because it relates to his present job, or to finish this course during this particular semester as he will be halfway done with his master's degree by then. The number of commitments that the instructor expects students to list as well as any relevant peer interaction criteria will have to be clearly stated.

Embedding a personal commitments task in your online course may be the most momentous instructional decision you make. As with the goals and expectations activity, commitments force learners not only to think of personal outcomes that they wish to accomplish but also to actually list them for later evaluation and reflection. In effect, posting commitments offers adults with chaotic schedules a definitive end state to work toward. Humans are goal-oriented creatures. This singular task makes it possible for them to reach toward some personally high standard of success or self-actualization.

In addition, this task makes explicit what was once internal and highly secretive or personal for each student, thereby allowing the entire class, and sometimes the world, to read and react to what is posted. By making such personal commitments, a class filled with adult learners (or even K–12 students) is less likely to experience drop-outs. Each person posting such commitments has decided that there are achievable course goals toward which he or she is investing personal time and energy to accomplish. Fellow students can then acknowledge and support each other in meeting those stated outcomes. Such support might compel a person who is considering dropping out to want to continue so as not to be ashamed (that is, to save face).

Skills and Objectives. These include idea generation, goal setting, working backwards, reflection, comparison and contrast, and analysis. This task helps students perceive possible course outcomes and work hard to make them happen.

Advice and Ideas. Most of the advice in the previous activity applies here as well. As with the goals and expectations activity, this task can be accomplished through a course discussion forum using a free computer conferencing system or available discussion forum in a course management system (CMS) like Desire2Learn, Moodle, Sakai, or Blackboard. The instructor may also use a course wiki to accumulate and expand on student commitments. Freely available wiki tools that many educators tend to use include Wikispaces, PBworks, and Wikis in Education. Another alternative is to ask students to create a blog for the course and post their course commitments publicly or privately within it. Privacy may be especially critical for students from different cultural or ethnic backgrounds. Be sure to make such privacy an option.

As with course goals and expectations, personal commitments are a window into the minds of your students. Each commitment is built upon previous accomplishments, backgrounds, and experiences. Instructors who read through these commitments gain a rich understanding of what their students aspire to be after they finish that course or their entire program of studies. Do not downplay this knowledge. It may help you change directions in a course when students seem apathetic toward selected tasks or particular course content.

Savvy instructors build on such information and refer to it often. Students will realize that their instructor has read their postings and genuinely cares about what they will accomplish in the online or blended course. This realization, in turn, will support and perhaps solidify their projected or hoped-for end states. Effective instruction could include student reflections on the commitments that they have in common with others in the course.

Variations and Extensions. Commitments posted in the first week of a course might be significantly modified a few weeks later. Given that likelihood, instructors should assign follow-up commitment tasks. As an example, ask students to post their commitments a few times during the course and then write a final paper on how their commitments changed during the course as well as which commitments they actually reached and when. If some papers are particularly insightful, instructors could ask their authors for permission to share them with students in the ensuing semesters or versions of the course or training experience.

Another variation of this task is to have students post their commitments to different discussion threads that are set up by age, gender, occupation, or student background. It would not be too surprising if students' course outcome commitments significantly varied between students in their 20s and those in their 30s and 40s with families and children to raise. They also may be drastically different from commitments coming from individuals nearing retirement. As an add-on or modification to this activity, you could ask students what they can contribute to the course using their personal expertise, experiences, or interests. In effect, this would be a set of personal commitments to help in the operation of the course, as opposed to commitments to achieving a certain state of knowledge or competence at the end of the course.

Key Instructional Considerations

Risk index: Medium
Time index: Low
Cost index: Low
Learner-centered index: High
Duration of the learning activity: 1 week

Activity 5. Eight Nouns

Description and Purpose of Activity. One of our favorite activities is called the "eight nouns activity." It is as simple as the name implies. In this task, everyone is required to post to a discussion forum eight nouns that best describe themselves (Dennen & Bonk, 2008). Learners should also describe why each particular noun selected is representative of who they are. Depending on the instructor preferences, such descriptions can be short, perhaps one or two sentences, or longer, extending for a paragraph or more.

The first few nouns often come fairly easily. For instance, Bonk will quickly list "pirate," "music lover," "roadrunner," "wind," and "traveler." For the final three, he often has to think for a while. Ditto for most of his students. It is in the last few nouns, however, that they often reveal aspects of themselves of which even they were not fully aware. Much of that information might find later use in the course. For instance, data from the eight nouns activity could prove valuable as a factor in grouping students for project work. It could also be strategically employed for engagement and curiosity when the instructor mentions a student interest, hobby, or accomplishment that was noted in the eight nouns task back in Week One.

The eight nouns activity is a common opening icebreaker for an online course. It helps students quickly grasp the backgrounds of others in the course. With so much personal information on display for peers and instructors to read, many barriers or walls come down that could have stood in the way of later interaction in the course. As with many of the tone and climate activities of this chapter, the eight nouns activity can find use in both brick-and-mortar classrooms as well as in virtual learning situations. And, given enough time, it also can be employed in nearly any discipline area or situation.

Bonk has used it in online courses as well as in F2F ones. Back in the fall of 2002, he had a live class which included a student named Ugar who had recently arrived from Turkey. Ugar included the noun of "dishwasher" with his eight nouns posting. He said that he loved to wash dishes. As a result, anytime people brought food to that class, they noted that Ugar would be happy to take care of any dishes. While a joke, it was said appreciatively, and Ugar soon became highly popular in that class.

Another student in that same class was named Riad. For Riad's eight nouns post, he included the word "technology" in his profile. He then added that if something had a power supply, he wanted it. Riad also noted that he was a "traveler" and did a road trip each spring to California. A few years later, Bonk observed Riad getting out of his truck, and, after remembering the eight noun activity, he asked Riad if he had been to California lately. At that point, Riad turned around and a huge smile beamed across his face. He then said, "I just got back from my annual pilgrimage. Here I am. You remembered. Wow." Coincidentally, just as we were beginning to write this book, Riad was in attendance for a Webinar given by Bonk and this story was retold.

A third student in that class, Raquel, said she loved music, especially the Dave Matthews Band. A few hours after her eight nouns post, a fellow student named Theresa responded to her post with the URL for an online radio station wherein she could listen to Dave Matthews 24 hours a day. Such peer postings are not unusual. Students find out pieces of information about each other in the eight nouns activity. This socially shared knowledge becomes the seeds for rich interactions and collaborations later in the semester (Salomon, 1993). As such, the eight nouns activity is a springboard to later learning. The exact amount or percentage of learning that ensues as a result of the method is impossible to quantify.

Keep in mind, however, this difficulty with measuring direct learning outcomes is the case with most of the methods outlined in this chapter. Nonetheless, a warm and accepting social climate is the starting point for learning. It sets everything in motion. If an instructor fixates on learning outcomes such as new behaviors and higher order reasoning skills and ignores the affective and motivational aspects of the learning situation, it is doubtful much learning will actually occur that extends beyond a single unit or lesson (Gunawardena & Zittle, 1997). In the eight nouns activity as well as most of the others listed in this chapter, there are socially shared understandings and a build-up of common knowledge (Schrage, 1990) from which to discuss, debate, and negotiate meanings.

Skills and Objectives. These include feedback, feelings of social presence and connectedness, socializing, sharing, student interaction, idea generation, appreciation of multiple perspectives, mutual knowledge, instructional immediacy, and community building. The eight nouns activity is a fun, nonthreatening way to interact with the course content.

Advice and Ideas. The eight nouns activity is most appropriate at the start of an online course. It may even be used a few weeks before a course begins, especially if that course is a summer intensive one or taught in a short time span, as in an accelerated program. In such a situation, students will build rapport with each other that can immediately be put to use once the course starts.

There are many subtle aspects to the eight nouns activity that make it work. First, the instructor should post her eight nouns list as well. Honest and thoughtful comments from the instructor will serve as a model for student postings. Similarly, instructors might post samples from previous semesters as a means to ease students into the task. In addition to those models, learners should be asked to respond to at least one such posting of their peers, though preferably several. Again, having personal traits and hobbies on display for others to read is useful, but not enough. Equally if not more powerful is reading through peer postings and forming connections and common understandings. Students should also be clear about the task expectations, including how much to post, where to post, and when to have the task completed by. If needed, create an instructional scaffold or job aid on how best to interact with peers on the eight nouns task.

Variations and Extensions. The eight nouns activity could be employed in a synchronous brainstorming session. In such an activity, there would likely be immediate feedback on each student post. Another variation or extension involves creating an activity based on the information students have posted in the eight nouns activity, such as a crossword puzzle with clues about each person in the class from the eight nouns posting. Similarly, the instructor might create some type of matching task or accomplishment hunt activity (see Activity 7) where students would have a competition to name the person with a particular trait, hobby, or background. Bonus points could be awarded to the winner as well as to the first one who completes the eight nouns activity.

Another alternative is an "eight adjectives" (e.g., lazy, powerful, shy, bored, exotic, cooperative, sloppy, ruthless, and so on) or "eight verbs" (e.g., coordinate, entertain, amuse, push, unite, beg, dream, publicize, and the like) activity to describe each course participant. To help in this effort, hundreds of sample nouns, verbs, and adjectives can be found in the website Moms Who Think listed with the resources of this chapter.

Key Instructional Considerations

Risk index: Low
Time index: Medium
Cost index: Low
Learner-centered index: High
Duration of the learning activity: 1–2 weeks

Activity 6. Two Truths and One Lie

Description and Purpose of Activity. The sixth activity for building a climate rich in socially shared knowledge is a fun and sometimes challenging one. In this activity, students must post two truths about themselves and one statement that is a lie. Fellow students in the course or module must attempt to determine which piece of information is a lie and which items are truthful. They can guess this after asking questions of that individual or exploring online information that is available on him such as a profile page of Facebook, LinkedIn, or some other website. The students who guess the most correct answers could be given a bonus point or two or be recognized in some other way.

As with most of the methods detailed in this chapter, the two truths and one lie activity is a means for students to share personal information about themselves and notice commonalities with their peers. Along the way, they will learn interesting facts about each other which may come in handy in later group activities. Such shared knowledge might be used later during the semester as a means to boost student curiosity and engagement in the course. Though this activity should work across educational sectors, it might be especially appealing in higher education and corporate or military training environments. In fact, Rick Kulp (1999) at IBM in Chicago told us that he found this technique quite engaging for adult learners.

Skills and Objectives. These include interactivity, dissonance, feelings of social presence and connectedness, mutual knowledge, community building, and prompt feedback. A primary objective is to share personal information that builds rapport and may be useful in later course activities.

Advice and Ideas. Before starting this activity, give students a few examples from previous semesters. In addition, you should post two truths and one lie about yourself and ask your class to ascertain the item that is less than honest. To further arouse student curiosity and engagement, you could give students a set amount of time in which to complete this assignment.

Do not let it drag on for more than a week or two. In fact, it could be billed as a one-day or 24-hour activity. For instance, the instructor might kick off this activity at 6 p.m. Monday of the first week of the course and expect all guesses to be posted by 6 p.m. Tuesday. The instructor could ask students to send her a private e-mail or text message identifying their lie so that she can determine the winner. She could also have students vote on the funniest lie or on the best liar. Virtual award ceremonies could even be held.

Variations and Extensions. If your class incorporates many team activities during the semester, students could work in teams to figure out the respective truths and lies, with some kind of recognition for winning teams. The activity could be modified in many other ways such as telling nine truths and one lie or listing five truths and five lies. You could also ask students to tell two truths and one lie about their professional lives and two truths and one lie about their personal lives. The possibilities are endless.

Key Instructional Considerations

Risk index: Low to Medium
Time index: Low
Cost index: Low
Learner-centered index: High
Duration of the learning activity: 1 week

Activity 7. Accomplishment Hunts

Description and Purpose of Activity. Another activity that we occasionally use in our online and blended courses is called an accomplishment hunt. This is a technique that typically is used in F2F classes or training events to foster knowledge sharing and provide a sense of pride among those enrolled. Normally, students are asked to list three or four accomplishments in their lives such as one from the preceding summer or year, one from their academic career, and one or two others of which they are especially proud.

The instructor then creates a sheet of paper with a few accomplishments listed per student but with no names noted. Instead blank lines are placed before each set of accomplishments. Students in the class are handed the sheet of paper and asked to walk around the room and determine the person with each particular set of accomplishments; however, they can only ask one simple yes-or-no question of their fellow classmates—namely, "Is this you?" If they have not identified the correct person, they move on. If there is a match, than they must request the signature of the person next to the appropriate accomplishments.

In the online version of this task, there are several options. In one of our recent courses, we simplified the task to the bare bones. We ask students to list a few accomplishments in a discussion forum thread with their names boldly attached to them. We also required them to comment on at least a few accomplishments of their peers. Though such an approach may not be as fun or interactive as the F2F version, it still fosters student pride, intersubjectivity, and sense of accomplishment. Our students have found the online version interesting and informative.

Skills and Objectives. These include social interaction, analysis skills, peer feedback, fun, adventure, curiosity, mutual knowledge, fostering building pride, and strengthening an online community.

Advice and Ideas. Consider whether this task will be most effective in a synchronous or asynchronous activity. If the accomplishment hunt is an asynchronous activity, keep it simple. You could, however, create secondary Web pages for students to obtain signatures, keep track of points earned, and reflect on their overall progress.

Be sure to monitor the activity. When appropriate, instructors might provide subtle clues, highlight successful identity matches, prod participation, and add additional accomplishments or information about each student in the course as deemed necessary. As in the two truths and one lie activity, instructors may choose to establish a time period in which the activity will start and end, anywhere from a day to an entire week.

When done, the instructor should post an announcement about how well the activity went, including information on the winners and a final list of student names and their respective accomplishments.

Variations and Extensions. There are many alternative versions of this task. As an example, students could post future accomplishments or targets for their lives instead of those they have already completed. Such an approach fosters student creativity and goal setting. Another variation would be for students to write a creative short story including the accomplishments of two or more peers in the class. Students could vote on the most unusual, interesting, risky, and humanitarian accomplishments, with awards given out in each category.

Key Instructional Considerations

> Risk index: Low
> Time index: Medium
> Cost index: Low
> Learner-centered index: High
> Duration of the learning activity: 1–2 weeks

Activity 8. Course Fan Pages

Description and Purpose of Activity. By 2012, there were more than 1 billion users of Facebook. In fact, at that time, more than 70 percent of the active Internet users in the United States were Facebook members (Swartz, 2011). Along these same lines, over 60 percent of adults who use the Internet had signed up for one or more social networking sites (Hampton, Goulet, Raine, & Purvell, 2011). Not surprisingly, college instructors are beginning to tap into social media in their courses (Moran, Seaman, & Tinti-Kane, 2011).

Social media can be used to enhance the climate, tone, and sense of belonging in an online or blended course or experience. With the explosion of interest in social networking tools like Facebook, LinkedIn, Google+, Ning, and Twitter, creating a fan page for your course in a system like Facebook might attract potential students to it. A fan page can be your marketing platform. In addition, anyone can then become a fan of your course and also contribute to the page as well as promote it.

There are many possible learning activities that differentiate a fan page from an individual's page on Facebook. For instance, if there are F2F events or meetings, you could take and post a class photograph. You may also create a task that asks students to contribute Web resource links, photos, or other relevant pictures to the fan page. Someone else might post questions to vote on in the course fan pages. After becoming a member of the fan page, students could create, post, and modify documents, create events, and chat with fellow group members. As an added benefit, alumni of the course and those who graduated from your institution but never had a chance to take the course could be informed of the fan page and encouraged to contribute something to it.

A fan page is a bridge between formal learning and informal learning. As such, it can ease students into a new course experience while enabling them to share aspects of their academic life with friends and family. It also legitimizes previous student knowledge about the functions and features of social networking technology. At its core, it is a form of invitational and personalized learning. Those who stop by are encouraged to check out the course.

Skills and Objectives. These include engagement, social interaction, friendship, networking, community building, course interactivity, feedback, idea generation, and sharing multiple perspectives. The fan page is also a means to market your course in ways that potentially could go viral.

Advice and Ideas. With social networking activities and sharing, the course builds immediate momentum. Having a course fan page is akin to having an annual department picnic late in the summer just before the semester or school year begins. Alternatively, some instructors may consider incorporating fan pages as an ending course activity as opposed to a beginning one.

Consider assigning each student a different role or task in building up the fan page. Some students can be in charge of polling site visitors and sharing the results of those polls with course participants. Other students can be responsible for creating links to videos that relate to the course, whereas still others can find an important role collecting text-based resources. In this way, each person has a role or identity in the external window you are building for your course. As such, it can excite students about the learning possibilities of the course.

If you find success with this task, consider expanding it to multiple fan pages, possibly one for each semester or section of the course. You might also create cross-institutional fan pages or pages that extend globally but are related to a particular content domain or topic. Such fan pages might eventually serve as a recruitment tool as well as a means to brand your school, university, training organization, or similar entity.

Social media technology is changing rapidly. You may consider asking students which sites they prefer using or are currently thinking about switching to. At the same time, you can explore the benefits of different social networking technologies through your own experimentations as well as from talking to colleagues and family members. Whatever you do, keep your antennae raised and alert to new possibilities.

Variations and Extensions. Instead of the instructor deciding on the fan page appearance, the students in the course could be charged with creating and maintaining one. Another idea would be to use the fan page as a means of recruiting students who have completed the course to come back as mentors to the new students in the course. Students could be matched with their mentors (or be able to select from a number of possible mentors) using the profile or other available information in the course fan page. A course attraction or homepage might also be created in a blog, wiki, or some other emerging learning technology.

Key Instructional Considerations

Risk index: Medium
Time index: Medium
Cost index: Low
Learner-centered index: High
Duration of the learning activity: 1–2 weeks (or possibly ongoing for entire course or semester)

Activity 9. Favorite Websites

Description and Purpose of Activity. We often start our online classes with students sharing a couple of their favorite websites. Such a "share-a-link" activity can be used to reveal student learning preferences and interests. You quickly discover what students know and do not know. Oftentimes their knowledge may extend beyond what you planned to cover in the course. Such link sharing can also be used to create mutual knowledge among the course participants. And, if the shared Web resources are highly integral to understanding the course content, this activity is a means to expand the available course materials for all the students as well as for the instructors.

Posting favorite websites starts the course off with a personally relevant activity. Just like dogs in the woods, students are marking their territory by posting the links to online resources that are important to them. Sharing links and online resources starts with what students know and find valuable, helping to create a tone that is more friendly and personal. Such a technique stands in sharp contrast to approaches wherein students read a chapter or watch a lecture filled with completely unfamiliar terminology.

Skills and Objectives. These include searching and filtering information, exploratory learning, analysis and evaluation, comparison and contrast, and feedback. Such an activity fosters twenty-first-century skills related to information search, selection, and critical analysis, while simultaneously empowering students with a personal voice and self-directed learning. A key goal of this activity is motivating and retaining students through personal relevance, openness, and building on what they already know.

Advice and Ideas. Assign students to post one or more of their favorite websites to the resources section of their course management system. Consider using a wiki or collaborative group tool such as Google Groups for such sharing. In addition, be sure to require students to explore a certain number of the websites posted by other students, and rate or comment on them. If you incorporate some type of rating system, be sure to specify the criteria in advance. If the posted websites have to relate to course content, students could be asked to examine resource links posted by those enrolled in previous years. They might write compare and contrast papers or some form of reflection paper on the sites listed across the years or semesters in which the course has been offered.

The information that an instructor gains from this activity helps to identify students' interests, which can be built on as the semester or term unfolds, thereby making the course more relevant and personally meaningful. For example, students can be assigned to be resource persons or experts in their areas and asked to contribute their knowledge in a joint problem-solving or collaborative learning activity. It is important that information asked from students in early course icebreakers or social activities be used and built on subsequently in the course where appropriate. Otherwise students may feel that the activity was merely added on without any relevance to their learning in the course.

Khoo has heard from disgruntled online students who had participated in a similar type of activity that had not been structured well or coherently designed into the course. The lecturer intended for the activity to be a quick first-week course social icebreaker before proceeding with what she termed "the real business of learning" in the rest of the course. The course continued without incorporating any of the information gained from students in the activity. Students felt the activity was a waste of time and irrelevant to their learning. The fact that students worked in pairs and were only asked to comment on one other person's shared websites diminished their need to interact with other peers. Such a technique missed a huge opportunity as it bypassed the collective wisdom shared by the entire class. Moreover, as part of building a community of learners, the instructor should have also participated in the activity.

Variations and Extensions. Instead of sharing favorite websites, students might post other preferences. For instance, they could list their favorite movies, foods, sports teams, cities, countries, vacation spots, courses of all time, news headlines, jokes (clean ones), cartoons, and the like. You could ask them to write a short reflection paper critiquing or promoting websites posted by one or more of their peers. Alternatively, using preestablished criteria, students could vote on the quality of all the websites posted. There could also be competitions for students to provide top-ten website lists on topics that will be explored later in the semester. Another idea is to consider inviting the designers of the top two or three ranked sites for an online class chat about the purpose and intent of their sites.

Key Instructional Considerations

Risk index: Low
Time index: Medium
Cost index: Low
Learner-centered index: High
Duration of the learning activity: 1–2 weeks

Activity 10. Online Cafés

Description and Purpose of Activity. An online café can be created as a special place and social space for learners to "hang out" informally. Here, students can post questions and comments on personal interests, pertinent items in the news, and so on. They could in fact discuss anything they want. The online café is a safe haven that operates within as well as outside the course. It is in this virtual space where formal meets informal. The online coffeehouse or café is a place to get to know peers and perhaps the instructor without worrying about the degree to which each comment relates to the topic of the week, or to any part of the course for that matter. As such, this technique helps to personalize the course and establish a learner-centered course philosophy.

From our experience, students post a range of topics in the online café. Sometimes students will post questions about technologies that they heard are popular. They might ask their peers about where they can get a good deal on a computer or smartphone. We have seen students post information about job openings for those who are looking for a position. Still other threads in the café will typically be about the course itself. Students could be looking for confirmation of ideas that they have for final projects, or ask for clarification on potentially confusing aspects of the course or topics. We have found that issues that are resolved in the café tend to lower learner tension and anxiety. Hence, this activity has emotional as well as cognitive ramifications.

The online café builds bonds between and among students enrolled in the course. It is in the café where everyone can act as they do in everyday life. They can let their hair down a bit. Over time, students come to know each other and respect each other's opinions. Trust, empathy, and respect emerge. It is also in the café where the sparks for an online learning community might first be seen. If properly nourished and managed, such sparks become flames. As is obvious by now, while the activities highlighted in this chapter emphasize the social and emotional aspects of learning over the cognitive side, such techniques often elevate the success of the online course to new levels. In addition, they provide the lasting course memories which members of the class fondly recall and tell others about.

Skills and Objectives. These include social interaction, questioning, feedback, course review and planning, connections to the real world, peer interaction, and social presence. A key goal is to foster a sense of trust and community building.

Advice and Ideas. What you create during this activity is definitely not yours. This is one resource that students will quickly assume control over and typically not seek your assistance or advice. The online café or coffeehouse is for them. This does not mean that they will totally ignore your advice or not welcome you in. However, you must proceed with caution. If you assume control over one or two discussion threads in the café, it may be fine. Answering all student questions and concerns and joining in every thread in the online café will discourage student interaction and personal honesty. Some instructors have chosen not to participate in this area, thereby allowing their students space just to hang out. Create this resource for them and then step back and watch it grow. Of course, some semesters and courses will see much more activity in the café than others. Despite our combined decades of online learning research and instruction, we admit that we do not fully understand why this is the case.

If a student does become a leader in the online café and offers extensive advice and directions to others, it may be important to recognize such leadership. Perhaps a bonus point or two for such an individual might suffice. Alternatively, you could simply acknowledge such café contributions in one of your weekly course announcements and reminders.

Variations and Extensions. Some of the hot topics and key concerns raised in the online café in previous semesters could be inserted as discussion starters in a new semester's café. Students from previous semesters could be asked to monitor the social cafés, thereby both freeing up instructor time while creating a space where students do not have to worry about instructor agendas and interference. You may also decide to have students from the current semester sign up to monitor particular weeks of the online café.

We have found that online cafés can get particularly interesting and lively when students from other sections of the course or from other institutions altogether are invited to participate. Back in 1997, Bonk created the "café latte" for preservice teachers from his institution as well as those in the United Kingdom, Finland, Korea, Peru, in addition to those from Texas A&M University and the University of South Carolina in the United States. In the café latte, students from around the world discussed their field experiences in their respective schools. In the process, they brought up case problems or situations, differences in the education-related laws and rules of different countries, pending educational policy, career aspirations, and so on. Needless to say, it was always quite informative and lively.

Key Instructional Considerations

Risk index: Low to Medium
Time index: Medium
Cost index: Low
Learner-centered index: High
Duration of the learning activity: Weekly or as needed

Final Reflections on Tone/Climate

This chapter explored many activities that can help establish a safe and inviting tone for an online or blended course or training event. We have used all of them in our university courses as well as in other adult training and professional development settings. At the same time, most if not all of them can be modified, tweaked, or rethought for nearly any educational level or situation.

As with all 100 activities that we lay out in this book, these first 10 should be viewed as instructional guides or templates, not as prescriptions. Change, combine, or eliminate any part of them to suit your own needs. Still not satisfied that they will work for you? Well, before discounting or saying "no way" to any of them, reflect for a few minutes on how you might creatively apply them. Trust us, they can work nearly anywhere with the right modifications. Perhaps start with one or two of the online icebreakers that you feel comfortable with. You might look for the low-risk, low-cost, and low-time activities.

This is just one set of tone and climate activities. There are dozens more that we wanted to include in this chapter but lacked the space. For example, learners can explore alternative ways to introduce themselves such as in relation to an online news story, cartoon, or video. If the instructor is keen on gaming, the syllabus, or aspects of it, could be turned into some type of learning game like *Wheel of Fortune, Jeopardy,* hangman, crossword puzzles, or perhaps even a 3-D world. You could place the course syllabus in a wiki that enrolled students can easily modify. Another way to enhance the course tone or climate is for instructors to create weekly podcasts or videos on aspects of the course and post them to a special channel on YouTube or YouTube EDU. As you can see, there are countless ways to acclimate learners to the course and establish that important sense of trust and community.

At times, you may need to turn on your creative thinking cap and exercise your risk muscle. Many social icebreaking and introductory activities can be fun. Though extensive sharing of personal information may not be the norm in F2F classroom settings, online students will often write pages about themselves in the hope of establishing connections. At times, they may reveal more about themselves than they would face-to-face. Instructors will need to monitor student frankness. Keep in mind, however, that such text-based sharing is just one of the ways for students to discover their commonalities and differences; video introductions or personal stories can also be employed, with perhaps even better results.

Another benefit of this first component of TEC-VARIETY is that instructors can insightfully refer back to the messages generated by these activities. When this happens, students get a better sense of who their classmates and instructors are. Knowing that the instructor is a "pirate" or "roadrunner" and one of their classmates is a "tea kettle" or "knitter" may have hidden benefits as the course proceeds. We have seen firsthand how such commenting can foster curiosity, laughter, trust, mutual respect, peer support, extended interactions, and high doses of learner course participation.

No matter how well conceived the idea, if the instructor is not modeling the behaviors expected, the activity will soon flounder. If eight nouns are asked for, the instructor should be creating her own list of eight and immediately sharing it. Students can then see that the instructor is a real human being with her own particular interests, strengths, and experiences.

One benefit of activities related to tone and climate is that everyone gets a chance to participate and share ideas and perspectives. As is evident in this chapter, there are a wide variety of activity frameworks from which to select, including posting and reacting to favorite websites, listing two truths as well as one lie about yourself, posting personally relevant questions and issues in an online coffeehouse or café, brainstorming nouns or adjectives to describe yourself, and so on.

If you are using some type of synchronous technology for any such activity, you will need to create procedures for taking turns and interacting with one another. If you do not, it will be extremely difficult to hear from all course participants. If, however, you are using asynchronous technology, students will likely not read all their peer postings and may only selectively post or perhaps contribute something at the last minute. To foster student reading of what is posted, you will need to embed some type of requirement for replying to peer postings or summarizing the postings of a set number of peer statements in reflection papers. No strategy or idea is foolproof or guaranteed to work. Each requires careful planning and deftness on the part of the instructor or instructional designers of the course or online learning experience.

Even considering all the various possible tone-related activities described in this chapter, your first attempt may not work. The recommendations and guidelines that we provided here for each activity should elevate your chances for success. Nevertheless, you must refashion each strategy according to your own situation or context. No strategy will work exactly the same way each time. And if you do not find success the first time, you can modify or tweak it slightly and try it again. Often amazing results will occur after a minor fine-tuning. But if it does not work to your satisfaction in the second attempt, then we recommend that you reconsider using it.

Your tone- and climate-related strategies will need to evolve with the technologies of choice. Today, social networking technologies are all the rage. Those working with adult learners might try Twitter, Facebook, and LinkedIn as ways for students to interact. K–12 teachers, however, will need to abide by school district policies and practices. We fully realize that there are significantly more security concerns and procedures when working with children. At the same time, we believe that there are dozens of activities found in this book that can be easily incorporated into blended or fully online learning in the K–12 classroom despite pervasive firewall and security issues.

Given the explosion of interest in social networking, and online socializing in general, the coming decade will likely be filled with interesting experimentations using online icebreakers and course introductions. Soon social networking technologies will be integrated into course management systems. If that proves insufficient, social networking technology will probably take over many of the duties of such systems. In fact, some instructors are already experimenting with using aspects of Facebook as a course management system and are finding mixed results (see Wang, Woo, Quek, Yang, & Liu, 2011). No matter what happens, instructors will undoubtedly find increasingly interesting ways to foster a safe and personal learning climate.

The first component of TEC-VARIETY is loaded with learning opportunities to capture student interest and help them commit time to the course. Without this first component, which is the backbone for everything else, it is extremely difficult for instructors to find ultimate success online. And yet, as essential as this component is, it is not on its own sufficient for online teaching and learning success. As you should be aware by now, as important as it is to establish a safe and productive tone or climate, there are nine other motivational principles that we detail in this book that are just as important. We now push on to the second principle, which involves the feedback and support mechanisms embedded in the course. For the purposes of the TEC-VARIETY framework, the word "encouragement" is emphasized. And so we encourage you to read on.

CHAPTER FIVE

PRINCIPLE #2 ENCOURAGEMENT

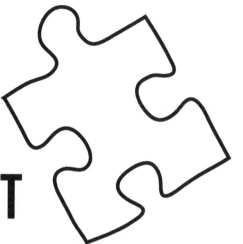

(Includes Feedback, Responsiveness, Praise, and Supports)

> Nine-tenths of education is encouragement.
>
> —Anatole France

Singer-songwriter and poet Patti Smith once reflected, "I've always thrived on the encouragement of others." Just as cheering and praise from fans and friends are the life-blood of the so-called "Godmother of Punk," it is equally vital for your students when they venture into new waters such as fully online and blended learning. Such encouragement and supportive feedback is exactly what the next principle of the TEC-VARIETY framework is all about.

Feedback is central to education and training systems because it serves as a means to let learners know whether their performances are meeting course or instructor expectations. Motivation is sustained and enhanced in the monitoring of progress toward that goal (Anderson, 2001). Whereas grades on tests and other assignments is often the primary form of feedback in F2F courses, those in online courses appreciate feedback at more formative points in time (Dennen & Bonk, 2008).

Support and feedback requirements in online courses are different from F2F settings. Unlike students in F2F courses, online learners seek feedback on nearly everything they submit. They may also need more direct forms of encouragement and praise. In traditional walled classrooms, instructors and trainers generally offer feedback to a few people during the class or workshop time period. Such an approach will not suffice on-line. Lack of feedback is deemed to be one of the main reasons for withdrawing from an online course (Ertmer et al., 2007).

There are numerous reasons why online learners seek so much feedback and encouragement to continue in the course. First, online learning might be a new experience. If that is the case, students will need reassurance that they are on the right path to success. Without some sense that they are doing well, they may lean toward dropping out of the course. Second, and related to the first point, there is often a lack of social presence on the part of instructors in online courses (Rourke, Andersen, Garrison, & Archer, 1999). Feedback gives students a feeling that someone is there who cares about their progress.

In addition to those two issues, learners have been programmed since kindergarten to expect feedback on any assignments that they turn in. In F2F classes, however, much student work is never submitted. For instance, small-group discussion is oral and feedback comes from those in the group or class. Discussion might be on reflection questions related to the readings or lectures, case problems and scenarios, debates, and role plays. In a live class, learners might be vicariously reinforced when they witness instructors giving feedback to a few of their peers on the same answers that they came up with (Bandura, 1986).

In contrast, in online classes, such activities are predominantly text-based (Lapadat, 2002). Unlike most F2F class discussions, there is a permanent record of online postings. It is not too surprising, therefore, that there is an expectation for instructor and peer comments on any text that online learners produce; written feedback has been the norm since they first started to write. At the same time, as will be shown in this chapter, such writing offers opportunities for real-world audiences and multiple forms of encouragement and advice on students' work.

As indicated in the previous chapter on tone and climate, there are many motivational tactics that have consistently been found to be effective in traditional classrooms. According to this research, instructors who attain better results create a supportive but challenging environment, project enthusiasm and intensity, provide choice, create short-term goals, and offer immediate feedback on student performance (Pintrich & Schunk, 1996; Stipek, 1998). In accordance with the TEC-VARIETY framework, there are many strategies that coalesce into successful instruction.

Decades of research on classroom-based forms of motivation have resulted in many guidelines and caveats for teachers. For instance, when providing feedback, it should be timely, genuine, appropriate, and sent by a credible source. Positive feedback gives students a message regarding their competence and mastery of the content (Reeve, 1996). It also provides a sense of support and public recognition as well as a record of that support. Feedback in the form of points earned is an indicator of whether the student has measured up to some preestablished standard of performance.

Research related to feedback is thorny and complex. After reviewing hundreds of studies related to schooling and achievement, many of which focused on feedback, Hattie and Timperly (2000) proposed a model of feedback that incorporated four levels or types of feedback including task- or product-related feedback, such as whether or not student work is correct; process feedback related to information on what the learner still needs to accomplish; self-regulation feedback; and personal feedback directed at the learner (e.g., "you are a great learner").

According to Paul Pintrich and Dale Schunk (1996), if you are attempting to encourage learners with praise, it should be simple and direct, unambiguous, and aimed toward positive learning progress and outcomes. The focus of that praise and feedback should be on areas that learners can control, such as their effort and strategy use, not on something deemed more static and highly difficult to change, such as intelligence (Pink, 2009). Ineffective praise, in contrast, is delivered randomly or unsystematically. Other signs of ineffective praise are when it is rather bland and uniformly presented, provides little or no information, is given without regard to effort or successful performance, and rewards the mere fact that the student participated in the activity or event (Brophy, 2010).

Prompt feedback online is not particularly easy to achieve given all the work students submit each week. Instructors might rely on peer feedback as well as that from experts or practitioners. Feedback could also be built into the online system or resources. Finally, feedback can be in the form of students' self-assessment and self-reflection on their progress and performance.

Technologies for Principle #2: Encouragement

The technology tools for encouraging and supporting student online learning quests are wide ranging. In online courses, encouragement and feedback are often asynchronous in nature. When the two of us teach online, we often make announcements in the CMS or via e-mail that include information on recent student performances. As with most online instructors, we also post comments and observations in discussion forums. In fact, this might be the most frequent method of feedback that we use. Peers, experts, and alumni of the course can also leave feedback in our course discussion forums.

In addition to feedback in discussion forums, some instructors might rely on annotation tools such as those found in Word or some other word processing system and attach these marked-up documents in their e-mail or upload them to a dropbox. Other instructors may make direct changes to a document in a wiki, thereby leaving their feedback markers in the document history section. Still others might require students to reflect on the weekly or unit readings with blogging tools. Instructors and peers can then leave comments within them.

Some tools might be purposefully designed to provide feedback. For instance, in the 1990s, Bonk fashioned a 5-point rating system on student-posted Web links. He also created portfolio tools wherein student work was accumulated and commented on. At the same time, he experimented with posting student work to an online gallery or exhibit hall, thereby allowing experts and alumni of the course to view the work and offer candid evaluations.

Online reflection questions and self-check lists are other forms of feedback often seen when a course is globally distributed to tens of thousands of learners, such as courses on

Java programming from Sun Microsystems (Wenger & Ferguson, 2006) or router training from the Cisco Networking Academy (Dennis et al., 2006). Along these same lines, many online courses rely on the CMS or learning management system (LMS) to monitor online quizzes and tests. Feedback could be in the form of a score, or perhaps explicit information on items that students got wrong as well as information on how to solve such problems. System feedback need not just be for examinations. Technology tools can be programmed to give feedback on case solutions or responses to practice problems as well as to provide insight or suggestions related to progress in a game or simulation.

The preceding examples tend to emphasize the asynchronous side of learning. Learner support can also take place in a chat window or via text messaging. Synchronous chats with peers or experts in Skype or some other system can offer students immediate feedback on their ideas and solutions. Webinars with experts or lectures presented synchronously—using tools such as Adobe Connect, WebEx, Blackboard Collaborate (formerly Elluminate), or Go2Meeting—often include time for student question-and-answer sessions.

Clearly, there are a plethora of technologies that can help support student learning with timely and appropriate encouragement, feedback, and overall responsiveness. Survey research conducted a decade ago by Bonk confirmed that instructors in higher education and corporate training recognize the benefits of responsive feedback as well as incorporating relevant materials, goal-driven activities, personal growth, choice or flexibility, and interactivity and collaboration (Bonk, 2002a, 2002b). Unfortunately, many of these principles are rarely employed (Bonk, Kim, & Lee, 2004). Our hope is that the various examples provided in this book will not only convince people of the need for motivational techniques, but will help them implement these techniques and activities in creative and powerful ways.

Ten Online Activities in Principle #2: Encouragement

There is little doubt that encouragement and feedback are vital to online learning success. Activities that provide explicit forms of feedback should lead to higher student course satisfaction and overall success. Though there are many forms such support can take on, we offer 10 pedagogical activities in this section. In some cases, the encouragement and feedback will be coming from the instructor, whereas in other examples it will be from peers, well-known experts, practitioners, the system, or the learners themselves.

As with the tone and climate principle, this second principle of the TEC-VARIETY framework finds its way into many of the examples in other chapters of this book. In fact, it is likely that all the activities outlined in this book entail some form of feedback; the 10 included here give a sense of the range and types of learner encouragement, support, and feedback that are now possible online. And, again, though many of the ideas in this chapter are reflective of our present positions in institutions of higher learning, we believe that most of them can be applied in other educational settings, albeit with some creative insights and modifications for many of them.

Activity 11. Critical Friends

Description and Purpose of Activity. Educators are always seeking low-cost resources to use in their F2F and online courses. Among the cheapest and most useful resources that can be tapped into are the course participants themselves. Many online instructors have discovered that the learners enrolled in the course are highly trainable and typically quite willing to help out. In our classes, we have often paired students to provide weekly or monthly feedback to each other. As research has shown, the incorporation of peer support is a huge relief for the instructor, especially because course quality can be maintained when peer feedback is used in lieu of instructor feedback (Ertmer et al., 2007). One form of peer feedback is called the "critical friend" technique. Keep in mind that this instructional method has many other names including constructive friends, e-mail pals, Web buddies, and ePals. Critical friends and Web buddies provide constant feedback, reminders, advice, and encouragement throughout an assignment or the entire course.

In traditional classrooms or work situations, the critical friend is a trusted person who asks provocative questions, supplies alternative points of view or data contrary to a particular perspective, and submits a critique of someone's work as a friend. In an online environment, the critical friend may provide reminders of task due dates, clarify items listed in the syllabus, respond to partner blog or online forum postings, and offer other forms of encouragement, feedback, and support. We often ask that critical friends provide weekly feedback on their partner's blogging reflections, podcast performances, or discussion group postings.

Students can be paired up as critical friends in many ways. Selection of critical friend teams might be according to personal or professional interests, prior experiences or backgrounds, age brackets, or year in the program. Assignment might also be purely random. If you have a F2F experience early on in the course, you might match students up according to their degree of confidence in the class from low to high (with a highly confident person paired with a much less confident one).

Most critical friend activities in online courses assume that interactions will be via text only. Instead of text-based interactions, however, critical friend pairs could interact in Skype, Google Hangouts, or via the video chat tool within Facebook and other social media (Baig, 2011). At present, the use of Skype within Facebook is best for paired interactions, whereas Google Hangouts is ideal for teams (Arrington, 2011). In a few years, video-based interactions may, in fact, be more pervasive in online courses than text-related ones.

Skills and Objectives. Includes timely and extensive feedback, feelings of social presence and connectedness, socializing, sharing, student interaction, self-monitoring, and planning. This technique is a means to keep students on track while fostering a highly interactive learning community.

Advice and Ideas. The critical friend task can be highly effective if you appropriately structure and monitor this task. Students will appreciate having someone provide them with weekly feedback and course reminders. However, many critical friend partners habitually fail to provide weekly feedback and many others do so at the last minute. When that happens, you will hear complaints. Listed here are some ideas that we find work well online.

First, provide students with an instructional scaffold or job aid on how to be a good critical friend. Spell out what your expectations are for this task, including the timing, type, quality, and quantity of any feedback. Of course, not only should students know that the template or job aid exists, but the instructor should explain how to use it.

Second, assign points for providing peer feedback. These might be mastery points for completing a set number of peer feedback posts. Alternatively, you could look at the quality of those posts based on criteria such as helpfulness, relevance, timeliness, coherence, persuasiveness, and depth of feedback. Some online educators opt to assess both the quality and quantity of critical friend feedback. If this aspect of the course is limited to a few points (e.g., 15 or 30 points for 15 peer feedback posts), then a quantity rating is all that is likely needed. If, however, the task is worth a substantive percentage of students' grades in the course, you may engage in a more extensive and transparent evaluation method.

Third, monitor the critical friend feedback by reading and responding to some of it, and send out reminders from time to time about the task. As students become aware of the instructor's presence, they will participate in more timely and effective ways.

Fourth, at the end of the course, you may require a brief reflection paper on the critical friend activity. In such a task, the students can review their feedback and mentoring techniques, and discuss what they learned—and what they might otherwise not have learned—because of their role as a critical friend.

Finally, you could include course evaluation questions related to the critical friend activity and how it could be improved.

Variations and Extensions. As you try out this technique a few times, you may start to tinker with it and perhaps even transform the method into something radically different. For instance, in a semester-long activity, critical friends could be rotated at the end of each unit or perhaps at the end of each week. With rotation, students are less likely to complain that their critical friend was not responsive to their needs.

Another idea is to create groups of three or four people as critical friends and to require them to offer feedback to all of their teammates each week. Although such an approach requires a tad bit more work each week from your students (i.e., responding to two or three of their peers instead of just one), it will expand the range, quality, and quantity of feedback. Naturally, students will appreciate the greater opportunities for receiving feedback and support on their posts. Their motivation for the activity will undoubtedly increase. To further spark such motivation, sets of critical friend teams might be monitored by students who previously took the course. Our attempts with the latter approach have resulted in quite marvelous interactions and course insights.

Key Instructional Considerations

Risk index: Low to Medium
Time index: Medium to High, depending on support and structure
Cost index: Low
Learner-centered index: High
Duration of the learning activity: Throughout the course or as needed

Activity 12. Student Polling and Voting

Description and Purpose of Activity. One way to engage students while eliciting feedback at the same time is the use of student surveys and polls. At the beginning of a course, students can be polled about their preferences for instructor office hours and times for any synchronous webinars or online course meetings, given that they may be working and have minimal openings in their schedules. During the course, students can also be asked how the course is going in general and asked to give their rankings among possible assignments and activities. Such formative feedback is extremely valuable for making subtle and timely adjustments to an online course.

If you are teaching a blended course with some live meetings, or if there are weekly synchronous sessions scheduled, you may want to poll students about a topic or issue before the class meeting. During the live class, instructors can then foster discussion on the minority point of view, based on the preclass polls, before those in the majority view dominate the discussion. Students could also be surveyed about the course and its activities at or near the end of the course.

Soliciting input provides learners with some control over the course while it is occurring. With student polling and voting, students have a voice in the direction and overall quality of the course. Their attitudes, preferences, rankings, ratings, and open-ended comments are not only feedback for the instructor and others helping to manage that course or unit, but they can also be shared with the fellow students in the course. Students will quickly become aware of aspects of the course that are more appealing or important to their peers. They may realize that their ideas on what the course should address may be in the minority. Along these same lines, if the instructor makes valid attempts to address any of the minority views, students may come to appreciate the course even more.

Skills and Objectives. Includes course interactivity, student feedback, responding to student needs, personalizing the learning environment, social presence, and collecting student perspectives. A really interesting poll or survey question can capture student's attention and foster discussion and community building.

Advice and Ideas. Pay attention to student preferences and ideas that are suggested in any online student surveys or polls. In addition to sharing the results of some or all of those polls, indicate how you are addressing them. If students noticeably prefer a particular task over others, reflect on how you might alter the course direction to incorporate that task. Also carefully ponder how such a task or activity can be expanded or altered the next time you offer the course. As part of such reflections, consider saving those polls and sharing the results with the next class.

There are many tools and resources for polling and surveying students. Some are built directly into the CMS or LMS. Besides internal systems, Web-based survey tools such as SurveyMonkey, Zoomerang, and SurveyShare are popular and have free limited-use versions. Dozens of other such survey tools exist, from low-end to extremely high-end options. Online survey tools are powerful in the hands of learners. They can collect information related to concepts and ideas from the course. For more details on how to design such an activity, Bonk and Zhang (2008) outline examples of how to engage students in Web-based survey research in their *Empowering Online Learning* book mentioned in Chapter One.

Simple polls are also popular and effective for gathering feedback from students. There are dozens of technology-driven polling methods to choose from. In traditional classrooms, instructors are increasingly using student response systems or clickers as a means to engage and involve their students. At the same time, interactive whiteboards and smartboards such as those from Smart and Promethean can engage students with polls and interactive questioning. Another technology growing in popularity is the use of mobile audience response systems like Poll Everywhere to collect data from students. Unlike costly clicker systems, Poll Everywhere can be used for free and it allows for comments and open-ended responses.

Online instructors can rely on one of the many Web-based polling tools when conducting a class poll. Among them are Mister Poll, Blogpoll, Blog Polls, Micropoll, Pollcode, Poll Host, and Polldaddy (Andrew, 2009). Before selecting among them, explore product examples and review company policies. Many offer a few free polls per month or per year, which should more than meet most instructors' needs. Some tools, like Polldaddy, allow for the collection of responses via a website, e-mail, Facebook, Twitter, iPad, or some other technology. Most polling tools generate easy-to-read results which can be immediately shared. Perhaps do a poll on the polling tools, asking your students which ones they prefer.

Variations and Extensions. A student or a team of students could design polls for each other related to the course contents and activities. The data that they collect can be submitted as a report to the instructor on how to improve the course. Students could also employ surveys and polls to arrange group meetings. If there are multiple sections of the same course or training experience, surveys and polls could be used across them and then shared so that instructors and students could note any similarities and differences across the course sections.

Key Instructional Considerations

Risk index: Medium
Time index: Medium
Cost index: Low to High (depending on system or tool selected)
Learner-centered index: High
Duration of the learning activity: As needed

Activity 13. Online Suggestion Box

Description and Purpose of Activity. An online anonymous suggestion box might be built for a course as a means to improve it continually. If you do not have the resources to create a website or system for student suggestions, you might try using a wiki tool that keeps the names of the participants anonymous. In addition, in a wiki, students could build on each other's suggestions.

We recommend keeping the suggestion box open for the entire semester, even though it may be used only at the end of the course. Keeping it open would grant students a sense of power and control over unclear assignments, areas of the course that they believe could be improved, and any dilemmas or frustrations that they are experiencing. As indicated in Chapters Two and Three, students' feelings that their ideas are being respected should help with course retention and satisfaction.

Skills and Objectives. Includes analysis and evaluation skills, idea generation, creativity, and reflection. If the suggestion box or tool is viewable for the class to read, learners can build on each other's ideas; in that case, collaboration and comparison-and-contrast skills would be emphasized as well.

Advice and Ideas. Do not worry about assessment of this task. However, you might provide bonus points to what you feel are the best suggestions. Because there is no grade attached to this item, be sure to remind the students that the online suggestion box exists and that you are checking it from time to time. Watson (2000) recommends that instructors not only keep track of the suggestions, but to post them along with the instructor's corresponding decision about each one. In fact, you could maintain a list of suggestions from previous semesters along with brief descriptions of how they each were addressed. In this way, students know that their ideas and perspectives matter. They will also realize that the instructor is concerned with improving the course.

Variations and Extensions. The suggestion box could be used across different sections of the same course. You could hold a competition between classes with prizes for the class or for the individual student with the most interesting or useful suggestion. Alternatively, such a competition could take place between students in the same class who are grouped by career interest, year in the program, gender, or some other variable. High-scoring classes or teams would be recognized with some award or incentive, such as the instructor posting the names of the winners to an online course Hall of Fame.

Key Instructional Considerations

> Risk index: Medium
> Time index: Low
> Cost index: Low
> Learner-centered index: High
> Duration of the learning activity: Throughout the course or as needed

Activity 14. Minute and Muddiest Point Papers

Description and Purpose of Activity. Another way to be responsive to learner needs in your online course or training event is to have students reflectively write from time to time on how they think they are doing in the course. Ask them to write an e-mail for one or two minutes about what they have learned from the readings or lectures as well as what they did not learn so well. When posting, learners could elaborate on the cloudy, confusing, or muddy aspects of the class. Some refer to this activity as a "minute paper" or "muddiest point paper."

These short reflections help learners review key points and summarize the content, which the instructor can then check for understanding. The review process need not be long. All it takes is a few minutes of reflective writing for students to solidify their learning. Instructors who can promptly and thoughtfully respond to student comments and address their "muddy" or unclear points or areas of felt tension will likely find more success than those who do not.

There are many technologies at your disposal for this particular activity. One alternative to e-mail is to ask students to write their minute papers in a wiki that accumulates their posts; another idea is that they post these comments to a discussion forum or to an individual or team blog. There are also online collaboration tools that could handle this activity. The main objective is to provide an opportunity to formatively evaluate aspects of the course (Brown, 2002).

Such moments of evaluation help instructors as well as the designers of the course understand what is and is not working and then make attempts to improve it. At the same time, instructors can respond to the student comments with feedback on how the course or unit might be altered. In this way, feedback and support travel back and forth between students and the instructor.

Skills and Objectives. Includes idea generation, critical analysis and reflection, and writing as thinking. Another key objective is to record ideas that may be troubling the learner, thereby freeing up mental capacity for other course tasks and activities.

Advice and Ideas. Be specific about what you expect students to include in their minute papers. Consider including a few examples of minute papers from previous semesters of the course. In addition, use this technique sparingly. If you collect minute papers weekly, you may overwhelm your students as well as yourself. If you are constantly collecting formative feedback, you will have less time for day-to-day course management issues. However, the amount and timing of this activity will vary depending on the type and level of course, the tools available, and many other factors.

Variations and Extensions. Instead of giving instructor feedback, you could consider having students post minute or muddiest point papers to a discussion forum for peer feedback. Alternatively, students might be required to use their weekly or monthly minute papers as the basis for end-of-semester super summary assignments on what they have learned and not fully learned in the course. Another variation of this task would be to ask for the "clearest point papers" wherein they write about the concepts and principles that they have solidly learned that day or week.

Key Instructional Considerations

Risk index: Medium
Time index: Medium to High
Cost index: Low
Learner-centered index: High
Duration of the learning activity: As needed

Activity 15. Comments and Annotations

Description and Purpose of Activity. Sometimes feedback is indirect and subtle. Other times it is direct and pointed. Annotating text is one example where that feedback is typically more direct. For instance, you can give students a writing assignment where a partner or team member must edit, comment on, and annotate that work. Critical friend or team member feedback in the form of comments and annotations can help students to see problems in their text and think of ways to address them. For instance, there might be a series of flow issues, a lack of depth, areas needing additional support or justification, and so on. Alternatively, a student may simply be stuck and not know what to do next.

Sometimes students are lost or not sure of the quality of their writing. Comments and annotations help shape the document. The instructor can decide to have students do everything in Microsoft Word, Google Docs, or some other system. Microsoft Word, for instance, captures comments and edits in different colors for each reviewer or partner with its Track Changes feature. Feedback from fellow students would be at a highly personal level and within their zone of proximal development (Vygotsky, 1978). Feedback could also come from experts and students who have taken the class in the past.

Skills and Objectives. Includes social interaction, critical analysis, writing, professionalism, the juxtaposition of comments and ideas, and gaining diverse perspectives. A key objective of annotating writing is to obtain feedback of some type on a work in progress or near-final draft as well as to have an audience beyond the instructor.

Advice and Ideas. We find tracking changes in Word to be highly beneficial though it can require much time. Whatever system you choose, be clear about the processes and procedures for annotation. Set the due dates and forms of paper exchange (e.g., course system dropbox, e-mail, physical meetings, and the like). If there are multiple rounds of feedback or multiple providers of that feedback, consider creating an online partner sign-up form. You should also monitor the process and send task requirements and due date reminders when appropriate. If you are using a wiki tool, edits are immediately made in the document. As a result, changes are much more difficult to track.

Variations and Extensions. Instead of student comments and annotations, the feedback partner could be real-world practitioners, well-known experts, or former students of the course. Another alternative would be for one student to annotate a paper and forward it to another student for additional annotation.

Key Instructional Considerations

Risk index: Medium
Time index: Medium
Cost index: Low
Learner-centered index: High
Duration of the learning activity: As needed, depending on assignment

Activity 16. Screencasted Supports and Directions

Description and Purpose of Activity. There are many forms of online mentoring and support. Some rely on text-based instructional scaffolds such as think sheets, job aids, assignment templates, and worksheets. Instructional designers might encourage using an online tutorial or wizard that provides an overview of expectations. Instead of sophisticated lecture capture tools like MediaSite, Tegrity, and Echo360 or multimedia and Web production tools like Camtasia, Adobe Captivate, or Articulate Storyline, tutorials can be created with much less effort and expense.

Sometimes an instructor's goal is to illustrate concepts and ideas on a computer screen. With the emergence of the Web 2.0, technologies for producing these help systems and demonstrating procedures and products have become much easier to use and often require minimal training, if any. One type of software to accomplish this is called "screencasting." Tools such as GoView, Screenr, Jing, Overstream, and Screencast-o-Matic are among the more popular (Mukherjee, 2011) and most have free versions.

A screencast is akin to making a movie of your computer screen in order to demonstrate a technology tool or resource that you are using in the course. You could also be mapping out specific steps or procedures for a particular task. At the more basic level, the user speaks as he explores or showcases particular websites or items in a website. Once done, a link to the file can be shared. Some tools allow for quick posting on YouTube or sharing links within Twitter, Facebook, or Flickr. Given that these are free tools, there are typically limits to the number of minutes for each screencast file. Some tools like Screencast-o-Matic allow for a video of the user as well as added text or animations. Additional sophistication will undoubtedly be added during the coming years, including features that enable users to edit their files and automatically share them to a range of social networking sites and groups.

Screencasting systems have many roles in online education and training. The video demonstrations that they produce are often available on demand for the mobile learner. These on-demand systems help focus the learner on critical aspects of a Web resource or tool that the instructor has incorporated into the class. They also personalize the learning and bring a sense of the instructor's social presence.

Skills and Objectives. Includes feedback, listening skills, the ability to follow directions, reviewing key course concepts, self-directed and on-demand learning, reflection skills, understanding sequential flow and procedures, and discriminating among particular tool or resource features. A key goal of this activity is to provide expert guidance and just-in-time support.

Advice and Ideas. First, ask learners about unclear assignments and difficult-to-navigate resources and tools used in the course. Second, think about all the other online tools and resources you plan to use in the online course. Then jot down a list of possible tools, resources, and activities that may require a screencasted session. Organize notes and ideas about each one. If you want to create extremely high-level demonstrations that are usable beyond your class or training situation, check on possible funding sources or internal support for the production.

Be sure to script each show and produce a couple of practice screencasts. Once done with a production, usability is a key issue. Test out each screencast before actually using them in the course or program. To determine bottlenecks or problems, ask usability testers to think aloud as they use your screencasted video. In addition, during the semester, gather feedback on each screencasted tutorial or help system that you have created. Review questions may make each video more engaging for the users. After such review, consider making that content object a free and open educational resource available to the world community.

Variations and Extensions. Many of your students will be more technologically savvy and have experience and interests with online social media and digital tools. You could solicit their support in creating screencasted videos that can scaffold the use of new online tools and resources in your course. In fact, each student (or pairs of students) might be assigned to create one such screencast demonstration during a course. Alternatively, you could allow them to eliminate or drop an assignment in return for producing a set number of screencasted tutorials, wizards, job aids, and help systems. You may even coordinate a screencast movie night or class press conference for their productions. Consider offering incentives and awards for the most informative, creative, and well-designed screencasted tutorials and help systems. The judges can be former students, experts in the field, colleagues and other instructors, and fellow students.

Key Instructional Considerations

Risk index: Low
Time index: Medium to High (depending on the number that need to be produced as well as familiarity with this type of task)
Cost index: Low to High (depending on whether you use free systems and tools or those that contain more features and are costly)
Learner-centered index: Medium
Duration of the learning activity: As needed

Activity 17. Embedded Reviews and System-Scored Practice Tests

Description and Purpose of Activity. One area of rising importance in the world of online learning is to embed different types of system checks and reviews of student learning in the course. Such system reviews and self-check examinations are especially useful for courses heavy in terminology, such as introductory and advanced courses in biology, psychology, anatomy, business management, and zoology. Actually, progress in most disciplines could be enhanced and perhaps accelerated with timely and appropriate use of embedded practice tests and reviews that are immediately scored by the system. Students want to know that they know the content. At the same time, instructors need help in providing adequate feedback and support. In addition, administrators want to standardize the content as well as establish quality standards for their online courses and programs.

The Khan Academy, for instance, is a popular website for skill-based learning among teenagers and young adults (Koelber, 2011). With over 2,300 videos for learning basic facts in science, mathematics, business, history, statistics, computer science, and other areas, there is much to choose from. In basic math facts, students can ask for hints, watch a video explaining a problem, and accumulate "energy points" for effort. Various target point totals are intended as student motivators. These types of motivators and system supports will undoubtedly increase in the near future thanks to funding from the Gates Foundation and from well-known entrepreneurs (Ferenstein, 2011; Kaplan, 2010).

The system that the Khan Academy currently has in place recognizes a learner as competent in a skill after correctly completing 10 problems in a row. Data that a teacher, mentor, parent, and student can access is displayed showing the time the student has spent on specific problems, videos, and so on. The exact problems that a student got right and wrong are saved by the system database and can be displayed immediately upon request. As learners accomplish more, they can earn Meteorite, Moon, Earth, Sun, and Black Hole merit badges, each indicating higher levels of competencies. As will be explained in the next chapter, such gamelike features are highly motivational. In effect, the system is tracking student progress and providing a custom profile on each learner.

As with this second principle of the TEC-VARIETY framework, encouragement, support, and feedback are critical aspects of the Khan Academy. And more forms of individualized feedback and assessment will emerge as their student tracking and assessment systems are upgraded, expanded, and tested with the influx of new capital it has received. Keep in mind that the Khan Academy is free and is targeted at the K–12 level. Countless other sites charge a monthly subscription, such as Virtual Nerd for math and science learning, ePrep for standardized exam preparation, and Vocab Sushi for learning vocabulary.

Many such tools and systems are available for higher education and corporate training as well. There are medical cases online wherein the learner solves problems and the system evaluates the response. For instance, a popular blood pressure simulation from California State University at Chico provides information, demonstrations, and actual blood pressure testing sounds. It ends with a series of true/false self-check questions and very simple feedback (i.e., "yes, that is correct" or "no, that is incorrect"). Learning a foreign language online through systems such as Livemocha might also entail earning points as a student identifies words to use, proper grammar or sentence structure, or matches the correct sentence with an audio file or picture.

Suffice it to say, all online learning stakeholders want to empower the learner and provide a more personalized and individualized form of instruction. Embedding concept reviews and practice tests in a course makes a lot of sense. Such system feedback saves online instructors an exorbitant amount of time; it is no small wonder that these computer-based forms of feedback are growing in popularity.

Skills and Objectives. Includes reviewing facts, concepts, and principles, trying out concepts, immediate system feedback, self-directed learning, self-monitoring, repeated practice, reflection on the knowledge acquired, and knowledge recognition and application. To be properly assessed, most practice test items are designed at the knowledge or basic fact level (e.g., online flashcards); higher-order cognitive skills are much more difficult to analyze but undoubtedly will be targeted in the coming decade.

Advice and Ideas. If your discipline or subject matter area is constantly changing or is relatively new or unique, you may need to design your own review items and practice tests. Before you do, be sure to check for internal as well as external funding sources. Once you have found or created the necessary content, do not simply make such content available; instead, require students to complete a certain percentage of it. Consider setting a criterion score or master level of performance such as 75 or 80 percent before students are allowed to move to the next level. In some systems, the instructor must make a decision about how many retakes will be allowed.

Variations and Extensions. One option or extension for this task is to have competitions with other sections of a course or with learners at other locations. The class with the highest percentage of learners reaching a certain level of performance could be recognized in some fashion. Students could also build some of the practice questions or examinations, or even design the embedded practice tests for future students in the course. Their completed work could be entered into a national competition or submitted for a conference.

Key Instructional Considerations

> *Risk index: Low*
> *Time index: Medium to High (depending on the availability of premade content)*
> *Cost index: Low (depends on systems selected)*
> *Learner-centered index: Medium*
> *Duration of the learning activity: As needed*

Activity 18. Asynchronous Expert Feedback and Mentoring

Description and Purpose of Activity. When the Web was just beginning to be used as a platform for delivering online learning back in the mid-1990s, Bonk quickly became mesmerized with the potential of the World Lecture Hall (WLH) from the University of Texas at Austin. College instructors from around the world were posting their syllabi to the WLH. Amid the excitement, there was discussion about whether college instructors might someday be replaced by free online courses and resources.

A few years later, Bonk and his colleagues began to analyze WLH syllabi for the types of online interactions that they incorporated (Cummings, Bonk, & Jacobs, 2002). They wanted to know the degree to which students were being required to interact with other students in those courses. They also sought to determine how often students were interacting with instructors as well as outside experts. Similarly, they wanted to know the percentage of tasks within each posted syllabus during which instructors interacted with other instructors as well as with students and with practitioners. They found that the least used form of interaction was between students and experts or practitioners. Such a finding was quite ironic given today's emphasis on real-world experiences and interactions combined with the power of the Web to make it possible.

There are assorted reasons for practitioners and real-world experts to offer feedback to online learners. First, it creates an authentic audience for learner products and reports. For instance, as noted in an earlier example, you can bring in a few graduates of the course to provide feedback for your students or offer important course reminders. Second, such an activity helps to situate student learning in the real world. Third, external experts can help judge or rate projects and products such as the quality of case solutions. Fourth, practitioners could offer advice and insight about how particular topics and skills are actually applied in the real world. They may also have heard about entry-level positions that are currently open in their field or perhaps even offer an internship to one or more students. Along these same lines, they may collaborate with students on projects or perhaps serve as a project adviser or mentor.

When we have embedded such expert interactions in our online courses within our asynchronous discussion forums, our students are extremely excited to hear the insights and adventures of the expert (Lee & Bonk, 2013). Sometimes they even gain their specific feedback and mentoring on their class projects. It is a new form of cognitive apprenticeship which is becoming increasingly highly used and valued.

Skills and Objectives. Includes connecting content knowledge from books and lectures to the real world, the identification of key concepts and principles, timely and thoughtful feedback, an appreciation of multiple perspectives, and learner engagement. A key goal is the creation of a cognitive apprenticeship in which learners become budding novices within an established learning community.

Advice and Ideas. Publications, conference papers, presentations, and social networks can increase the profile of your course or idea. We have often been contacted by potential course mentors after giving a conference talk or presentation. In addition to such external support, you could ask students to come back and help when they complete your course or training experience. Keep track of those who express interest. Be clear about the roles and expectations for those external to your course who are asked to provide feedback and mentoring. Provide appropriate forms or guide sheets on what you are expecting the mentors and experts to do. Make sure that they have access to the asynchronous conference forum or system and know how to use it effectively. During the course, be sure to monitor mentor and guest expert responses, especially those who are new to your course or situation.

At the end of the course, solicit feedback on the overall activity as well as advice on the guide sheets and scaffolds provided. Perhaps one or two of the external experts will offer support for updating them. A couple of students in the course may also offer their perspectives on how the mentoring might be enhanced in the future. Finally, be sure to thank everyone involved.

Variations and Extensions. Ask students to reflect on the various forms and types of mentoring that they have received during the course. In that reflection paper, it would be wise to ask them to link the forms of mentoring to the content of the course as well as their career aspirations. Also consider asking the practitioners and mentors to respond to the reflection papers.

Key Instructional Considerations

Risk index: Medium
Time index: Medium
Cost index: Low to Medium
Learner-centered index: High
Duration of the learning activity: Weekly or as needed

Activity 19. Synchronous and Mobile Mentoring

Description and Purpose of Activity. For those interested in the role of experts in online classes, April 7, 2011 was a landmark day. That was the day that Tutor.com, which claims to be the largest online tutoring and homework help service available, announced that its services were now available for mobile devices (Tutor.com, 2011). Students could suddenly use applications on their iPhone, iPod Touch, or iPad to connect to an expert in real time to answer their questions, problems, and homework help needs. There is good reason to believe that such services will be the norm within 5 to 10 years, not just in middle and high school settings, but in any education or training situation. Recent reports from the Pew Internet and American Life Project show massive societal changes toward the use of mobile devices, especially among minorities in the United States (Smith, 2010).

Mobile interactions can individualize instruction and offer support on demand; in effect, an instructor is available when needed. To introduce students to this kind of interaction, you could assign students to solicit the help of a mobile mentor at least once a week in the online course. Students could not only ask questions about problems that they are facing, but they could take a picture of their problem and send it to their tutor or mentor. The mentor would then review the situation and offer guidance, share Web resources, and chat with the student.

These forms of interaction will become increasingly widespread during the coming years with Web conferencing, interactive whiteboards, video capabilities on smartphones, video-enhanced discussion forums, and other related technologies. Wearable computers like Google Glass are projected to have an impact on professional fields like health care and business with immediate mentoring and expert support systems (Aungst, 2013; Poulos, 2013). As such technologies proliferate, the supply of mobile mentors and synchronous or real-time forms of interaction will escalate. So, too, will the forms and levels of expertise that they offer. Imagine, if you can, a decade or two down the road when learners can excitedly explore any path while knowing that expert supports are always available when problems or confusion arise.

Skills and Objectives. Includes on-demand learning, problem clarification, connecting content knowledge from books and lectures to the real world, questioning skills, the identification of key concepts and principles, and learner engagement. As with the previous example, a key goal here is apprenticeship into a content area or field.

Advice and Ideas. You might create a mentoring or support network application for student mobile devices where none exists. Before adding someone to the mentoring network, screen all mentors and provide them with expectations or guidelines for support. Assign students to particular mobile mentors based on their interests and backgrounds. Share the activity with colleagues and discuss how the mobile mentoring network could be expanded and fine-tuned. You might consider conducting action research on the effectiveness of the mobile mentoring application.

Variations and Extensions. Students may be asked to find and select a mobile mentor whom the instructor must approve. They could also design prototypes of a mobile mentoring application. Students could present their final products at the end of the semester. In fact, consider creating a competition for the best mobile mentoring application in your content area.

Key Instructional Considerations

Risk index: Medium to High
Time index: Medium
Cost index: Low to High
Learner-centered index: High
Duration of the learning activity: Weekly or as needed

Activity 20. Learner-Self Interaction and Self-Feedback Forms

Description and Purpose of Activity. This chapter's previous nine examples involve many forms of encouragement and feedback. Activity 12 entailed feedback from students to instructors in the form of surveys and polls, whereas the first activity of this chapter employed critical friend or peer feedback experiences. Some of the others highlighted expert or practitioner feedback to students. And still other activities threw the human out of the feedback loop altogether and had the system or machine evaluate and respond to student submissions. In such situations, learners interact with the online content instead of with peers, experts, or instructors.

All these forms of interaction—learner-learner, learner-instructor, and learner-content interaction—are based on decades of distance education theory (Moore, 1989). In 1998, Soo and Bonk (1998) introduced the idea of learner-self interaction. This type of interaction refers to a learner's personal reflection on the learning-related content, the learning process, and her personal understanding. In learner-self interaction, there is an inner dialogue about the ongoing learning process. The learner constantly rethinks and reframes her understanding of the content through this inner dialogue. With enough learner-self interaction activities, the learner can develop self-regulated learning skills and become a self-directed and independent learner.

Learner-self interaction can be fostered in many ways. First, the online course or experience might have self-check and reflection questions embedded at key points in the process. In a business management class at MIT on Generating Business Value from Information Technology (MIT, 2011), students are given discussion question such as:

- Describe UPS and its business environment, and,
- Critique UPS's strategy for online business and its business model.

These discussion questions, found at the MIT OpenCourseWare site, though excellent for spurring class discussion and reflection, might be reshaped for learner-self interaction as follows:

- What did you learn about UPS and its business environment from the case that was presented? Ask yourself: What did I fail to learn? What other types of information resources would have helped me learn more? How might I have acquired such resources?

- Think about what you have learned about online commerce and the business models of other companies. What ideas and learning resources were critical to this new learning? Write down some key principles that seem to work. Then critique the online business approach and model used by UPS based on your new learning.

These are just a few examples of learner-self interaction types of questions. Instead of such open-ended queries, learners might simply respond to a checklist of skills and competencies to indicate if they have acquired them or not. Learners could submit their responses individually in an online form after which they could read their peers' responses. Additional reflection papers or activities could wrap around such a submission process. Other options could have students personally reflect in a wiki that accumulates all student posts, or requires them to reflect individually on their learning progress (or on a set of questions like those in the MIT example) in a blog. Yet another possibility would be to use a threaded discussion forum for student reflections. Each student might post a designated thread.

Skills and Objectives. Includes personal reflection, review concepts learned, concept attainment, comprehension and application skills, the development of self-regulatory and metacognition skills, and personal awareness and feedback. The key is for students to take time out and think about their learning journey. Feedback is drawn from within instead of outside.

Advice and Ideas. In some ways, this might be a novel activity for learners. If it is, be sure to provide examples from previous semesters or versions of the course if available. Keep in mind that students are often highly critical of their own work. As a result, some of them may need timely doses of encouragement and advice after reflecting on the skills that they learned. In addition, consider looking for common themes across the student self-reflection posts and list them.

If unique online forms or reflection templates are created, you could reuse such forms in later semesters or versions of the course. A vast system of reflection activities could be embedded into the course to foster student self-directed learning and reflection.

Variations and Extensions. Instructors could weave several learner-self interactions in a series of activities, followed by individual summary reflection papers that are shared with a critical friend or learning partner. The two individuals could also reflect on differences in their learning approaches as well as the results.

Key Instructional Considerations

Risk index: Low
Time index: Medium
Cost index: Low
Learner-centered index: High
Duration of the learning activity: As needed

Final Reflections on Encouragement

In building on Chapter Four's emphasis on the creation of a safe and engaging online climate for learning, this chapter highlights the forms and types of feedback and encouragement that can communicate to online learners that they are on the happy road to success. As indicated, there are many types of instructional supports or scaffolds that can be embedded into fully online and blended courses to elevate learner motivation as well as the learning outcomes. When this occurs, course satisfaction and completion rises, as does overall program completion.

The 10 activities highlighted here showcase the assorted ways in which feedback occurs and the numerous dimensions of feedback that must be considered. In addition to instructor feedback, many online instructors now embed peer-related feedback like critical friend or Web buddy activities in their courses. Others utilize system and outside expert feedback. And still others embed opportunities for self-feedback and reflection.

No matter the setting or the instructor's experience, each type of feedback has merits and should be considered when designing and implementing an online course experience.

As suggested regarding the ideas related to tone and climate in the previous chapter, we encourage you to find encouragement and feedback mechanisms that work for your situation. You know your course goals, materials, and audience best. You might decide to merge expert feedback with your own. Or perhaps you will choose to incorporate system feedback for certain tasks, weeks of the course, or milestone markers.

For some of you, the ideas of this chapter will save you time as you rethink your feedback strategies. After testing some of them out, be sure to share those that work well with your colleagues and ask for their feedback. Also consider expanding on the suggestion box idea in Activity 13 to solicit formative and summative feedback from your own students. Effective feedback need not be just "for" the learners; it can also be "from" them.

Keep experimenting with these ideas and then go beyond them. To do this, we suggest you read other books and materials or attend conferences. Those who feel adventurous can browse the Web for examples of instructional supports and feedback mechanisms. From that browsing, such individuals can also get a sense of how other online instructors encourage and support student course success. If you find something of interest online, ask the developer how he responds to student needs. What types of rewards does he use? Have any of your colleagues created a job aid or online tutorial that you might use in your own courses?

You need not create a feedback system from scratch. Open educational resources can be mined for feedback and support ideas. Those in higher education should look for online course resources posted to MERLOT, Connexions, or the Open Educational Resources Commons. If you are at the K–12 level, we recommend that you try out resources at Curriki as well as Connexions. Tired? There is also much in the OpenCourse-Ware project from MIT, the National Repository of Online Courses (NROC), and Jorum (from the United Kingdom). See the course Web resources at the end of this book.

If you have decided that peer-based feedback will be a key part of your feedback system, you must train your students to do this properly. They should not just randomly comment on fellow student work. Once in place, feedback can have a significant impact on the amount of work you face. If the rubric clearly specifies the assessment criteria and standards (Conrad & Donaldson, 2004), students will be well-armed assistants. And when their feedback is combined with instructor and system feedback, there are many valuable opportunities for student reflection and improvement.

The forms of encouragement, feedback, and overall support will vary depending on whether the activity is synchronous or asynchronous. In synchronous situations, students can immediately ask for clarification and elaboration on points made. At the same time, in many systems, once the synchronous session ends, the feedback vanishes. Instructors relying on synchronous activities should inquire about ways to archive sessions and make them available for later viewing. We have found that placing links to each synchronous session in the resources section of our course management system or class wiki is sufficient. In asynchronous forums, feedback may extend over several days or weeks, resulting in more opportunities for highly reflective feedback. However, the amount and timing of that feedback must be considered. If the student never reads it, it does no good.

As we draw to a close on the second component of TEC-VARIETY, we should re-mind the reader that Web-based instruction is relatively new. More innovative forms of learner support and feedback will undoubtedly emerge during the coming decade. Already we see this happening with social networking technology currently entering the academic world. Remember, too, that as stated in the opening section of this chapter, students want feedback on everything they do. Given this, we could easily make the case that encouragement, responsiveness, and feedback is the most important component of the TEC-VARIETY framework. Without effective feedback and support components in place, most students will flounder online just like Patti Smith would likely flop on stage without her adoring fans encouraging her.

It is now time, however, to explore the third component of TEC-VARIETY related to fostering student curiosity. Those curious about the contents of Chapter Six need only turn the page.

CHAPTER SIX

PRINCIPLE #3 CURIOSITY

(Includes Surprise, Intrigue, and Unknowns)

> We keep moving forward, opening new doors,
> and doing new things, because we're curious
> and curiosity keeps leading us down new paths.
>
> —Walt Disney

The first two principles of the TEC-VARIETY framework lay the groundwork for a high-quality course. First, you want learners to feel comfortable in the online course or training experience (Chapter Four, Principle #1). Second, you want to provide feedback, encouragement, and timely support for what they are learning (Chapter Five, Principle #2). While those first two principles are vital for student motivation, the third component of the TEC-VARIETY framework is essential for most courses and learning situations. Curiosity is said to have killed the cat. Put more positively, it is the spark of life for tens of thousands of learning situations taking place around the globe as you are reading this very page. In some ways, curiosity is what learners live for.

Our microbiologist friend, Brian J. Ford from Cambridge University, cautioned us against mentioning that old cat saying. When we spoke with him, Brian argued that "curiosity is actually the driver for humanity, the creator of society, the bearer of wisdom." He then took note of our book title and added, "The point about the Web (and e-learning access) is that it offers a way for people to satisfy their innate curiosity, irrespective of where or who they are."

Brian was spot on as usual. Curiosity arouses human interest in pursuing some intriguing piece of information or kernel of knowledge and the Web is filled with enticing resources and learning nuggets that can spark it. The satisfaction of our curiosity, temporary as it may be, brings deep-rooted pleasure to our lives. As Noble Prize–winning American chemist and peace activist Linus Pauling put it, "Satisfaction of one's curiosity is one of the greatest sources of happiness in life." If Pauling is right, this third component of the TEC-VARIETY model may be the most vital of them all.

Clearly, scientists, inventors, and world leaders recognize the importance of curiosity and inquisitiveness. What about educators and psychologists? In his 1996 book, *Motivating Others: Nurturing Inner Motivational Resources,* Johnmarshall Reeve proclaims that "Curiosity is a cognitively based emotion that occurs whenever a student perceives a gap in his or her knowledge" (p. 158). That sense of bewilderment or "gapness" nudges the learner into finding out more information. There is something intriguing about the content. Some unknown or missing piece of information that must be filled in.

Curiosity need not mean enjoyment. Steven Reiis (2004) contends that notions of intrinsic enjoyment exaggerate the importance of pleasure in motivation. He rightfully points out that highly curious people desire knowledge so much that they will overcome momentous challenges along the way, including a series of failures, extensive criticism, personal tension, and many forms of frustration. Still they march on to seek new information or some sense of learning accomplishment. People desire competence. This is universal.

Curiosity is internal. It is not some external coercion tactic. There are no carrots and sticks. Instead, there is a felt discrepancy between the knowledge that a learner possesses and that which he needs or desires to complete a task or gain a new competency or skill. There might also be a sense of wonder or suspense about something not previously known.

According to Paul Pintrich and Dale Schunk (1996), the discrepancies between the new information and what learners already know must be modest; large discrepancies are rapidly dismissed as highly implausible. Using Piaget's terminology, significantly different information is too difficult to assimilate or accommodate within our existing mental structures (Piaget, 1963). When a person, let's call her Rosie, expects something to happen but another event occurs, she enters a state of cognitive dissonance (Festinger, 1957). From there, curiosity and wonder are roused to life. Rosie may feel that her present state of knowledge is inadequate. At the same time, she is aware that she has the capability to learn more and overcome it. Such situations help bring Rosie to an optimal state of arousal for exploring her surrounding environment for the answer. And explore she does.

For decades now, researchers and educators interested in applying aspects of Piaget's theories of cognitive development to the classroom have relied on emerging technologies to exemplify certain principles in action. In particular, Piaget's ideas related to how learners construct and internalize new knowledge have been extensively explored (Pea, Kurland, & Hawkins, 1985). Remember back to Chapter Three, which referred to the allure of gaming as researched by Thomas Malone at the beginning of the personal computer era. He noted the motivational appeal of hidden or secret information, uncertain events and outcomes, and event randomness. In a game, we do not truly know the winner until the end. In real life, elements of surprise as well as strange, novel events can challenge our thinking and force the evaluation of inconsistencies in personal mental structures. This sense of challenge to fill in the gaps creates an intrinsic need to push ahead and learn more in order to succeed at the task.

The instructor who wishes to spur learner curiosity and some sense of unknown has many techniques at his disposal. He can throw out questions that do not have clear answers at the present time (Stipek, 1998). For example, "If we are in the age of the Web 2.0, what will the Web 5.0 look like?" Instruction can also start with questions and hypotheses that students might want to raise (Brophy, 1998). The instructor can also ask his students to converse about their views, and during the discussion, he can incorporate different forms of media to illustrate unexpected results. As errors in their thinking become obvious, students will seek more information. As illustrated in the Rosie story, Piaget referred to this as being in a state of disequilibrium (Piaget, 1969; Reeve, 1996). Such cognitive conflict or dissonance can be unnerving at times; however, when events violate expected standards or norms, interest is aroused and this often leads to extended learning quests for additional information and answers.

Curiosity might be cultivated with highly open-ended tasks with many possible learning paths. For example, instructors might insert open weeks in the schedule, thereby allowing learners to select their content for the week. Exploring ideas beyond those presented by the instructor or course resources will expand viewpoints that the class can access. In addition, guest speakers might be invited to present in a synchronous session followed by an asynchronous reflection in a class discussion forum. Students may search for further information that the guest has discussed. Yet another idea for fostering curiosity would be to arrange for learners to be mentored electronically by peers and practitioners throughout the semester. With this assembly of diverse views, students will perceive inconsistencies in their thinking and find themselves in a state of cognitive dissonance—a situation which is ripe for curiosity and learning to flourish.

Technologies for Principle #3: Curiosity

Web-based technology can foster curiosity and a sense of the surprise, intrigue, and the unknown. There is quick hyperlinking from information node to information node. The thoughtful combination of audio and video streaming can stimulate the senses, and thus enhance learner curiosity. Examples of how Web technology can spur curiosity include instant messaging with peers on Facebook, scanning daily events in Yahoo! News, searching for current research in Google Scholar, online brainstorming in a wiki, listening to an author explain the premise of a newly released book in a podcast, glancing through questions posted by the instructor to a discussion forum, and reading blog posts of a research team after they have made an exciting new discovery. Such technology resources are increasingly common and can be quickly embedded in fully online and blended learning experiences.

There is much that an instructor can do today to maximize the curiosity principle. She might design a website portal for someone famous in history. The site could be loaded with information nuggets in the form of quotes, digital news clippings, and stories that students may not have been heard before. Another way to provide such intrigue would be to invite a mystery guest to an upcoming online chat or Webinar. During the chat, the guest expert could sprinkle in facts and stories that are interesting but not common knowledge. Yet another technology tool for fostering curiosity and intrigue is to assign students to watch a live event somewhere around the world via a Web stream. For example, in a European history class, students may have watched the royal wedding of William and Kate on April 29, 2011, as it took place live on BBC News or CNN International. Alternatively, they might view it later in archived footage found while exploring the Royal Channel in YouTube.

Students could be pushed into dissonance or disequilibrium in online discussion forums. To prepare for these forums, instructors would assign them to particular perspectives or sides of a debate. As part of such an activity, they would be asked to propose and agree to a compromise position. When properly structured, online forums engage students with the voices and opinions that make up their particular class. Such voices will often ring out even when the class size reaches into the thousands or even tens of thousands of participants in a MOOC. In a MOOC, course participants can also be part of a world community discussing a controversial comment or an event in the news and their respective perspectives on it. Everyone reading that post or the associated news story undoubtedly would have an opinion to share.

The argument could be made that nearly everything that appears in the news each day can be used to spur dissonance and learner quests to know more. Some events are, of course, more heated than others. But any situation can arouse sadness, happiness, or other emotions in students. A view into the day in the life of a scientist, writer, or historian is now possible with videostreams of the news, audio files from a podcast series, live feeds from Twitter, interviews posted to a blog, and so on. Live science can stream to learner mobile devices and desktops from anywhere in the world. And when a Webcam can directly bring into your class a well-known scholar or team of researchers—who during the previous week announced an astounding discovery—many highly memorable learning activities are possible. Each time you turn on that Webcam, perspectives are shared, the relevancy of new findings can be explained, and intriguing questions for the future can be posed and discussed.

Questions and activities can wrap around each of the technology tools and ideas we have mentioned in ways that engage and arouse student learning. Perhaps the ideas of this chapter can unveil new ways to design learning environments that contain heavy doses of suspense, timely elements of surprise, and extended learning quests into the unknown.

Ten Online Activities in Principle #3: Curiosity

The information-intense world in which we live is filled with points of wonder and delight. Those teaching and learning online can tap into such wonder and delight on a daily basis. If you are a curiosity junkie, there is a fix awaiting your every keystroke or finger swipe. Many of us were born in the days of physical encyclopedias that often required us to borrow from a neighbor or hike to the local library to look up a fact or two. Today, there is much to quench our thirst for knowledge in the Web of Learning. We live in an age of fingertip knowledge, an age that we will someday come to call "The Learning Century."

Unlimited online resources and novel technologies are only part of the greater learning equation. In fact, Reeve (1996) cautions that effective instructors must also rely on deft pedagogical skill to raise learners' curiosity to an optimum level. For instance, instructors can foster suspense by leaving key pieces of information missing while presenting sketchy but enticing preview information, as is standard practice in any newscast before breaking for commercials. An instructor might also design games involving some form of guessing or predictions that have prompt feedback on the correctness of the guess. Whodunit mysteries, controversial issues and debates, and responding with contradictions to individual guesses and solutions all energize the learner to find additional information.

With proper course planning, we would have to wonder how someone would not be curious to know more in this age of information abundance. This third principle of the TEC-VARIETY framework is the starter fuel for many of the others described in this book—just as it is for most activities you hear about at conferences or read in reports. As with any motivational principle, curiosity is hard to bottle up, or constrain to a single chapter. You will find much to attract and engage your learners' attention throughout this book. Arousing curiosity, in fact, is part of the intent of the TEC-VARIETY framework itself.

Activity 21. Online Events in the News

Description and Purpose of Activity. It is likely that news of the day has been woven into learning for millennia, whether we were sharing information on how to fashion some type of stone tools, design a clay pot, or prepare a meal of fish, vegetables, roots, and nuts. News is engaging as it typically provides some unique piece of information and life interest stories that had not been known previously. And stories are easy to recall, put to use, and share with others.

You can likely find several news items relevant to your class each day. Not all of them will spark intense learner curiosity, but with some creative pedagogy most will. What if you were in the following three situations?

- You are an online instructor for a paleontology course in the fall of 2009 when a miniature version of a Tyrannosaurus Rex is reported. It was originally unearthed in northeastern China but secretly and unlawfully found its way to the United States. The tiny T. Rex disrupts much of the facts and theory related to the evolution of what we know about the gigantic version (Fountain, 2009). You could make use of this controversy about how the mini prototype Tyrannosaurus got out of China in the first place by sparking class discussion and debate about ethics in the field paleontology and related disciplines.

- You are a retired general assisting in a course on military leadership or tactical maneuver training during the spring of 2011. On May 1, 2011, Osama bin Laden is killed in a firefight with US Special Operations Forces (CBS News, 2011). In a few simple Google searches you find extensive video clips, maps, drawings, timelines, interviews, and text to incorporate into your class.

- Your specialty is the culture, history, or religions of India. It is July 4, 2011, and, earlier that morning, you opened the local paper and read a short caption about a temple of gold in India with a treasure trove of items unearthed. Not much more was said. Curiosity piqued, you soon scavenge the Web for more details and read articles from the *New York Times* and other places. In them, you learn about a temple in the southern part of India from the sixteenth century called Sri Padmanabhaswamy where diamonds, coins, jewels, and sold-gold statues of gods and goddesses have been found in vaults beneath it. Initial estimates indicate that they are worth at least $22 billion (Bajaj, 2011). This is the largest such find ever in India. It is something out of an Indiana Jones movie epic adventure. Of course, if, instead of religious studies or history, your area is acting, screenwriting, or film production, a few moments of creativity might turn such news into a highly engaging online or blended learning activity for your class.

Online events in the news can help develop or support prime knowledge related to concepts and ideas from recent lectures or help draw interest in a presentation that is about to start. News events can also help with learner attention and comprehension of assigned readings. Students quickly understand that the course content has relevance and application in the real world. The news item can be used as an advance organizer for knowledge that will be presented later in the semester. It can also anchor that learning in a context. News, however, is often incomplete. There is only so much time available and news reporters cannot be experts on most of what they cover. As a result, they provide only a thin slice of any topic they write about—which can be an incentive for learners to find out more.

Skills and Objectives. Includes linking discipline knowledge to current events in the news, learner curiosity in content, encoding news information both verbally and visually, observational skills, and critical analysis and application of concepts. This technique extends the course to the real world and to facts, trends, ideas, and opinions that may not have been addressed otherwise.

Advice and Ideas. Innumerable activities can spin out of any news item. We often put online news events related to each week of our online and blended courses in a section of our syllabi that we called "tidbits." These tidbits are extensions of the required course content into the real world. There are often 5–10 or more tidbits each week to select from. We have our students decide which ones to read and respond to in their weekly blogs or discussion forums, though there is often a targeted number of tidbits that they must read and reflect on by the end of the course. During the course, we notify students of current events in the news related to the class as they come up. Notifications can be sent via e-mail, announcements in the course website, the instructor blog, the class wiki, or in discussion forum posts.

Instructors can do many things with these articles, videos, or special reports. As indicated, you could require learners to refer to news items in their weekly discussion forum postings; items that link to course content might be highlighted or analyzed. And there could be competitions to see who can identify the most course-related concepts and principles in a particular news story. The instructor may also refer to the news articles during an online lecture or Webinar. Such content would then be fair game for later quizzes and examinations.

Variations and Extensions. You may prod students to venture beyond one or more current events stories that interested them, suggesting that they extensively research such topics for a final paper, report, or presentation. The news article, therefore, becomes a springboard to greater depth of learning. This approach fosters curiosity for each student on different feature stories or news items. Students could also search for trends buried in the news content or to predict future trends. To further spur curiosity, instructors could specifically mention the most intriguing pieces of an old news story or provide parts of that story that students might not be able to find online, building up to a climax when they uncover the rest of the story.

Key Instructional Considerations

> Risk index: Medium
> Time index: Medium
> Cost index: Low
> Learner-centered index: High
> Duration of the learning activity: Throughout the course or as needed

Activity 22. Live Science, Creative Expression, or Artistic Invention

Description and Purpose of Activity. Activities 22 and 23 will engage your learners with scientific discoveries, unique creations, and innovations as they are happening. In Activity 22, your class could attend an online ceremony for a new book or report, and then take part in a virtual book signing after the event. They could find out about discoveries announced in shared online video sources like the Discovery News Video, BBC News Video, Earthwatch on YouTube, National Geographic Video, CNN Video, or CurrentTV. Announcements could also be found online from an NPR station or some other radio show or podcast.

Want more? Well, there probably are podcasts of interviews with writers, scientists, poets, musicians, and inventors. A much-heralded and unique musical performance or play could be streamed live to students' desktop or mobile units. Perhaps there is an exciting new finding from an ancient burial chamber in Egypt or Mexico (Huffington Post, 2011). Or maybe you are about to watch the first live Webcast of a brain dissection (Chronicle of Higher Education, 2009). Still need more? Well, in 2010, there was an announcement of more than 40 new plant and animal species found in Indonesian waters as captured by robotic vehicles and high-definition cameras (Associated Press, 2010). Two years before that, there was a news story about a colossal squid that was accidently caught in Antarctic waters and was being examined by scientists after being on ice for nearly a year (Black, 2008). It was the first discovery of its kind. Such scientific, artistic, and cultural events are increasingly common.

Take the case of Dr. John Ballard, a former US Navy officer and professor of oceanography at the University of Rhode Island. Ballard is an explorer and underwater archaeologist who has a history of locating famous shipwrecks including the Titantic, the World War II aircraft carrier USS Yorktown, and John F. Kennedy's PT-109. Today, he is heading up the Nautilus Live project. As an example of live or "immediate" science, there are researchers and scientists on board the Nautilus Live. Students can ask questions via the Web about various aspects of their expeditions, including encounters with sharks, monkfish feeding, ancient ship and artifact locating and recoveries, and more. Each event is designed to captivate students' imaginations about the real world.

Skills and Objectives. Includes connecting content knowledge from books and lectures to the real world, identification of key concepts and terms, appreciation of expert viewpoints and insights, and curiosity and engagement. A key goal of such an activity is to apprentice students into the field and give them a taste for what is presently interesting or exciting to leaders in the field.

Advice and Ideas. Given the endless stream of news at one's fingertips from around the planet today, there will come times when some of it will be directly related to the class or training event that you are teaching or online programs you are administering. You must plan ahead, therefore, for how that course, module, or program might take advantage of live news feeds and events. Many tasks and activities can be connected to the live event, including student-generated podcast reviews, compilations of students' reflective writing, student and instructor blog postings, and online class discussions. The exact form of the activity chosen may vary quite significantly each time.

Variations and Extensions. Assign students to search for live science, creative expression, or artistic invention events. Each must come up with one such event during the course or training experience. They should post a link to it in the course website and make an announcement to the class. Attending the event may be optional or you may request students to attend a set number of them during the class. A short reflection paper can be assigned requiring students to link concepts, themes, and ideas in the course to the live event. Unique connections and insights might be acknowledged and praised. Once again, students could be given bonus points or be allowed to delete any one assignment if they contact the original researcher, artist, or inventor. Any response from that person that is shared with the class would be worth additional points.

Key Instructional Considerations

Risk index: Medium
Time index: Medium
Cost index: Low (assuming any videostreamed activity is free to attend)
Learner-centered index: Medium
Duration of the learning activity: 1–2 weeks

Activity 23. Live Scientific Discovery or Invention

Description and Purpose of Activity. As seen in the previous activity, new discoveries and inventions occur each day. Increasingly, however, researchers, institutions, and publishers work together to synchronize the announcement of a unique finding, life-saving product, or controversial new theory. In effect, science can be immediately felt in the classroom and in everyday life. A snowball of activities can occur that make it seem that the idea, concept, species, entity, principle, theory, and so forth had been known for some time.

As an example, immediate science took place on May 19, 2009, when Dr. Jørn Hurum, a paleontologist from Oslo University's Natural History Museum, announced what appeared to be a vital missing link in human evolution called "Ida" (Randerson, 2009). Across the ocean that same day, one could walk into Barnes and Noble, Borders, and many other bookstores throughout North America and find a brand-new book on display at the front of the store called The Link (Tudge, 2009). If a reader did not understand aspects of the book, a website for the discovery went live as well on May 19, 2009, and could explain many aspects of Ida.

For scholars interested in what the discovery meant, a research article on Ida was simultaneously published in the Public Library of Science (PLOS) (Franzen, Gingerich, Habersetzer, Hurum, von Koenigswald, et al., 2009). Importantly, all PLOS articles are free and open to the world community. To better understand the finding, photos were released on the homepage as well as a video from Sir David Attenborough that explained the importance of the finding.

At about the same time, *National Geographic* discussed aspects of the finding while posing serious questions and concerns. It also added to the mix of immediate learning possibilities with a link from their article to an interactive prehistoric timeline on the Web (National Geographic News, 2009). So much occurred on that one tiny day in May! Science was finding its way into K–12 and university classrooms as well as research labs around the planet on that same day. Young students learned about Ida exactly when most scientists became aware of the findings—not months, years, or decades later, as is often the case. With such activities occurring regularly online, there is much opportunity for fostering student curiosity and motivation. The Web certainly offers remarkable opportunities for surprise, intrigue, discovery, and sharing. Take advantage of it and you too will spring to life with learner curiosity.

Skills and Objectives. Includes connecting course content knowledge from books and lectures to the real world, extending knowledge to the edges of the field, appreciation of expert viewpoints and insights, multitasking, and learner curiosity and engagement. A key goal of such an activity is to apprentice students into the field and give them a taste for what is presently exciting people.

Advice and Ideas. Students can be tasked with exploring different aspects of the finding or invention. They could also work in teams, with one student reviewing available multimedia of the finding or invention (e.g., pictures, audio, or video resources), another finding and reading primary news reports and blog commentary, and a few other students reading and summarizing any available research reports or books on the topic. You could require this team of students to come up with a report, critiques, or reaction papers on the discovery or invention.

Variations and Extensions. Students could write to the scientist, explorer, inventor, or members of the research team for additional information, with the goal of pushing into areas beyond what has been reported in the news. As part of this project, they might produce individual, group, or entire class blog posts or podcasts about the discovery or invention.

Key Instructional Considerations

> Risk index: Medium
> Time index: Medium
> Cost index: Low (assuming accessing information related to the event is free)
> Learner-centered index: Medium
> Duration of the learning activity: 1–2 weeks

Activity 24. Just-in-Time Syllabus

Description and Purpose of Activity. The previous activity relied on current events in the news to spur student curiosity and course interest. It was just a small taste of what is now possible with online resources for this third principle of TEC-VARIETY. Back in 2002, Shyamala Raman from Saint Joseph College, Jean Shackelford from Bucknell University, and Kim Sosin from the University of Nebraska Omaha, coined the term "Just-in-Time Syllabus" (JiTS). In their undergraduate economics courses, they would incorporate time-sensitive data from the real world as it occurred. As economic conditions changed, so did their syllabus.

According to Raman, Shackelford, and Sosin (2002), their innovative use of online materials enriched and energized traditional textbook content. In economics, as with many other disciplines, information is quickly outdated. Worse, it is often presented in a boring manner. If, however, a syllabus is designed as a shell with key themes outlined, additional content and applications can be infused into the course according to student interests as well as prevailing societal trends and conditions.

For example, students majoring in business management might have different examples and case situations from those in public policy or environment science departments. Concepts like supply and demand and elasticity might be linked to breaking news from the Gulf region with protests and potential leadership changes from Oman or Bahrain, rolling blackouts in California, or the infamous BP (Deepwater Horizon) oil spill of 2010. Over time, sets of articles on a particular topic could be handled by different students or groups in the course and each person or group would have to glean from these resources relevant information to make sense of the situation from an economics stand-point. They could discuss price elasticity or the determinants of supply.

When the three scholars mentioned earlier designed their JiTS approach, the Web was still in its infancy. Today much more is possible. It is important to point out that Raman, Shackelford, and Sosin were attempting to foster student critical thinking and the sharing of perspectives. Other skills and competencies they targeted included collaboration, synthesis, literacy, and responsiveness. They also hoped to foster four levels of thinking from receiving information (Level 1), to observing and comprehending it (Level 2), to personally developing alternative interpretations (Level 3), to analysis and synthesis of it (Level 4).

There are many ways that the idea of a JiTS might be incorporated into an online or blended course. Following are three examples.

- Suppose you are teaching a course on Middle East culture, civics, economics, or political science and there is a major political revolution or a so-called "Arab Spring." To you and your students' surprise, you locate an online interactive timeline of news events by date for each country in the Middle East as reported by the British newspaper, *The Guardian* (Blight & Pulham, 2011). Articles related to protests, political moves, international responses, and regime changes are noted in different colors as you scroll through time. In this way, the Arab Spring timeline and associated navigation bar provide a highly unique way to synthesize events of the past while dynamically adding new ones as they transpire. Clicking on any link in the timeline leads the user to a news story for a particular date and country. For instance, assume it is July 8, 2011. A link in the Libya timeline indicates that on that particular date there was a news story about Muammar Gaddafi threatening attacks on Europe (Smith, 2011). The news from Saudi Arabia, Lebanon, and Egypt was different that day. You soon realize that each node is an opportunity for student exploration, reflection, and discussion. The comprehensive timeline from *The Guardian* is like a supplemental reader for the course. Some instructors, in fact, might take it so far as to replace the standard course syllabus with that one interactive news timeline. As the timeline changes, so, too, would the course; it would be constantly evolving. This would be the ultimate JiTS.

- Imagine that you teach a course in physical geography, world cultures, or emergency preparedness. For each major earthquake, tsunami, or hurricane of the past decade, there are likely online maps, interviews, video footage, news articles, and live accounts that can be used to excite learners to complete particular course activities related to these events (Shahid, 2011). With geographical and climate information in the news each day in addition to thousands of relevant blog posts, resources like Earthwatch and National Geographic, and portals of images online in Flickr or Picasa, a course could tap into a rich tapestry of supplemental resources each week. And that course would evolve day by day.

- Similar possibilities arise for a course on emerging technology for learning intended for undergraduate pre-service teachers as well as graduate students. Each day is replete with technology news from CNN, the *New York Times*, eCampus and eSchool News, and other online resources. As a result, there could be links each week to new research reports, technology announcements, and interesting tools and applications related to content in the course; the course would thus evolve depending on news related to learning technologies. For instance, an article appeared about the South Korean government's committed $2.4 billion to a project that would see all K–12 textbooks digitized by 2015 (Haq, 2011). Students could discuss the ramifications for the world as well as issues of mass adoption and scalability to other emerging technologies. Then the instructor could provide the following quotation from the article, "The digital conversion is part of a project to create 'smart schools' across the country, according to South Korea's Education Ministry. The state says it plans to incorporate 'smart' features such as video, animation, virtual reality, and hyperlinks, in its digital curriculum." With that new information, students would discuss the theoretical underpinnings of each form of technology. They might even create prototypes of a "smart school" project or write to members of the South Korean government for sample content or virtual demonstrations.

Skills and Objectives. Includes analysis and evaluation skills, multitasking, linking new knowledge to current events in the news, learner curiosity in content, encoding the news information both verbally and visually, flexibility in thinking, and critical analysis of concept application. This technique provides the skeleton, shell, or base knowledge extending to online information in the form of news, research reports, trends, or opinions.

Advice and Ideas. We place our syllabi online for our students. Such online documents are especially handy to look things up, even when not teaching the course. As new articles and resources appear, they can be added on the fly to that online syllabus. New course activities can spin out of those recent resources. Though highly engaging, such an approach requires much time, effort, patience, and persistence to generate and maintain. To save some time, you might consider allowing one or more students in the course to drop one assignment in return for helping you review and update the online course syllabus and associated contents.

When you rely on evolving trends to augment and supplement traditional course materials, you are taking a risk regarding the content that will come up. Perhaps the exact example you were hoping to embed in the course will not appear in the news that semester. Be honest with your students. Tell them that you may alter your plans based on what is available online to supplement the course.

As more materials are placed online, the role of the instructor shifts from that of deliverer of content to online concierge and curator of content. Such a shift is simultaneously exciting and difficult to master. Few instructors have had the necessary training to be an online concierge, counselor, or curator. Nevertheless, these are often the new roles.

Variations and Extensions. The course could be divided into two parts: Part 1 for delivering some set content that the instructor or administrators of the program believe students need to be aware of; and Part 2, which relies on JiTS ideas.

Key Instructional Considerations

Risk index: High
Time index: High
Cost index: Low
Learner-centered index: High
Duration of the learning activity: Throughout the course or as needed

Activity 25. Just-in-Time Teaching

Description and Purpose of Activity. A similar method to the preceding is called Just-in-Time Teaching (JiTT). The essence of JiTT is to have students complete some task or assignment prior to class. So if you are teaching a psychology of learning course and the current unit is on cognitive psychology, there may be a short quiz online about concepts such as working memory, knowledge transfer, accommodation, metacognition, and so on. The form of the exam could be objective and easily scored or more open-ended and subjective. With a large class, objective measures naturally are much easier to embed.

JiTT often involves a set of test or reaction questions delivered to students prior to class. Students could first read chapters of a book or several articles; alternatively, they may watch and analyze an important video segment, complete a case problem or simulation, or analyze a set of data. Questions related to each JiTT activity can be posted in the course website or within some other tool. To foster efficiency, give students a set amount of time to respond. As with the JiTS activity, JiTT allows for more student engagement and participation than traditional lecture-based classrooms. JiTT activities can be extremely open-ended and conceptual in nature. At the same time, they can also include highly objective questions and activities that are easily scored by an online program.

This idea was originally developed for physics content with support from the National Science Foundation (Novak, 2000). While physics instructors were the first to rely on it, the JiTT approach soon expanded into other disciplines such as biology, chemistry, journalism, language education, business, and many other areas. In the beginning, JiTT was intended as an online warm-up activity for a later live meeting.

In journalism, for instance, Professor Claude Cookman at Indiana University has found a way for his students to reflect online each week using a series of thought-provoking questions he provides. His primary goal is to help them critically analyze and process the readings prior to coming to a live class session (Cookman, 2009). Cookman refers to his method as "Thinking About the Readings" or TARs.

When employing TARs, he asks his students to write short essays on oppositional readings. He and his grading assistants then provide extensive positive feedback as well as constructive criticism on those essays. A key advantage of TAR assignments is that the instructor can more readily know student perspectives on different issues. With that insight, he can spur intense debates, address misconceptions, conduct interesting surveys and polls, and spin out other activities as needed. In terms of critical thinking skills, the instructor can nurture compare and contrast skills as well as those related to summarization, formulating points of view, defending positions, and critical reflection.

Online warm-up activities like JiTT and TARs give instructors the opportunity to analyze the information collected from students and alter their classes or upcoming activities accordingly. A well-designed JiTT activity is akin to a brain surgeon opening up someone's cranium and taking a peek inside. With that information, the instructor can then devote more time, resources, and attention to areas in need. Concepts and principles that students were having difficulty with can be directly pointed out. In addition, supplemental readings or video demonstrations of key course concepts can be placed in the course website based on the JiTT results. Instruction becomes tailored or individualized according to student needs.

Skills and Objectives. Includes self-testing, analysis and evaluation skills, linking new knowledge to prior knowledge, priming knowledge stores, learner curiosity in content, and concept application. This technique starts with a skeleton, shell, or base of knowledge which then extends out to online information in the form of news, research reports, trends, and opinions. Another key objective is to record course concepts that may be difficult for the learner.

Advice and Ideas. Students should have examples of the task expectations or the quality of answers that the instructor is looking for. JiTT questions should be designed clearly and appropriately for the intended audience. In addition, the results should be shared quickly and with the entire class.

The resource center at Carleton College in Northfield, Minnesota, has designed online resources to guide faculty members through the Just-in-Time Teaching process. Their online JiTT resource details what JiTT is, how to use it, and its benefits to students and instructors. It also details how to get started, the research on JiTT in fields such as physics, economics, biology, and history, and how to review and assess student responses. In addition, this resource offers more than a dozen JiTT examples in earth science.

One such JiTT warm-up activity is on groundwater and archaeology in a course on geoscience created by Laura Guertin from Penn State University Delaware County (Guertin, n.d.). Her JiTT questions include:

- What is causing the groundwater to rise to the foundations of Egypt's archaeological structures? What damage is the groundwater doing?

- Describe at least two different solutions that have been proposed to combat the problem of the rising water table damaging the monuments. Which do you think is the better one, and why?

- In your opinion . . . do we even need to save these monuments? Why? I mean, what are they really worth—are they worth anything?

Instructors may choose to grade student responses to randomly selected JiTT exercises, or perhaps for a random selection of students for each exercise. Instructors may also grade any JiTT task for simple completion rather than accuracy. In any event, the act of grading or assessment will encourage students to do the course readings and activities prior to class time. The percentage that such tasks will represent in the course grading system might be as low as a few percent of the total course points to perhaps 25–30 percent or more.

Variations and Extensions. Ask the students to design the JiTT activity or set of preclass questions for students taking the course in the future. Perhaps have a different volunteer each week. Students can also analyze JiTT and TAR results and explain them to the class.

Key Instructional Considerations

Risk index: High
Time index: High
Cost index: Low
Learner-centered index: High
Duration of the learning activity: Throughout the course or as needed

Activity 26. What's My Line Guest Games

Description and Purpose of Activity. Students may not be aware of the background, accomplishments, interests, and experiences of synchronous and asynchronous guests. In this activity, you would invite an unannounced guest for a presentation or discussion. First, however, ask your students to determine the occupation or expertise (i.e., line of work) of the guest or the actual name of this famous mystery person. Questions from panelists or participants can only be in a yes-or-no response format. If there is a pair of guests, there could be multiple rounds of probing and guessing.

Once the person's identity is determined, there may be additional competitions to locate information about him or her. Based on the clues received, students could conduct searches in places such as: (1) Google Scholar for papers the person has written; (2) Google Books or Amazon for books by him or her; (3) Google Images, Picasa, or Flickr for pictures or images of the mystery guest; (4) Facebook for personal and professional information; (5) YouTube, Google Video, or other shared online video sites for presentations, interviews, news stories, and documentaries; and (6) online news, biographies, blogs, or podcasts for still other insights on this individual. To focus their searches and create team spirit, you could number students from one to six and assigned one of these six places to search; in addition, students could accumulate bonus points as individuals or teams for correct guesses.

As a result, students will learn about the background of a key individual in a field in some depth. In addition, much more content-related information on the person will be available for later discussions and activities.

Skills and Objectives. Includes social interaction, search skills, critical analysis, connecting course content to important people in the field, curiosity, and dissonance. The key is to arouse student curiosity about someone or something that they are known for.

Advice and Ideas. There are many possible formats and procedures. The format selected might become enhanced and fine-tuned over time. If you do a "What's My Line" activity every week, the students you allow to guess the identity of the individual could rotate each week on a "What's My Line" panel. If this is only a one-time or occasional activity, the entire class might be asked to participate. Be sure to clearly spell out the rules of the activity, including the start and end dates. Students incorrectly guessing the occupation or name of the guest should be eliminated from competition. Hints might be offered by the instructor as necessary.

Variations and Extensions. Instead of a synchronous session with the guest or expert, the instructor could detail clues each day about a mystery person in an asynchronous discussion forum and have the students determine the person's identity. Once they have properly guessed the occupation or name of the guest, that person could be invited in for a synchronous chat or to comment on the discussion that had taken place thus far. Alternatively, the expert may never appear and may, in fact, have lived centuries or millennia ago; thus, instead of a live appearance, you could have students simply reflect on, write about, discuss, and debate the ideas of that person. Dressing the part, of course, is always optional for the instructor or any guests.

Key Instructional Considerations

Risk index: Low to Medium (depending on how effectively the technology works)
Time index: Low to Medium
Cost index: Low
Learner-centered index: Medium
Duration of the learning activity: As needed

Activity 27. A Day in the Life of a Scientist, Scholar, or Celebrity

Description and Purpose of Activity. One way to excite students about the content is to have them track one or more famous people in the field. The assigned task could be to write a blog post, paper, or discussion forum entry on an imaginary day in the life of an award-winning scientist, well-known scholar, or celebrity in a particular field. You may request that they respond to particular questions or issues in their writing. For example, who were the person's friends, what were her hobbies, what items of significance did she produce in her life, how did her career change and when, and so on.

To aid in task support, students might be given a list of well-known people in a field with brief one- or two-sentence biographical sketches about each one. You could include relevant links to biographical information on each person. To streamline the activity, students could be asked to sign up for a particular person to investigate by completing an online form. Alternatively, students might brainstorm which leaders in a field to investigate based on their prior experiences and readings to date in the course.

Once a person has been selected (or while still mulling it over), students might explore his homepages and blogs, subscribe to his Twitter feeds, watch his videos, or read his online news. Instead of writing one blog posting or discussion forum entry, students could write a series of such postings on that individual for a week. Alternatively, you could ask them to post brief reflections on multiple people in the field. Their postings should note particular contributions of that person as well as significant changes or evolutionary steps in his professional careers.

When completing the assignment, ask students for a final reflection paper discussing how what they learned from researching that person relates to specific topics and ideas in the course, including new concepts, theories, principles, and related fields of study. Such a tactic should help to synthesize student learning and excite them about the field.

Skills and Objectives. Includes self-directed learning, motivation and engagement, appreciation for a topic or field, analysis skills, personalizing learning, reflection, and analysis skills. The key aspect of this activity is an indirect apprenticeship into the field.

Advice and Ideas. Perhaps have students explore sites of famous people from an online portal or resource. In that portal, you might have links to Wikisource, the Encyclopedia of World Biography, Biography.com, FamousPeople.co.uk, FamousPeople.com, Biography Online, Wiki-quote, Turning the Pages from the British Library, Google Books, and other such websites. Constrain student searches by providing instructional scaffolds of your expectations as well as examples of prior student work. Before they start, request that students select a couple of potential people to study and then turn in one- or two-paragraph justifications for researching each one. Instructor or peer feedback will help shape their ideas and explorations.

Remember one of the opening quotations to this chapter about the importance of curiosity from Brian J. Ford from Cambridge? Not heard of him? Students locating his homepage online will find out that he has over 30 books to his credit, including *Sensitive Souls*, *Patterns of Sex*, *The Digital Microscope*, and *Future Food*. He also has a new book on secret weapons of WWII and several others in the works (Ford, 2010). The online biography on his homepage will also inform the learner that he is not only the founder of *Science Now* and *Where Are You Taking Us?* for the BBC but also a former TV game show host. There is also a Wikipedia page on Professor Ford which contains dozens of interesting information tidbits that you can learn nowhere else. To see him in action, you need only go to the Tellymonitor channel in YouTube for examples of saved video footage. Once there, students can watch candid interviews, stunning presentations and lectures, and become immersed in his travels. Professor Ford's Twitter feed provides occasional current and ongoing information. On top of that, students can send Brian Ford an e-mail with questions and then find him on sites including Facebook, LinkedIn, Bebo and MySpace. E-mails to him are always answered.

If, instead of a biology course, suppose you were teaching something in computer science, engineering, psychology, marketing, video gaming, or entrepreneurship. In any of those situations, someone like Nolan Bushnell, founder of both Atari and the Chuck E. Cheese's Pizza-Time Theaters chain, might be the perfect celebrity guest for one or more of your students to investigate. As noted in his Wikipedia page, Bushnell is considered a founding father of the video gaming industry. The history of the field of video games as well as many aspects of home computing can be revealed to students by investigating the long career of this one individual. In addition to Wikipedia, you can also find informative articles on Bushnell in *Inc.* magazine (Chafkin, 2009) and interviews of him in places like *Gamasutra* (Sheffield, 2008). Want more? Google can also provide a timeline view of search results from his birth in 1943 to today. And like Brian Ford, you can follow him in Twitter as well as friend him on Facebook. Once connected, you can send him a private message and await a response. Many additional links for Nolan Bushnell, including decades of images, interviews, company reports, and so on await your searching pleasures.

These are but two examples of what is possible today. Both illustrate the fact that much is possible today online to foster learner curiosity and engagement. Much that was once unknown, rumored, or misunderstood can now be investigated and verified or refuted with the simple click of a mouse or swipe of a finger and some seasoned critical thinking skills. These are exciting times to be able to follow the world of a scientist, scholar, or celebrity.

Variations and Extensions. If their selected person is still alive, ask students to write to the scholar. If not, they might write to someone connected to that individual (e.g., a direct descendent or relative, the director or board member of a foundation, or a curator of an online resource for that person). Students could also engage in an online role play or debate where they must assume the characteristics of the person that they have been tracking. If the class is fully online, the role play might take place live in a Webinar or chat, or by asynchronous discussion posting. If the course is blended or F2F, students could physically assume the persona of their character in front of their peers.

Key Instructional Considerations

Risk index: Medium
Time index: Medium
Cost index: Low
Learner-centered index: High
Duration of the learning activity: 1–3 weeks

Activity 28. Cultural or Contextual Blogs and Resources

Description and Purpose of Activity. Traditional textbooks are often criticized for their homogeneous and bland content. Part of the intrigue with Web-based courses is that they can tap into rich online content as well as connect with people around the world. Learner curiosity can be aroused with content that they might not normally encounter.

As an example, instructors teaching about the Stó:lō people or other First Nation tribes and cultures in British Columbia from over 10,000 years ago or some distant culture in Ecuador or Albania could rely on blog postings of archaeologists discussing customs, newly discovered artifacts, rituals, maps, and personal accounts (Bonk, 2009b). There are even interactive online archaeology sites and art museums for students to experience particular events, peoples, and projects from ancient Minoan life in the second millennium B.C. to the Roman Empire to the Middle Ages and on to the Renaissance. For those teaching American history courses, similar online interactive sites now exist for historic Jamestown in the 1600s, Colonial Williamsburg in the 1700s, Civil War prisons in the 1800s, the growth of personal computing in the latter part of the 1900s, and the impact of hurricanes and tsunamis in this century.

Cultural and contextual enhancements need not be limited to history, archaeology, and anthropology courses. Accounting and finance students might listen intently to business executives on the podcast show, "Wall Street Confidential," where guests explain their perspectives on recent events in the news or changes in government legislation. They might also listen to free podcasts from the *Wall Street Journal*. Similarly, nursing students might gain insights about their chosen field from listening to podcasts found at "The Nursing Show" or "Insights in Nursing: Interviews on Trends and Careers in Nursing." Courses in religious studies or world cultures can tap into online photo websites displaying different customs, rituals, historical sites, common rituals, and other religious practices as well as online museums of well-known statues, tools, books, and so on. In fact, dozens of expert blogs, podcasts, and news reports exist on nearly any subject area.

As an example, Professor Kim Foreman at San Francisco State University created a blog called "Come and See Africa" (CASA) (Foreman, 2010) where she documented missionary work that she and her husband, Chris, conducted in different parts of Africa. For more than a decade, they traveled to Rwanda, Burundi, Congo, and Uganda. Many pictures and stories showcase their journey, including the people they met and the places they had been. An associated website, Come and See Africa International, has additional documentation including links to pictures for each trip, videos, mission statements, and seminar notes from different educational and religious speeches given (see Figure 6.1).

FIGURE 6.1: KIM FOREMAN (THIRD FROM RIGHT) AND CHRIS FOREMAN (SECOND FROM RIGHT) DURING THEIR MISSIONARY WORK IN RWANDA.

This is but one example of the endless opportunities for adding culture and context to course or training experiences using online resources. Sadly, Kim Foreman died in a car accident during a missionary trip in the summer of 2010, yet her blogs and documentation from previous trips continue to live on. In effect, any documentation of culture or society can be reusable for years and even centuries to come. Every blogger today is a historian of some aspect of twenty-first-century society. Each insight, comment, and resource posted might be used in different ways to spur student interest in a topic. For instance, Kim Foreman's final blog posts could find use in pre-service teacher education courses as well as those on African history, pastoral ministry, higher education policy, and many other disciplines and situations.

Skills and Objectives. Includes cultural curiosity, reflection, seeing multiple perspectives, and global understanding and appreciation. Central to this activity is the opening up of perspectives beyond limited views from textbook authors, instructors, and standard course resources.

Advice and Ideas. Find a quiet location and spend one or two hours brainstorming a list of possible course extensions and open educational resources that might prove valuable in one or more of your courses. Next, prioritize that list and search the Web for information related to it. Keep a log or database of what you have found. During the ensuing months or years, keep updating that log or list. Share what you have found with colleagues and ask for their recommendations. You could also ask students for their advice about contextual and cultural information that they are aware of. They might make recommendations about the inclusion of such content. The instructor should evaluate any cultural and contextual content found online that is used.

Variations and Extensions. The instructor could obtain the e-mails or physical addresses of some of the people referred to in a blog post, podcast, or online presentation or resource. Once obtained, those enrolled in the course could write to some of these people for an update on their lives or to ask them to respond to other questions or issues that they have generated. Students can write reflection papers on their findings; they could also write to the original creator of the online content and ask for additional information and insights as to why the content was originally posted.

Key Instructional Considerations

Risk index: Medium
Time index: Medium to High
Cost index: Low to High
Learner-centered index: Medium
Duration of the learning activity: As needed

Activity 29. Extreme Learning

Description and Purpose of Activity. The past decade has seen a proliferation of ways in which people learn and teach. Humans take learning to the extreme edges of the planet and beyond. Students can now control submarines from their classrooms, send research questions to explorers excavating Mayan ruins, comment on blog posts of teenagers attempting to become the world's youngest global solo sailors, interact with Space Shuttle astronauts, and read dispatches from adventurers on their way up Mount Everest. They can even sit in the tropics and interact with scientists studying polar ice, the Antarctic toothfish, or penguin populations. And there is much funded research and curriculum innovation at the K–12 level for such types of learning.

During the past several years, such projects have expanded and multiplied. Among them are the Polar Husky project (also called GoNorth!), the Journey North, Earthducation, Geothentic, the Last Ocean Project, North of 60, the Jason Project, and the Ice Stories project from the Exploratorium in San Francisco. This area is known as "adventure learning" (Doering, 2006).

Among those at the cutting edge of such curriculum design and research are Aaron Doering, Charlie Miller, and their colleagues at the University of Minnesota (Miller, Veletsianos, & Doering, 2008). Grounded in experiential and inquiry-based learning, Doering and his colleagues define adventure learning (AL) as "a hybrid distance education approach that provides students with opportunities to explore real-world issues through authentic learning experiences within collaborative learning environments"

(Doering & Veletsianos, 2008, p. 25). AL is a means of engaging students in asking questions, solving local as well as global problems, and becoming curious about environmental, scientific, and geographic problems and issues. It is authentic and anchored in real-world environments (Doering, 2006). AL has become so popular that unique instructional design models have been developed for it (Veletsianos, & Klanthous, 2009).

AL is often limited to K–12 situations. Consequently, we will use the phrase "extreme learning" here which will include adventure learning. Bonk and his research team refer to extreme learning as any use of technology in unusual or nontraditional ways to learn or teach (Bonk, 2012). Today people can learn while in a plane, ship, bus, train, or car, or even when climbing mountains or out on polar ice (Bonk, 2009c). Extreme learning can also occur within the confines of your own home.

For instance, anyone can now learn at home from some of the foremost experts in the world such as professors at MIT, Yale, UCLA, Oxford, Columbia, and Stanford. There is now a video database to tap into lectures from a portal called "Academic Earth." One hour you might view a course lecture from Paul Bloom at Yale on Freudian psychology and the next hour you could learn about the stock market from a computer science lecture and simulation from Eric Grimsom and John Guttag from MIT. In addition to Academic Earth, you can watch TED talks from internationally prominent people such as Sir Ken Robinson and his discussion of how schools kill creativity; teenager Adora Svitak telling us "What adults can learn from kids"; Mary Roach discussing her book about sex; or Jill Bolte Taylor describing her insights from a stroke. Given the passive nature of watching such shared online video content, some people may consider this a modest version of extreme learning. Nonetheless, there is an amazingly diverse range of learning choices from such shared online videos now available to people in the comfort of their own homes.

Extreme learning certainly need not be passive viewing. In a project called Take Two, students can also learn from editing professional-grade video footage of a world crisis or issue. Such issues might include water emergencies in the Sahara, education problems in Sudan, or conflict in the West Bank. As a learning goal or outcome, students might use this footage to create and submit their own video projects to YouTube or CurrentTV.

Other forms of extreme learning include students learning English at LiveMocha, English Central, Babbel, or BBC Learning English. They can go on a hike and collect, record, and analyze data with their mobile devices. Each of these activities is within the definition of extreme learning.

What should be apparent by now is that extreme learning can take many forms. There is no standard description or set of procedures to follow. Instead, it is tremendously open-ended at this time; however, in the context of a course, the length of the activity should be clarified. When done, students could write a reflection paper about the experience or discuss the situation in an online discussion forum.

Skills and Objectives. Includes student excitement for learning, intrigue, learner motivation into the unknown and unusual, engagement in real-world learning pursuits, expert modeling, and awareness of concept use in the real world. At its core, extreme and adventure learning activities stretch student thinking about learning, education, and career possibilities.

Advice and Ideas. There are many types and levels of extreme teaching and learning. Often, however, extreme learning is a high-risk endeavor because the technology may not work. In addition, it may only marginally relate to your course syllabus plans and objectives. Despite the risk, it can help students find a niche area to explore or perhaps even a future career. To succeed, you must be willing to accept failures if the technology does not work properly or if your students become highly engrossed in materials that are only tangentially related to your course topic.

Extreme learning opportunities can arise at any point in a semester or learning experience. Keep your eyes and ears open. Be sure to include enough flexibility in your course agenda and syllabi to take advantage of them when they appear. If you want to preplan the event, you can create a list of extreme and adventure learning opportunities. Ask students to rate or evaluate them. Whatever is selected, be sure to record the events so that they can be shared later with others.

Variations and Extensions. Consider having your students write reflection papers or book chapters on their experiences during the extreme or adventure learning project. That book of experiences could include interviews with fellow students as well as others around the world taking part in the adventure. Such extreme learning stories could accumulate over time.

Key Instructional Considerations

> *Risk index: High*
> *Time index: Medium to High*
> *Cost index: Low to Medium (depending on the task and equipment*
> *   or technologies required)*
> *Learner-centered index: Medium*
> *Duration of the learning activity: 1–4 weeks*

Activity 30. Quests and Probes on the Web

Description and Purpose of Activity. This technique asks students to jot down questions that they have about a topic and then search the Web for information. Although language learning is the primary example we insert here, the technique can be implemented in any discipline. The key is to personalize the learning with items of interest to the learner.

There are a vast array of pedagogical ideas documented in the research literature on computer-assisted language learning (CALL) (Egbert, 2005; Meskill, 2005; Murday, Ushida, & Chenoweth, 2008; Savignon & Roithmeier, 2004). Among such activities include using online dictionaries and other referenceware, blog writing and reflection, Web engine searches, and reading and summarizing online news. In a report by Liang and Bonk (2009) on English as a Foreign Language (EFL) instruction in Taiwan, one activity intended to arouse student curiosity was titled, "Inquiring Minds Want to Know." In this activity, students are asked to think of a new topic of interest to them. Next, they write down five questions related to it. After that, they must search Web resources such as CNN News International, BBC News, MSNBC Headline News, Google News, and Yahoo! News for information on their topic. When they have found an article of interest, they read it, and during their reading, they write down search words and additional questions that have sprung up in their heads. They also can ask a series of generic questions when searching and reading online texts.

Skills and Objectives. Includes authentic learning, learner motivation and engagement, reading skill and comprehension, inquiry and questioning skills, reflective writing, feedback, and following procedures. A primary objective for language learners is to be situated in real-world contexts where they can witness the nuances of language use and reflect on them. In other disciplines, this activity is the spark to future quests and explorations and deeper probes into the content.

Advice and Ideas. Caution students that answers to their questions may not be immediately found. Given the possibility for frustration, consider assigning each student a Web buddy or partner who can be e-mailed at any time for support. And be sure that the task procedures are well laid out. Initial answers to student questions could be shared with the instructor to determine whether students are floundering or proceeding as intended. For further support, you could develop an online job aid. When the task is completed, be sure to ask students about any bottlenecks or difficult moments in the process. At the end of the task, celebrate students who find answers to most or all of their questions. Upon completion, a follow-up task might be designed to build on that learning.

Variations and Extensions. Once students have located part or all of the information they are seeking, ask them to blog on their online learning experience. In their blog posts, they could list each question as well as the answer that they obtained online. Alternatively, they might post their questions to an online discussion forum thread for the course. Fellow students could respond to the reflections of one or more peers. A third option would be a reflection paper or worksheet with the students' questions and answers.

Another option would be for students to find two or three news stories related to their interest and compare and contrast the information that each provides. Pushing them further, the instructor could ask students to find at least one article that contains multimedia, such as a video, audio interview, or interactive timeline of events. Yet another idea would entail instructors requiring students to use online referenceware to find their answers, including online thesauri (e.g., Roget's Thesaurus, Thesaurus.com, and the Visual Thesaurus), dictionaries (e.g., Dictionary.com, Merriam-Webster's, YourDictionary.com, and so on), and encyclopedias (e.g., Encyclopedia Britannica, Encyclopedia of World Biography, Gale Encyclopedia of Children's Health, Wikipedia) for answers. Another variation would be for the instructor to craft all the questions and randomly assign them to students.

Key Instructional Considerations

Risk index: Medium (directions may be confusing for nonnative speakers)
Time index: Medium
Cost index: Low
Learner-centered index: High
Duration of the learning activity: As needed (depends on the type of course)

Final Reflections on Curiosity

In this chapter, we have detailed only a few examples of the pedagogical activities that might spark your learners' curiosity and sense of wonder. As is clear, opportunities to ignite curiosity pervade Web-based learning contexts. New cultures and customs can be brought directly into an online or blended class where and when needed. Events that are groundbreaking or outside the norm might be highlighted, analyzed, and discussed years before they are even considered for a course textbook or study guide. The requisite syllabus from now on may be organized just-in-time and in a state of constant flux. The learning participants using that syllabus can be following an online adventure even while engaged in one. Learning may even bend toward the furthermost edges of what is now possible and push into nontraditional or extreme learning territory.

As alluded to at the beginning of this chapter, however, heavy doses of suspense, curiosity, and intrigue are not always fun or pleasurable events. Searching, finding, and filtering through the relevant information sources each day is cognitively as well as physically demanding. At the same time, the tools and resources for fostering curiosity are all around us. Be mindful of them. Talk to colleagues about what they are experimenting with to arouse student learning and increase retention rates. Seek advice and suggestions from your students as well; they are the ones with whom you will be using these strategies.

This latter point was underscored and expressed through the disappointment of an online student interviewed by Khoo. He was asked how it felt when instructors failed to allow for learner curiosity and experimentation to flourish. He stated, "The disappointing thing was that the discussions didn't really happen. They [the lecturers] didn't make it a place for experimentation, for learning. That was a bit disappointing."

Not all of the ideas presented in this chapter will work for you. Find those that will and polish them up in your own inventive ways. Consider those that may not work and alter or perhaps transform some aspect of them to make each more suitable to your intended audience. Fostering curiosity may not be the first consideration when designing or delivering online instruction. Perhaps it should be.

There are over seven billion humans on this planet seeking knowledge in an attempt to better their lives. As such, there may be no motivational principle that is more important than Principle #3 of the TEC-VARIETY framework. With curiosity and personal desire to know more, learners can jump through new learning vistas.

Some of you will earmark or bookmark this chapter on curiosity, surprise, and intrigue. You may consider it central to your online teaching plans and the very core of the TEC-VARIETY framework. Others will say, "Wait a minute! I thought variety was the spice of life. And I thought learning was supposed to be fun?" We would agree with aspects of that perspective as well. And so now we turn to the fourth principle of our framework which highlights online learning variety as well as online fun, fantasy, and novelty.

CHAPTER SEVEN

PRINCIPLE #4 VARIETY

(Includes Novelty, Fun, and Fantasy)

> The secret of happiness is variety, but the secret of variety,
> like the secret of all spices, is knowing when to use it.
>
> —Daniel Gilbert

Hank Stram, the Super Bowl–winning coach of the Kansas City Chiefs, was once asked about his coaching philosophy. In response, Stram said, "My philosophy? Simplicity plus variety." Stram was known for his innovative play calling and groundbreaking motivational techniques. Given his induction into the American Pro Football Hall of Fame in 2003, his use of variety and simplicity certainly worked.

Variety is also vital across educational settings. The term *variety* is equated by teachers with the use of atypical activities, resources, and experiences (Brophy, 1998). In F2F settings, those less than common events often include guest speakers, field trips, and unusual artifacts. Such events are relatively common in online courses and might not be considered variety at all. When you're teaching online, variety could mean almost anything.

As implied in the underlying mnemonic of this book, variety is a key component of the TEC-VARIETY framework. It is also the fourth principle of the TEC-VARIETY mnemonic. In fact, it is crucial for any type of training or educational experience, no matter the age of the participants, their backgrounds, or the level of the course. Variety is needed to maintain learner alertness and interest. How many classes or professional development experiences have you had in the past that were stagnant, or worse, lifeless and awaiting a coroner's reporter to explain the cause of death?

Repeating tasks might be beneficial for those new to an online course and highly tense about the learning activity or situation. However, such repetition will quickly turn to boredom if you do not properly gauge the learning context and fail to engage your learners. Students appreciate variety and the sense that there is something new to master, whether it is a novel use of a technology tool or a set of concepts to learn that are displayed in a unique manner. With the range of online activities in this book, instructors have much to contemplate to ensure that their students are not bored. Instructors might rely on brainstorming to inject new life into an otherwise dull experience. Online brainstorming can happen in a discussion forum, wiki, chat, or Twitter feed, to name just a few options.

The variety principle also includes elements of novelty, fun, and fantasy. Prolific inventor and shrewd businessman Thomas A. Edison once claimed, "I never did a day's work in my life. It was all fun." In a similar vein, American writer and lecturer Dale Carnegie stated that "People rarely succeed unless they have fun in what they are doing." What both Edison and Carnegie realized is that when we are in a state of flow there is less of a sense of looming failure or task difficulty. Instead, we are focused on finding needed knowledge and crafting a viable, if not award-winning, solution. Having fun along the way is intrinsically motivating. So much so that students tend to forget that they are, in fact, learning something that previously was quite difficult or beyond their reach.

The problem is that the fun aspects of education are too often seen as frivolous and unrelated to the goals of mastering the assigned material. Such notions are so pervasive that most traditional forms of learning end up so dreary and mind-numbing that learners often sleep through their F2F courses and drop out of their online ones. There is nothing that excites them. Learning need not be boring or rote, however, to have impressive results. For instance, as shown later in this chapter, popular songs and sonnets can be repackaged by instructors and students to learn the history or science content in a unique and highly memorable way.

Fun, fantasy, and novelty are often synonymous with the use of computer games for learning. As mentioned in Chapter Three, in his dissertation research on computer games at Stanford over three decades ago, Thomas Malone (1981) discovered that fantasy and fun fulfill significant emotional needs for players of such games. As we shall see, the types and delivery formats of computer games have exploded all these years later. Mobile games are fast becoming ubiquitous and highly popular in both formal as well as informal education. Students enjoy games. Not too surprisingly, then, enjoyment is a key variable in predicting student motivation to succeed in online courses (Teng, 2008).

Building on the importance of enjoyment, play, creative expression, and choice in learning, in their book, *A New Culture of Learning: Cultivating the Imagination for a World of Constant Change*, David Thomas and John Seely Brown (2011) detail a movement toward a new model of learning. Their model emphasizes learning environments in which digital media offer a rich array of information in addition to intensely engaging opportunities and options to play and experiment with knowledge. In these digital worlds, students participate in a specific culture or practice instead of simply being taught about it. In contrast to education as a series of tests on what we know or have effectively received from others, in this new age we must ask questions about what we do not know, ponder what-if scenarios, and engage in inquiry for incremental as well as exponential results. We no longer simply learn about the world; instead, in this new culture of learning, we help re-create it.

In the spirit of this chapter, Thomas and Brown argue that change in education is a constant. In past centuries, information that was taught in most courses and disciplines was altered or updated at a relatively slow pace. Given the stability of most knowledge, it could be taught directly to passive learners. Teaching in such a manner had long-term benefits for the learner as well as the instructor. Everyone was happy.

Echoing the sluggish pace of change in education, the evolution of learning technology was monumentally slow too—at least until online technology emerged on the scene. As Thomas and Brown note, widespread adoption of color television evolved over 70 years after the initial invention of the color television signal in 1929. Today, technologies like YouTube, Twitter, and Wikipedia take less than a year for educators to begin to embrace and integrate into their courses. Even more amazingly, millions of people adopted mobile technologies like the iPhone and iPad seemingly overnight.

Although educational and training norms and practices of the previous century align well with the overriding stability of knowledge, this century requires educators and learners who can embrace the changes happening around them and are looking forward to what is on the horizon. From the viewpoint of Thomas and Brown, "Change motivates and challenges . . . change forces us to learn differently" (2011, p. 43). They further argue that this transformational perspective requires us to begin to view the future from the standpoint of unique possibilities and the ability to take advantage of a world in motion. We can no longer be taught or trained for each tool, procedure, or policy that we will encounter in the real world.

Finally, Thomas and Brown point out that successful participation in this highly digital world requires extensive opportunities for play as well as sharing, messing around with ideas, and simply hanging out with others. When learners work out creative solutions in their minds as a result of messing around with remixed film footage, alternatives in an intense game, or information in an online database, they have the chance to generate and contribute knowledge, not just receive it. Play connects the information networks we hang out in, such as Facebook and Ning, to the active experimentation now possible in the Web 2.0 with massive multiplayer online games, virtual worlds, and online science experiments. Thomas and Brown emphasize the connection between play and imagination. For them, we no longer just learn to play—we play to learn.

This fourth principle of TEC-VARIETY, involving variety, fun, fantasy, and novelty, does just that. There is much serious play here. The 10 activities in this chapter offer glimpses into what is possible online in this new culture of learning, especially with intense episodes of play.

Technologies for
Principle #4: Variety

Given the pace of technology change in the twenty-first century, it is difficult to equate Principle #4 with any particular learning technology. Fun, fantasy, variety, and novelty—such words raise the eyebrows of administrators, while at the same time grabbing the attention of learners across age groups. Any teenagers spontaneously flipping the pages of this book and suddenly stopping on this page or chapter might be saying, "Where do I sign up?" They can easily envision scenes where mobile games and virtual worlds stream to them at a moment's notice.

What about older learners? Today, some may consider interactions in virtual worlds or learning games and simulations on a mobile device a healthy and fun change of pace. Many others will not. Some might want synchronous experiences with experts and re-assurance that they are on the "right" learning track. Others will savor the chance for personal discovery in some type of self-directed learning system.

Tomorrow, the more intriguing technologies might be the use of artificial agents, robots, and three-dimensionally displayed learning portfolios that capture, analyze, and then categorize real-world footage of a student's learning journey. Think about the immediacy of learning with wearable computing like Google Glass, for instance. In later tomorrows, electronic mentors and guides available on demand might provide a highly essential and intriguing addition to an online class or training program. Video content streamed to a watch or displayed on the outside of a coffee mug might be extremely novel today and ho-hum news tomorrow. In ten years, we might be watching that same video on sides of buildings or displayed on buses as we walk past, or perhaps even projected on the backs of people in front of us as we stroll through cities.

The technologies for varying the learning environment may also be contingent on the content area or discipline, time of day, year in the program, or progress in the course. For instance, early in a course, a blog reflection or discussion board could seem unique. Later in that same course, a chat with a guest expert or a live experiment from another corner of the world might be better to capture student interest. Of course, with a little imagination, the same technology tool or resource can be used in dozens of engaging ways. Such variety is always within reach. It may be time to reach out.

In terms of true novelty, an activity that you have designed for your course could be something no one in the world has previously attempted. Back in 1995, for instance, Bonk and his colleagues at Indiana University linked two videoconferencing systems together—CU-SeeMe and PictureTel—as a means to bring in guest speakers whose articles his students were currently reading (Bonk, Appelman, & Hay, 1996). That may have been the first such linkage of these two separate videoconferencing systems for one instructional event. Fortunately, it worked even better than planned. The students had read and critiqued the articles of the guests in an asynchronous discussion forum prior to the live event. Students who had previously found little or nothing to like about the assigned articles and associated topics (which included the impact of computer programming on thinking) were the same ones who were agreeing with everything that both the guests said during the live discussion. The guest videoconferencing experience totally changed their perspectives.

Such an idea represented novelty and variety back in the 1990s. In this century, we will find ourselves coming face-to-face with a sea of technology-enriched situations that we have yet to dream about. Dream big dreams, and be prepared for a fun but bumpy ride.

Ten Online Activities in Principle #4: Variety

Activities to vary or modify the instructional setting are nothing new for those with teaching experience. Teaching online and blended courses, however, presents instructors and training coordinators or directors with more opportunities for changing the learning environment than ever experienced before. Some of the ideas we describe will be filled with fun. Others will engage learners in fantasy or dream worlds. And you will likely consider many, if not most, of the activities quite novel.

Keep in mind, however, that as with curiosity in the previous chapter, there may be some activities at the high-end risk continuum that you may need to modify or skip for now. An online séance, anyone? How about venturing into extreme teaching or giving your students a second life? You may decide to skim quickly through these ideas. That is fine. We are not expecting anyone to try them all. They will await your return on another day.

Activity 31. Online Séance or Roundtable

Description and Purpose of Activity. One popular method that we use to engage people in fantasy worlds is to hold some type of live online meeting or asynchronous discussion forum where students take on different personalities or personas. Students can engage in a role-play situation in which they each sign up to take on the persona of an influential figure in the field. Before carrying out the role play, they could be assigned articles, chapters, news reports, or biographies to read about (or written by) that person. If available, they could also watch popular video lectures, virtual presentations, or online interviews of that person.

With such resources to immerse students in, mock trials or courtroom simulations are possible. For the purposes of this activity, we will focus on the idea of an online séance or roundtable. For those interested in more information on how to conduct an online role play or mock trial involving personality traits or types of people, see Bonk and Zhang (2008).

To set up an online séance (or roundtable), have students brainstorm a list of famous people from the field who are no longer living. Each individual mentioned might be added or fictitiously enrolled in the course. Based on this list, students would enter the course discussion forum or synchronous conferencing system posing as a particular individual. Once logged in, they could make entries or contributions from the perspective of that person.

In an online séance for a psychology course, for example, students might be Jean Piaget, Sigmund Freud, B. F. Skinner, Abraham Maslow, Carl Rogers, and so on. You could assign them a particular news item, government policy, or current issue in psychology to discuss and debate. If an asynchronous discussion forum is used, ask students to show up in costume after dark and make contributions by candlelight. If the session is a live synchronous session, students could use their Webcam and come in costume. Stretching this activity further into the land of fun and fantasy, they could also make a mask of their assigned person using a photo found online. Colleagues could enter as guests taking on the roles of people not chosen by the students in the class. In responding to the selected issue, topic, or event, students could read direct quotations from books and articles written by or about their assigned person.

Skills and Objectives. Includes appreciation of multiple perspectives, content review, concept application, critical thinking, problem identification, and problem solving. This technique forces students to reflect on how the content they are learning generalizes to people and places around the world.

Advice and Ideas. Be sure to define all roles and activities in sufficient detail. Students must understand where to post, the timing of the event, and how much and how often to respond. The first time you use this method, allow students to sign up for particular roles. Give much choice and freedom. If it is a séance, you will need to find a medium to conjure up spirits. See what happens. Based on that experience, you may have to create more structure or assume greater control over the activity. If you run this activity more than once or on multiple weeks, you could allow students to change roles.

The role of the instructor or trainer is to facilitate the activity with prompts, hints, ideas, additional Web resources, and personal opinions. Perhaps near the end of the activity, you could ask students to explain how their personal views differ from those of the individual they were assigned.

Variations and Extensions. If an online séance is deemed too risky, you could refer to it as a roundtable activity, akin to King Arthur's Knights of the Round Table. As with King Arthur's knights, everyone would have equal status at the roundtable. In taking advantage of such equal status, each assigned knight at the table could represent a different person in your field. In addition to the discussion of some prearranged topic or event from that perspective, other course issues, disputes, and ideas could be brought up in a roundtable type of meeting.

Key Instructional Considerations

Risk index: High
Time index: Medium
Cost index: Low
Learner-centered index: High
Duration of the learning activity: 1–2 weeks

Activity 32. Virtual World Role Plays

Description and Purpose of Activity. One current trend in education is the use of fantasy worlds for reenactments of historical events, decisions, and problem-solving situations.

When engaged in such activities, students can understand the complexity of issues and problems within a topic or field of study. They might also feel empathy for those less fortunate or who have been portrayed unfairly or negatively in the press. At the same time, these fantasy worlds can help students reflect on the interconnectedness of ideas.

For instance, in April 2011, Dr. Monica Rankin's History 4359 course on "The Cuban Revolution" at the University of Texas at Dallas engaged in a role activity in Second Life. One group role-played scenes from the 1960s in Cuba involving Fidel Castro (the event was titled "Castro Salvado"). Some of Rankin's students were assigned to be sympathetic to Castro. They portrayed Castro, members of his military, and his Soviet collaborators. Questions were related to various charges made against the revolutionary government of Castro and measures to defend what they have done. Students also pondered the response from the United States should Cuba and the Soviet Union form an alliance.

During this role play, students had to reflect on differences between the culture and history of Cuba and those of the Soviet Union. In effect, they had to put themselves in Castro's shoes as well as the people of Cuba. Personal beliefs about Cuba, Castro, and the United States could, at least in part, be separated from what really happened.

While that was transpiring, a second group role-played "No Country for Old Castro," in which President Barack Obama is perplexed by his low approval ratings as "hope" and "change" had not worked. His administrative assistant suggests that he "could always find a way to kill Castro." Former presidents such as Kennedy, Carter, Reagan, and Clinton soon separately enter a dream Obama has wherein he asks them for their advice. He then hears what happened under each of their watches regarding Castro.

To be successful in their performance in Second Life, students in Rankin's class had to dig deep into the literature. Students even used the accents of the people that they portrayed. As a means to scale up the project and support others, each of the Second Life scenarios was captured and made into a YouTube video. Dr. Rankin's reflections in YouTube indicate that student creativity, engagement, and freedom to explore ideas were among her chief course goals. Also important to Rankin was seeing key historical issues from other points of view.

This is a prime example of how technology can foster respect and understanding of multicultural points of view (Rasmussen, Nichols, & Ferguson, 2006). Real-world content can be experienced in innovative ways with such technology. Students are in the driver's seat. Of course, instructor support and peer interaction, conversation, and collaboration are vital.

There are many other ways in which Second Life can be used in education (Atkinson, 2008). For instance, online court forums can be held when real-life ones are unavailable. Students can tour virtual art galleries; explore discoveries and inventions in history; make patient diagnoses in a health care setting; explore ancient worlds (e.g., the Forbidden City in China), experience a tornado, earthquake, or tsunami; and learn about the solar system through three-dimensional environments (Park & Baek, 2010). Want more? Megan Conklin details more than a hundred uses of Second Life (Conklin, 2007).

Skills and Objectives. Includes appreciation of multiple perspectives, learning by doing, connecting content knowledge from books and lectures to the real world, and fantasy. A key goal of such an activity is to push students' thinking beyond their preexisting viewpoints and biases.

Advice and Ideas. This is a high-risk activity which typically requires much time to create and implement. Not many instructors are willing to allot class time for virtual worlds, games, or fantasy activities. Warn students that it may not work as planned. Talk to colleagues about what has worked for them. Evaluate each activity immediately after it occurs. And share the results.

Variations and Extensions. Ask students for suggestions for follow-up activities on the method or script. Perhaps even allow students to create the script or scenario. You might even place them in charge of production.

Key Instructional Considerations

Risk index: High
Time index: Medium to High
Cost index: Low (if using a free system)
Learner-centered index: High
Duration of the learning activity: 2–4 weeks

Activity 33. Mobile and Social Networking Content Games and Apps

Description and Purpose of Activity. As with the online séance, roundtable, and virtual world role plays in systems such as Second Life, games and simulations offer a chance for students to take on different personas and enter fantasy worlds. Of course, they also are flavored with fun and highly novel learning experiences or problems to solve. For many years now, students have played games online as a means to review and apply content learned. There are games for basic and advanced accounting principles (e.g., *Bean Counter Free Accounting, Bookkeeping Tutorials,* and *Biz/Ed Virtual Worlds*; see Anderberg, 2010), civics issues (e.g., *iCivics*), and public health crises (e.g., the *Point of Dispensing [POD]* game). In *iCivics,* for instance, students learn how different types of taxes, tax rates, entitlements, and cost decisions affect the federal budget. While engaged in such an activity, students are learning critical thinking skills including finding and evaluating available evidence, identifying reasons and rationales, analyzing trends, crafting arguments, and comparing and contrasting information provided. Former United States Supreme Court Justice Sandra Day O'Connor was involved in part of this civics literacy and education project in an attempt to prepare the citizens of tomorrow to better understand and form their own arguments around pressing issues.

In recent years, massive multiplayer online games (MMOGs) like *FarmVille* have become popular on social networking sites like Facebook and on mobile devices (Schroeder, 2010). Rather than the violence found in games like *Grand Theft Auto, Halo, Mafia Wars,* and *World of Warcraft,* in *FarmVille* users learn the ins and outs of managing a farm. They plow land, grow and then harvest their crops, plant bushes and trees, and raise pigs and cows. To get started, each player must create an avatar which is customizable and changeable. In *FarmVille,* the player progresses through different levels of farming expertise. Their level of play is indicated by different experience point (XP) levels. XP points are earned through such activities as harvesting crops and visiting neighbors (FarmVille, 2011).

There are many other types of mobile games online for learning languages, grammar, math facts, the laws of physics, geography, and so on. Mobile learning is turning smartphones, iPads, and other devices into multimedia study guides and reviews. However, their power extends far beyond simple flashcard technology. When needed, students can access video and audio clips as well as other interactive features.

Most such mobile games are content specific. For basic mathematics, there are dozens of drill games (e.g., *Math Drill* from Instant Interactive) that can be downloaded from Apple's iTunes store and used with the iPhone, iTouch, and iPad (eSchool News Staff, 2011). In spelling, there are applications for the iPad like *Miss Spell's Class*. This tool offers a series of ever more challenging vocabulary words and forces students to decide if a word is spelled correctly or not. In addition, dozens of mobile dictionaries and language games can be used at the K–12 and college levels.

Professional fields like medicine, engineering, and business have increasingly incorporated mobile study aids and games. Peter H. Abrahams from the University of Warwick in the United Kingdom, for instance, has designed a series of nearly forty short films as well as a reference manual for his clinical anatomy classes that work on the iPhone (Young, 2011). In these mobile videos, different scenarios and problems are presented (e.g., trouble with the cardiopulmonary plexus, the arch of the aorta, and so on). After viewing the scenario, students must answer quiz questions about this situation including naming the relevant body parts.

Abilene Christian University (ACU) has embraced a campuswide adoption of the iPhone since it first came out (Abilene Christian University, 2008). In March 2011, Stephen Baldridge, an assistant professor of social work at ACU, had students use their phones in a campus scavenger hunt based on the TV reality show *The Amazing Race* (Young, 2011). In his cleverly designed *Amazing Nonprofit Race*, Baldridge had his students find service-related organizations on the ACU campus. His role was that of a guide who built clues into the system that could be accessed during their exploration.

These are but a few of the social networking games and mobile apps available today. The coming decade will see an explosion of apps for education. Most tasks and activities previously conducted in lecture-based classrooms will be eventually supplemented, extended, augmented, or repeated using mobile technology. As this occurs, our mobile lives will become our learning lives, and vice versa.

Skills and Objectives. Includes learner engagement, comprehension and application skills, practice, problem solving, trial and error testing, and identification of key concepts and terms. A key goal of such an activity is to allow learners to practice their skills wherever they are in the world, at any time, and receive feedback on it.

Advice and Ideas. Determine whether there are mobile games related to your content or discipline. You could do this by conducting literature reviews, talking to colleagues, keeping up with the news, attending conferences on gaming or technology in education, or exploring open educational resource portals such as MERLOT and Connexions, mentioned earlier. You might recruit colleagues to test a new simulation in related courses or different sections of the same course. And when done, conduct reflection and debriefing activities.

Online simulations and games often require special hardware and software to access or use. Test the technology. Perhaps watch students as they use it and see if they are encountering any problems. Ask students if they have the necessary technology or backgrounds to use a particular simulation or mobile application. If they do not, consider making the use of that particular mobile application optional. Be sure to create online and offline guidelines and job aids for any learning activity involving such technology. Monitor the activity as much as possible.

Variations and Extensions. Assign reflection papers on what students have learned from the activity. They might reflect on their planning and decision-making processes while playing the game. In fact, each game could have a checklist of skills for learners to reflect on. A further extension of this assignment would be for students to think aloud while playing the game for 5–10 minutes and record their thoughts for later personal review and retrospective analyses. Papers could be exchanged with peers who would read and comment on those reflections.

Key Instructional Considerations

Risk index: Medium to High (the risk index will lower in the coming decade)
Time index: Medium to High
Cost index: Low (if using a free system)
Learner-centered index: High
Duration of the learning activity: 2–4 weeks or as needed

Activity 34. Educational Music Videos

Description and Purpose of Activity. One way to add some novelty, fun, and variety to a course is to link the content to memorable and relevant resources. For instance, events in history or literature can be summarized and presented in the format of poems, sonnets, songs, mottos, hymns, tales, stories, and adventures. Such approaches are powerful and exciting given the capability of humans to remember stories and anecdotes more readily than facts (Driscoll, 2005; Goldsmith, Kaye, & Shelton, 2000).

For an extremely novel and engaging example, take a look at one or more videos at the "History for Music Lovers" channel in YouTube. This site offers a series of videos based on popular songs from the past few decades rewritten and remixed to detail important moments or people in history. The brains behind this highly creative channel are Amy Burvall of the Le Jardin Academy in Kailua, Oahu, and her colleague Herb Mahelona, choir director at the Kamehameha Schools Hawaii Campus (Strauss, 2010). Each of their videos is witty, entertaining, and covers a wide range of historical content. In addition to being a high school history teacher, Burvall is quite the performer and musical artist. In fact, she has written lyrics for more than fifty music history videos including Elizabeth I ("She's Not There" by the Zombies), Charlemagne ("Call Me" by Blondie), The French Revolution ("Bad Romance" by Lady Gaga), and the Trojan War ("Tainted Love" by Soft Cell). Those watching the last one will hear words such as:

In Homer's Epic Tale of
Ancient Greece in order to
Make some peace at a wedding
The handsome Paris had to make a choice
Who was most fair
Of all the goddesses there . . .

As in this example, many historical facts and sequences are embedded in each video. Equally important, each video is filled with creative expression. Comments on Burvall and Mahelona's YouTube channel indicate that many people are addicted to their videos and want to purchase their music. Watch any one of them and you will immediately understand why. Although designed for 15-year-olds, there are many college professors and adult educators using them (Strauss, 2010).

Skills and Objectives. Includes creative expression, design, planning and coordination skills, content review, and linking course content to multimedia resources (e.g., visuals, audio files, and animations). This type of activity helps students learn factual knowledge as well as higher-order thinking skills.

Advice and Ideas. Similar videos exist for other content areas including science music videos explaining topics like DNA, the Periodic Table of Elements, and Space Junk (Rowe, 2009). Many are highly popular. In fact, nearly 3 million people have watched the Hui Zheng lab at Baylor College of Medicine, which studies Alzheimer's disease, parody Lady Gaga's "Bad Romance" with their science research twist called "Bad Project." Like those found at the "History for Music Lovers" channel, these science videos are funny, catchy, and informative. Take an hour to explore the Web and you will likely find one or more useful videos that can inform as well as entertain your students in new and imaginative ways.

If you do not discover any, however, consider creating one or more on your own. The act of creating something new is personally empowering. At the same time, keep in mind that it can take extensive planning and development time. For high-quality contents, the cost of production may be prohibitive. When done, consider contributing your musical creations and other productions to the world community at such sites as Creative Commons, Curriki, or MERLOT. If applicable, obtain permission from sponsors. Sharing online resources will save others time and money. In addition, you might advertise these resources through your homepage, blog, Twitter account, online communities, and other such places.

Variations and Extensions. As discussed in many other activities described in this book, students could design and write the lyrics, poems, or videos. If you take that route, you could arrange an end-of-course competition for the most creative or useful product. Another idea would be to curate and perhaps extend existing musical resources found online that relate to your domain. You and your class could index, categorize, rate, and share them.

Key Instructional Considerations

Risk index: High
Time index: High
Cost index: Low to High (low to watch, medium or high to develop)
Learner-centered index: Medium
Duration of the learning activity: As needed

Activity 35. Database Problems and Search Competitions

Description and Purpose of Activity. One activity that is fun for many people is to search the Web for information. In formal educational settings, information search competitions could be intended to test student search skills or problem-solving abilities. There are many databases now for students to practice their skills. The instructor could create an asynchronous activity akin to an online scavenger hunt, but instead of testing student search and access skills for a wide variety of online contents and resources related to the course, such an activity would test student skills within just one Web resource or tool. For example, you could have students search for factual answers in Wolfram Alpha, a highly innovative and comprehensive online answer engine for search queries. Some examples are below.

- In an algebra course, students might be given a particular mathematical equation. Next, they might be asked to use Wolfram Alpha to find alternative forms of that equation, derivatives, and the type of geometric figure that it represents. Students could work on a series of such problems.

- Instructors in educational leadership courses could assign one group of students to find comparison data on universities such as Harvard University and the University of Houston, including date founded, tuition, population of the city it is located in, number of undergraduate and graduate students, and so on. Instructors could have a second group get ACT scores in a state like New Mexico, and ask them to follow up with probes about the population, land area, water area, housing units, poverty rate, and mean household income in New Mexico.

- In a finance class, students could analyze stocks and mutual funds using Wolfram Alpha. For instance, they might quickly determine the market cap for automobile stocks like Ford, Tesla, and Hyundai. They could also gather their prices on different dates in history, find data in analyst reports, and compare different stock ratings.

- Students in a course on nutrition, fitness, public health, or biology could access the food and nutrition area in Wolfram Alpha. Once there, they could gather information such as the calories of a breakfast meal of orange juice, a banana, a cup of coffee, and a bowl of cornflakes.

If you have done all of these activities, you will likely say to yourself that Wolfram Alpha is an amazing resource. Look again—there is so much more to explore. Topics within Wolfram Alpha include particle physics, electrical engineering, geology, weather, airplane flight data, diseases, mortality rates, political leaders, mountains, time zones, and much more. You should be cautious, however, as the answers it provides are not always correct. Bonk once typed in the question, "Who did North Korea defeat to get into the 2010 Men's World Cup tournament in South Africa?" and the response he received was about the current weather in North Korea.

Instructors can use this database and others as a way to start a class and prime student knowledge. In a live class or Webinar, they could pick a topic and arrange 5–10 questions for students to quickly look up. They might also post a few starter questions each week or each day to an asynchronous forum thread where students can submit responses, perhaps awarding a bonus point to the first one with the correct answer each week. Creative instructors could randomly post such questions at different times each week as a means to get their students to check in on the class.

Of course, there are many other types of online databases besides Wolfram Alpha. A second example is the Worldmapper tool. It allows users to access data such as pancreatic cancer deaths, primary school spending, adult literacy, sanitation, and infant mortality rates and then display it on a map of the world. Those countries or regions of the world with higher numbers or percentages of a certain variable or item (e.g., traffic fatalities) are displayed as fatter or bulkier. Countries or regions with lower amounts are smaller or skinnier. The Worldmapper is a fascinating database for learners to manipulate and begin to understand vital data on health, education, housing, fuel, manufacturing, disease, and so on. For instance, a visual portrayal related to infant mortality (i.e., babies who die during the first year of life) shows India and many parts of Africa as larger than their true size, whereas Canada, the United States, and much of Europe and South America appear to be quite tiny in comparison to their actual size. Pollution, income, fuel, education, and other related types of data searches will reveal world maps of very different compositions.

Students in a sociology course, for instance, could be asked to locate the countries in the world with the lowest and highest rates of literacy. After that, their assignment could be to determine the countries with the highest rates of polio or malaria, enrollment in primary education, percentage of territory with rain forests, sewage sludge, or carbon emissions. In contrast, a graduate course on qualitative research might start with such visual data and then engage students in search activities from oral history databases as a way of personalizing it (Wolverton, 2011). Next, these students could compete to find different quotations, comments, or themes from those databases. The instructional possibilities are endless.

Skills and Objectives. Includes information access, search, evaluating the credibility of sources, comparison and contrast, and communication skills. While most such competitions focus on basic facts, the ability to display trends as well as to compare and contrast data with tools like Wolfram Alpha and the Worldmapper indicates that higher-order thinking skills are also involved.

Advice and Ideas. One of the issues for instructors to consider is teaching students effective search strategies for a particular program. Screencasting tools, mentioned earlier, allow instructors to create effective tutorial or help systems.

Keep in mind that this type of activity can quickly become routinized and lose its luster. To avoid this turning into a monotonous weekly requirement, create a unique game, perhaps with a game show host, name, and set of rules. Winners (i.e., those with the most correct answers each week) can accumulate points for increasingly higher-level competitions. Weekly competitions might lead to an event at the end of the course or semester. To further arouse student interest, consider including some items from these database competitions on course quizzes and examinations.

Variations and Extensions. Students could take turns in creating the weekly questions or information items to explore. They could also find new databases to mine as well as set up or change the rules for their own search competition game. Team competitions are another option.

Key Instructional Considerations

Risk index: Low to Medium
Time index: Low
Cost index: Low
Learner-centered index: Medium
Duration of the learning activity: As needed

Activity 36. Task and Activity Randomizer

Description and Purpose of Activity. Some instructors try to avoid ruts in their courses by allowing students to vote on the type or order of activities for a week or unit. Sometimes they give learners alternative formats to select from. Instructors may also randomly go through the activities that they planned or, better still, rearrange them in reverse order. We find that such randomness keeps our courses and our delivery fresh and alive. In addition, there may be holes or open weeks in the syllabus which have no preplanning. Such weeks add to the variety, suspense, and spontaneity felt within the course.

Changes to the routine are especially important in online courses. It breaks students from the excessive monotony or repetition seen in F2F courses. Today there are dozens of online tools to help randomize events. There are random number generators, coin flippers, dice, playing card shufflers, clock time generators, integer sequence generators, string generators, research subject randomizers, and so on. If you had 12 items listed for an online class meeting, you could use an online pair of dice to pick the number of the task or activity to start with. Alternatively, you might use a random sequence generator and put in a minimum of 1 and a maximum of 12 and have the tool randomly select the order of activities for the entire class session. This same tool can be utilized to select the order of student presentations.

Skills and Objectives. Includes variety, flexibility, creative expression, freedom to explore, freshness, and tolerance for ambiguity. With such an approach, there is a sense of unknown and the spark of spontaneity.

Advice and Ideas. The tools for random course events are available for F2F, blended, and online instructors. Be sure to check that the randomizing tool you are using suits your needs and is still active. Such tools often change. There are many such tools listed in the resources section related to this chapter. In addition to the options listed, you should conduct a quick search of the Web for other tools and resources that may more directly relate to your content area.

These tools can add a spark of excitement and fun to a course. If your students are complaining about the lack of variety, try one out in a small pilot experiment and see how it works. Afterward, collect feedback from your students. You may even become bold enough to randomize the entire course sequence. Of course, randomness might soon run through your veins, allowing you to discard such online tools and rely solely on your intuition and judgment.

Variations and Extensions. We have a lateness policy where students are always allowed 24 hours extra for any assignment as long as they do not abuse the policy. You could use the randomizer to determine how many hours late you will accept an assignment (e.g., from zero to 48 or more). To pique student interest, instructors could announce the day and time when they will spin or use the randomizer. Alternatively, they might select a random type of class event early in the course. Later on, instructors could allow students to suggest other ways to use the randomizer. Students could come up with ingenious ideas on how the class format, activities, and events might be made more motivational.

Key Instructional Considerations

Risk index: Medium
Time index: Low to Medium
Cost index: Low
Learner-centered index: Medium
Duration of the learning activity: As needed

Activity 37. Time-Constrained Presentations

Description and Purpose of Activity. Akin to the course randomizer detailed in Activity 36, one activity that we use to bring a diversity of perspectives and more spirited participation in our courses is the use of timed activities. There are different types of technology tools that you can use for both synchronous and F2F class events. For instance, there are 99-second timers as well as those you can set for any length of time. Such tools might display as stop watches or countdown timers; some of the latter appear as bombs with a long fuse that explodes when you run out of time.

In such an activity, you force students to make a statement or set of statements within an allotted time period. For instance, you might give students 99 seconds to summarize the readings for the week. Alternatively, they could be asked to bring one or more quotations from the readings and explain, in the specified amount of time, why they selected those particular sections as important to their learning. Once the clock expires, so too does their moment of fame and attention turns to the next person.

This kind of timed activity forces students to reflect on the truly important content as well as how to present it to others. Simultaneously, it encourages students to voice their ideas and opinions, instead of listening solely to the instructor. Each student is granted a platform on which to speak, effectively shifting learning from instructor-centeredness to learner-centeredness. And although the activity is highly structured in terms of time, it is open-ended in terms of everything else.

Skills and Objectives. Includes planning, rehearsal, information summarization and distillation, comprehension skills, engagement, and communication. The key aspect of this activity is condensing information into a useful summary for both yourself and others.

Advice and Ideas. For those of you who do not think this strategy will work with adults, our friend Dr. Sivasailam "Thiagi" Thiagarajan uses timers in many of his online and live courses and workshops with clients such as AT&T, Chevron, IBM, Intel, and United Airlines. He also uses the 99-second activity at conferences. We have seen him bring in 20–30 of the most famous people in the fields of performance technology and instructional design to preconference symposia, workshops, and institutes and then give them each just 99 seconds to make a point. Each person is allowed to present on anything; however, when the 99 seconds are up, Thiagi politely yanks them off the stage. It is one of the most informative and entertaining methods we have ever seen. And all it takes in terms of technology is an extremely minor piece of software that you can find online for free. To boost the fun and intensity of the timer activity, instructors could create incentives or competitions within the timed activities.

Variations and Extensions. There are hundreds of uses for timers, including group or team situations, online panel presentations, or online symposia. A virtual conference conducted with class members and outside guests could have set starting and ending times for each presentation or panel.

Key Instructional Considerations

> *Risk index: Medium*
> *Time index: Medium*
> *Cost index: Low (unless you want to purchase something highly sophisticated)*
> *Learner-centered index: High*
> *Duration of the learning activity: As needed*

Activity 38. Virtual Community Brainstorming

Description and Purpose of Activity. A sense of déjà vu caused by instructional repetitions or redundant activities gets old quickly. Online instructors can rely on brainstorming to inject new life into an otherwise dull experience. When teaching online, such brainstorming can happen in a discussion forum, wiki, chat, or Twitter feed, to name a few. Many interactive learning technologies can be used to spark a new idea and resuscitate a course.

Brainstorming and idea generation activities start with nothing. All lists are blank. Students are asked to respond to a comment, question, goal, or event. They can piggyback on ideas that are generated; however, they are not allowed to evaluate or rank them. Working in this type of an environment, they can say what is on their minds without having to back up their claims, demonstrate the practicality of an idea, or worry too much about fellow students' laughter. There is less pressure to perform and fewer embarrassments. Such an open approach frees up mental energy.

As indicated, students can make their suggestions to a course wiki or within a live chat session window. They could also type messages to a class Twitter account to which fellow students have subscribed. Other such microblogging tools include Plurk and identi.ca. If, however, you want privacy and a system where teams can post to other team members in a group communication hub, you might try GroupTweet. A group account in GroupTweet receives direct messages from group members. Those in the K–12 space might consider Edmodo, a private online social platform. With Edmodo students and teachers can share files, links, ideas, events, and assignments.

Much is possible with microblogging technology. Tools like Twitter are well suited for sharing short inspirational moments and ideas. Anything that pops into your head can be immediately typed and shared. As a public notepad, it is ideal for creative expression

(Parry, 2008). The same might be said about wiki-like collaborative tools like PiratePad and MeetingWords. Both are open environments allowing anyone to participate with contributions marked in different colors. Changes to a document or a list of ideas are immediately displayed on all screens. If you prefer visual brainstorming, a relatively new tool we are experimenting with from the LT Media Lab at the University of Minnesota is called Flipgrid. With Flipgrid, you can post a question, issue, or comment in video format for others to respond to. In contrast to asynchronous discussion forums, when you include video and audio, you will elicit responses that are often more sincere, thoughtful, and connected.

Skills and Objectives. Includes excitement and enthusiasm for learning, fun and suspense, creative expression, class diversity, student voice, and engagement. Such an activity is well aligned with the rapid-fire approach to learning to which young people are accustomed.

Advice and Ideas. This may be a totally novel activity for the class. If it is, create an instructional scaffold for your students. In the job aid or guide sheet, lay out your expectations in terms of the timing of the posts, post length, and kinds of ideas that are acceptable or unacceptable. If you are using Twitter, create a class account for students to send their tweets. You might also provide tips on how to create hashtags (the "#" symbol) to help categorize their posts. Similar advice applies to the use of wikis. Whatever technology or system that is ultimately selected, be sure to run a pilot of the activity, especially if there will be points assigned for completing the task.

Once ideas begin to accumulate, consider expanding the activity with some type of discussion of the suggested ideas where students can elaborate and combine ideas. In addition, they may vote on which ones are the best, the most practical, or the most unique, with the instructor sharing his votes and opinions as well. If you are using Twitter or some other microblogging technology, you can track conversations among students (i.e., the "backchannel") outside of the main course Twitter feed (Reinhardt, Ebner, Beham, & Costa, 2009). As will be discussed in Chapter Ten, in the backchannel there is intense interactivity, near-instant feedback, and currency to the information shared.

Variations and Extensions. Consider empowering each student once during the course with selecting the brainstorming topic of the week. You could also start creative expression competitions between groups in the class or between classes around the world, with the student, group, or class posting the best or most ideas receiving public recognition. You could also create a Twitter or wiki activity hall of fame wall or list.

Key Instructional Considerations

Risk index: Medium
Time index: Low to Medium
Cost index: Low
Learner-centered index: High
Duration of the learning activity: As needed

Activity 39. Extreme Teaching and Online Mentoring

Description and Purpose of Activity. In the previous chapter, we discussed extreme learning. Now we shift gears to "Extreme Teaching," or teaching with technology in new or unusual ways, in addition to other forms of volunteer teaching or mentoring situations online. There are a growing number of extreme teaching situations that students can be engaged in to use or extend the knowledge that they are learning in your course. When a student is the teacher, he will most certainly learn the material better. Such an approach is especially pertinent in teacher training, though it has benefits in nearly any field or discipline. When the learners take over all or a portion of an instructional situation, they are empowered.

As an example, adults could use a Webcam to mentor children in South Africa whose families have been affected by HIV/AIDS (Berger, 2011). In one such project from Infinite Family, hundreds of South African teens have been connected to volunteer mentors from around the world. Such services are crucial given that over 15 million children in Sub-Saharan Africa are orphaned due to HIV/AIDS. These "Web Buddies" help provide role models as well as valued educational services and support.

Other forms of extreme teaching or volunteer mentoring include signing up to teach a language at Mixxer or Livemocha. Someone might also lead a discussion wherein users practice a new language such as French, Spanish, or English in threaded audio discussions with people around the world in Voxopop. Students could broadcast a weekly webcast or podcast production on a special topic such as seen at EdTech Talk. In each situation, the learner is helping others to learn something or gain new skills. Such online teaching or mentoring can remain local with fellow students or expand to a global stage. As with any teaching professional, if your students are involved in online teaching or mentoring, they should have opportunities to reflect on how well it went and what they might change next time.

Skills and Objectives. Includes content preparation, interaction, communication skills, content delivery, support skills, and leadership. Assuming the role of teacher is courageous and fosters a sense of responsibility and caring for the learning of others.

Advice and Ideas. Teaching and mentoring elevates the students in your class to one of the highest levels of human expression. Provide them with instructional support and advice to help in their successes. When issues that concern them arise, be available for support. And reward students when they take initiative to help in the lives of others. Such rewards might be explicit recognition, bonus points, or recommendation letters. We often allow students to replace an assignment with their online mentoring or teaching if they include a short reflection paper on the experience. Of course, the reward or incentive for such a task can also be more implicit in nature.

Variations and Extensions. Students could work in pairs to collaboratively teach or mentor online. Each team could then write one or more reflection papers based on their experience.

Key Instructional Considerations

Risk index: High
Time index: Medium to High
Cost index: Low to Medium
Learner-centered index: High
Duration of the learning activity: As needed

Activity 40. Exploring Dynamic Web Content

Description and Purpose of Activity. Content changes fast in many fields. One way to encourage variety or novelty as well as add a bit of fun to a class is to have your learners explore the most recent online resources, posts, comments, and so on. Alternatively, you could have them look for the most viewed, debated, or shared resources. Here are some examples of what is possible.

- Suppose you were teaching a course on computer programming, business management, or the entertainment industry. You could assign your students to read the highest-rated news items for that day in Digg, Reddit, Drudge Report, Fark, and Slashdot, and then write a reflection paper or some type of summary on what they learned. Sites like Slashdot and Digg are Web aggregation and social news websites where users vote on the news, up or down, and even submit original content. Drudge Report, on the other hand, consists of links to stories from mainstream media related to politics, entertainment, and current events, and could be useful in political science, law, sociology, policy studies, venture capital markets, and American government classes.

- Instructors might require students to subscribe to StumbleUpon and enter a few topics of interest to them related to their course. In a course on "East Asian Religious Thought and Culture," for instance, students might enter topics of interest such as Buddhism, Taoism, and reincarnation. They might hit the "Stumble" button and see what news articles or Web resources on those topics float to the top for them to read.

- In a course on pop culture or new media, students can be asked to click the public timeline for posts on Twitter or identi.ca. The instructor could ask them to click it at least fifty times during an hour and to record or capture what people are currently microblogging about. A public timeline provides a highly dynamic and varied record of what is of interest to people around the globe. International students might especially appreciate posts in their native language.

These are but three examples. There are myriad random Web explorations possible with online portals of famous people in your field as well as from lectures found in Academic Earth from award-winning professors, new talks posted to iTunes University or YouTube EDU, and so on. In each case, students will be confronting content that was previously unknown and often in the midst of transformation.

Skills and Objectives. Includes extending beyond standard course content, connecting course material to current events in the news, discovering new trends, seeing relationships, learner curiosity in new content, exposure to fresh and novel material, and excitement for the topic. This activity helps the learner perceive the connectedness of concepts and ideas.

Advice and Ideas. Although this task would be fun for students, it could also be highly confusing. Be clear on your expectations in terms of the amount and timing of student searches as well as any reporting back of their explorations. Examples or testimonials from previous semesters or course experiences would undoubtedly prove beneficial.

In setting up the task, randomly assign students a database, portal, or website to explore. One student could be assigned to Twitter for the week, another to YouTube EDU, still another to Wikinews, and so on. They would track how their site changed or evolved during that week in terms of the class or a particular topic within it and report back to the entire class. Such reporting can be in the form of an online discussion, webinar, chat, or class wiki; when done, have students write a reflection paper on what they found.

Variations and Extensions. Students could work in pairs or teams on such a task. Each observation might then build on the other and result in a deeper and more informative report. Another idea would be to have their random exploration of Web content merge together into a class technical report that is made freely available to the world community. This activity could evolve into their joint statement on what was happening on this date in history.

Key Instructional Considerations

Risk index: Medium
Time index: Medium
Cost index: Low
Learner-centered index: High
Duration of the learning activity: 1 week or as needed

Final Reflections on Variety

Much variety is possible with the Web. As a result, it is truly an adventure to teach as well as learn online. Variety is the core or focal point of the TEC-VARIETY model. What is considered variety today, however, quickly becomes commonplace tomorrow; it is a constantly moving target. And if online instructors repeatedly select particular tasks, students may no longer consider that activity as novel or engaging as it once was.

Some readers of this book may have already tried a Second Life simulation, an online séance of long since departed founders of your field, or a mobile game. If so, you are taking bold steps to shift the balance of power in the teaching-learning equation toward your learners. Such risk takers allow students opportunities to teach or mentor others in the course as well as generate knowledge for the next class. Risk-taking instructors may also leave gaps or spaces in the syllabus or course schedule for their students to fill in.

This chapter not only emphasizes variety but also ideas related to fun, fantasy, and novelty. Considering the generation of learners brought up in the age of the Internet, Principle #4 might be one that they appreciate more than most. How will you convey notions of fun and fantasy in an online class? Will you ban joking from your online discussion forums? We have seen some instructors in the early days of Web-based instruction do just that. What about novelty? Will you be allergic to testing out emerging technology tools or resources when they are announced? Is your risk muscle well developed? Or will you be among those who stay with practices that are tried and true? If so, no variety for you then! Move on to one of the other nine principles.

You must be starting to realize that teaching and learning online, be it in a blended or a fully online mode, is not the same as F2F courses and experiences. Sure, many of the 100+ activities outlined in this book will work in F2F settings. Nevertheless, how each one is implemented and evaluated is vastly different when teaching online.

When you use the TEC-VARIETY framework, variety will be jumping out at your every turn. You will undoubtedly develop your own notions of what variety means to you and your students. When you do, share your ideas, results, and insights with others. The variety you seek might be personal so as to avoid boredom and burnout. It may also be variety for the learners in your online courses but not for others.

The next principle of the framework moves us into the section that more directly emphasizes the learner part of the equation. The watchword of the next chapter is autonomy. As we stated with the first principle of TEC-VARIETY, learners should have freedom to learn. They should control their learning destinies. Choice, control, flexibility, and opportunities are part of that fifth principle. And these are often the very principles that many educators argue are the key advantages of online learning. No matter the delivery mechanism, a learning environment filled with autonomy and ample choice is central to learning success today. Of course, you now have a choice of whether or not to proceed to the next chapter. We certainly hope that you will.

CHAPTER EIGHT

PRINCIPLE #5 AUTONOMY

(Includes Choice, Control, Flexibility, and Opportunities)

> To me, success is choice and opportunity.
>
> —Harrison Ford

American psychiatrist William Glasser, author of *Choice Theory: A New Psychology of Personal Freedom,* argued that the daily personal choices we make are critical in determining our mental health. It is better to make internally motivated choices and enter into caring relationships than to be externally driven (Glasser, 1998). As Glasser puts it, "We almost always have choices, and the better the choice, the more we will be in control of our lives" (1998). Of course, our age of information abundance offers many learner choices. Not too surprisingly, Dr. Glasser's ideas have been applied in a wide array of schools and business training settings.

Glasser's theories about personal control are well suited for this age of learner-centered education. Principle #5 of TEC-VARIETY, in fact, has to do with learner choice and autonomy. Previous chapters addressed climate and feedback variables as well as how to generate curiosity, variety, fun, and fantasy. Those aspects of motivation, though seemingly learner-centered, are actually often under the control of the instructor. As a result, Glasser and his followers might applaud this chapter as it ventures into territory that tends to be outside the direct control of the instructor or curriculum developers. They realize that making choices is part of what we do as autonomous beings, whether in school, home, or business.

Opportunities to choose and to act on their learning choices can have a powerful influence on learner satisfaction and performance (Pink, 2009). Any felt increase in autonomy enhances intrinsic motivation and offers learners a sense of control over their learning situation (Stipek, 1998), instead of feeling controlled or manipulated by someone else. In an educational setting, students could have a voice in the rules, procedures, tasks, activities, test questions, and many other classroom variables. It is vital to note that such autonomous motivation is linked to higher levels of comprehension, enhanced persistence, better grades, and less burnout.

There are decades of research to back this up. Edward Deci and Richard Ryan are well known for their work on self-determination theory (SDT). According to SDT, there are innate psychological needs that all humans seek. These needs include basic desires for competence, autonomy, and relatedness (Deci & Ryan, 2008). Deci and Ryan argue that the creation of environments or social contexts that support these needs foster intrinsic motivation and persistence toward goals. When such basic needs are frustrated, there is less intrinsic motivation. There are substantial benefits to be gained from autonomous regulation as compared to more controlled regulation. From this perspective, teachers should create an environment that respects student agendas, provides extensive choices and options, and designs activities that are highly relevant to student interests. Such actions are known in the motivational literature as autonomy support (Reeve, 1996), which refers to the amount of freedom that a teacher grants to students to pursue their passions and interests.

As was noted in earlier chapters, learners need opportunities and extensive freedom to learn and, ultimately, express themselves. They also need heavy doses of choice and volition. It is such volition or purposeful striving toward some action or goal that is at the heart of self-directed learning; that is, there is an inner will or determination to succeed. Daniel Pink (2009) argues that this internal drive system is focused on getting better at something that matters or is personally meaningful.

Ryan and Deci (2000) contend that extrinsic educational practices such as grades, detentions, and honor roles can undermine our intrinsic desire to learn. The extensive research that they document show that threats, surveillance, demands, deadlines, evaluations, and rewards undermine autonomy and can reduce creativity, complex problem-solving abilities, deep conceptual processing of information, and learner satisfaction. They find that the degree to which autonomy can be supported in the classroom, as opposed to the external controlling behaviors noted earlier, ultimately determines the level of student commitment and engagement in the learning process. Not too surprisingly, it also has a direct impact on the resulting learning outcomes.

Managers across business sectors have become increasingly aware of the importance of autonomy for new product development and overall success. Google, for instance, uses autonomy with its well-known policy of 20 percent time. At Google, engineers can spend one day a week doing what they want, including fine-tuning an existing product or dreaming up something totally new. This policy often results in more than half of Google's annual new product line (Pink, 2009). Products developed at Google during 20 percent time include Google News, Gmail, Google Talk, and Google Translate. Clearly, providing employees with choice, control, and a sense of freedom to allocate time when, where, and how they see fit is a work world much different from that of the prior century.

Interestingly, the cofounders of Google, Sergey Brin and Larry Paige, attended Montessori schools when they were young. So did Jeff Bezos who founded Amazon. As many are aware, Maria Montessori created a curriculum filled with choice, collaboration, play, exploration, self-directed learning, and learner autonomy (Montessori, 1912). Montessori believed in a multisensory approach, hands-on activities, and unrestrained liberty for the student. Small wonder, then, that Brin and Paige attribute their success to such a system. Their prior experiences and dispositions allowed them to create a company environment where employees ignore existing rules and orders of how things are normally done. They also question what is going on in the world and have extensive opportunities for freedom, personal choice, and intrinsic motivation.

Are online educators willing to do what Glasser, Montessori, and other educators and psychologists have long argued for? Not only must educational settings prepare workers for environments like those found at Google and Amazon, such open and collaborative approaches simply result in better learning. Think about how ceding 20 percent of class time to students might result in a dramatically changed environment. No longer will students wait to be taught. Instead, they will think, collaborate, and develop products light years ahead of course objectives.

Each learner enters your class with a set of personal goals and beliefs. By embedding opportunities for choice and personal exploration in an online course, learners can feel in charge and in control of their learning environment (Bonk, Fischler, & Graham, 2000). With choice, flexibility, and autonomy, learners tend to make a personal investment in the course (Maehr, 1984). They want opportunities to learn, not restrictions from it. Nevertheless, online courses are notorious for being overly regimented or scripted. Too often, there are few, if any, options or choices. Instead, everyone must follow prepackaged content in lockstep order. No exceptions.

The good news is that during the past decade increasing experimentation has taken place in online environments. Students can be given choice in the discussion forums to participate in, the cases to respond to, and the assignments to select. They can even play a role in helping create weekly discussion topics, finding resources to share, or inviting guest experts. In some online and blended learning courses, students could take a lead in a discussion forum or concept demonstration. They might also sign up for a particular personality type or persona to role play. Across these techniques, instructors are giving learners choices in how they will meet course objectives. And, as is apparent by now, such choices and flexibility are highly motivating and personally valuable.

Technologies for Principle #5: Autonomy

There are innumerable ways that autonomy, choice, control, flexibility, and opportunities are possible online. The technologies might be as simple as a sign-up page on the Web, a set of open educational resource portals to explore, or a discussion forum with multiple tracks or themes to select from. An opportunity to explore one or more learning portals or Web resources is common today. In addition to sign-up pages and portals, learner choice and autonomy are evident when students select an expert podcast to listen to, a blog to read, or a conference speech to watch and take notes on. Students may also select from a range of shared online videos to watch or engage in different virtual world meetings and interactions. With their avatars in place, learners can decide on which virtual meetings and learning experiences they want to investigate. Such opportunities to explore and self-determine their learning are increasingly common practices.

There are times when the learner should have the choice of which tool to use to best accomplish an assigned task (Jukes, McCain, & Crockett, 2010). There are often dozens of tools available for any particular digital activity or task. If the assignment involves educational blogging, list the ones you know about and allow students to suggest others. The same is true regarding the creation of shared online videos, podcasts, or animated characters. Skills for manipulating photos, sound, or video evolve from engagement in those activities. Find and use the technologies that are allowed. There will be plenty to choose from despite extensive lists of banned technologies.

The new digital landscape that we have entered over the past decade or two is rich with options and possibilities. Let students engage with new technologies. Let them have a sense of control and personally designed destiny.

Ten Online Activities in Principle #5: Autonomy

The activities listed here for Principle #5 are intended to enhance opportunities for learner autonomy and choice. Giving students a choice on their assignments and activities builds commitment and passion for learning. These activities involve increasing degrees of choice and freedom to learn from selecting a resource to showcase for a particular week, as apparent in Activity #41, to opening up the course not only for your own class but also for the entire world to take part in, as seen in Activity #50.

Activity 41. Cool Resource Provider

Description and Purpose of Activity. A prime example of a task offering student autonomy as well as choice, control, opportunities, and flexibility is the notion of the "cool resource provider." Bonk coined this method a few years ago in one of his graduate courses, but the idea could be used in any education or training situation from the very young to senior learners. The cool resource provider explores and finds Web resources related to the course for a particular week or unit. To allow for student choice, the instructor posts a form online with blank lines for each week for students to submit their names. Alternatively, a wiki could be used.

Student cool resource exploration extends beyond instructor lectures, text resources, class archives, and assigned supplemental materials. If there are synchronous or F2F meetings, the assigned cool resource provider could be required to make a short presentation to the class of one or more resources found. Such a presentation might take place for 5 to 10 minutes at the start of a class.

In Bonk's learning psychology course, such resources often include online psychological tests and instruments, simulations, animations, models, videos, or audio clips. Students have found videos of famous psychologists such as Albert Bandura, B. F. Skinner, John Watson, Jean Piaget, Lev Vygotsky, and others (see the Web resources associated with this chapter).

In one instance, a student found an old video of Bandura explaining his famed Bobo doll experiments from the early 1960s. The video included original film footage in black and white. In that particular research, children who watched aggressive and violent actions from an adult model were more likely to engage in such acts. Reading about the study is vital to student learning; however, seeing the original research unfold is much more powerful. And it is a video snippet that Bonk continues to use in his courses. This is just one of dozens of instances where the use of the cool resource provider assignment helped to extend and even transform one of his classes.

As is evident, the cool resource provider role grants students a voice in the activities for the week. Instead of subjecting students only to the limited views of their instructors or course designers, this activity empowers them to go far beyond.

Skills and Objectives. Includes student autonomy, empowerment, and choice, the appreciation of multiple perspectives, content review, sharing, learner interaction, and critical analysis of concepts and applications. This technique extends the course in interesting directions and forces student reflection.

Advice and Ideas. The assignment should be clear. For instance, the instructor might ask students to find 5–10 or more Web resources for the particular week of the course that they signed up for and submit them to her for approval at least two days prior to class. A corresponding handout may be required. If it is an online class, students might post their resources to the course website. In a F2F class, students would present a few of these resources at the designated time (e.g., the start of class). Their presentation might take 5 to 10 minutes followed by questions and comments from the class.

Students could sign up for this role once or twice during the semester. To add a greater sense of instructional as well as intellectual power to this activity, the cool resource provider(s) may also be asked to help moderate discussion for the week by providing four to six starter discussion questions, or to generate a couple of debate topics, or to pose a few controversial issues. In terms of grading, we often make this a mastery assignment with full credit if done well.

Be sure to save all the Web resources contributed by the cool resource providers. They can be used in following semesters or versions of the course. In addition, ask students to rate or evaluate the resources found. Then archive the highest-rated resources for future students. You might also share them with colleagues who teach similar courses. Instructors can take advantage of this extended support for their classes, and, over time, their collection of class resources noticeably appreciates. The list of video resources for Bonk's learning and cognition class, for instance, has built up over the past few years and is now quite extensive with links to videos found in YouTube, TED, the George Lucas Education Foundation, and other places.

Variations and Extensions. We often have students work in pairs as cool resource providers. A paired approach offers additional support and analysis that often results in higher-quality work. An option to weekly cool resource provider activities would be to allocate one day of the semester for cool resource presentations or sharing. In fact, you might have cool resource provider competitions with awards at the end. To boost the quality level even further, there could also be competitions across classes or institutions. Another option would be to vary the type of cool resources shared each week. For instance, Week One for text resources, Week Two audio, Week Three video, and so on.

Key Instructional Considerations

Risk index: Medium
Time index: Medium
Cost index: Low
Learner-centered index: High
Duration of the learning activity: Throughout the course or as needed

Activity 42. Technology Tool Demonstrator

Description and Purpose of Activity. Akin to the cool resource provider idea is the technology tool demonstrator. In this activity, students contact the instructor and explain the technology tool that they want to demonstrate to the class. The instructor must review the tool as well as the justification from the student and approve it. If it is a blended or F2F class, the instructor might reserve a computer lab for the technology demonstration. The length of the presentation will vary depending on the course as well as the complexity and utility of the technology tool. Perhaps 15–30 minutes would be sufficient for such a presentation. If it is an online class, you might allow a similar amount of time in a synchronous class meeting using Web conferencing tools available within your organization or institution or some other freely available tool like AnyMeeting. Alternatively, students could screencast a simple video explaining or demonstrating the particular tool.

During the past decade, we have had students demonstrate collaborative technologies, blogging tools, and tools for creating 3D animated characters in movies. In terms of the latter, GoAnimate and Xtranormal are popular among students as they are easy to use. With such tools, students in blended courses could post video supplements to their live demonstrations.

There are various ways to reward students. We often allow students to drop an assignment if they present a new technology to the class. Keep in mind that most Web tools demonstrated will immediately be used by someone in the current course or training experience. The technology tool demonstration, therefore, is a way to extend the class in exciting new directions.

Skills and Objectives. Includes student autonomy and empowerment, resource exploration and selection, sharing, presentation and communication skills, and learner interaction. This technique temporarily places students in the role of instructor.

Advice and Ideas. There are innumerable benefits from this task including student respect, empowerment, and expertise. Be aware, however, that the activity can chew up a significant amount of class time; you may choose to limit such technology demonstration sessions to just one or two during the course term. In any event, ask students to create a handout or guide sheet for the technology or resource. Also, be sure to maintain a list or database of all previous technology tool demonstrations.

Variations and Extensions. The instructor could designate a day for student demonstrations of new technology tools that relate to the course. Another idea would be to have multiple people spotlight various technology tools for the class on a few select dates during the semester. At the end of the session or semester, the class might vote on the most useful, unique, or relevant technology tool.

Key Instructional Considerations

Risk index: Medium
Time index: Medium (in terms of class time)
Cost index: Low (assuming the technology demonstrated is free)
Learner-centered index: High
Duration of the learning activity: Throughout the course or as needed

Activity 43. Starter-Wrapper Technique

Description and Purpose of Activity. Another online activity Bonk has experimented with is called the "Starter-Wrapper" task (Bonk, Ehman, Hixon, & Yamagata-Lynch, 2002). When using this technique, students sign up to lead or end the discussion on the assigned book chapters, articles, videos, and other resources for any week that interests them. The discussion takes place in designated threads in an asynchronous discussion forum. Most learners find a week that interests them. Students can also sign up in teams or in tracks. For instance, one person could lead a track for those interested in working in the corporate sector and another for those interested in working in higher education. A third track might be for K–12, informal environments, military training, or something else.

Akin to the highly popular and effective reciprocal teaching method (Webb & Palincsar, 1996), the starter assumes some of the teacher roles for the week by summarizing the assigned content for others. That person is also the discussion facilitator or moderator. To be effective, he would read ahead and summarize the week's content before others are required to enter that discussion thread. The assignment might also call for him to post a few questions to get the discussion started. Once replies are posted, he would read the comments and pull out controversial, interesting, or important issues and themes. This switches him to a moderator role.

At the end of the week, the discussion "wrapper" would summarize the discussion that took place, including any themes, debates, and remaining open issues. The course instructor would act as a second moderator and wrapper. With such an approach, instead of "lectures" coming from instructors, students lecture to each other. In the starter-wrapper technique, the instructor would point out any student misconceptions, errors, and areas that they forgot to mention or where they did not go into enough detail.

This method works. Research indicates that it focuses student interactions and provides a structure for their discussion (Hara, Bonk, & Angeli, 2000). When used effectively, there is often much depth and insights within the discussion. As the weeks unfold, student interactivity becomes more apparent and complex as students get to know each other better. However, if a student who has signed up as the starter for a week drops the course or fails to perform, the discussion will likely flounder. Be sure to quickly replace people who are no longer in the course or who fail to contribute in a timely manner. Bonus points might be offered to replacements.

Skills and Objectives. Includes choice and control, engagement, feedback, comprehension skills, and overall skill internalization. Students quickly learn the routine and have a place to review their learning.

Advice and Ideas. Provide examples of previous starter-wrapper activities. Perhaps ask students from previous semesters to provide testimonials on how it worked. You might also create a list of guidelines and caveats.

All discussions can be printed out for later review. The discussion forum is a living record of their teaching and learning in the course. In a F2F course, you could have your students print out one or more of their weekly discussion transcripts and bring them to class, with key concepts circled and open questions noted. Your students might also make presentations based on the weekly transcripts. Instructors could also create quizzes based on them.

Some semesters we establish a minimum number of student postings per week. We also ask students to respond to at least one peer comment each time they post. Finally, we often require posts to have a minimum of three sentences. We put this rule in place because the first sentence is often an agreement or social acknowledgment of the previous post, whereas the second sentence tends to be an opinion that starts with "I feel," "In my opinion," or "I think." In the third sentence, they finally must say something substantive.

Variations and Extensions. One variation we have tried that works is to have the same person be the starter and the wrapper. In effect, that person is the moderator of the discussion. If you take this approach, you might rename the method "Starter-Moderator." Another way to expand on this technique is to have students write super summaries of their learning in the course based on their discussion transcripts. Often students ignore the posts of the wrapper. To address this issue, we sometimes require students to quote directly from or at least refer to the posts of four or more starters and four or more wrappers in their super summaries.

Key Instructional Considerations

Risk index: Medium
Time index: High
Cost index: Low
Learner-centered index: High
Duration of the learning activity: Throughout the course or as needed

Activity 44. Shotgun Questioning

Description and Purpose of Activity. Options are important. In the preceding starter-wrapper technique, you allowed your students to pick issues or questions to respond to. Another option is for the instructor to post a series of questions or issues to discuss and debate each week. Instructors can literally fire them out and see what happens. Students can then decide which to respond to.

For instance, there may be 10 issues or key questions each week. Students could be required to respond within three or four of those discussions. Alternatively, there could be one or just a couple of discussion threads; however, each may be loaded with questions on a common theme or target area (e.g., art periods in an art history class, work settings in a business management class, or ages of clients in an occupational therapy course).

Skills and Objectives. Includes choice and engagement, flexibility, feedback, comprehension skills, linking content to student interests, and overall skill internalization. Students quickly learn the routine and have a place to review their learning.

Advice and Ideas. Instructors or instructional designers of the course might create separate discussion threads for each question. As discussion proceeds, they could add new pieces of information or additional questions. For discussions that are fairly intense, there may be less need to intervene. For lightly populated discussions, interesting quotations, facts, and other data might entice student reflection and commenting.

During the semester, take note of the types of questions and content areas where students tend to post more heavily. Adjust questions and issues appropriately. We find that the discussion thread title and first few postings are strong influencers of the ensuing discussion patterns. Monitor them closely.

Variations and Extensions. Students could select 10 of the key discussion forums that they entered and contributed to during the semester and write a reflection paper on their learning within those discussions. The instructor may also ask them to reflect on fellow students' misconceptions and any interconnections between different discussion threads. To foster learner self-monitoring and other metacognitive skills, they each could reflect on how well the shotgun approach aligned with their particular learning style.

Key Instructional Considerations

> Risk index: Medium
> Time index: High
> Cost index: Low
> Learner-centered index: High
> Duration of the learning activity: Weekly or as needed

Activity 45. Hot Seat Questioning

Description and Purpose of Activity. Similar to the time-constrained presentations mentioned in earlier chapters and the starter-wrapper technique outlined in this chapter, in this activity students sign up to be in the "hot seat." The term *hot seat* is used in many environments, from witnesses testifying in a courtroom, to a corporate official reporting in a congressional hearing, to a suspect being interrogated in a police station (wiseGEEK, n.d.). Often, the person is in a hot and uncomfortable environment. At the extreme end of the spectrum, a hot seat includes painful shock treatment or even the electric chair. In any event, the hot seat is hardly where anybody wants to be, but an online hot seat activity encourages students to display their newly discovered skills or learned competencies. Clearly, with such an activity label, students know that they will be challenged.

The designated person in the hot seat must attempt to answer all questions posted during the week by fellow students in the course as well as by the instructor. Essentially, the person in the hot seat plays the role of resident expert. She would not only read the assigned content, but also potentially dozens of additional sources. This requires depth of thought on the part of the student and the ability to think rapidly. The hot seat activity could take place either in a live Webcam conference or in an asynchronous discussion forum.

In terms of student autonomy and choice, students select the week that most appeals to their interests and expertise. Many students enjoy the chance to field questions on a wide range of topics and issues. They might even develop a sense of expertise in certain areas that fellow students continue to ask them about later in the semester or even after the course ends. Importantly, later assignments might utilize that growing knowledge base. The hot seat activity could serve as a base for budding expertise and perhaps even useful products and papers.

Skills and Objectives. Includes choice and engagement, flexibility, feedback, comprehension skills, linking content to prior knowledge and interests, and overall skill internalization. Students quickly learn the routine and have a place to review their learning.

Advice and Ideas. Instructors can create an online form for learners to sign up to be in the hot seat or use a wiki for students to negotiate or even bid on weeks. Monitor the hot seat activity. Before commencing the activity, the instructor may have to train students in how to interact in socially appropriate ways with each other. If a student is experiencing difficulty with a particular question or fellow student in the course, the instructor could offer her additional information or resources directly in the discussion thread or privately via e-mail to help the student manage it. If the student is handling questions extremely well, however, the instructor might challenge that student with harder or more complex problems. What becomes clear is that the instructor's role is to provide instructional support and scaffolding, while also pushing students to reach the outer edges of their competencies and comfort zones.

Variations and Extensions. Students might work jointly in the hot seat with a peer, such as their designated Web buddy or critical friend. They could also be assigned to write a short reflection paper or blog post on how well their particular week went, reflecting on their content knowledge acquired, knowledge deficiencies, and areas that they still want to explore. All references and resources used during the week should be noted. If it is a paired activity, students should also reflect on their respective contributions and how well they worked together as team members.

Key Instructional Considerations

Risk index: Medium
Time index: High
Cost index: Low
Learner-centered index: High
Duration of the learning activity: Weekly or as needed

Activity 46. Open Exploration Weeks

Description and Purpose of Activity. Another way to build autonomy and choice in classes and training events is to leave designated openings and opportunities for that to occur. One activity discussed in the *Empowering Online Learning* book (Bonk & Zhang, 2008) is called "Library Day." In Library Day, students must find and summarize a pre-determined number of articles in a week or a day, instead of reading a set of articles selected by the instructor. In contrast, Activity 46 allows students to do anything that they want. They can watch a set number of online videos, find and read articles, correspond with others in similar classes, explore simulations and games, listen to a number of podcasts, read through and summarize dozens of articles, or perform a combination of these activities.

First, however, students should be required to submit a short proposal on what they plan to explore that must be approved by the instructor. They could also share their plans with their assigned Web buddy or critical friend in the class or with the entire class in a discussion forum thread. During the week or at the end of it, students would reflect on their learning from their activity.

Skills and Objectives. Includes student autonomy and choice, exploration, addressing student interests and individual differences, and extending the course to additional topics and emerging areas of interest. Using such a method can help guarantee that the instructor will address student needs at some point during the semester. It can also reveal to students topics or areas that currently have limited information or resources to learn from.

Advice and Ideas. Provide scaffolds and job aids for the open weeks. Be clear about your expectations in terms of the number of articles read, websites visited, videos watched, podcasts listened to, discussion posts made, and so on. It is extremely important to have students reflect on how well the assignment went and what they learned from it. Examples from previous semesters as well as ideas on what students might explore could be used to entice student learning pursuits.

Variations and Extensions. Open weeks for exploration are quite popular with our students. They often ask for more such weeks. In response, you could offer two open weeks, one in the middle the semester and one just before students' final assignments are due. Alternatively, you could place two open exploration weeks back-to-back. You may also consider letting students decide when the open weeks will occur during the semester.

Key Instructional Considerations

Risk index: Medium
Time index: Medium
Cost index: Low
Learner-centered index: High
Duration of the learning activity: 1–2 weeks as needed

Activity 47. Open Educational Resources Explorations

Description and Purpose of Activity. Sometimes we offer our students a chance to explore a list of resources related to the week. Each student in the class might have a different assignment. For example, in a course on instructional or educational technology, students could investigate and report on open educational resources as a topic. Sample open educational resources are listed in the resources section associated with this chapter. You could assign students to review and report back on a set number of them. In addition, give students a handout with questions or criteria listed that they must address. For instance, one question could ask about the ease of navigation as well as the depth, currency, utility, and relevance of the resources found at each site to which they are assigned. In a fully online course, their completed reports may be presented in a synchronous Web meeting or in an online discussion forum. In a blended course, they could demonstrate each site in a F2F class meeting and offer their suggestions for improvement.

The preceding example is just one quite obvious application of this type of task. Not everyone teaches an educational technology course focusing on open education, however. In other types of classes, such as English literature, the open educational resources for Jane Austin, Ernest Hemingway, William Shakespeare, and Edgar Allen Poe listed in the Web resources section of this chapter provide a starting point for further exploration. The instructor or course designer would find additional sites and design exploration and evaluation criteria and forms. Similarly, physics instructors would find more sites like the Einstein website. And courses in biology or anthropology could start with the Darwin website as well as articles from the Public Library of Sciences (PLoS), and Scitable from *Nature*. They might also browse through the Trailblazing website, which holds 350 years of Royal Society Publishing. Courses in photomedia could have students exploring sites like Panoramio and EveryStockPhoto.com. Much is possible with careful plans and thoughtful reflection and exploration.

Clearly, this activity should find utility in any type of online or blended course. It shifts the learning burden from the instructor toward the students. That is not to say that the instructor is unimportant in the process; in fact, instructor creation of the task and selection of resources is what makes it possible. As we mentioned in previous chapters, the instructor assumes the role of online concierge and curator of course content. Such a role is not as difficult as it may sound. We find that it typically does not take more than an hour or two to locate enough open educational resources for an entire class to explore in a week. We urge you to allocate this time. Without a doubt, the role of the instructor is more varied and complex when teaching online. It can also be much more fun!

Skills and Objectives. Includes student autonomy and choice, student exploration, addressing student interests and individual differences, depth of learning, developing expertise in a particular issue or topic, and extending course resources. The exploration of Web resources takes advantage of the power of the Web.

Advice and Ideas. There are many ways to scaffold this assignment. In addition to a guide sheet or online form for website evaluation, there would likely be tasks for students to locate certain data, summarize what they have found, and link the website content to one or more concepts discussed in the course.

There is also a need to consider and perhaps find ways to constrain the amount of work associated with this task. If there are 30 students in the class, each could be assigned one of 30 online resources that the instructor has found (see example in the Web resources section of this chapter). If there were 15 students, each would be assigned two of them. If there were 10 students, each would get three. If there were more than 30 students, the instructor could expand the list or perhaps assign students to work in teams.

Variations and Extensions. Instead of instructor-selected resources and learning paths, true learner autonomy would happen when students themselves find open educational resources to explore for the week. To enhance this search, students could work in teams or groups to locate and select what they feel are the best open educational resources, and then share the resources found and their ratings in a class wiki or in an online discussion forum thread. Final reflection papers or presentations on the process might be required.

Key Instructional Considerations

Risk index: Medium
Time index: Medium
Cost index: Low
Learner-centered index: High
Duration of the learning activity: 1–2 weeks or as needed

Activity 48. Pick and Choose Options

Description and Purpose of Activity. For centuries, educators were limited in their course resources options. Higher education was a land where the scarcity of knowledge was the norm. The same was true at the K–12 level as well as most corporate and military training settings. Publishers often dictated what went into a course. Given such limitations, there was not much the instructor could do to support learner autonomy. Today, however, those norms are being reversed. Learners and instructors have a plethora of options for learning. There are podcasts, shared online video clips, expert blogs, and so on.

With this learning resource explosion comes a tearing down of predefined course structures and an expansion of learner options and opportunities. For instance, for every case or scenario you find on the Web related to your course, there are dozens more to choose from. Content and tasks that at one time were extremely rare and far too expensive, such as simulations, animations, and video, are now increasingly common and often free.

When Bonk taught a technology integration course to practicing teachers in the late 1990s that was primarily online but with a couple of F2F meetings, he failed to adjust his teaching to the new delivery format. He decided to assign all students the same four tasks and set of readings. He also created a series of debates with preassigned debate teams. There was minimal choice. Bonk soon found that his choices of tasks did not fit his students' needs. His rigid course structure was not amenable to full-time working adults with families.

The next time he taught the course, he offered ten task options for the course and allowed the students to pick any four. Notice that the amount of work remained the same. In addition, there were no assigned course readings. Instead, students could select their readings from a collection of articles found in a popular book that each student received for free from the project. The learners picked the tasks and articles that appealed to them. In addition, with instructor approval, they could substitute other articles that they found. Moral of the story? Options! Students love options.

A couple of years before that, Bonk taught an educational psychology course to pre-service teachers. Instead of assigning them to read and solve a set of 5–10 cases that he had designed and used in previous semesters, Bonk had his students write cases based on their field experiences in Indiana schools while responding to the cases of their peers. In addition, students from other universities in the United States as well as the United Kingdom, Finland, Korea, and Peru added to those field experience cases. They had thousands to pick and choose from. It was a highly interactive and engaging global educational experience.

Those are but two examples related to giving students options in online and blended courses. As is apparent, choice and options are increasingly the norm and the role of the instructor is one of learning guide or concierge for her students. But first she must be an effective and efficient curator of online course content. Following are 10 ideas for such an open-ended activity.

1. Detail 10 task options for the semester or course and allow students to select any four or five.

2. List multiple cases (e.g., Case A and Case B) and allow the students to select which ones to answer.

3. Have multiple final project options (e.g., research reports, grant proposals, special topic reviews, wikibook chapters, super summary papers, short videos detailing their learning, summary podcasts, and so forth).

4. Require three or four short reflection papers during the semester. Provide examples of different types of reflection papers to select from (e.g., current trend papers, course journey reflections, article summaries, expert or scholar reviews, thought papers, website exploration reflections, book or special journal issue reviews, and so on).

5. Create a database of online papers tied to weekly topics and allow students to select three or four of them each week to read.

6. Create a database of videos related to the course and require students to watch a few of these each week and then reflect on them in an online discussion forum.

7. Ask students to review one expert blog or podcast show each week from a list of 10 or 20.

8. List online conferences, summits, institutes, and similar events and ask students to watch and reflect on one or two of the keynote speeches or invited talks.

9. List e-books and special journal issues related to the course that are freely available online and have students write a critique or review of one of them.

10. List technology tools or resources related to the course and ask each student to write a review of one of them or a compare and contrast paper of two or more such tools or resources.

Skills and Objectives. Includes student excitement and enthusiasm for learning, fun, student autonomy and choice, student exploration, decision making, communication skills, and addressing student interests and individual differences. Such a method helps to personalize the learning process, allowing students to have a voice and a sense of control over their learning journeys and destinies.

Advice and Ideas. Clearly, in such an activity, the skill of the instructor or course designer will be in scaffolding or guiding the learning process. Given all the options, the refinement of your feedback and grading system may take time. Not every task or option will work. Ask students to evaluate these options and suggest new ones. Remain open to new ideas. And be sure to catalogue what worked and share it with others.

Variations and Extensions. There might be designated points of reflection within the course for students to debrief on the activity and share what they learned. The assignments might also recursively build on each other, perhaps ending with a task in which students compile their learning journeys into a portfolio or online gallery. Or students could be asked to compare their learning journeys to that of their Web buddy, critical friend, or others in the course.

Key Instructional Considerations

Risk index: Medium
Time index: High
Cost index: Low
Learner-centered index: High
Duration of the learning activity: As needed

Activity 49. Open Syllabus Course Portal with Options

Description and Purpose of Activity. Many of the previous activities described in this chapter included options and choices for a particular week or activity. The final two relate to the entire course. Many instructors already use a CMS or LMS and upload links to articles, e-books, shared online videos, and other Web resources. However, this is just part of the course resources.

Imagine what happens when the entire course is available online and filled with options—and there are no required books or F2F meetings. Back in 2005, some instructors started to use tools like Pageflakes and other Web resources as a portal to their course. Each "flake" in Pageflakes could offer different course content including calendars, notes, Web searches, bookmarks, photos, social networking tools, examples of prior student work, RSS feeds from blogs or podcasts, and so on. For some instructors and students, such a technique was overwhelming and quickly caused cognitive overload. For others, it was ideal.

One approach that some instructors and trainers increasingly use today is to post the course syllabus on the Web with every assigned article, video, or Web resource available as a clickable Web link. Bonk has employed such an approach the past few years in his course on the emerging learning technologies and open education. In 2007, his course syllabus was 27 pages long. It mushroomed to 75 pages by the spring of 2013. At that time, he nicknamed it "the monster syllabus."

In this course, there was nothing for students to purchase; instead, every journal article, report, and resource was available online. Each week, students were asked to choose three or four main articles to read from about six or seven that were available. He also posted a dozen or more "tidbits" or recent articles in the news for each week of the semester, of which students were expected to read two or three each week as well.

Placing the entire syllabus online with every article or resource available for free allows students to explore the course contents at will. They can enter a website or peruse an article and decide if it meshes with their needs. Students can embark on a learning journey and the instructor's role becomes that of expedition leader. Given that the syllabus is open to the public means that countless others can learn from that course portal. At the same time, anyone can also make recommendations for improvement or extension of the course materials.

Skills and Objectives. Includes student excitement and enthusiasm for learning, adventure, fun, student autonomy and choice, student exploration, extended course connections, student multitasking, addressing student interests and individual differences, and sharing course content with the world community. Such a method helps to personalize the learning process and grants control to learners based on their interests, prior knowledge, and future directions.

Advice and Ideas. The open course syllabus and associated content are not only available to students at any time but also to the instructor, departmental colleagues, and anyone with a casual interest in the topic. There are many people relying on the accuracy and currency of the information. As you might expect, such a course requires serious attention to detail. Instructors and course designers must stay abreast of current trends in the field and update the online syllabus on a regular basis. They might bookmark relevant Web links according to current topics and interesting articles related to the course. Such files can be reviewed and updated at any time.

Consider recruiting a former student or some other Web-savvy individual to help maintain the site. That person could check the links from time to time, post updated syllabi, let you know when a course resource is no longer available, and discuss changes in the format of the content. Alternatively, one or two students might help with any course maintenance and updating at the end of the course. Such course review and maintenance activity might be an optional end-of-course assignment.

Variations and Extensions. Instead of posting the entire course at the start of the semester, pieces of the course can be revealed over time. In addition, an interactive course timeline or concept map for the course could be created that provides a visual overview of the online syllabus or course portal. An optional assignment in the course might be for students to evaluate the linked course contents and overviews, using an item evaluation or ranking form that you have prepared. You could ask them to select their favorite and least favorite items in the course. Given sufficient data, the instructor can then make changes to the course portal.

Key Instructional Considerations

Risk index: High
Time index: High
Cost index: Low (assumes access to all articles and resources linked to the course are freely available)
Learner-centered index: High
Duration of the learning activity: Every week

Activity 50. Open Teaching and MOOCs

Description and Purpose of Activity. At the high end of the risk continuum today are those instructors who decide not only to make their course materials available online for people to browse and use, as in the previous example, but to allow anyone around the world to participate in and contribute to the course itself. Increasingly, instructors like David Wiley of Brigham Young University allow a modest number of people from around the world to sit in and participate in such an open course. At the end, they might receive a badge or certificate of completion (Young, 2008). We call this "open teaching." Open teaching typically allows for much student choice and autonomy.

Other instructors are even more ambitious and simultaneously deliver a free and open course to thousands or tens of thousands of people around the world. The phrase "massive open online course" (MOOC) is used to refer to this situation. According to Wikipedia, "A massive open online course (MOOC) is a course where the participants are distributed and course materials also are dispersed across the web" (Massive Open Online Course, 2011). Of course, it is typically the intrinsically motivated learners who do not require a grade, course credit, or gold star who complete a MOOC (Fini, 2009).

During the summer of 2011, Dr. Ray Schroeder, professor emeritus at the University of Illinois Springfield, offered a massive open online course in education (eduMOOC) titled "Online Learning Today . . . and Tomorrow" (Parry, 2011). Within a couple of weeks of its announcement, Schroeder had more than 2,600 people registered, representing some 80 countries including Morocco, Vietnam, Guyana, Fiji, Sudan, India, Cyprus, and Belgium. When Bonk interviewed Schroeder about his observations halfway through the course, Schroeder replied that a MOOC is ideal for ideas related to learner autonomy and choice. As he stated, "This addresses individual choice, access, and flexibility. In the end, there is an awesome resource site with a rambling network of interested individuals, blogs, wikis, G+ circles, etc." Schroeder then added, "The motivation mostly comes from the broad range of professional colleagues that are engaged. The enthusiasm, knowledge, interests of the individuals raises [the level of learning of] all who read/view/hear what they share on the topics" (Bonk, 2011).

With a MOOC, you can reach a vast number of people in a short amount of time with just-in-time content. According to Schroeder, "This is a natural for professional development/training. . . . This would seem to be a great fit for courses and topics where there are new developments, new issues, new topics" (Bonk, 2011). Intrigued with the idea of a professional development MOOC, in the spring of 2012, Bonk offered a MOOC on how to teach online titled, "Instructional Activities and Technology Tools for Online Success" (Bonk, 2013; Chronicle of Higher Education, 2012). CourseSites, a free course management division within Blackboard, was the sponsor of the MOOC. Over 3,500 people initially enrolled in this five-week course and many more have enrolled since then. There were weekly synchronous sessions using Blackboard Collaborate (previously called Elluminate) as well as online discussions, extensive resource sharing, student use of blogs and wikis, and so on. The course is still available for anyone to enroll in and receive a badge for completion.

Although an open syllabus offers extensive autonomy and choice, there tends to be even more with a MOOC. There is also a unique sense of excitement and energy because enrolled students can interact with global peers who are keenly interested in the topic. Enrolled students are often inspired by the people who want to sit in and learn something that can help them in their careers. In terms of autonomy, with freely accessible course materials as in the case of open teaching, participants can choose the materials that they want to access and read or use. In a MOOC, such materials are often quite extensive and of high quality. Participants can decide on the modules or units in which they want to participate. And they can typically select their learning partners or study group team members. To personalize the experience, MOOC participants tend to form local chapters that meet up in cafés and bookstores to discuss their learning. In effect, a MOOC or open class is all about such choice, control, and learning opportunities. Though perhaps deemed risky today, open teaching in the form of MOOCs will become a common practice in the coming decades (Chronicle of Higher Education, 2010). You too can be a part of this exciting trend.

Skills and Objectives. Includes flexibility, choice, openness, a culture of sharing, appreciation of multiple points of view and diversity, learner interaction and debate, participatory learning, exploration, extended course connections, addressing student interests, and welcoming the world community. Open teaching exposes students to a wealth of opinions and levels of expertise.

Advice and Ideas. Start small. Invite a few visitors or lurkers into your online or blended course. Once you have pilot-tested the course, consider opening it up to the world. You might ask enrolled students for their opinions about opening up the course before you do so, however. If they approve, scan previous MOOCs for ideas on how to run one. In addition, you might watch the four-minute YouTube video from Dave Cormier from Prince Edward Island, Canada, in which Cormier uses his experience with MOOCs to explain what a MOOC is.

It takes time to get adjusted to this type of course. There are many challenges and items to consider. In Bonk's interview with Schroeder, he said, "The volume of users is daunting in the first week or so. Getting everyone registered and receiving the listserv is a challenge when there are more than 2,600 in the group. But, once it is running, the participants take over. We continue to populate each week's webpage with dozens of resource links and conduct the panel discussion with knowledgeable people."

Variations and Extensions. Consider working with one or more instructors who have also placed their syllabi and extensive materials online. Resources from each open access course could be used and evaluated by students across institutions or cultures. Or perhaps two instructors offering MOOCs on distinct but related topics could have one or more cross-course collaborations. For example, in a series of professional development courses related to training instructors to teach online, there may be separate MOOCs on understanding students and their needs, emerging technologies for learning, copyright and plagiarism, quality and assessment, and online delivery and facilitation. Such courses might have common assignments or occasional student interactions.

Another idea would be to have students in a traditional class explore online MOOC materials that are openly accessible. You could ask these students to find resources and evaluate those related to your course. Be careful, however, as not all MOOC vendors allow their contents to be used in other courses. Check that you have the appropriate copyright clearances.

Key Instructional Considerations

Risk index: High
Time index: High
Cost index: Low to high (depending on the technologies selected)
Learner-centered index: High
Duration of the learning activity: Every week

Final Reflections on Autonomy

Counting all the above activities and their respective extensions and variations, there are dozens of ideas to select from to create autonomy support in your online courses. Online learners will respond in highly positive ways to the choices and options that you provide as long as they are supported with clear and direct explanations. Try the cool resource provider, starter-wrapper, Case A and Case B, or some other idea. Openness, options, flexibility, and choice are really what differentiate Web-based forms of instruction from other formats. When you place your focus there, you are giving your students opportunities to learn and to make personal decisions about their learning present and futures. As you begin to experiment with some of these ideas, in addition to your own ideas, you will have the kernel or shell for developing your own self-determination theory. You can be the Deci and Ryan of your online class.

You will have to decide the type and degree of learner autonomy in your online and blended classes. There will be many extreme highs and lows when you initially cede control to your students. Some of your students may prefer the old ways in which they were taught; they might find security in set lectures followed by assessments of that knowledge. Of course, all learners want some sense of learning guarantee that they have obtained the main objectives and can now apply the key concepts. In our fast-changing society, however, such methods no longer suffice. The twenty-first century needs human beings who are independent and self-directed learners. These are the kinds of learners who will find success in companies like Google, Apple, and Amazon.

This chapter addressed the fifth principle of the TEC-VARIETY framework. We now turn to the second half of the framework. In building on ideas related to learner autonomy, choice, control, and flexibility expressed in the current chapter, the sixth principle addresses the relevance and meaningfulness of the learning situation—a key component of any motivational approach or theory related to self-directed or self-determined learning. When learners find meaning in tasks, they will strive to complete them. We hope that by reading the next chapter, you will feel comfortable in designing highly authentic and interesting tasks that are relevant to your learners.

CHAPTER NINE

PRINCIPLE #6 RELEVANCE

(Includes Meaningful, Authentic, and Interesting)

> Always desire to learn something useful.
>
> —Sophocles

We have finally arrived. No, not simply to the start of the second half of this book; rather, we are now located in what many consider to be the crux of any plans for motivating and retaining online learners. We have arrived in the land of learning relevance. The lack of relevance in educational tasks and tests has been an issue for centuries. Reflecting on his scientific training, Albert Einstein once remarked, "One had to cram all this stuff into one's mind for the examinations, whether one liked it or not. This coercion had such a deterring effect on me that, after I had passed the final examination, I found the consideration of any scientific problems distasteful to me for an entire year" (Goodreads, 2013).

Shoving content into his head in order to pass an exam did not sit well for Einstein, nor does it for savvy technology learners of this digital age. Without relevance and its associates —meaningfulness, authentic learning, and personally interesting content and tasks—there will be perpetual distractions that keep learners occupied in alternative activities, including games, texting their friends, and updating their social networking accounts. Suffice it to say, learners will fail to tune in. Make learning interesting and personally meaningful, however, and you will dig into a rich vein of online learning success.

Principle #6 of the TEC-VARIETY framework reminds the course developer or deliverer that, whenever possible, tasks should be relevant and meaningful. In his highly popular treatise on the "First Principles of Instruction," eminent instructional technologist David Merrill (2002), supports the primacy of relevance. He argues that student motivation increases when the activity entails some sense of solving real-world problems or engagement in authentic tasks of some type. When learners can incorporate the new knowledge of a course into their personal or professional lives, they will be more motivated to master that material (Keller, 1983). In some ways, this sixth principle of TEC-VARIETY is strongly linked to the final one related to designing or producing products, given that creating authentic or meaningful tasks often entails building, designing, or crafting something for a wider audience than the instructor. In fact, derivatives of several activities mentioned in this chapter are detailed in Chapter Thirteen on yielding products.

As might be expected, scholars have found that contextually rich cases and scenarios are highly empowering (Williams, 1992). Research from Singer, Marx, Krajcik, and Chambers (2000) at the University of Michigan reveals the importance of tasks that are meaningful and problem-based. Such consistent findings in this area in many ways signal the obvious: learners are drawn to activities which they believe are meaningful, authentic, and relevant (Blumenfeld, Soloway, Marx, Krajcik, Guzdial, & Palincsar, 1991). Much of this research, however, has occurred in physical classroom spaces, not virtual ones. In such places, students can be corralled into an activity or event without much difficulty. In online spaces, however, the degree of task meaningfulness appears to play a more vital role.

As we have discussed, one commonly employed online technique is the use of real-world cases and scenarios. Rich multimedia components (text, audio, animations, graphics, videos, and so forth) can enhance the user experience. Learners can discuss their perspectives and experiences relative to these various scenarios. In addition to cases, learners can respond to a set of reflection questions related to their job, internship, or field placement. Alternatively, they could write case problems and questions for their peers to solve based on their current job situation or field placement (Bonk, Daytner, Daytner, Dennen, & Malikowski, 2001). In such activities, students are practicing their newly learned skills and can compare their answers with peers who might be located anywhere on the planet.

Creating authentic and personally relevant tasks is often not easy. How realistic should your tasks be? Will learners be satisfied with a case presented in text with still images or prefer a more rich and engaging video scenario packed with interesting context variables and cues? In their book, *A Guide to Authentic e-Learning,* Jan Herrington, Tom Reeves, and Ron Oliver (2010) summarize a series of studies that indicate that a high degree of physical reality is typically not that important to the creation of an effective and engaging online learning environment. What is more critical is the development of realistic and engaging ideas within the task or activity, or what they term "cognitive realism." The real question is whether the task fosters the type of problem-solving processes that you want, not whether the activity is presented at the highest level of fidelity. Just like going to the movies, a key part of that success depends on the willingness of the participants, at least temporarily, to suspend their disbelief. If the context of the situation or scenario is acceptable to the learner, the quality of the surrounding graphics and images are far less of a concern.

Herrington et al. (2010), nevertheless, caution that learner sense of authenticity comprises many components. For instance, there must be an authentic context that approximates or reflects the type of knowledge or skills used in the real world. Does it capture the scene or situation well enough? Second, the task selected must be authentic. Does it seem genuine or realistic given the audience, future uses of that skill or competency, and later expectations of assessment? Third, are the resources and guidelines provided to enrich or supplement the task meaningful for the learners to reflect upon and use as they deem necessary? Workplace materials or examples, websites, open access journals and articles, and other primary resources may be appropriate for one audience or point in time, but knowledge in most domains is rapidly changing today. As a result, what is authentic or relevant one year may not be in the next.

Another factor affecting perceived authenticity involves the levels and types of learning supports. Such supports may entail interactive timelines and knowledge maps, guidelines and templates for producing high-quality products, and feedback mechanisms built into the course. Other examples include instructor interventions, peer interaction, and opportunities for reflection and discussion.

Adding to this research base, Kyong-Jee Kim (2009) found that when self-directed online courses offered more interaction and authenticity, often in the form of simulations and animations, they were deemed more motivational by the study participants. A couple of years later, Kim and Frick (2011) reanalyzed this data and discovered that the more students believe that the learning goals are personally relevant, the more likely it is that they will achieve the stated goals embedded within the course learning objectives. It is clear, then, that relevant, meaningful, and authentic e-learning is vital to overall course and program success.

A final motivation-related component of this chapter is "interest." Whereas curiosity may be fleeting and highly situational and then disappear as rapidly as it arose, when learners develop an interest in something, it tends to be more enduring (Reeve, 1996). As might be expected, when a person is interested in a topic, he or she will devote more cognitive resources and attention to the task at hand, which in turn will determine overall comprehension and later recall (Hidi, 1990). Stated another way, if learners are interested in the topic or task, they will make a consistent personal investment in the task. There will be deeper processing of the content with elaboration and organizational strategies, instead of simple reliance on surface-level forms of repetition and rehearsal of content in their heads (Pintrich & DeGroot, 1990). Over time, as we gather rich and meaningful life experiences in an area, we refine and develop our skills, and from this work a unique set of expertise often emerges. As this happens, the value we place on a particular topic or activity increases as well as our prior knowledge or competence about it.

Of course, what is highly valuable for one or a few of your students may not be of importance to everyone in the class. Hence, as noted in the previous chapter, personal choice or selection remains vital.

Technologies for Principle #6: Relevance

For decades there has been talk that some types of educational technologies and activities can foster learning environments where students construct and negotiate knowledge. Seymour Papert (1980, 1993), the father of constructionism, was among the most persuasive advocates of making learning relevant and granting the learner as much control over the activity as possible. From his perspective, such environments would spawn intensely engaged and active learners because they would be creating something new while being immersed in heavy doses of relevancy. As the technologies for the Web have evolved during the past few decades since Papert's (1980) momentous book, *Mindstorms: Children, Computers, and Powerful Ideas*, opportunities for learners to generate knowledge with technology have vastly increased.

An educational technology historian might discuss the levels of authenticity rising from simple games of *Pong* in the early days of personal computing to systems with much higher levels of fidelity (e.g., *World of Warcraft*) in this age of augmented reality, virtual worlds, and haptic or touch-based systems. Now, learners can be fully immersed in the learning process. Though questions remain about whether learning is enhanced as fidelity goes up, there is little doubt that learning feels more realistic. Realism, however, does not necessarily result in perceived relevance of the learning materials or context.

There are numerous ways to enhance the sense of authenticity and relevance of the learning environment. For instance, being up close with guest experts or a group of peers from another country, school, or university via videoconferencing will typically elicit an immediate sense of relevancy. Expert podcasts, such as online interviews of researchers about their latest findings, books, or other publications, lend an air of authenticity to the learning situation. In addition to podcasts, the Web is a storehouse for countless on-demand maps of the weather, travel destinations, census records, and so on. There is a never-ending cascade of data and information that includes business financials for a cost accounting course, survey reports on the latest in teenager technology-use patterns for a course in marketing, voting records for courses in politics or sociology, and current news reports for any course or topic. And the available data may change on a day-to-day or even minute-to-minute basis and require extensive student monitoring, analysis, distillation, report generation, and communication skills.

The Web is filled with opportunities to arouse student interest with authentic tasks. Herrington et al. (2010) list a wide assortment of such activities, including the use of virtual microscopes in biology classes, conducting research on different military battles or on a particular soldier, and exploring the Web for resources related to one or more key issues facing a local government. They also point out that there is a mass of data now available on the Web, including online newspapers going back more than 150 years, online census records for decades in the United States alone, millions of digital videos and open access text documents, and countless pictures and biographies of famous people of past centuries. With this vast array of documents and image files, courses on research methods, history, and social studies as well as any course with an inquiry component lend themselves to innumerable online possibilities. Such resources can be employed to create contextually rich cases and scenarios that foster deep reflection and extended discussions (Williams, 1992).

Of course, the technological resources for data gathering and analysis will only become richer in the coming decades. Some of these ideas will become clearer after reading the various activities detailed in the next section of this chapter.

Ten Online Activities in Principle #6: Relevance

As in the five previous chapters, there are 10 activities for Principle #6. Keep in mind, however, that aspects of personal relevancy are probably embedded in most of the 100 activities described in this book. The extensive possibilities for relevant, meaningful, authentic, and personally interesting activities in this age of the Internet made the selection of the 10 activities outlined in this chapter a particularly difficult task. Note also that these 10 activities do not appear in any particular order of importance or pragmatic use; there is no one task or activity that we deem to be any more meaningful or authentic than any other. Ideally, several of them can serve as a base for your personal thinking about this topic.

Activity 51. Multimedia Case Vignettes and Decision Making

Description and Purpose of Activity. Students enjoy being close to the content that they are expected to master. Case vignettes and scenarios are one such opportunity. Since the times of Socrates and Plato in ancient Athens, cases have been used to foster student analysis, discrimination, and evaluation skills. The cases and scenarios insightfully employed in the days of Plato's Academy, however, were orally delivered. Today, as Internet bandwidth rises, storage capacities expand, costs of such storage drop, and software becomes simpler to use and deploy, it is relatively easy to add a multimedia component to such cases in the form of animations, simulations, graphics, pictures, videos, and sound. Each layer of context can help offer the learner a distinct learning cue (Mayer, 2001). At the same time, too many forms of media can be distractive and present a heavy cognitive burden on the learner (Moreno & Mayer, 1999). The amount and types of media you use, therefore, need to be thoughtfully selected and integrated.

Rich multimedia cases have wide acceptability and applicability in higher education settings, especially as the average age of a college student rises and the type of student shifts from full-time young adults to middle-aged adult learners in the workplace. With their years of practical experience, those more seasoned learners can often relate to contextually rich stories as well as offer personal cases of their own.

Not surprisingly, many professional schools are known for their use of case situations. Education cases may be embedded in a school context with video interviews of teachers, principals, and parents as well as the interview transcripts, classroom and student pictures, and detailed problematic situations. Business law cases can show plaintiffs, defendants, juries, judges, witnesses, and the various complex issues that they are dealing with, and possibly include a simulation of key court proceedings. Business management and cost accounting cases, on the other hand, could include graphs detailing days of inventory items, links to financial statements over a period of time, animations depicting particular problems or situations, and descriptions of prior accounting or business management practices.

Skills and Objectives. Includes critical thinking skills such as inferring, analyzing details, deductive and inductive reasoning, comparing and contrasting, evaluation or judgment, breaking down case situations or problems into component parts, and the application of concepts and terminology to real-world situations. Multimedia cases also foster the ability to sift through extensive content and prioritize masses of information, and, accordingly, include reflection skills as well as learning in a context.

Advice and Ideas. One of our colleagues, Mark Braun, a pathology professor at Indiana University, has designed a series of modules for second-year medical students engaged in a year-long general and systemic pathology course. In the 25 units that students complete during the year, each one has clinical vignettes that represent a common medical condition (e.g., an elderly man with chest pain, a woman with morning stiffness, a man with abdominal pain, a young woman with blindness, and the like). The modules typically are sequenced at the beginning of each unit, thereby allowing students to learn the content at their own pace. Along with each module there is an online graded component. According to Dr. Braun, these cases foster clinical application of the course content.

There are many forms of media used in these cases. For instance, most are patient-interview driven. As students work through them, additional information is offered such as medical history, lab tests, and X-rays. Students can access the results of chest X-rays, blood counts, chemistry profiles (e.g., calcium glucose, cholesterol, protein, uric acid, and so on). Different slides offer images and descriptions of various diseases (e.g., pulmonary, cardiovascular, liver, and infectious diseases). Opportunities for content review dovetail with the progression of each case. Naturally, every case concludes with students making a list of plausible diagnoses, before the correct diagnosis is provided. Braun uses a set of 10 to 15 nongraded and self-paced online quiz questions that cover the main points of each module. After students learn their scores, they can revisit and complete each module as many times as they wish. Questions on their graded exams are drawn from these self-paced clinical cases.

Braun's case-based learning approach is a splendid example of how to use Web resources to enable more authentic and meaningful forms of learning. His surveys and evaluations of the cases confirm that students find them very relevant to the course because they closely mimic their real-world encounters in later clinical experiences. Professor Braun cautions, however, that the creation of these modules has been a multiyear process. Depending on their complexity, each module can take up to several weeks or even a month to develop fully and deploy. On average, case creation time is roughly 40 to 60 hours. And though they are already quite well received by his students, Braun hopes to embed even greater interactivity in the future, including the use of more animations and multimedia components.

The previous example is but one kind of multimedia case. You might explore Braun's cases and others and reflect on your own discipline or content area. Not everyone has the time, technology skills, and interests of Professor Braun. Fortunately, nearly every field likely has a rich array of cases or scenarios that exist online in places like MERLOT, Connexions, and the Open CourseWare Consortium. Those in K–12 settings might explore Curriki, Share My Lesson, and HippoCampus.

Each country around the world probably has similar specific content available at a government, nonprofit, or university site. For example, in terms of science-based curricula resources in New Zealand, where Khoo is employed, there is the Science Learning Hub and the New Zealand Biotechnology Learning Hub. Both provide freely available contextualized multimedia resources rich with teaching strategies, interactive content, and timelines for teachers to promote student interest and engagement in science. These websites also contain contacts and links to real-life scientists as well as scientific organizations. When accessing these experts and organizations, teachers and their students can communicate, ask questions, and pursue personal interests and ideas so that they can better understand the connections and relevance of scientific research to their everyday lives.

Variations and Extensions. Consider creating a repository of case solutions from previous semesters or versions of the course. You could also record and post all-time high scores as a means of motivating students to take the cases seriously. Activities can be designed to critique, extend, and combine previous case solutions. In addition, consider designing a set of more difficult challenge cases, possibly enlisting former students who are now practicing in the field to serve as online mentors or tutors to offer advice to students when they get stuck or have a question.

Key Instructional Considerations

> Risk index: Medium
> Time index: Medium to High
> > (depending on whether usable case materials or resources exist)
> Cost index: Medium to High
> > (depending on whether usable case materials or resources exist)
> Learner-centered index: Medium
> Duration of the learning activity: 1–4 weeks or throughout the course as needed

Activity 52. Job Connection and Strategic Planning Papers

Description and Purpose of Activity. One of the best ways to establish meaningful and authentic tasks is to link them to students' personal or professional lives outside the course or program of study. If there is an audience beyond the instructor, there is greater likelihood that student ideas or products will be shared, discussed, and potentially acknowledged and even celebrated. Such is the case of job connection and strategic planning papers. When learners can connect course content to their work lives and perhaps immediately apply it, they obtain professional recognition for their coursework and validation that what they have taken the time to study can have an impact in their work lives on a daily basis. For instance, they may receive recognition in the form of praise, bonuses, assignments to interesting projects, and even new positions or job duties.

A job connection or application paper basically forces learners to think about how one or more course concepts could be applied in their particular job setting. Students who previously may have thought that they were going to be wasting time in a course often make a 180-degree mental shift and become excited when faced with work-related possibilities.

Skills and Objectives. Includes student choice, resource exploration and selection, sharing, presentation and communication skills, and learner interaction and feedback. This technique temporarily places students in the role of instructor.

Advice and Ideas. Give students some examples of job connection or application papers from previous semesters. If they are thinking about doing a strategic planning document, action research project, or some type of technical report for a particular organization or a department or unit within it, share relatively recent examples to scan through. Perhaps ask prior students of the course to offer suggestions on how to locate sample reports and insights on achieving success in this task. The paper might be modest in length (e.g., 2 to 3 single-spaced pages) or a much longer technical report or strategic plan. It is vital that students obtain approval for their initial idea before commencing—not only from the instructor, but possibly also from their work supervisor(s).

Be sure to post your evaluation criteria and grading rubrics ahead of time. Alternatively, you could have students work in small groups to create rubrics for final project evaluations. Consider also offering students the option of turning in drafts of their work for feedback from peers or the instructor. Any feedback given should be genuine, timely, and specific. Try to incorporate episodes of meaningful peer feedback and support whenever possible.

Variations and Extensions. There are a slew of variations for a job connection or application paper. For instance, the papers can be anonymously entered into a class competition in which peers or external experts vote on the best ones, with awards handed out for the highest-rated papers. As part of such a competition, top papers can be placed in an online gallery of papers for students to read through in the following years. Student papers can also be repackaged into an online course compendium, uploaded as a digital book to a website like BookRix, or made into a wikibook at Wikispaces, PBworks, or Wikibooks which can be modified and extended by students in future semesters of the course, or by peers around the world in similar courses.

Key Instructional Considerations

Risk index: Low
Time index: Medium to High
Cost index: Low
Learner-centered index: High
Duration of the learning activity: 1–2 weeks during the semester (if a brief paper);
	4–5 weeks (if a final project or strategic planning document)

Activity 53. Wiki Editing Projects (including Wikipedia)

Description and Purpose of Activity. Some online tasks and activities have benefits inside as well as outside the class. Such is the case of student projects to edit, or more significantly, to improve a wiki resource of some type. For example, a class of students could edit and expand a wiki glossary or wikibook from previous semesters of the course. They could update a database of articles in a wiki, or add to editorial content and critique comments made in a wiki on one or more research articles. In the midst of such a project, they should begin to understand how knowledge, at least in some fields, is socially constructed and negotiated. They may also begin to grasp the fluidity and impermanency of text in a wiki, where anyone can edit, change, add, combine, remix, or delete ideas.

There are a series of initiatives today to improve the quality of Wikipedia pages. As an example, the Wikipedia Education program mobilized graduate students from around the world enrolled in public policy courses and programs to edit Wikipedia pages as a means to enhance the use of Wikipedia as a teaching tool or platform. Georgetown University, Indiana University, Harvard, and George Washington University were among those participating in the public policy project (Kolowich, 2010). Other organizations involved include the Moscow Institute of Physics and Technology and universities in Mexico and Macedonia (Wikipedia Education Program, 2012). To foster success, students in public policy courses were specially trained by Wikipedia Ambassadors to participate.

With such a project, individual students as well as student teams contribute to the growing knowledge base in a field. As an additional benefit, they have to be extremely meticulous because untold people will browse and read these open access articles. In many graduate courses, students conduct literature reviews and then synthesize and summarize what they have found. Such a project vastly extends the potential audience and purpose of student coursework.

Skills and Objectives. Includes paying attention to detail, Web searching and filtering, synthesis skills, the ability to digest and condense extensive amounts of knowledge, write for a generalized audience, handle feedback, collaborate in a team, and negotiate knowledge.

Advice and Ideas. Consider assigning students to edit Wikipedia pages in your discipline. Alternatively, you could become part of an education project sponsored by the Wikimedia Foundation to improve Wikipedia. Perhaps assign students specific pages or topics to read and edit in Wikipedia or have them sign up in a wiki for the pages that they would prefer to work on.

The role of the instructor is crucial in such an activity. First of all, the instructor should set clear expectations including the type and amount of edits expected, the respective due dates and timelines for the project, and the associated assessment or grading criteria. Second, if possible, examples of work from previous semesters should also be made available. Third, the instructor should also be involved in the project as a role model. Fourth, online scaffolds or job aids should be created to help guide the learner. At the end of the module or semester, student progress on different Wikipedia pages should be shared with the class.

Variations and Extensions. Wikipedia editing could take place across sections of the course or in collaboration with other schools or universities. You could create a competition for best improvements made to a Wikipedia page, possibly offering awards for different categories of achievement.

Key Instructional Considerations

Risk index: Medium
Time index: High
Cost index: Low
Learner-centered index: High
Duration of the learning activity: Throughout the course or as needed

Activity 54. Language Learning Conversations and Mentoring

Description and Purpose of Activity. The tools and resources for learning a language have proliferated during the past decade. Lesson guides, podcasts, word lists, exercises, dictionaries, thesauruses, and other referenceware are found in many of them. But that's just a start! Some provide interactive flashcards, pronunciation labs, grammar lessons, voice games, quizzes, and progress reports. Relevant language learning tools can be found at About.com (e.g., ESL, French, German, Italian, Japanese, Mandarin, Spanish), BBC Languages, ChinesePod, Coffee Break Spanish, Duolingo, Learn-Korean.net, LoMasTV, Mango Languages, and Japanese Online.

Increasingly, language learning tools and systems extend beyond such technologies and resources to the human side of learning. A conversational partner or set of partners may assist in an online chat, peer-to-peer conversation class, and general online tutoring and mentoring sessions. Systems that foster such interaction include Babbel, italki, Livemocha, The Mixxer, Palabea, PalTalk, and Voxopop. Livemocha, which started in 2007 and reached over 14 million users from 195 countries by 2012, was recently acquired by Rosetta Stone. With Livemocha, you can sign up to take or teach pretty much any language. The next generation of Web-based language learning is found at English Central where you can compare your speech delivery to those given by famous people like Steve Jobs, Lady Gaga, and Angelina Jolie.

These systems can be used to supplement student learning while extending the resources available in a class. Each resource adds something unique; however, the ones that help situate student learning in a context are likely the most powerful. As a result, tools to practice language skills with human or computer feedback can accelerate and elevate student mastery of a language. No longer must a language instructor rely solely on notes, lectures, and selected text materials.

Skills and Objectives. Includes choice, engagement, feedback, interactivity, flexibility, language comprehension and communication skills, speaking in a context, skill discrimination, and goal setting. Such tools and resources can foster basic language learning skills and competencies as well as more advanced language competencies.

Advice and Ideas. Instructors and instructional designers should review the online language learning tools, programs, and systems mentioned here and listed in the Web resources associated with this chapter. As you do, make note of the features and ease of use of each system. In particular, explore the systems that have online conversation options. After finding one or more online language learning tools that are appropriate for your course, ask your students to become members of one and acquire a language learning partner. Alternatively, if none of the language exchange resources you review are appropriate for your learners or content area, find and contact one or more scholars or experts from your language area to talk to your students via Skype or Google Hangouts.

Variations and Extensions. Assign students to language partners within the class to practice their conversational skills using Skype, Google Hangouts, or some other technology. Try pairing students by interest, location, language competence, confidence (less confident with more confident), or some other dimension. When their conversations are done, have students write a reflection paper or create a term glossary based on their experiences.

Another idea is to contact instructors from other countries who might be interested in a cross-institutional partnership between their students and yours; for example, the students can engage in a joint project across regions of the world that requires them to practice their language skills in context-sensitive ways. Once again, a reflection paper or creation of a term glossary might be assigned as the capstone experience.

Key Instructional Considerations

Risk index: Medium
Time index: High
Cost index: Low
Learner-centered index: High
Duration of the learning activity: Weekly or as needed

Activity 55. Online Current News Feeds and Streaming Data

Description and Purpose of Activity. Similar to Activity #21, "Online Events in the News" (Chapter Six), this activity builds from emerging news stories and live data. Each day, there are unique and context-rich events that occur and are quickly reported. When they do, the data, videos, reports, interviews, animations, reactions, and so forth pour in. Such immediate news feeds are now an expected part of our daily lives; as events unfold, different pieces of data emerge and are offered in ways to arouse people's interest. Hence, they link to Principle #3 on curiosity.

Savvy instructors, however, can do more with such reports than simply grab the attention of learners. Effective online and blended learning instructors find ways to push student thinking about that data or report. How does it relate to the topics or concepts of a course or perhaps extend these subject areas in new directions? How might such data change commonly held scientific views of some phenomena? What analyses and special reports could the class make with such data?

This particular activity focuses on the live and fast-changing data as it is shared. Static news reports and press releases have existed for eons. Today, however, we can access and subscribe to live news feeds. There are videostreams of weather maps related to tropical storms and hurricanes as they form and later expand to cause havoc. There are pitch-by-pitch baseball games on display in ESPN.com as well as many other live sporting events. Rock concerts, stock market ticker tapes, political convention polls and speeches, and religious gatherings are streamed live each day on the BBC, CNN Live, CNN International, MSNBC, Fox News, and Yahoo! News. Science experiments and research findings are also instantaneously streamed for all to witness on Discovery News or Explor.TV. And many institutions of higher learning and other organizations are using Livestream and Ustream to broadcast their unique news and events. With such connections, you can get live feeds of sharks and turtles from the Monterey Bay Aquarium, daily events at NASA, and speeches from politicians like Hillary Clinton (USA), Park Geun-hye (South Korea), Jean-Marc Ayrault (France), Julia Gillard (Australia), or David Cameron (UK).

Remember the explosion aboard the Deepwater Horizon oil rig on April 20, 2010? An underwater Webcam at the site of the famous BP oil spill during the spring and summer of 2010 offered live shots of the 53,000 barrels (2.2 million gallons) of oil leaking each day until it was repaired (Hoch, 2010). Fortunately, with pressure from the US Congress, the vast majority of the time BP kept open the live video feed of the ruptured pipe that was gushing oil into the Gulf of Mexico. CNN, PBS, and other news agencies broadcasted the flow as BP attempted to seal the well with "top kill" and other procedures (CNN, 2010).

Now, imagine teaching a petroleum engineering course or one on safety management during that time. How could you use such live data feeds to teach issues of safety, ethics, leadership, teamwork, or management? Perhaps students in a mathematics course could run comprehensive calculations on how much marshland was being affected by this oil disaster. Alternatively, they might contact scientists, engineers, BP officials, community leaders, and reporters for updates on the data and their impact.

A similar explosion of media was received when a tsunami struck the northeast coast of Japan on March 11, 2011, killing over 15,000 people and injuring more than 6,000 others (Harris, 2012). There were live video feeds, twitter and blog posts, news reports, pictures, and a barrage of news-related announcements (e.g., CNN, 2011; Young, 2011). The pool of data was being updated every few seconds. These types of live streaming events will become increasingly commonplace in the coming decades. Students will expect course content to be supplemented with such materials; thus, it is vital to begin to design innovative forms of instruction to incorporate this new technology.

Skills and Objectives. Includes linking new content knowledge to current and fast-changing events in the news, encoding news information both verbally and visually, learner curiosity in course content, observational skills, and concept application. This technique extends the course to the real world, including facts, trends, ideas, and opinions that may not have been addressed otherwise. It forces students to analyze such data in rapid sequences.

Advice and Ideas. Students can write articles or reports and design presentations based on the live data, possibly linking together information from two or more related news sources. In mathematics or statistics classes, they could perform specific calculations or analyses based on the data that have been provided. Teams, in fact, could compete in making meaningful predictions or forecasts related to the data.

There is a never-ending supply of such data available each day. Keep searching for relevant news and reports that can augment or enhance what is known in your field or subject area. Perhaps assign your students to find such data on a weekly or monthly basis.

Variations and Extensions. An instructor could have students search for the latest news data and reports related to the class and post them to a wiki or course discussion forum. Consider offering bonus points for finding and sharing high-quality content that is relevant to your courses. Perhaps have students take two of more of these resources and write compare and contrast papers or peer critiques of each website or resource.

Key Instructional Considerations

Risk index: Medium
Time index: Medium
Cost index: Low
Learner-centered index: High
Duration of the learning activity: Throughout the course or as needed

Activity 56. Cross-Cultural Web Conferencing and Interactions

Description and Purpose of Activity. As Merry Merryfield (2007) states, "By introducing students to diverse people within a country, a teacher can help students learn to appreciate complexity within cultures and the dynamics of how cultures change" (p. 270). She further argues that new technologies for globalization flatten the educational world but simultaneously challenge us to develop curricula that help introduce students to the diverse people and cultures of the world. Given this, some may suggest that this activity is the most vital idea described in this book.

Interactive videoconferencing technology and simple laptop Webcams provide convenient ways to connect learners with experts and speakers from remote locations (Lee & Bonk, 2013). From primary grades to MBA classrooms to military training units, interactive and collaborative technologies offer unique opportunities for increased global awareness and understanding through engaging presentations, discussions, and debates (Lee & Hutton, 2007; Schrage, 1990). During such events, learners from young to old can better understand the life experiences, struggles, and daily life patterns of those in vastly different environments. For decades, educators have argued for the importance of global understanding, social perspective taking (Selman, 1980), and curricula that promote cross-cultural understanding and world peace (Longview, 2008; Merryfield, 2007, 2008; Merryfield & Kasai, 2009; Riel, 1993; Schrum, 1991).

Much research validates these arguments. For instance, Sugar and Bonk (1998) found that sharing perspectives with Internet technology can enhance perspective taking and the social cognitive abilities of young learners. Importantly, in this study, students asked higher levels of questions when engaging in collaborative role play online.

Intriguing ethnographic research from Mimi Lee at the University of Houston details how technology such as videoconferencing and Web conferencing can connect young learners in previously isolated or rural parts of the world to experts while fostering greater cross-cultural awareness and understanding (Lee & Hutton, 2007). As Lee astutely argues, intercultural educational events can promote shared understanding, dignity, respect, and the exchange of current information as well as enhanced interpersonal skills (Lee 2007, 2010). More recently, she and Bonk recapped a series of Web conferencing and videoconferencing events that they have individually used with guest experts during the past decade or two to help apprenticeship learners into a specific field or topic (Lee & Bonk, 2013). What becomes clear is that the pedagogical possibilities for online apprenticeship and global education continue to expand in exciting directions.

At the K–12 level, there are many global education projects for instructors to select from, including the Flat Classrooms Project, ePals, iEARN, TakingITGlobal, RoundSquare, the World Class–World Vision Canada, and so on. In Seeds of Empowerment, for instance, Paul Kim and his colleagues at Stanford have used mobile storytelling among Palestinian and Israeli youth and with young people in Rwanda, Tanzania, and India to show how technology might lead to greater cross-cultural awareness as well as higher-order thinking skills (Buckner & Kim, 2012; Kim, Higashi, Gonzales, Carillo, Gàrate, & Lee, 2011). For those in higher education settings, programs such as Soliya can connect your students to those in the Middle East. Before and after such videoconferencing events, learners can rely on other learning technologies to gather data on and discuss a particular culture or topic. Researchers have noted that the benefits of collaborative technologies such as e-mail, chat, asynchronous conferencing, and videoconferencing include greater perspective taking, critical thinking, task engagement, and overall sensitivity to cultural differences (Bonk, Appelman, & Hay, 1996; Merryfield, 2003). These types of tasks, therefore, should be well planned for maximum impact and engagement.

Skills and Objectives. Includes the appreciation of multiple perspectives and diversity, interpersonal and intercultural skills, global and cultural awareness, critical thinking, feedback, interactivity, creative expression, student autonomy, exploration, knowledge construction and negotiation, student participatory learning, and active learning. Many additional benefits of global and cross-cultural interaction are likely but difficult to specify in advance.

Advice and Ideas. There are unlimited possibilities for cross-cultural Web conferencing today. World experts as well as students from other cultures can enter your course at any time and often without much planning or prior notice. Such an activity can be a singular course event or part of a series of meetings. Those who are more ambitious might consider arranging for students across different classes or locations to work on collaborative projects and share the final results during a videoconferencing session. As part of those efforts, students in crosscultural teams could jointly write books or proposals, create online news shows, or peer critique each other's work.

Following an interactive videoconference, students could create a digital story of what they have learned from the experience and post it on YouTube. Alternatively, you could have them reflect on their learning in a blog or podcast, including listing questions from the session for others to answer, or creating online photo albums or scrapbooks of objects and cultural artifacts of those with whom they have corresponded. At the macro level, the entire class could create and maintain a wiki with audio, video, and text-based Web resources of that culture. Whatever the topic (e.g., Hungarian Gypsy music, Japanese Zen gardens, music from Zimbabwe, or Mexico's Day of the Dead) (Lee & Hutton, 2007), there are new ways to communicate that open up avenues to mitigate the stereotypes and misconceptions that are sometimes transmitted when the main source of information about people of other cultures is limited to mass media.

Variations and Extensions. The cross-cultural Web conference can be a weekly or monthly course event. Before each session, students could vote on the people or places around the world to meet or which events to engage in. Once you determine a set of destinations or cultural events, write to colleagues, Twitter followers, or friends on Facebook or LinkedIn for recommendations, or make new connections with those at the respective locations. Be clear about the level and type of participation you are asking of others.

Key Instructional Considerations

Risk index: Medium to High
Time index: Medium
Cost index: Low to High (depend on the system selected)
Learner-centered index: High
Duration of the learning activity: 1 week or session as needed

Activity 57. Instructor Online Video Demonstrations

Description and Purpose of Activity. For decades, video has been used to anchor instruction in a familiar and replayable event or episode sequence. John Bransford and his colleagues in the Cognition and Technology Group at Vanderbilt (CTGV) (1990, 1991) used short snippets from movies like *Raiders of the Lost Ark* to teach complex science and math concepts in a meaningful and interactive way. The rich video segments that they later produced in the "Jasper Woodbury" series could be used to situate learning in a story or context from which students will later discuss, problem solve, and reflect. As that happens, knowledge becomes more richly connected instead of inert.

A key to these video episodes was the macro context within each of them that provided a shared learning space that could be replayed and revisited as needed. Today, there are millions of shared online videos that have the potential to anchor student learning, including those found in TVLesson, TED, Academic Earth, BBC Videos, LinkTV, Big Think, and MIT World. Such portals of shared online video continue to expand. Bonk has created a portal of such websites and has published an article that describes 10 learner-centered uses of such video as well as 10 other activities that are instructor selected or coordinated (Bonk, 2011).

In addition to the work of John Bransford, many educational psychologists such as David Ausubel (1978) argue that knowledge is hierarchically organized. As a result, educators should find ways to help learners subsume new concepts and ideas within their prior experiences. Ausubel suggested that when you link new terms and concepts to learners' prior knowledge, that information is going to be richly and meaningfully anchored or attached to what they already know. Shared online videos like YouTube, YouTube EDU, SchoolTube, and MedTube, therefore, can foster such new conceptual ties.

The shared video clip can be an advance organizer for later instruction and discussion, providing the conceptual connections or glue among the learning concepts that are deemed vital for basic factual information and higher-order thinking skills. Video clips guide learner attention to critical elements of the learning module or concept (Pan, Sen, Starett, Bonk, Rodgers, Tikoo, & Powell, 2012). When effectively employed, instructors and instructional designers can help learners organize the content and draw out the new relationships that are forming.

A third theoretical perspective comes from Allan Paivio from the psychology department at the University of Western Ontario in Canada. Paivio (1986) posited that visual information is stored separately from verbal information in long-term memory. His research demonstrated that when learners possess text or verbal components as well as images or visual components, that the learning will be more strongly encoded; what was once tip-of-the-tongue knowledge (i.e., available with sufficient prompting) is now more easily accessible and usable. He called this concept dual coding theory (Paivio, 1991). The use of shared online video in fully online and blended courses, as well as F2F ones, is an example of dual coding in action when students also have lecture and textbook materials. With short video clips from YouTube, TED Ed, or CNN to start a class or unit, there is immense learning power, and the class often explodes with energy and enthusiasm.

So much is now possible with the tens of millions of shared online videos available today that can be employed as concept anchors for instruction. Importantly, "anchoring instruction with online video content can happen at any moment—at the start of class, at the end, or whenever deemed necessary or advantageous" (Bonk, 2011, p. 20). It is now vital for instructors to begin to reflect on the power of such online video technology, to experiment with its use, and to share the results. With anchored instruction nearly any lesson can quickly come alive.

Skills and Objectives. Includes analysis and evaluation skills, reflection, grasping visual cues, forming conceptual linkages, and deeper understanding of course content. Another key goal is to extend student learning beyond prepackaged course materials or lectures developed and delivered by the instructor. You can update instruction with rich new video content that has yet to find its way into books. Such content will appeal to students who are visual learners as well as those who prefer multimodal learning activities to solely text-based ones.

Advice and Ideas. As indicated, there are dozens of ways to use shared online video; some are more instructor-centered and some are more learner-centered (Bonk, 2011). Some instructors may employ them at the start of a class or unit as a conceptual anchor, whereas others may use them selectively to demonstrate key concepts as they lecture or as students are exposed to different portions of the course content. Preferably, the videos will be short. In fact, they might be extremely short. If you discover a relatively lengthy YouTube video that provides an excellent overview of a concept or idea, consider using a tool like TubeChop that enables you to quickly and easily select the precise clip of the video you want to show; in many cases, a mere 10 seconds may prove long enough to get the point across.

You can give students a handout or think sheet to reflect on the concepts embedded in each video listed or shown in class. There could also be an ending quiz, crossword puzzle activity, or general discussion about the different concepts explored in the videos shown. For his learning theories class, Bonk has developed a portal of shared online videos for each week or unit of the course. He has videos of famous psychologists and researchers such as B. F. Skinner, Ivan Pavlov, Jean Piaget, John Watson, Lev Vygotsky, and Albert Bandura that explain different concepts from behavioral theory, cognitive theory, constructivism, social learning theory, and others. In the behavioral ones, for instance, there are demonstrations of positive and negative reinforcement, shaping, and fixed and variable schedules of reinforcement. In his live classes, he might spontaneously pause the video and ask students to yell out key concepts that they have observed. Of course, they must also explain the concepts that they have observed.

If you are teaching a fully online course, such video demonstrations could take place during weekly synchronous sessions, if applicable. Alternatively, students could watch selected shared online videos on their own and discuss the concepts learned in a discussion forum. That is the approach that we tend to use in our own online courses.

It is vital to keep updating the videos used for demonstrating course concepts. First of all, new concepts and associated videos might emerge. Second, archival video footage of famous researchers may be found and posted online. Third, movie and television show episodes might exemplify key course concepts. Be on the lookout for them.

We have found that the use of shared online video clips often elevates the class discussion and brings a class community to life. Concepts and ideas that were once difficult to explain or grasp now begin to make sense to students. Importantly, because many video segments are relatively short, instructors do not have to give up much class time. We recommend that you keep the video activity short. In fact, a video of two or three minutes typically suffices. As indicated earlier, it often just needs to be a few seconds. When effectively used, the learning payoff is potentially immense as the learner can now recall the information through both verbal and visual channels.

Variations and Extensions. Instead of the instructor of a blended learning course deciding when to pause the video and asking students to yell out concepts that they observe, the students could yell "Pause!" at any moment in the video sequence to make their observations. In addition, the instructor could replay a video one or two more times while prompting the class to reflect on additional concepts embedded in it that they forgot to mention in their initial viewings.

Other variations include students creating the shared online video demonstrations and anchors to illustrate key course concepts. For instance, each student could be assigned to find and bring one video to class and explain how the clip is related to course concepts. In a fully online course, students can post these videos to a specific discussion forum or course wiki. A coinciding handout of videos and concepts is recommended. Consider creating competitions for finding the most appealing or highest-rated clips. Students can also use shared online videos to illustrate pro and con sides of debates (Bonk, 2011).

Key Instructional Considerations

Risk index: Medium
Time index: Low to Medium
Cost index: Low
Learner-centered index: Medium
Duration of the learning activity: Anytime as needed

Activity 58. Video Study Guides, Tutorials, and Microlectures

Description and Purpose of Activity. Sometimes relevance and meaningfulness can be found in a brief recap or review of articles of key points in a lecture or book chapter. Today, video snippets might also be used in such an activity. Since the late 1950s, students have been using CliffsNotes as a means to learn a topic. Why? Students simply want more avenues to master the content that they know they will be tested on. In the past, supplemental course resources from CliffsNotes as well as all major book publishers were primarily text-based. Today, such resources are increasingly in video format. Just like movie trailers, many books, lab projects, and scholarly competitions come with video supplements and introductory aids. Thousands of video tutorials for mathematics, science, English, and technology now exist at Sophia, LearnZillion, Grovo, the Khan Academy, Lynda.com, and WatchKnowLearn.

CliffsNotes, in fact, recently announced that they will build a series of one- and five-minute short video study guides for major works of literature such as *Romeo and Juliet, The Scarlet Letter,* and *The Odyssey* (Collins, 2011). Students will not simply watch them but will be able to comment on them as well. Other websites like 60 Second Recap have been offering such recaps for several years now. The 60 Second Recap website includes most popular English literature such as *Fahrenheit 451, The Adventures of Huckleberry Finn, Macbeth, The Catcher in the Rye,* and *A Tale of Two Cities.* Each book recap has 10 one-minute videos including a teaser trailer, the overview, the plot, meet the cast, themes, in conclusion, and a few other video segments specific to that particular book.

Students can use such videos when they need to and as many times as they want. As described in the previous activity, the videos provide a context for their discussion and overall learning of each book (Brown, Collins, & Duguid, 1989). In addition, as Paivio (1986) indicated, such resources extend learning beyond text to visual or episodic memory, thereby increasing retention of that information. As in anchored instruction, such videos also provide a commonly shared experience for learners to discuss and reflect upon the concepts and ideas (The Cognition and Technology Group at Vanderbilt, 1990, 1991). The videos can also be used as an advance organizer for later class discussions, lectures, and other activities (Ausubel, 1978). Finally, as part of a participatory learning culture, these videos can be watched, shared, or commented on (Brown, 2006; Brown & Adler, 2008). There are countless ways that these kinds of video tutorials and study guides will play a role in teaching and learning in the coming years.

Skills and Objectives. Includes choice and selection of content; content review; reflection; grasping themes, plots, and main points; forming conceptual linkages; and deeper understanding of course content. Such material offers a chance to review content at a place and time that is most convenient; hence, the learning experience is more personalized.

Advice and Ideas. Inform students of the various video tutorial and study guide websites in your field, and discuss how students in previous semesters have used them. Many course activities can spin off from these sources. First, students might nominate the videos or study guides that offer the most conceptual linkages to your course. Those that garner the most votes are the winners. Second, online discussion forums could be established for each video tutorial and study guide site. Third, students could suggest test questions based on the sites that they have observed. Fourth, students could recap each respective video in a text transcript or set of guidelines in a wiki.

Another adaptation of this idea is for the instructor to create his or her own series of one- to three-minute lectures. Such microlectures are used in places like San Juan College in New Mexico in courses on occupational safety, veterinary studies, reading, and tribal governance (Shieh, 2009). In these courses, instructors introduce key course concepts in video format to serve as a lesson overview or advance organizer for later learning. As such, they prime the learner to complete later tasks and assignments. Boiling lectures down to such key points forces the learner to reflect on the value and importance of different course concepts and to prioritize them. Alternatively, students could create these microlectures with the best ones posted to a student video gallery.

Variations and Extensions. Consider asking your students to draft critiques or reviews of the videos in one or more video tutorial, study guide, or microlecture sites. Student reviews could also be in a video format and perhaps placed in a YouTube channel. Alternatively, younger students can post their own video recaps of the respective books that they have read in ClubRecap, an online community of learners for 60 Second Recap.

Key Instructional Considerations

Risk index: Low
Time index: Medium
Cost index: Low
Learner-centered index: Medium
Duration of the learning activity: Anytime as needed

Activity 59. Pubcasts and Researcher Interviews

Description and Purpose of Activity. One way to help students connect with research that they are reading is to embed supplemental or blended content from the Web. Fortunately, opportunities for blended learning have exploded during the past decade. Prior to the emergence of the Internet as a learning tool, students were fortunate to hear from a book author or researcher via a letter, e-mail, or telephone call. The privileged few might interact with that person when at a conference or during a rare colloquium appearance on campus or in the local community.

Today the potential to enhance course content with the scholars, experts, researchers, or known authorities on a topic or trend have mushroomed well beyond what any sane person might have predicted a few decades ago. A short visit to the Web will yield you the slides that the researcher, whose article you have been assigned, used to explain a new discovery, research finding, or trend. In addition you will likely discover the papers and proceedings that he presented at a recent conference.

One particularly promising technique is to obtain a podcast or video interview of a researcher or scholar about her new findings or book. A video connected to or embedded within a research article is called a "pubcast." The pubcast can be enhanced when there is video timecode or an index that you can use to select snippets of the author interview that relate to certain sections of the published article.

The term "pubcast" was coined by Phil Boune, cofounder of SciVee, a Web 2.0 science-related website (Hane, 2007). SciVee, which was formed back in 2007, is a YouTube-like outlet for scientific research, which allows scientists to communicate their research findings and other works in an enriched multimedia format. SciVee journals include the *American Journal of Preventive Medicine, Bioscience, Computers & Geosciences,* the *Journal of Nutrition,* and many more. Another example of a journal with videos is the *Journal of Visualized Experiments* (JoVE) which is a PubMed-indexed video journal. Notably, JoVE includes rich animations of concepts and procedures with its articles.

For scientists, the pubcast is a monumental innovation. With this invention, seminal scientific research can be explained orally to the masses, not just in text or to those fortunate enough to attend the scientific conference where it was announced or to subscribe to the journal where it was later published. Using SciVee and JoVE, scientists and even ordinary people can see the experiments of researchers around the world, not simply read about them. In this way, the pubcast broadens and speeds up the dissemination and understanding of any breakthroughs and discoveries as well as significant modifications or extensions of existing scientific knowledge.

In SciVee, you will often find very sophisticated and narrowly focused studies with interviews of one or more authors. One such pubcast is titled, "Early participation in prenatal food supplementation program ameliorates the negative association of food insecurity with quality of maternal-infant interaction." In it, Amy Frith of Ithaca College reads her article while a set of slides or images parallel her talk (see Figure 9.1).

Others might explore important areas such as "The deceptive nature of UVA-tanning versus the modest protective effects of UVB-tanning on human skin." Imagine how effective video footage would be with that research paper and what an impact it could have on undergraduate college students just prior to spring break. Other topics found at SciVee are concerned with such diverse topics as drinking water in Africa, bionic legs, rocks in Antarctica, early cancer screening, the rising of marshes and sea levels, visualizing galaxies, bonobos and chimpanzees, skin-mounted electronics, and disappearing red shrimp.

SciVee is not just a place for one-way communication from researchers to readers. In fact, others can respond with pubcasts of their own or comment on a pubcast. For learners, a pubcast can help them see the relevancy of the research that they might not have grasped when reading a textbook or research article. Author insights can arouse learner interest in the topic. In general, there is an enhanced sense of learning authenticity when supplemental materials such as pubcasts are employed.

Skills and Objectives. Includes richer connections to course content (encoding both text and visual cues), enhanced course interactivity, excitement and enthusiasm for learning, and sense of research applicability. The method helps learners to focus on key course content instead of on peripheral issues.

Advice and Ideas. Find and embed pubcasts and other forms of supplemental author, scholar, and researcher information in the course. Your search may turn up conference or seminar interviews or keynote talks; alternatively, you may locate an open access interview that the researcher has granted to a particular organization or institution. If you are in a science-related field, browse through websites like SciVee to determine if there are pubcasts that you might assign to your students. As part of such tasks, you could

FIGURE 9.1: EXAMPLE OF A PUBCAST FROM SCIVEE (Amy Frith of Ithaca College).

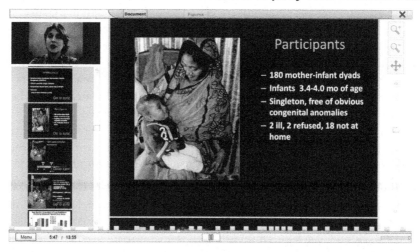

assign reflection papers or online discussions of the course content, asking students to include information on how their learning was enhanced from the additional video content. Some students may even write to the author of the pubcast and ask for an update. Along these same lines, you could invite the researcher into the course for an intimate discussion session, in person or via a Web conference or videoconference.

Variations and Extensions. Students could be required to find one or more multimedia components that augment an assigned research paper, earning bonus points for finding actual author interviews or pubcasts. Alternatively, you could assign them to interview the author of a research paper using a tool like Skype or Adobe Connect Pro and make that pubcast or audio interview available for the class. Consider placing these interviews, pubcasts, and additional resources into a course portal that continually expands. As it grows, a community will begin to form among current and prior students of the course, and perhaps even extend to peers around the world in the same course areas.

Key Instructional Considerations

Risk index: Medium
Time index: Medium to High (depending on the type and format of existing resources and how easy they are to locate)
Cost index: Low to High (once again, depends on the resources available)
Learner-centered index: Medium to High
Duration of the learning activity: 1–2 weeks

Activity 60. Oral History or Situational Research

Description and Purpose of Activity. No matter your topic areas or the age of your learners, reading through historical archives, watching historically important video footage, and listening to interviews of experts, practitioners, and people who lived through a particular experience is a means to excite students and bring an air of authenticity to your course. Advice, insights, and wisdom exhibited in those interviews can foster learner enthusiasm for the content that they are learning.

Students can explore images and interviews of a particular time period. They can also compare and contrast perspectives related to different Supreme Court cases, controversies within a person's life, or issues surrounding particular battles within wars. For instance, they may listen to audiotapes used in the Nixon Watergate trials, watch speeches of significant political leaders during the Cold War, read interview transcripts of former slaves in America, and learn from comments of march leaders and activists prominent (and not so prominent) during the civil rights movement. They could also browse through documents from artists and thinkers involved in the early conservation movement in the United States, listen to stories of Native American culture, or gather data from a historical timeline of innovators and entrepreneurs of the dot-com era, as well as those who helped develop Silicon Valley to what it is today.

Fortunately, with Web-based search engines, it is much easier today to identify interview and oral history materials relevant to your course and particular student interests. One starting point might be the Oral History Association Wiki. Among those listed is the Louie B. Nunn Center for Oral History at the University of Kentucky, which has more than 8,000 oral interviews primarily about the political history of Kentucky as well as interviews related to Kentucky writers, Appalachia, agriculture, and education.

Other resources found at the Oral History Association Wiki include the United States Holocaust Memorial Museum, Archives of American Art from the Smithsonian Institution, and Densho: The Japanese American Legacy Project. The latter project is an award-winning website that documents the oral histories of Japanese Americans who were incarcerated in "internment camps" by order of President Roosevelt during World War II. Not only is this a comprehensive history of these times, but Densho resources can enhance students' exploration of issues surrounding democracy, intolerance, racism, civil rights, citizenship, and hysteria during times of war. Most important, students can engage in ethical decision-making and critical thinking activities around these resources.

For those interested in military history, there are many oral history and photomedia sites available. As an example, in the Rutgers Oral History Archives you can find stories of men and women from New Jersey who were involved in World War II, the Korean War, the Vietnam War, and the Cold War. Those interested in more recent conflicts could search the oral histories on the Gulf War. For instance, there is Frontline, a program from PBS that has provided insightful information from the decision makers at the time (e.g., Colin Powell, Chairman of the US Joint Chiefs of Staff; Margaret Thatcher, Prime Minister of England; analysts; military commanders, such as General Norman Schwarzkopf; and various Iraqi officials).

Before the Web, instructors (and students) had to weed through hours of tape or hundreds, if not thousands, of pages of transcripts for selections that were relevant. In contrast, today instructors can more easily locate specific quotes, sections of content, and themes to include in course materials. And, as seen with the previous pubcasts activity, e-publications of the authors or researchers restore the oral tradition to the level of importance that it had thousands of years ago in Ancient Greece and Rome.

Skills and Objectives. Includes the ability to sift through masses of data, interpret results, grasp possible audiences, filter information, synthesize various information sources, appreciate multiple points of view and diversity, and extend course connections, listening skills, and various inquiry skills. Oral histories help situate student learning in specific events, people, and places for later class activities and events.

Advice and Ideas. The instructor can provide a list of oral history websites to select from. Alternatively, students could search as individuals or teams to find such resources and make recommendations for their inclusion to the instructor. Subsequently, they can write reviews, reports, or critiques on the interviews that they listened to or watched. In such papers and reports, students could be required to create a set number of course connections.

For those seeking support on how to locate and use oral history sites, the website History Matters: U.S. Survey Course on the Web from George Mason University has much advice on evaluating and using oral history websites. Among their tips for evaluation include the following questions that students might ask: Is the purpose clearly stated? How or why might others use this website? Who is the audience? Is the site well designed and easy to navigate? And are the materials current and relevant?

Still more questions can be asked. For instance, are the interviews presented in text, audio, or video format? Are these full interviews or selected excerpts? Did anyone summarize them? Is the quality of the sound adequate? Are there pictures or other resource linkages with each interview? Is additional context provided with each interview? Is there some background information on why each interview was selected and conducted? And are there references or citations for additional resources? Without a doubt, much learners will need much guidance using oral history websites.

Variations and Extensions. Consider having students compare and contrast findings at two or more oral history resources or sites on the same topic (e.g., Women in Journalism, the Civil Rights Movement, the Battle of the Bulge in World War II, or the Cuban Missile Crisis). Another idea would be for them to generate and record unique themes or topics across one or more oral history websites, possibly writing to the developer of the particular sites with questions, comments, and recommendations.

Key Instructional Considerations

> Risk index: High
> Time index: High
> Cost index: Low to High (depending on the actual technologies and resources
>   available and used)
> Learner-centered index: High
> Duration of the learning activity: 3–5 weeks at the end of the term

Final Reflections on Relevance

There is little doubt about the importance of relevance in learning. Educators hear about the lack of relevancy as the key reason that students drop out or disengage from the learning process. Finding relevance in your content area is just like finding relevance in life. As shown in this chapter, relevant and meaningful tasks shine through in many ways. Technology can bring real-world data and situations into the online or blended classroom. Students can juxtapose that data with previous information as well as review it, test it, analyze it, and extend it with data from other sources.

The case can be made that this sixth principle of the TEC-VARIETY model is the most important. Without felt relevance, students will most likely just be biding their time. Keep in mind that both the context and task should be as authentic as possible (Herrington et al., 2010). You must always be asking how the knowledge you are teaching will actually be used in real life. You might incorporate the job application paper activity as a means to generate an immediately relevant task. At the same time, online news and other Web reports can be incorporated to generate ample real-world context. Live news feeds find their way into a course at a moment's notice; no longer is there a span of three or four years to wait for such material to find its way into textbooks. And rich multimedia scenarios, cases, and pubcasts allow the learner to decide which aspects of the task will bring about a sense of authenticity and a personally meaningful situation. At the same time, students might be charged with finding the latest information resources and adding them to an existing article or course portal from a previous semester.

Authentic content could come not only from Web resources and technologies but from human experts, who can be invited into your class or task to offer their erudite opinions and reviews. Alternatively, one or more members of the class could interview historical figures or local experts for an interesting set of oral histories that might find extensive use outside your particular course. As shown in this chapter, the technologies of the Web make such a scenario increasingly possible. Whether you want to reach someone from the Royal Society or someone from the local rotary club, both are now possible to contact and interact with within seconds.

And so concludes what many believe is the most relevant and meaningful chapter of this book. We have come a long way already through six key principles of the TEC-VARIETY framework. You must be contemplating, "What comes after a chapter on relevant, meaningful, authentic, and personally interesting learning?" Well, oftentimes such relevant learning must be rooted in a context in which there are other participants. The task must also be interactive and engaging. Without interactivity and engagement, the most relevant and meaningful idea you can think of will quickly flounder. We push on, therefore, to the seventh principle, detailed in Chapter Ten on interactive, collaborative, and team-based learning. The chapter will also address aspects of community building. After that, you will find Chapter Eleven on the eighth principle of TEC-VARIETY, namely, engagement. The associated goals of such engagement are sustained effort, involvement, and excitement related to the task or activity.

We recommend that you read those two chapters consecutively and then reflect on some of your present instructional activities as well as your personal learning preferences. When you do, you will see that life as an online or blended instructor does not start and end with meaningful and authentic learning. There are a multitude of factors that have an impact on online motivation and retention. Fortunately, the tools and techniques for fostering interactivity and engagement are rapidly increasing and, at the same time, becoming less expensive. Read on.

CHAPTER TEN

PRINCIPLE #7 INTERACTIVITY

(Includes Collaborative, Team-Based, and Community)

> People enjoy the interaction on the Internet, and the feeling of
> belonging to a group that does something interesting:
> that's how some software projects are born.
>
> —Linus Torvalds

Helen Keller once said, "Alone we can do so little; together we can do so much." Today the possibilities for working together have expanded to new heights. Social networking technologies such as LinkedIn and Twitter as well as collaborative tools like Google Docs and Wikispaces provide virtual avenues for rich collaboration among learners in different parts of the world. Students can basically pick their peers and learning partners. They can form teams and communities outside of those enrolled in their school or university, or employed in their work setting. As this happens, they have opportunities for sharing ideas, perspectives, and strategies that can result in unique course products and solutions.

Despite the expanding possibilities for online interaction and collaboration, interactivity in distance learning courses is difficult because there is a separation of time and place between learners and instructors (Willis, 1993). Online students are deemed to be at a distinct disadvantage as they lack the rich and sophisticated support systems that are typically available to on-site students (Hodgson, 1993). The physical distance shifts what was previously a high-fidelity and synchronous learning event under the tutelage of an expert instructor into one that requires self-directed learning skills and heavy doses of perseverance and grit. Without a doubt, online learning is more flexible and convenient than traditional instruction.

Tony Bates (1991, 1995) argues that high-quality forms of interaction with the learning materials, other learners, and the instructor are essential for effective distance learning. Interactivity, however, comes in many formats and flavors. Such interaction can involve dialogue about the instructor's questions and answers; control over the pace, order, and timing of content; purposeful searching for and selection of additional information; manipulating the content or presentation in some way; and the selection of and navigation through different pieces of content (Moreno & Mayer, 2007). The dilemma for instructional designers, therefore, is to find ways to reduce extraneous cognitive load while increasing interactivity in ways that are more germane to the learning process (Maddrell, 2008).

As mentioned in Chapter Five, more than two decades ago Moore (1989) proposed three key types of interactivity: (1) learner interaction with content or the subject of study, (2) learner interaction with other learners with or without the instructor, and (3) learner interaction with an instructor or other experts assuming the role of instructor. As detailed in Activity #20 in Chapter Five, others have expanded on this model by exploring learner-self interaction that relates to learners reflecting on their own learning and new understandings as well as possible misconceptions or inaccuracies (Soo & Bonk, 1998). Still others have focused on learner-interface or learner-technology system forms of interaction (Hillman, Willis, & Gunawardena, 1994). In the next chapter we will focus on different types of learner-content and learner-technology system interaction (e.g., interactive timelines, glossaries, dictionaries, and so on), many of which are quite exciting.

In this chapter, much of our focus will be on learners interacting with other people. In fact, interactions with the instructor, expert guests, or practitioners in the workplace are critical in applying new knowledge. Learner interaction with practitioners or community leaders might be vastly different from their interaction with instructors and tutors. Practitioners may foster an apprenticeship to life in the real world. With global technologies, the possibilities for this form of interaction are endless and often fairly inexpensive and easy to incorporate. The 10 activities in this chapter will include such forms of interaction, but will also include many team- or peer-based collaboration examples.

Though the field is still evolving and filled with much debate and controversy, research has generally confirmed and extended Moore's ideas that interaction is vital to learner success across the various forms of distance education (Kelsey & D'souza, 2004). Research by Khoo, for instance, has revealed that when interactions are highly intellectual as well as social and emotional in nature, there is a better chance for a productive learning community to form online (Khoo & Forret, 2011; Khoo, Forret, & Cowie, 2010). Khoo and her colleagues found that in courses where peers extensively asked each other questions, elaborated on issues, and generally provided high levels of feedback, not too surprisingly, learners exhibited deeper reflection and discussion than those in courses that did not use these techniques. Interestingly, when students in these online courses delegated tasks and engaged in team-based communication and decision making focused on team products, they displayed a special type of social glue or group cohesiveness. Third, Khoo and her team also discovered a need for emotional support. The forms of such support include addressing one another by name, asking about each another's welfare, and sharing a joke or humor in online activities. Clearly, online interaction is complex and multifaceted.

As Khoo's dissertation (2010) research revealed, all three forms of interaction—intellectual, social, and emotional—are crucial to the success of an online class. To create such courses, therefore, online instructors need to provide guidelines for interactions as well as carefully monitor the resulting class interactions and discussions. Suffice it to say, productive peer interaction depends on thoughtful use of online pedagogy (Khoo, 2005; Khoo & Cowie, 2011).

Fortunately, with more than two decades of Web-based education in the books, there are hundreds of Web-based pedagogical activities that have proven valuable for peer interaction and collaboration (Dennen, 2001). Among these instructional methods include press conferences, online symposia, panel discussions, and interactive role plays, or debates. Another technique that is often used is called the "critical friend" or Web buddy technique which we detailed in Activity 11 in Chapter Five (Bonk, Ehman, Hixon, & Yamagata-Lynch, 2002). Collaboration can also take place in cross-cultural wikibook projects or interactive Web conferencing (Lee & Bonk, 2013). Some of these activities will be discussed in this chapter.

The forms and instances of interactivity and collaboration, however, will vary by course level and the age or maturity of the students. Such key components of distance learning courses will also depend on the nature of the learning materials or contents, the instructional philosophy of the course designers, and the technology systems and tools employed in the course (Moore & Kearsley, 1996).

Technologies for Principle #7: Interactivity

Educational researchers and psychologists have been advocating a more sociocultural view of learning in technology-rich environments for decades. The key premise is that social interaction and dialogue is central to learning new skills and strategies (Bonk & King, 1998; Scott, Cole, & Engel, 1992). These skills first appear on a social plane with adults and more capable peers and are later internalized as independent problem-solving skills (Bonk & Cunningham, 1998). In fact, learner social negotiation of meaning is salient as it exposes learners to the unique skills and strategies of their peers and instructors. Technology-based collaboration allows learners to test the viability of personally constructed ideas as well as to internalize some of the skills displayed on the social plane.

Stanford Professor Roy Pea (1996) predicted that distributed learning environments would eventually transform education. He argued that such a transformation would take place when collective and collaborative learning communities emerge and become filled with highly interactive multimedia conversations. Pea was spot-on: think Facebook, Twitter, Course Networking, Piazza, Google+ Hangouts, and Ning. According to Pea, such technologies awaken educators to the overreliance on transmissive models of education and communication.

Clearly, a shift in educational models is overdue. A shift toward a more sociocultural view or perspective of education would emphasize the use of telecommunications to foster a sense of shared space or place for learners to participate as members of a learning community (Lave & Wenger, 1991; Schrage, 1990). As education has opened up during the past decade (Bonk, 2009c), a rich array of online resources and experts has been made available for learners to be apprenticed by more mature members of an online community (Collins, Brown, & Newman, 1989). At the same time, they can interact with other learners on a local or perhaps even a distinctively global cooperative learning team (Riel, 1996).

Pea was not speaking from thin air. Technologies for collaboration have existed for decades (Koschmann, 1996). Bonk and his colleagues—Padma Medury and Tom Reynolds—conducted an extended review of collaborative technologies back in the early 1990s (Bonk, Medury, & Reynolds, 1994). At that time, there were dozens of tools for synchronous and asynchronous writing and brainstorming. Back then, there were five levels of such tools that ranged from basic e-mail collaboration to what was labeled cooperative hypermedia. Each level was extensively researched at Indiana University during the 1990s (Bonk & King, 1998).

Fast-forward 20 years and the tools for collaboration and human-human interaction are once again in the limelight. As the proliferation of collaborative learning tools and resources occurs at an ever faster rate, educators are having difficulty keeping up. For those expecting students to collaboratively brainstorm, share, and negotiate knowledge, there are wiki tools like Wikispaces and PBworks mentioned in the previous chapter. Others might choose Google Docs or Meeting Words for document co-creation. To represent such knowledge, students could collaboratively build concept maps, glossaries, timelines, and hypermedia-based forms of representation. And for course content discussion and question-and-answer sessions, there is Piazza. Alternatively, for users of shared online videos, tools like Flipgrid and Vialogues can foster intense interaction around such videos. Of course, there are also many synchronous conferencing tools for learner interaction, including Skype, Google Hangouts, Adobe Connect, and Blackboard Collaborate. Many of these collaborative tools and systems will be central to one or more of the 10 activities of this chapter.

Each tool has specific features to take advantage of. For instance, one free social software tool, Loomio, enables discussion groups to be formed around topics or projects. As part of this system, members can vote and make decisions on ideas generated by the group through a user-friendly polling system (e.g., Yes, No, Abstain, Block). The results can be visualized instantly as a pie chart, allowing members to view the most popular idea options, thus informing the collective decision-making process of their group. Such features make it possible for an individual's ideas to be negotiated so members can share and learn from one another. As will be shown in this chapter, such types of collaborative technology can enrich learners' projects and products as well as their overall problem-solving processes.

Each of these tools can be used in local or global ways. Although educators are often well meaning in terms of infusing their courses with global issues and the development of multiple perspectives through cross-cultural, project-based approaches, most such activities are quite isolated events. As prominent global education consultant Jennifer Klein accurately points out, part of the problem is teacher training and part of it is a lack of recognition by administrators and the surrounding community of the value of global forms of learning (Klein, 2012). Many educators merely lack awareness of just how pervasive and simple global collaborative technologies are today (Lindsay & Davis, 2013; Peters, 2009).

Whether you are in K–12, higher education, or corporate or military training settings, most kinds of collaboration that previously took place in walled classrooms can now happen effectively online. You have likely experienced the tremendous shift we have been witnessing during the past decade toward learning tools that are increasingly interactive and learning activities that are highly collaborative and enhance community building. Ideally, the following set of ideas will spark an idea or two in your brain that you might try out in your courses or with departmental colleagues or with others located in distant places across this planet.

Ten Online Activities in Principle #7: Interactivity

Even more than in previous chapters, the importance of peers is fully revealed in this chapter's 10 activities. Interactive and collaborative learning, especially in a global or international sense, has become much more common today than it was prior to the Web. Each activity detailed here can have a local classroom flavor of collaboration or entail something much more complex and global. If you seek the latter, be sure to set aside ample time to plan the event, negotiate the details, and reflect on the outcomes. And if it does not work, do not give up on the idea immediately. We find that a minor tweak can often lead to rich success.

Activity 61. Scholar, Scientist, or Innovator Role Play

Description and Purpose of Activity. Educators have experimented with forms of online role play for nearly two decades. Personally, we have attempted to stretch our risk muscle with online mock trials and séances. We have also incorporated various forms of role play including student assignments by type of occupation (e.g., real estate agent, teacher, corporate executive, politician, and so on), personality type (e.g., optimist, pessimist, sage, comic, slacker, leader, coach, and so forth), online activity or role (summarizer, starter, devil's advocate, questioner, and the like), level of thinking and questioning (such as knowledge or basic facts, comprehension, synthesis, evaluation or judgment), and types of commenting expected. For instance, you could assign every person in your class a different personality or role. Alternatively, you could juggle a few select roles among several students and allow the others to assume any position or role that remains open.

We have conducted online role plays many times. We have also assigned students the names of famous people to assume during that role play such as Mother Teresa, Jacques Cousteau, the Dalai Lama, Dian Fossey, Eva Perón, Stephen Biko, Ernest Hemingway, or Anna Freud. As indicated in the previous chapter, such a task can elevate student perspective taking and level of thinking (Sugar & Bonk, 1998). There are countless ways to engage students in the content using online role play. Fortunately, the tools for doing so are becoming increasingly sophisticated and available. For example, next-generation collaborative tools for online learning environments, such as Piazza and Course Networking, both described later in this chapter, could be used for online role play.

Students should be given specific tasks or problems to discuss within such roles. In our education and technology courses, these problems often relate to school reform, some new law that was proposed or recently passed, or the costs of purchasing new technology (e.g., iPads). Embedding specific problems and events around the role-play activity encourages students to comprehend the dynamic nature of the surrounding educational system or political climate. They can begin to grasp the viewpoints of different stakeholders who are concerned with the costs, traditions, achievement test scores, or other impacts. Instead of a one-off course task, you could create a series of assignments that are recursively embedded to foster systemic ways of thinking about such problems.

In other courses, students may be discussing and debating the causes and implications of a recent catastrophe or event in the news (e.g., South Korea's renewed whaling plans, a series of European monetary bailouts for Greece, or bloody violence in Syria or Egypt). In typical online role-play situations, students would contribute to the discussion based on an assigned personality type, occupation, thinking level, experience level, task, or skill. If the role-play situation calls for each student to assume the personality or experience level of a particular person, learners will be obliged to research their assigned person and his or her domain area in order to be successful during the event.

One idea we extensively use is called "scholarly role play." In scholarly role play, we have our students assume the voice of someone whose articles, books, or press clippings they have read during the semester, or whom the class has discussed, watched, explored, or referenced. They must enter all posts and responses from that specific role or point of view.

Alternatively, they could engage in a "scientific role play" where students would assume the personas of leading scientists and engineers making particular breakthroughs or coming up with one or more inventions (e.g., Edison, Tesla, Lovelace, Marconi, Curie, Bell, and Ford). Again, they would have to research their assigned person and his or her invention or innovation prior to any online discussion and interaction with peers.

Skills and Objectives. Includes creative imagination, spontaneity, application of skills learned, appreciation of other viewpoints, discovery and exploratory learning, problem solving, and flexible application of learned concepts and principles. Scholarly and scientific role play breaks learners out of their present mindset and requires them to envision a situation from another perspective.

Advice and Ideas. Carefully plan the role-play task or activity. Be clear on the roles or tasks, the types and timing of interactions, grading criteria, and other expectations. Offer plenty of options. At some point during the activity, you will need to explain the purpose as some students may find online role play highly frivolous or insignificant to their completion of the course or overall program of studies. In some cases, the explanation of the purpose should take place prior to starting the assignment, whereas sometimes it may need to wait until the very end.

If training is required for different roles, then offer it. Provide instructional scaffolds such as a list of relevant Web resources for the roles that students will be playing. Consider allowing students to pick the scholar or scientist that they will role-play. If necessary, find a way to "enroll" those individuals into your course management system or discussion forum tool. Role assignment from lists of those fictitiously enrolled might be random, purposeful, or student selected.

As an example, Bonk has experimented with role plays of pioneers in the field of open source software. Using a blended learning format, students research their characters online and come to a physical classroom for the role-play experience. The role-play activity is held as a mini-institute or one-day conference event attended by the famous open source developers, educators, and advocates that the students were assigned. In fully online classes, Bonk uses a combination of synchronous chats with asynchronous discussion activities for the same activity. Such combinations tend to yield highly rich and creative interactions.

Online role play is possible in most any field. Those teaching courses on computer technology, engineering, or entrepreneurship might enroll people like Steve Jobs, Steve Wozniak, Bill Gates, Michael Dell, Sir Tim Berners-Lee, William Burroughs, Mark Zuckerberg, Linus Torvalds, Sergey Brin, and William Hewlett. Alternatively, such instructors might focus on women of the Silicon Valley such as Marissa Mayer, president and CEO of Yahoo!, Pooja Sankar of Piazza, and Meg Whitman, president and CEO of Hewlett-Packard (Shontell, 2012). Fortunately, there are websites emerging like Women 2.0 and ForbesWoman (Chang, 2012; Swartz, 2012) where students can read about such individuals (Sankar, 2011). After role-playing innovators, entrepreneurs, or scientists, there could be a follow-up assignment wherein students envision their own companies, products, and business plans.

Instructors have much to keep track of during the role-play experience. For instance, they should facilitate the online role play with questions, management guidelines, tips, task-structuring cues, and timely reminders to participate. Course instructors should also be alert to ways that they could address any conflicts between assigned roles and student personal viewpoints or opinions. Once the assignment is over, students could write reflection papers or engage in some type of summary assignment. In addition, episodes of debriefing and group discussion regarding the role play will reinforce and extend that learning.

Variations and Extensions. As in the online role play and séance activities mentioned in Chapter Seven, students can conduct extensive research on their assigned people, perhaps reading biographies, watching movies about their lives, or reading about their primary work done prior to becoming famous. In addition, if students' assigned people are still alive, they could write to them with a set of questions or ask for new research findings, reports, or ideas. They might even invite their scholar or scientist to join the class in a synchronous conferencing session. If successful, instructors could offer bonus points or some other type of award or recognition. The invited person could even enter the course role play and contribute to it. The possibilities are endless.

Key Instructional Considerations

Risk index: High
Time index: Medium
Cost index: Low
Learner-centered index: High
Duration of the learning activity: 1–2 weeks

Activity 62. Interactive Learner Questioning and Discussion

Description and Purpose of Activity. In online courses, much of the learning takes place in the course discussion forums. Recently, however, there is an emphasis on student questioning and responding within those discussions. In the Stanford Mobile Inquiry Learning Environment (SMILE) project, for instance, learners can type content-related questions that are distributed via their mobile phones for their peers to answer (Seol, 2012). All student-generated questions are collected and instantly made available to the class. Students can add multimedia elements such as photos of certain diagrams found in their textbooks or notes from key lectures to include with their questions. Using the SMILE system, students can also rate inquiries based on their perceived relative merit.

The developer of SMILE and founder of Seeds of Empowerment (which is testing SMILE), is technology maverick Professor Paul Kim from Stanford. According to Paul (personal communication, July 8, 2012), "Our ultimate goal is to bring about a *seismic pedagogical paradigm shift* in classrooms around the globe. While we recognize that technology can never—and should never—replace teachers, we do believe that technology can empower students to take their learning into their own hands, and make them active agents of their own learning." Paul has tested SMILE in remote and urban communities in India, Tanzania, Argentina, Indonesia, and Thailand with stunning results (Buckner & Kim, 2013).

Another interesting Web 2.0 tool for interactive questioning is Piazza. Piazza is currently a free service employed in higher education settings. In fact, many professors shift their physical office hours to the Web using Piazza and others use it to help students form study groups (Young, 2012). Importantly, learners can choose to be anonymous in Piazza, thereby freeing them up for participation. The nonhierarchical and interactive functionality of Piazza nurtures an environment rich with student questions and associated answers (Qasem, 2012). Answers to student questions can arrive in minutes, or even seconds. Moreover, using Piazza, previously shy students can participate anonymously as well as find answers to questions that they may be hesitant to ask despite the anonymity.

Among the users of Piazza are entire MBA programs as well as professors of topics like Computational Fluid Dynamics, Linear Algebra, Contemporary Civilization, Introductory Chemistry, Engineering Entrepreneurship, and Introductory Computer Programming. In a software engineering course, Jeff Offutt of George Mason University used Piazza with his students as well as those from two universities in Sweden. By incorporating cross-institutional collaboration, Offutt was assured of sufficient diversity in student backgrounds, perspectives, and answers. In this course, students paired off into teams to review research papers each week. After that, they led discussions about the research in Piazza. Moreover, in this highly ingenious activity, a third student was assigned the role of dissenter who was required to disagree with the conclusions of the other two students who drafted the summary.

Students ended the course with an online miniconference of student research paper presentations between students in the United States and those in Sweden. Their research designs were posted and discussed within Piazza prior to the conference. As a result, the discussions were at a deeper and higher level than those experienced previously.

Piazza and SMILE are not alone. In fact, many new course tools and social networking systems (e.g., Course Networking and Canvas) are taking on flavors of tools like Facebook by having students post questions on a wall for others to answer. Given their familiarity with Facebook, such systems are relatively easy for students to adapt to.

Skills and Objectives. Includes discussion skills, formulating questions, inquiry, choice, feedback, empowerment, idea exchange, appreciating different perspectives, analysis, resource sharing, and evaluation and analysis skills. Through this activity, learners pool together their knowledge.

Advice and Ideas. This instructional approach and the tools employed may be unfamiliar to students. They may not be used to such challenge questions coming from their peers. If that is the case, create tutorials around the system that you have chosen to use. For F2F classes, consider taking students to a computer lab for a demonstration as well as to test out their passwords. Otherwise, create help systems, screencast videos, or other types of tutorials.

Instructors and their assistants should participate in the question-and-answer sessions. Instructor modeling will foster more intense student participation. To fuel discussion even further, you could acknowledge the more active students with special certificates, praise, bonus points, or some other type of course credential. Course Networking, for instance, offers motivational incentives in the form of "pomegranate" points.

Be sure to structure the task. Indicate how often and how much to post as well as how students will be assessed. It is also helpful to provide examples of the types of postings that are expected. If you do, emphasize making substantive postings rather than, for example, simply stating, "I agree with Sheryl and Jay." Monitor the system. If anything mentioned is incorrect, intervene in a timely and appropriate fashion with the correct answer. Extend student answers with additional resources.

Variations and Extensions. Ask students to sift through the question-and-answer pool and generate themes or metaquestions. Ambitious students or teams could enter sample content into a qualitative research tool for in-depth analyses. The metaquestions uncovered may be listed at the start of the following semesters. Students could also create a wiki of frequently asked questions (FAQs), which can evolve over time. The most common ones could be used as a filter or lens from which to update the course syllabus, exams, and course resources; naturally, such questions are indicators of what students consider important. Use them as a guide in course redesign when possible.

Key Instructional Considerations

Risk index: Medium
Time index: High
Cost index: Low
Learner-centered index: High
Duration of the learning activity: Every week

Activity 63. Jigsaw the Online Content

Description and Purpose of Activity. The jigsaw method has its roots at the University of Texas at Austin where it was designed by Elliot Aronson. Though is it more common in K–12 classrooms, we have used it in higher education settings and at various corporate and military training events.

There are many components to the jigsaw method. At base level, groups are formed and each student in a group is assigned a different task or area of study. Students then find ways to obtain the needed expertise. Next, they break out into temporary expert groups with students from the other teams who have been assigned the same role or purpose. At that point, students study, learn, rehearse, question, negotiate, and share content with other members of their expert group. At some point, students move back to their home or jigsaw groups and share their new knowledge. There could be an ending quiz, presentation, game, or some other type of capstone event to summarize what was learned.

The prevailing literature is filled with various K–12 applications of the Jigsaw approach, but we have employed the jigsaw method in F2F, blended, and fully online college courses. For example, in the late 1990s, Bonk apportioned a 10-chapter book by David Perkins called *Smart Schools* (Perkins, 1992) to small teams of five students each. The first student in the group was assigned to become an expert on the content in chapters 1 and 2. The second student was told to master chapters 3 and 4. The third student had to learn chapters 5 and 6, and so on. In the online version of this course, students discussed their respective chapters in expert groups, so that all the students reading chapters 1 and 2 discussed and summarized that content in a specific discussion thread for those chapters.

Once that was complete, students engaged in synchronous chats as well as asynchronous discussions with other team members about the content in their assigned task. Today they would place that knowledge in a wiki or collaborative document specific to their group. In blended courses with final class meetings, there can be a series of final presentations as well as group papers. The presentations offer a sense of completion, camaraderie, and community. Such a method is even more efficient with the rise of digital books. Some digital books have built-in tools for sharing, commenting, and discussion among those reading that particular book.

Skills and Objectives. Includes teamwork, group interaction, knowledge negotiation, communication skills, interpersonal skills, and learning depth. There is a sense of identity or self-worth from this task.

Advice and Ideas. The Jigsaw method can require extensive planning, especially in online and blended courses. When properly detailed, however, there are numerous benefits. For example, the jigsaw method will bring out a sense of commitment from students. It will also efficiently utilize student resources in the course. As a result, instructors can cover more material at a faster pace than with most other instructional methods. At the same time, the students are forced to learn the content in a deeper and richer manner than most traditional approaches allow. Coordinating the Jigsaw method is not easy, however.

As is clear by now, the Web is filled with rich digital content. Assume that the instructor had 20 students and one or more key topics that she wanted to end her course with. Students could be divided into groups of four people and assigned to learn from different Web resources, shared online videos, simulations, biographies, open access articles, digital books, blogs, and podcasts related to such content or topics. For example, one person could be required to find expert blogs on a topic, a second group member could be charged with researching one or two central people in the field, the third person could be asked to listen to relevant podcasts, and the fourth person could watch dozens of online video resources that are available on that topic. In addition, they could all read a particular book or set of articles for background materials. Those individuals reading blogs could correspond with each other in a discussion thread, as could students with the podcast, video, and biography assignments.

Clearly, there are many possible spin-offs of this technique. For instance, some parts of jigsaw might be abbreviated or eliminated as needed. Experiment and see what works. What is certain, however, is that online course contents will continue to proliferate. Methods like jigsaw will help students make sense of them.

Variations and Extensions. There are many variations as to what students may turn in at the end of a jigsaw activity involving the analysis of a book or report. For instance, groups could present their summary of the book in a synchronous Web conferencing presentation. Alternatively, they may write a group report or create a video summary of their learning. Students take pride in the fact that they have contributed something beneficial to their group.

Instructors who are open to global collaboration could establish jigsaw student groups across sections of the course or across different institutions. Their cross-institutional or global activities might be posted to a wiki and discussed in a social networking community like Ning.

Key Instructional Considerations

Risk index: Medium
Time index: High
Cost index: Low
Learner-centered index: High
Duration of the learning activity: 2–4 weeks or as needed

Activity 64. Flipping the Class

Description and Purpose of Activity. Paralleling the growth of methods of delivering educational content since the emergence of the Web, there has been increased interest and experimentation in ways to transform traditional processes of teacher-centered instruction. Ideas stretching back hundreds of years about learner-centered instruction are now quite salient. Strained educational budgets, improved learning technologies, the availability of high-quality online content at low or no cost, a wealth of insights from cognitive psychologists on how people learn, and increased pedagogical experimentation have uniquely converged to alter the discussion about the best ways to deliver education (Berrett, 2012).

As these changes take place, new terms and ideas are coined to help people make sense of them. One such term is the notion of the flipped classroom. In a flipped classroom, students watch a video lecture or listen to a podcast of that lecture prior to coming to class. During class time, then, instructors can create a learning-centered environment rich with problem solving, reflection, and student interaction. Different types and forms of interaction can occur before, during, and after class. Students can be asked to comment on specific components or sections of the assigned video or audio file. Alternatively, all learners could view, listen to, or scan through each assigned resource prior to class but with different tasks or responsibilities. They could later follow up by sharing their observations in the F2F class or posting them to an online forum.

Some educators believe that flipping the classroom occurs solely when video lectures or podcasts are posted to the Web. That is not always the case (Sams & Bennett, 2012). A flipped classroom requires rethinking the entire educational environment and ceding more responsibility to the learners. Naturally, in many cases, this flipping may entail learners watching a series of video-based lectures (e.g., the Khan Academy) in their homes, offices, cafés, or hotel rooms. In other cases, it may entail reading the assigned chapters or articles and writing down associated questions and problems before they come to class.

The flipping does not just appear where and when the learning occurs. More importantly, this flipping is apparent when instruction shifts from whole-group or instructor-centered situations toward individualization of learning (Makice, 2012). As the flipped classroom proliferates in education, active learning and peer collaboration replace the passive instructor- and text-centered past.

As an example of active learning with technology, you might visit TED Ed, a spin-off from the now famous TED talk series (Byrne, 2012a). As the name implies, this video portal was created specifically for educational purposes. Multiple choice and short answer questions about a TED Ed video can be answered by students during or after viewing the video. By customizing lessons with TED Ed, teachers can flip the classroom and place students more in control of their own learning.

TED Ed offers quiz questions with immediate scoring and video hints for the ones they get wrong. In addition, there are open-ended questions and supplemental resources to explore. Teachers can edit the title, provide instructional context, select or deselect any quiz questions, and add additional reflection questions and resources. When done, a unique video URL can be shared with a class. Importantly, with this privately shared Web resource, instructors can track student progress. At the present time, instructors can perform these tasks with any TED talk, TED Ed video, or YouTube video. Stated another way, much flipping is now possible.

As should be apparent by now, shared online videos do not replace teachers. Online simulations do not replace teachers. And interactive digital books do not replace teachers. The role of the teacher is much more complex than many of those advocating posting video instruction to the Web would suggest, especially given that learners may not be used to being in charge of their own learning situation. Individualized and personalized instruction may be the ultimate goal of education, but such individualization requires deeply committed, caring, knowledgeable, and risk-taking instructors or mentors who are comfortable giving up some control over the delivery and timing of the content.

So far the news on flipped classrooms is somewhat positive. Students in introductory calculus courses at University of Michigan, for instance, exhibited twice the gains of those in traditional classrooms (Berrett, 2012). Similar gains have been found in physics courses at Indiana University and Harvard. And, as shown in Activity #51 in the previous chapter, flipping the class is popular in medical schools where lectures, cases, and other content can be placed online for students to explore and perhaps make diagnoses before a physical class session. They might, in fact, be selected purposefully so as to place medical school students in a state of bewilderment prior to class, thereby making them more attentive to instructor insights (Minenko, 2012).

Skills and Objectives. Includes choice, engagement, communication skills, self-directed learning, self-confidence, collaboration, and addressing misconceptions. One key result should be student ability to ask questions as well as solve problems in the field. Other goals include higher levels of attendance, increased student satisfaction, and elevated test scores.

Advice and Ideas. Flipping the classroom is a controversial topic. In fact, there have been heated debates for what seems like eons about the degree to which students should take more control over their own learning as well as what the role of the instructor and other experts will look like in that process (Berrett, 2012). We recommend that you think about what content is available to you to change your classroom structures. Are there online articles or books that students can all access inexpensively or for free? Would a set of lectures on critical topics in your field enable you to change the focus of any F2F sessions or synchronous Webinars? Technologies like Camtasia, Elluminate, Adobe Connect, Mediasite, Echo360, or just a simple Webcam on a laptop can help you create such video lectures. Find out what is available within your organization or institution.

Perhaps you only want to post audio files as a form of flipping. If that is the case, you might podcast your lectures, as has been done at the School of Dentistry at the University of Michigan. You could also digitize all your pictures, charts, graphs, and handouts for your students. We recommend that you explore the Web for at least one or two hours to determine if there are professionally produced cases or scenarios that you and your students can access. We also suggest that if the course has a F2F component, you might request a room in which the desks are not bolted down and where there is ample marker board space and projection units for learners to share their ideas. If the room assigned is not conducive to learner-centered instruction, consider the use of other spaces like hallways, outdoor classrooms, computer laboratories, and conference rooms. There may even be a "classroom of the future" that has been designed for your school, college campus, or executive training center that is just waiting to be put to work.

With this method, and many others in this book, you are changing the layout of the learning environment. You are shifting the ways in which students learn, the timing and delivery of that learning, and the ways in which that learning is assessed. Once again, when done, debrief on the purpose and effectiveness of the method.

Variations and Extensions. Consider "flipping" across two or more sections of the same course. To help students acquire basic knowledge, instructors might pose term-related competitions or challenges. For higher-end learning, they could structure cross-class-room or cross-institutional projects. Students in the flipped classroom(s) may have more time for global projects and presentations (Bergmann & Sams, 2012). Such internationalized courses are ripe for a student-directed approach to learning.

Another idea would be for students to spend the first four or five weeks or meetings of the class creating the podcasts, Webcasts, video lectures, and digital book material that the entire class would study and learn from during the remaining weeks of the course. This is definitely a high-risk strategy. However, we have seen it work at Old Dominion University where students in Professor Dwight Allen's Social and Cultural Foundations of Education course wrote book chapters in a wiki during the first month of the term and then read the chapters of their peers in remaining weeks of the course, instead of an expensive textbook (O'Shea, Baker, Allen, Curry-Corcoran, & Allen, 2007). Ask yourself: is there a little Dwight Allen in you?

Key Instructional Considerations

Risk index: High
Time index: High
Cost index: Medium
Learner-centered index: High
Duration of the learning activity: Every week or as needed

Activity 65. Product Brainstorming and Co-Creation

Description and Purpose of Activity. As indicated in the previous activity, we live in transformative educational times. In this unique learning age, every day brings a fresh technology tool or Web resource to explore that offers learners a chance to co-create knowledge not only within a class but with peers around the world (Lindsay & Davis, 2013). Instead of passively receiving knowledge from instructors and books, students can offer their own insights, ideas, and suggestions. Most learners, whether young or old, have rich prior experiences that they can offer to a class or project. The art of teaching is finding ways to pull it out in a manner that allows the learner to feel that it was his or her personal decision to contribute that knowledge, story, or insight.

In our own classes, we have been experimenting with many tools, resources, and pedagogical ideas for learner product creation. Sometimes, we arrange for virtual teams of students to contribute to an expanding knowledge base on a topic. Other times, we have pairs of students from two different universities act as a team to solve case problems or situations. And on occasion, we have students sign up to write a chapter in a wikibook that continues to evolve from year to year.

Fortunately, there is a wide array of collaborative technology on the Web for learners to jointly create, share, and negotiate knowledge. For instance, there are tools for joint document and database creation like Google Docs. Learners can also brainstorm ideas with simple yet robust resources like Meeting Words and PiratePad. With Meeting Words, every contribution is in a different color of text. Alternatively, learners could monitor projects or resources in a wiki. Given the wealth of tools at our disposal, instructors could have students rotate from one tool to another as they work their way through a particular problem-solving approach; in the process, students learn valuable digital literacy skills.

Skills and Objectives. Includes creative expression and insight, knowledge construction and negotiation, the appreciation of multiple perspectives, student-generated or participatory learning, collaboration, interaction, the application of course concepts and ideas, problem-based learning, and decision making. Many such skills are not found in traditional course syllabi.

Advice and Ideas. Brainstorm ideas for products that your students might co-create (e.g., podcast shows, mobile applications, video documentaries, multimedia glossaries, and the like). Discuss your ideas with local and distant colleagues. Talk to former students and ask what tasks they might have preferred in terms of generating and sharing knowledge. Share these insights with current or prospective students. What would they like to co-create with their peers? List some options but have current or future students extend them. Following are a few ideas of what students might jointly create in a wiki or some other tool:

- Strategic planning documents
- Wikibook chapters or a complete e-book
- Outline for a paper or project
- Course review quiz generation
- How-to videos, help pages, and tutorials (e.g., screencasts of how to use a piece of technology or how to perform a particular task)
- Engaging stories or narratives about some topic related to the course
- Class glossaries, study guides, or help books
- Databases of course articles and resources
- Course homepage, Facebook fan page, or Ning group
- Course identity—slogan, video overview, documentary, and so on

Perhaps attempt a pilot or small-scale version of the project before you start a major undertaking. We recommend that you solicit feedback on how well it went. When the project is completed, be sure that the students are given ample feedback and outlets to disseminate their work. In addition to feedback, there should be recognitions and celebrations. Celebrations could include showcases of student work, one-day institutes and summits to present projects in a conference-style format, video recordings of any presentations, certificates of achievement, award ceremonies, and retrospective round-tables and panel discussions (Lindsay & Davis, 2013). Think such rewards are only effective at the K–12 level? We have offered graduate students certificates of completion, personally signed books, and other recognitions when they design outstanding or highly creative course products. Unsolicited student feedback indicates that such rewards are extremely effective.

Variations and Extensions. Put the brainstormed list of co-creation ideas in a wiki. Ask previous students to add to that list. Former students could also serve as course mentors and tutors for current student projects or as project evaluators and knowledge disseminators. In fact, alumni of the course might sign up for one of the following roles: creative brainstormer, tutor/mentor, project evaluator, feedback giver, judge, knowledge disseminator, social networker, and so forth. Consider giving your support people and instructional assistants a certificate or badge for their service.

Key Instructional Considerations

Risk index: High
Time index: High
Cost index: Low to High (depending on resources required)
Learner-centered index: High
Duration of the learning activity: 2–5 weeks, typically at or near the end of the course

Activity 66. Collaborative Mind Mapping and Idea Visualization

Description and Purpose of Activity. Cognitive psychology has taught us that among the most important skills learners can have is the ability to organize and represent their knowledge in personally meaningful ways (Driscoll, 2005). For example, instructors could assign students to create concept or mind maps of a set number of chapters of a textbook. Student linkages between terms and their depictions of causal relationships would be key indicators of what they have learned from a lesson or unit. Putting their knowledge on display for others to observe and comment on forces thoughtful examination of conceptual understandings. Students must think about the causal connections, key ideas (i.e., macropropositions), secondary or less important information (i.e., micropropositions), and the coherence and completeness of the overarching structure.

For most of the 1990s, educators bemoaned the lack of technology for knowledge representation and visualization. Around 2005, a series of concept mapping and mind mapping tools became popular including Gliffy and Bubbl.us. However, most early concept mapping tools for the Web offered text-only options. Over time, these tools gradually evolved to allow users to insert pictures as well as links to external documents, videos, animations, and other media. Popplet is one such tool for idea visualization that is popular with educators. In educational settings, a learner could embed links to articles read in a Popplet for instructors and peers to browse through. There are now very rich and engaging multimedia and hypermedia components to online knowledge representations. And by using Popplet, they can be shared with colleagues and peers who can help in expanding them even further. Such tools operate the way the brain works. In fact, one such tool is called The Brain.

As these systems have evolved, they have offered increasing opportunities for team collaboration. Examples here include Mindomo, MindMeister, Creately, Comapping, and Webspiration. In the case of Comapping, learners can collaborate in a virtual student lounge where notes, links, and files can be shared in real time. As is the theme of this chapter and the next, these systems foster learner interaction and engagement. Without a doubt, we now live in a world of collaborative knowledge building and representation. What was once a solitary effort is now group-based and displayed in real time. There has never been an age like the present one.

Skills and Objectives. Includes reflection, clarifying relationships, concept review, juxtaposing ideas, prioritization, sharing knowledge, knowledge integration, critical analysis and evaluation skills, visual communication, and term or chapter review. Explaining what one has designed can provide further knowledge gains and interconnections.

Advice and Ideas. Test out at least a few of the many tools for mind mapping and collaborative knowledge building (see Web resources associated with this chapter). Each tool or system you discover for online collaboration and idea visualization will have different purposes. Some might be better for brainstorming, others for project planning, and still others for knowledge representation and decision making. Fortunately, many are free (Byrne, 2011). Select the one that looks most promising. Perhaps ask several former students or student assistants to test the tool out before creating an assignment using it, or try to use it for a personally important task before incorporating it into your online and blended courses. In that way, you will be able to empathize with your students should they experience difficulties with the tool features or overall project.

Be clear about the task. Instructors should indicate the number of concept or mind maps required, the multimedia elements expected to be embedded, the breadth of terminology covered, the size of project teams, the assessment criteria, and length of time for any associated presentations. Assemble outstanding work in a project gallery and include student testimonials about the assignment as well.

Students could be paired or assigned to groups by interest area, level of expertise, or prior experience and background. Each student team might be assigned a different chapter, unit, topic, issue, and so forth, to generate a multimedia knowledge structure. Consider assigning points for student presentations of their projects, especially if it is a blended course. There could be recognitions for uniqueness, diversity of media employed, logical flow and rationality, and persuasiveness.

Variations and Extensions. Consider asking students to build collaborative knowledge maps across disciplines. For instance, students in MBA programs, informatics, and computer sciences might use the concept maps as planning documents for jointly created business plans and technical reports. Many of the concept and mind mapping tools mentioned here are used in the business world. Hence, such an activity would be beneficial on many levels. Be sure to showcase the best of these efforts in a project gallery.

Key Instructional Considerations

Risk index: Medium
Time index: High
Cost index: Low
Learner-centered index: High
Duration of the learning activity: 2–4 weeks

Activity 67. Collaborative Video Annotations

Description and Purpose of Activity. Classroom discussions can be rich and deeply engaging. Unfortunately, topics that some students feel are worthwhile and engaging can be the same ones that others feel trail off on a tangent. Similarly, video can be extremely static and boring and just another talking head—or it can stir a passion in students to want to learn more. What if students were actively engaged and doing something while watching a video? What if their conversations had a video to focus them? Collaborative video annotations allow learners the time and space to participate to the fullest on the topics that they feel are important (Howard, 2011).

Using annotations as the spark for interaction and debate, students could discuss ideas on weekly course videos that parallel the course readings or instructor lectures. "Collaborative video annotations" is a term coined by Craig Howard when at Indiana University (Howard, 2012). As Howard describes the process, it is a way for people to talk asynchronously while they are watching a video (Howard, 2010). These video-annotated discussions are richer and more engaging than traditional discussion forum postings. With such an innovation, the video and text are closely aligned in a way that fosters deeper learning (Moreno & Mayer, 2007).

Video annotations empower the user. According to a YouTube blog post (YouTube, 2008), a user can now provide additional background information to a video, create branching stories, or add links to other YouTube videos or channels at any point in the video. As the user plays a YouTube video, he or she can insert personal comments by adding speech bubbles, notes, and highlight boxes wherever deemed relevant. Instructors or learners could also embed questions for assessment.

Annotations can be used to evaluate performances, give and receive feedback on performances, analyze the video message, discuss media produced by others, and analyze how messages are constructed. Comments, embedded in a timeline of the video, appear when selected. As such, annotations are an important tool to focus commentary and can elevate performances, foster deeper conceptual understandings, and stimulate student engagement in a previously passive task. See Figure 10.1 for an example.

The purpose of collaborative video annotation is to foster richer discussion about what learners observe in a video as it relates to a class. This activity is a prime example of student interaction and knowledge negotiation. The video provides a common frame of reference or base to refer back to and replay as necessary; as explained in Activity #57 in Chapter 9, the video is the macrocontext. Students can use collaboratively annotated videos for critiques, reflections, project collaborations, presentations, and topical discussions. Students may even use the platform to debate current issues in the news or prominent ideas within their fields (Johnson, 2010).

Not only is such a tool useful in teacher training, there are similar benefits for students planning to be school counselors, clinical psychologists, social workers, auditors, forensic accountants, lawyers, sales managers, nurses, or musicians. Video sequences of recent or distant performances can be inserted for annotations and other forms of feedback.

Skills and Objectives. Includes group interaction skills, sharing ideas and resources, reflection, critical analysis, problem solving, sequencing, conceptual insights, creativity,

FIGURE 10.1: COLLABORATIVE VIDEO ANNOTATION EXAMPLE IN A TEACHER EDUCATION COURSE (Howard, 2012).

deeper and richer understanding of course content, appreciation of the perspectives of others, and feedback. There is an overall focus on higher-order thinking in discussion.

Advice and Ideas. Select or record the appropriate video content for your course. In general, free accounts will allow up to 10 minutes of video. Post the footage to a videosharing site which allows for overlay annotations. In addition to YouTube, tools like VoiceThread, VideoANT, Bubbleply, and Viddler allow for user annotation (Johnson, 2010). Bubbleply, for instance, has options for adding stickers, photos, text, animated bubbles, and links as well as different fonts. Other tools like Viddler allow for text or video commenting; however, Viddler may not be an option as school or university firewalls may make it inaccessible (Byrne, 2010). Be sure to consider the access, security, and functionality of each tool before selecting one.

If you use YouTube, there will be an annotation link for each video you upload. Distribute that link to the appropriate group. Note that this link is different from the "watch link." It is available from the owner's upload confirmation page. You may have to upload the video multiple times in order to obtain a different annotation URL for each group or team.

As learners watch the video, richly annotated discussions will develop (Howard, 2012). Ask your students to rewatch the video after others have had a chance to contribute and then respond to initial annotations. Such an approach will create deeper discussions. Learners could be asked to insert multiple comments per video or multiple comments across all the videos made available for a particular unit or week. A final reflection paper on the experience would foster knowledge integration and summarization.

Variations and Extensions. Students could review annotations made from previous semesters or versions of the course; you could ask them to make metacomments over two or more such previous annotations. In addition, they could write reflection papers on the annotations made by these prior students. Alternatively, consider inviting former students back to comment on the video annotations that current students have inserted in these videos from previous semesters or in new ones.

Another idea is to have an optional assignment where students create a series of videos with embedded questions. As their peers get a particular question correct, they would proceed further into the interactive experience (see Interactive Shell Game in the Web resources section for an example). This task requires some technology skills, patience, time, and creative imagination. When done well, it can be a highly motivating and widely shared class resource.

Key Instructional Considerations

Risk index: High
Time index: Medium
Cost index: Low
Learner-centered index: High
Duration of the learning activity: Anytime as needed

Activity 68. Video Discussion and Questioning

Description and Purpose of Activity. Annotating video with comments and perspectives is one way to spur learner interaction and collaboration related to the course content. Embedded learner annotations have the advantage of being presented in unison with the content. They can be inserted at a specific moment in the video timeline. However, they do not reappear once you have pushed on to other sections of the video. In addition, the comments can be about insignificant or even frivolous aspects of the video (e.g., what someone is wearing or how their hair looks that day). In response, there are now asynchronous interaction tools for such videos like Vialogues and Grocket Answers (Byrne, 2012c). One can also use Flipgrid for video-based discussions of questions or issues. In addition, synchronous technology like Google+ Hangouts and Watch2gether allow for conversations or chats to flow as the video is being watched in real time (Byrne, 2012b).

As with annotations in the previous activity, learner conversations and commenting on video snippets transform this technology from static content into a more interactive and collaborative experience. To get a feel of what is now possible, there are assorted video examples on the homepage of Vialogues. Popular "vialogue" reflections found there include those on financial markets, cello performances, USA women's soccer, child poverty, and the impact of stress. Instructors or students have a choice of selecting an existing video from YouTube in which to have a discussion or uploading a unique one. The Vialogue can be public or private. Links can be embedded in a course management system, blog, or resource list (Byrne, 2012c). However, only the moderator of a particular Vialogue can post polling questions.

Grocket Answers is similar to Vialogues, though instead of the focus on conversation and dialogue around a particular video, it is annotated with questions and crowdsourced answers (Winkler, 2011). Anyone can ask a question or offer an answer and then pin it to a particular point in the video. Questions and answers appear at the exact point where they are relevant. In this way, at the exact moments when the video content gets complex or difficult to comprehend, questions and answers may arise in unison to clear it up. Such an approach allows the learner to focus on the remaining sections of the video and not give up or become overwhelmed. Each of these tools is a means for students to focus on particular content while interacting with their peers and others. They expand a video-watching activity into a more creative video production task.

Skills and Objectives. Includes group interaction skills; peer and instructor feedback; content review; reflection; grasping themes, plots, and main points; forming conceptual linkages; appreciating the perspectives of others; and deeper and richer understanding of course content. There is the potential for dual coding of the content with text juxtaposed against the video content.

Advice and Ideas. Once again, you must test or experiment with each tool or system privately before employing it in class. Some of the synchronous tools have freewheeling chat from around the world that would be inappropriate for youth to observe, much less engage in. Fortunately, most video discussion systems allow for private URLs that you can personally share with your learners.

We recommend that you ask your colleagues if any of them has used a video discussion, testing, or commenting technology. Once you have selected a tool, start small with perhaps a trial video segment. Be specific about expectations including the timing of student postings, the minimum length, the type of discourse expected, and so on. Once comfortable with the tool, you might consider embedding a role-play activity within the video discussion and commenting activity. Gather formative as well as summative feedback from students on that experience.

Coinciding with their video commenting and discussion activities, you could have students write reflection papers on the content of those discussions, possibly including a glossary of terms that they thought were important as an appendix at the end of their papers. As a class, individual students or pairs of students could be assigned to collect those term summaries and place them in a wiki glossary of all the terminology used in the video discussions.

Variations and Extensions. Consider asking your students to sign up for a week of the semester where they are required to find a few videos that are closely related to the course content. Then ask them to use an asynchronous discussion tool such as Vialogues and build discussion threads for one or more of these videos. At the end of the week, they could follow that up with test or review questions with Grocket Answers.

Key Instructional Considerations

Risk index: Medium
Time index: Medium
Cost index: Low
Learner-centered index: Medium
Duration of the learning activity: Anytime as needed

Activity 69. Word Cloud Interactions

Description and Purpose of Activity. As mentioned in Activity #49 in Chapter Eight, as the resource pools in course content library expand, the role of the instructor changes to one of concierge or tour guide. At the same time, students take on new roles through which they contribute to the Web instead of simply receiving from it. Participatory online environments offer opportunities for learners to contribute their ideas, insights, and personal views to the Web. Given the vast array of contributions coming from the instructor and the students, however, there need to be new ways to quickly capture, display, and comprehend what is initially available in addition to what people have contributed to the system.

Tags can add labels and associated meanings to digital artifacts related to the course. They are a means to index or catalogue the content. Another way to understand the content and contributions is to use a visual representation of it such as a word cloud (Lindsay & Davis, 2013). Word clouds help learners visualize word frequency in a dataset or document. The importance of each word may be represented by the shape of the word cloud in addition to the style and size of font, the color, and the word's position in the cloud. In addition, a word cloud can highlight key themes and common vocabulary used in the course or some section of it. The words represented in the cloud that are not familiar to the learners can be looked up prior to fully participating in the course. A word cloud can also introduce new and important terms prior to a class assignment or lecture.

As noted in Activity #50 in Chapter Eight, a massive open online course (MOOC) can generate thousands of participant postings (Kop, Fournier, & Mak, 2011). Tools like Wordle can help learners skim through the course materials and visualize the content of a particular document before reading it. With a quick glance, they can grasp the main topics of different conversations and then decide upon which ones to contribute something meaningful. Such word clouds can also help instructors stay abreast of what is occurring in their online courses in an efficient and sometimes quite motivating manner. And when text becomes visualized, there is an element of multimodal learning; in effect, there are two ways to retrieve needed information: (1) from the text document, and (2) from the visual representation of that text document.

Word clouds can be generated by the instructor or by the students in the course. Some tools create word clouds from a text document and others rely on URLs of blogs, blog feeds, and other Web pages. Word clouds can also be generated from bookmarked websites. There are a number of freely available social networking tools and systems for word clouds, including TagCrowd, Wordle, ToCloud, Tagul, Tagxedo, and Worditout (Hammad, 2012). Teachers of younger learners might try ABCya (Gorman, 2010). WordSift is another simplistic tool which has a unique link to a visual thesaurus for each word. That feature alone is very motivating and contagious. The user can often control the number of words, the minimum frequency of use, words to exclude or filter out, and the language in which to translate the word cloud results (e.g., Hungarian, Danish, Spanish, and so forth). Figures 10.2 and 10.3 illustrate the result of word clouds for the text at the beginning of this chapter using Wordle and TagCrowd.

Skills and Objectives. Includes visual representation of knowledge, discriminating concepts, comparison and contrast skills, spontaneity, reflection, synthesis and summary skills, and evaluation. A word cloud offers learners with visual learning preferences a chance to catch up to other learners in a text-dominated class or unit.

Advice and Ideas. Assign students to generate a word cloud from one key document assigned in the course or from a related document they found on their own and read. Next, ask them to write a short (1–2 page) reflection paper on their learning in that unit.

FIGURE 10.2: WORD CLOUD OF THE INTRODUCTION SECTION OF CHAPTER TEN OF THIS BOOK USING WORDLE.

FIGURE 10.3: WORD CLOUD OF THE INTRODUCTION SECTION OF CHAPTER TEN OF THIS BOOK USING TAGCROWD.

They should include at least 10 of the words listed in their word cloud. The third and fourth pages of the assignment might be reserved for the word cloud image and a student-designed glossary of key words listed in it. We suggest that you make your grading scheme clear and available in advance. Perhaps more important, we recommend that you place the highest-rated papers and word clouds in a project gallery for the course.

Variations and Extensions. One variation would be to assign pairs of students to create separate word clouds for each chapter or module. When complete, each pair could present their word cloud and associated interpretations of it in a short three- to five-minute presentation. From an instructional standpoint, each student would be lecturing on the chapter instead of solely relying on the instructor notes. Students (or the instructor) could vote on the best presentation, with the winner receiving bonus points or recognition in the course management system.

Another variation is to ask students to create two word clouds from the course content. First, ask them to reflect on the best text-based resource that facilitated their learning and generate a word cloud from it. Next, ask them to find the least known resource for this course that was highly valuable to them and generate a word cloud from it as well. Those two unique word clouds could be uploaded to a course gallery of word clouds.

Key Instructional Considerations

Risk index: Low
Time index: Low
Cost index: Low
Learner-centered index: Medium
Duration of the learning activity: 1–2 weeks

Activity 70. Backchannel Conference and Course Participation

Description and Purpose of Activity. Given the time, money, energy, planning skills, and commitment that are required to attend a conference these days, few students can attend them. Fortunately, online conferences are prominent today and many are free or offered at a significantly reduced price. In addition, many conferences post their keynotes and specially invited talks for free to the public. As a result, your learners can monitor a broad online conference such as the Global Education Conference or Global Learn, or one in a specific domain, such as Music Therapy or Cardiovascular Health.

Virtual attendance can entail many degrees of involvement and forms of interaction. With the rise of the backchannel, or the conversations that wrap around the events occurring during the conference, there is now an added layer in which to participate. Your students could help with fact-checking during a speech, offering links to resources, projects, and tools mentioned, noting and cataloguing themes within or across presentations, blogging on their opinions and summaries, and so on. As fact-checkers, students can verify claims and perhaps even communicate with the presenters during the actual presentation.

Live presence at a summit, symposium, public talk, or conference often allows for the same backchannel participation. With WiFi connections for their laptop computers, students can chat about the conference with other students. There might also be a conference hashtag for Twitter activities and quick response (QR) code for mobile applications associated with the conference that can be photographed or scanned in. When audience members add an event hashtag to their tweets, others can search and review all the background tweets associated with the event.

To be sure, backchannels have other uses in education besides conferences. Such uses include taking notes on lectures, asking questions of the instructor or others, offering advice on issues and topics, and sharing course resources between instructors and students. MOOCS, mentioned in Chapter Eight, are ideal for backchannel activities such as using Facebook, Twitter, and blogging (Kop et al., 2011), especially if there are synchronous sessions with the instructor(s) or other guest expert presenters.

At Purdue University, for instance, students can anonymously ask questions and offer real-time feedback using a mobile Web application. The tool developed at Purdue is called the Hotseat. It combines aspects of Facebook, Twitter, and text messaging for a unique class backchannel (Dybwad, 2009a). Unlike the hot seat activity mentioned in Chapter Eight, instructors at Purdue are often in the hot seat, rather than the students. Purdue is not alone. As an example, Twitter is also being required in journalism courses at Griffith University in Australia (Dybwad, 2009b).

Clearly, universities are beginning to see the importance of an online channel for more complex forms of interaction rather than relying solely on traditional instructor lecturing to the students. In her review of backchannel research and theory, Jennifer Maddrell (2008) noted that the benefits might include enhanced student participation, deeper processing of information, increased interest in the topic, peer support, and spontaneous discussions that lead to creative insights. Unlike a traditional classroom setting, learners can interrupt the backchannel conversation and ask for clarification (Warlick, 2009). Maddrell simultaneously is honest about the drawbacks, which include split attention, heavy cognitive load, redundancy, side comments that might be of limited interest or impact, and the general lack of time to process all the information.

Skills and Objectives. Includes the ability to monitor progress, synthesize trends, filter information, distinguish facts from themes, combine ideas, make creative insights, multitask, communicate events, and listen to others. The diverse views should help foster an appreciation for diverse ways of knowing and multiple perspectives. Involvement in the backchannel can apprentice novice learners into a field.

Advice and Ideas. Search for a conference, workshop, institute, summit, symposium, or other related event in your field. Find out all that you can about it and share that information with your students, including the conference homepage, Twitter hashtags, Facebook fan pages, wiki URLs, and associated conference resources. If you locate more than one online event related to your class or topic, have students vote on which one to attend virtually. You may have to write to the conference organizers to obtain a pass for your students. Be sure to test student access to that conference; perhaps take them to a computer lab to try out their passwords. Those wanting some bonus points might create a job aid or screencast instructions.

Embed assignments around key moments of the conference, but be sure to offer plenty of learner choice and control. For instance, you could include a reflective writing assignment related to the backchannel experience or content. Collaborative assignments with students in similar courses who are located in other educational settings or countries should foster greater interaction and collaboration.

Once the conference or event is selected, offer students reflection questions, issues, or areas to focus on. You may want to require some minimum number of postings to the conference Twitter feed. You could also create a separate Twitter feed about the conference or event just for your class. Perhaps have teams of students interview the various conference keynotes and plenary speakers. Alternatively, they can select topics or papers of personal interest to conduct some type of follow-up interview. Highlight such events as they occur and recognize any of your students who played a role in the conference from a distance.

Variations and Extensions. Julie Lindsay and Vicki Davis (2013) offer advice to those wanting to take a stab at creating their own conference within their class or across classes. Your students, along with local or global experts, could be the speakers and participants. As part of these efforts, instructors could post the title of their conference and list of speakers. A backchannel could be created through a conference blog. As mentioned in the previous chapter, presentations can be streamed through systems like Ustream or LiveStream. In addition, Facebook, Ning, and Twitter accounts might be created to which outsiders to the course could subscribe; students could be posting to each of these accounts as part of the class activity.

When complete, have students write a paper wherein they reflect on these experiences. And be sure to archive videos from the conference and everything else for which you have permission and then share it.

Key Instructional Considerations

> Risk index: High
> Time index: High
> Cost index: Low
> Learner-centered index: High
> Duration of the learning activity: 3–5 weeks at the
> end of the semester

Final Reflections on Interactivity

As shown in this chapter, interactivity comes in an array of forms. The type of interactivity emphasized in this chapter is with other people. We saw virtual team interaction with activities using such technologies as Popplet and Meeting Words to coconstruct a final course product that could be used by students in later versions of the course. Such teams could also present their ideas and products in an interactive online press conference or symposia, whereas others might rely on word clouds or mind maps to do their explaining. The important thing is to focus on learner ideas; have them generate, discuss, negotiate, and share new knowledge.

But we were not done. We also detailed various forms of class interaction in scholarly, scientific, and innovator role-play activities. Such activities give students license to be creative while exploring leaders in a field or topic in some depth. And then there were activities that highlighted the use of shared online video including video-based annotations in YouTube and discussions in Vialogues and Flipgrid. In addition, your class may interact in systems like Piazza about basic and more complex questions that are perplexing them. If some students lack access to such technology or find it too complex, jigsaw and other cooperative learning structures can still be formed to help them interact online and gain expertise in one or more areas.

Keep in mind that collaborative learning was a fixture of the learning technology world before the emergence of the Web. Researchers had advocated groupware products in the workplace as well as in higher education during the late 1980s and early 1990s. The Internet, in fact, spawned global collaboration in the 1980s with Usenet news groups, the Well, and other interactive group technologies. There were collaborative writing tools like Aspects, Conference Writer, BBN Slate, the Knowledge Builder, and Collaborative Writer long before the dawn of the Web (Bonk et al., 1994).

Sir Tim Berners-Lee's much-acclaimed Web invention only accelerated this trend. The emergence of the Web 2.0 offers even greater chances for active, participatory learning. Tools for interactive commenting, rating, ranking, discussion, and sharing now dominate the Web. Today, employers simply expect it. We can no longer train individuals for a solitary existence in the work world. Teamwork, communities of practice, and mentoring and coaching programs are pervasive in corporate, government, and military settings.

Given the endless opportunities for online interaction and collaboration today, no one can detail all the possible activities that you can now try out in a single chapter. Consequently, you will need to experiment with different ideas and explore the Web resources associated with this chapter as well as the other fourteen. In particular, we encourage you to refer to the 10 learner-content activities in the next chapter. As stated earlier, in many ways the present chapter goes hand in hand with the next one. You will, in fact, notice the word *interactive* within the descriptions of several of the activities outlined in the next chapter. In most of those tasks, the term signals interaction with the content or the system, whereas the activities of this chapter mainly entailed interaction with other people. Still, many, if not most, of these pedagogical ideas entail a bit of both.

As indicated, Chapter Eleven is on engagement and involvement in learning, while focusing on learner investment and effort in all aspects of the online course. The activities we outline will be part of the antidote to learner disengagement, passivity, and boredom. The goal is involvement in the learning process, as opposed to mere reception of some preordained learning path. When learners are excited, engaged, and involved, they will exert extensive effort. As this occurs, they will often discover personal passion for learning. And so we hope that you will turn to it now and perhaps discover new ways to help your students find their respective learning passions. As Captain Jean-Luc Picard routinely shouted aboard the U.S.S. Enterprise, "Engage!" And engage we shall.

CHAPTER ELEVEN

PRINCIPLE #8 ENGAGEMENT

(Includes Effort, Involvement, and Investment)

To begin, begin.

—William Wordsworth

Can there be a more pressing issue today in education, and perhaps society, than learner engagement? Walk down the conference hallways of any educational technology conference and then pop into any keynote address, invited talk, or expert panel session. No matter the room you enter, the drumbeat will be the same: you will undoubtedly hear a call for better understanding of how technology can engage students in the learning process (Stansbury, 2012).

That discussion will have you reflecting on the underlying theme of this book on online motivation and retention. As you have learned from the previous 10 chapters, motivated learners are the ones who are deeply engaged in the learning process. They are committed to learning and push hard to complete assignments at the highest possible level of quality. Decades of research on student engagement indicates that students who make an investment of extra effort in the learning process will see positive results (Kuh, 2009a). Simply put, when it comes to student achievement, involvement in the learning process matters.

The real inconvenient truth of our times, however, is the lack of learner engagement and all-too-often implicit contract of disengagement between overworked faculty members and students juggling multiple responsibilities (Kuh, 2003). As a result, students are not only failing to engage in their courses, but are dropping out of schools and universities altogether. Those who hang on often become savvy at meeting minimum course requirements, instead of attempting to connect ideas or read widely and deeply. As we know, when online courses are filled with authentic and meaningful tasks, as discussed in Chapter Nine, or when these courses embed thoughtful collaboration, as laid out in Chapter Ten, learner understanding of the content is deeper and more sustainable (Herrington, Oliver, & Reeves, 2003; Herrington et al., 2010).

But just what is engagement? According to Johnmarshall Reeve (1996), engagement comprises the intensity and the emotional quality of a learner's involvement in a school-related task or activity. Engagement is manifested in sustained behavioral involvement and overall positive affect or emotion in a task.

Disengaged learners, however, lack commitment to the learning situation or to school in general and often see no value in learning. As a result, they often withdraw or rebel. At the very least, they are bored. At the extreme, their career aspirations are lowered, they skip classes, and they have a negative attitude toward the class or learning as a whole. There is no learning involvement or investment. There is no commitment. And no tenacity or perseverance either. Simply put, there is no effort, no grit. As a result, their excitement or passion for learning is nonexistent.

All is not lost, however. As we highlighted in the discussion of Carl Rogers in Chapter Four, an environment filled with warmth, respect, choice, enthusiasm, and sincere praise can promote learner engagement and motivation (Reeve, 1996). Also helpful, according to Reeve, is modeling, guidance, and clear learning goals. Learners need to be involved and to have adequate support structures to find success. They need to belong to something or feel socially interconnected (Usher & Kober, 2012). At the same time, they need to sense that they are empowered to make some of their own learning choices. We addressed ways to build warmth, enthusiasm, and choice in Chapters Four and Eight of this book.

To understand engagement, such warmth and positive tone is not enough, however. Ingram (2005) suggested that engagement is made up of three variables: (1) deep attention to the learning task or situation; (2) the activation of effective cognitive processes (e.g., strategies of rehearsal, organization, visual imagery, monitoring comprehension, and so on); and (3) the social context or community in which learning occurs. According to Ingram, one cannot simply look at computer login data or the number of contributions a particular student posts to a discussion forum and make a determination about the level of engagement. The concept of engagement is far more complex than that.

As data from the National Survey of Student Engagement (NSSE) reveal, part of that complexity results from the degree to which online learner engagement can significantly differ across courses, programs, and departments (Young & Bruce, 2011). Many instructors and programs struggle with determining the types of tasks and activities suitable for engagement. The NSSE focuses on institutional characteristics or components of engagement as well as the time and energy that learners invest in educationally purposeful activities (Kuh, Cruce, Shoup, Kinzie, & Gonyea, 2008). Engagement is seen through the lens of the number of writing assignments, books read, and presentations made as well as obtaining prompt feedback, discussing ideas outside of class, interacting with faculty members and peers, and tutoring or mentoring other students. It is also shown through coursework emphasizing the analysis, synthesis, evaluation, or application of what the student has learned (Kuh, 2009b).

Tens of thousands of students from hundreds of colleges and universities across North America take the NSSE each year (National Survey of Student Engagement, 2006). From 2000 to 2011, more than 4 million students from 1,500 institutions in North America and several in Europe and the Middle East completed it. As George Kuh and his colleagues at Indiana University (IU) have found across these studies, the more students take responsibility for their learning, the more they become invested and committed in the activity.

Not surprisingly, the NSSE has expanded over the years to look at student engagement in distance learning. Interestingly, Chen, Gonyea, and Kuh (2008) found that students taking all of their courses online were more engaged than those on campus. Online learners were not only more challenged and engaged in higher levels of reflective thinking, but also indicated that they gained more practical knowledge and were generally more satisfied with their course experiences (Kuh, 2009b). There was more interaction between online learners and faculty members, especially among first-year distance learners. As a direct consequence, older or more experienced distance learners surprisingly perceived their learning environment as more supportive than did residential students sitting in traditional courses.

Technologies for Principle #8: Engagement

Year after year, we hear the steady mantra that schools, universities, or corporate training centers should purchase a particular technology tool because it will better engage their learners. Unfortunately, the technological resources that learners need keep changing. Today instructors engage students with online surveys and polls that can be completed on mobile devices. They also may rely on chat tools in a synchronous Webinar to engage the learner. Or they could connect an online news event to the current topic of discussion. That discussion might expand into a global or cross-cultural space as a means to pique learner interest and show the relevancy of the topic. At some point, this discussion might break out into small teams that complete a collaborative group task in a wiki or online document.

As inroads into the gamification of learning are made, it is increasingly obvious that learner engagement can also come in the form of educational games, whether they be solitary in nature or collaboratively pursued. For the very competitive or sports-minded, a soccer net could be set up to kick answers through. At the same time, a bell could sound, a light could flash, or a winning record can be displayed as a student completes an activity. Each game level completed can award the learner with a new status, points, or some other form of recognition. As accomplishments mount, learners will crave more of that sensation of winning or success.

Another place where learner engagement is apparent is in the use of Twitter, Facebook, and other social media. Educational activities in Twitter might include extended class discussions, sending task or campus event reminders, providing academic support information, organizing study groups, stimulating book reviews, and generally helping students connect. Research by Junco, Heibergert, and Loken (2010) indicates that such activities can foster student engagement and feeling of connectedness. Additional research with social media is now needed.

Still other forms of engagement can occur through voice instead of text or images such as in the use of VoiceThread or Vocaroo, or video and voice feedback with Flipgrid. In addition, natural language personal assistants such as Siri for the iPhone allow the user to ask questions and obtain personalized information such as stock or weather reports, recommendations for restaurants, directions to campus, and today's scheduled appointments (Pogue, 2011). Such immediate and personalized forms of feedback in the form of a voice, whether it be computer-generated or a real human, can arouse a sense of excitement and energy in the learner.

Suffice it to say, there is no particular "engagement" technology and no engagement guarantee. As should be clear from the previous chapter on interactivity, technologies can excite and involve the learner in many ways online. We have known students to work long hours when they are designing a technology product of some type. And we have heard stories of school administrators troubled by having to keep the doors to the school or university buildings open on the weekends or late at night. Clearly, students expend more energy when they realize that their products will be on display for others to view, comment on, share, and perhaps remix (Brown & Adler, 2008). Nevertheless, it is not the technology itself that determines learner engagement, but, rather, specifically *how* that technology is used.

Although many chapters of this book contain opportunities for learner engagement and involvement in the learning process, this particular chapter narrows the focus primarily to learner-content forms of engagement. Such technologies include elements that the learner can interact with such as an animation sequence, a novel timeline, a class multimedia glossary, or an interactive map. Learners may make decisions about artifacts found in a timeline. When they move up or down the timeline, additional data, interactive images, or other embedded media elements can appear. In some online timelines and databases, learner decisions and selections are immediately represented visually.

As Web technology advances and training opportunities increase, the forms and types of interactive content will no doubt skyrocket. Learners will not only find preselected content and objects to interact with, but will encounter greater opportunities to design the content that the class will explore and use. As this transpires, digital books and mobile technology will continue to evolve to offer new ways to engage with content. For instance, simulations and animations could depict famous scientific experiments, war battles, political decisions, geographic expeditions, or sporting events that can be accessed on demand while reading various sections of the book. At the same time, those learning languages are finding ready access to audio and video files as well as practice exams. Many such activities are detailed in this chapter.

Ten Online Activities in Principle #8: Engagement

In many ways, the 10 activities detailed in this chapter bring online course content to life. These activities go far beyond the mere reception of knowledge; instead, there is an element of learners doing something with the content. Such hands-on tasks might augment or expand online content as well as transform it. Many of the ideas here help learners interact with content in ways that inflame internal passions to play with ideas, make predictions about them, and generally want to know more. A timeline tool representing the United States in the 1950s may inspire someone to learn more about communism, mass transit, or civil rights. A timeline for Korea or Vietnam in the 1950s might also highlight communism, while raising issues of colonialism and the Cold War, just for starters.

As with the previous seven chapters, there are just 10 activities in this chapter on engagement. You might find some of the ideas listed here quite commonsensical or related to a discipline other than your own. If so, reflect for a minute or two on other ways to spur engagement. Perhaps you will add a global component to one or more of the activities listed here. Or you may find ways for your learners to develop and review the interactivity within different online learning content elements. Whatever you do, keep thinking. This is a topic ripe for further experimentation and development.

Activity 71. Interactive Maps and Databases

Description and Purpose of Activity. The Web is offering increasingly rich visual displays of data. Among the more educationally powerful and engaging visuals are maps. There are weather maps, climate change maps, political election maps, and maps showing college applications as well as graduation rates by states and counties over time. Josh Keller from the *Chronicle of Higher Education* has published a number of such maps with his articles on higher education including one concerning adults with college degrees in the United States. But this is hardly a static map. Instead, users can explore an interactive timeline of the changes in college completion rates from 1940 to the present for each county and state. The same dataset can be explored by gender, race, income, and size of population. Juxtaposing such information is quite illuminating (see Web resources associated with this chapter for links to maps).

In addition to college-related maps, the United States Department of Agriculture (USDA) has an innovative Plant Hardiness Zone Map that depicts the types of plants that can survive in different zip codes. Such data is helpful for gardeners and crop growers as well as stock exchange traders. Perhaps more important, this interactive GIS-based map shows the serious effects of global warming (Lloyd, 2012). In addition to gathering knowledge about meteorology and climate change, students can also learn about geography. For instance, they can observe how the location of crops near the coasts or in higher elevations can have a significant impact on growing seasons. Educators in agriculture, geography, meteorology, public policy, and environmental affairs courses could incorporate such maps in their courses.

Skills and Objectives. Includes interactivity, excitement for learning, visual discrimination skills, data analysis, evaluation, comparison and contrast, visual thinking, inquiry, self-directed learning and resource exploration, and application of what was learned. Learners must grapple with complex datasets as well as grasp different ways of representing knowledge.

Advice and Ideas. Read widely. Take note when your newspaper or some online resource includes an interactive map or visual display. Explore the associated website and save pertinent information related to the article. Reflect on how you might incorporate such maps into your courses; perhaps you will simply use them as supplemental resources. Alternatively, you could assign a series of activities or calculations that require data interpretation or calculation skills. Students could form small groups to explore different aspects of the data embedded in a particular online map.

As an example, for the pollution database in the World Mapper, some students may explore greenhouse gases by country, whereas other groups could be assigned to nuclear waste, hazardous waste, carbon emissions, sulfur dioxides, and so on. Each group may find a different hot spot or zone in the world with significant pollution problems.

Variations and Extensions. Instead of exploring a particular map, have students compare and contrast two different maps (e.g., US state or presidential election maps from Fox News, CNN, and the Huffington Post). They could form teams and make predictions about a particular race or margin of victory. Often such maps allow the user to change the color of a state to indicate their opinions about which candidate or party will win a particular state or region. Student predictions would then be compared to the final results. Teams with the best predictions could be granted bonus points or some type of course recognition. In contrast, with different weather maps and norms for particular cities as well as scientific trend maps for the next few months or coming seasons, students could make predictions about cities that will experience different forms of weather during the coming months (e.g., drought, blizzards, rain, and so on) and the implications of these on infrastructure planning and development.

Key Instructional Considerations

> Risk index: Low
> Time index: Medium
> Cost index: Low
> Learner-centered index: Medium
> Duration of the learning activity: 1–2 weeks

Activity 72. Interactive Multimedia Glossaries

Description and Purpose of Activity. Too often students are limited to the text resources that are provided by publishers and the instructor. Traditional books are mostly static documents allowing for only one type of learning modality. As indicated in prior chapters, psychologists have long realized that people learn more effectively when ideas are represented both visually and verbally (Paivio, 1986) or when multimedia is properly employed (Mayer, 2001).

One particularly engaging and interactive activity we have seen emerge recently is the use of a multimedia course glossary. For example, an online glossary for the course on "Essential Genetics: A Genomics Perspective" includes an interactive term list (e.g., candidate gene, mutant, ribonucleic acid, and the like) as well as practice quizzes, links to Web resources with further descriptions, flash cards, and additional research and reference materials. Some of these resources include pictures, video, and sound. Another such resource, "The Glossary of Computer and Internet Terms for Older Adults" from the National Institute on Aging, is a simple alphabetic listing of 37 key terms with associated definitions, many of which include a visual image or picture.

Requiring your students to browse through such multimedia glossaries can help them grasp key terms as well as feel more comfortable in knowing that they have a supplemental and handy resource base. Instructors could use these at the start of a class lecture or unit to provide a conceptual anchor and retrieval cues for later learning.

Skills and Objectives. Includes term recognition and recall, content review, dual coding of content (e.g., visually and verbally), comparison and contrast of terms, inquiry, self-directed learning and resource exploration, and the application of what was learned. Harkening back to Chapter Four, students find psychological comfort and safety in knowing that the content is available for review at any time.

Advice and Ideas. Multimedia glossaries are a treasure trove of course activities. Spend a few minutes searching in your area to see whether any such resources exist. If you find one of high quality, you may tell your students that a certain percentage of exam items will come from the glossary or that you will have a weekly quiz or crossword puzzle based on it. In addition, students could write reflection papers that reference examples from the multimedia glossary. An alternative writing assignment is to critique the glossaries or write a design document on how they might be extended. Once completed, students could also extend them further in a wiki. They could also use such interactive resources to augment class presentations and discussions.

Variations and Extensions. Ask one or more students to volunteer to create an interactive glossary with links to videos, documents, and animations that illustrate key terms. Once completed, that interactive glossary can be refined and expanded each time that the course is taught. Your overriding goal may be to create the world's best interactive glossary on that particular topic. You could hold competitions between classes within the same institution or across the world for the best interactive glossary. If a single student generates such a glossary, that student might be allowed to drop any other assignment.

In Bonk's class on learning theories, he included a link in his syllabus to a theory-in-to-practice database that had a comprehensive glossary. Although all the terms had embedded hyperlinks with rapid access to other terms or prominent people, it was unfortunately a text-only glossary. One of his students, Umida Khikmatillaeva, decided to create an interactive course glossary that contained many multimedia components. Not only were terms defined, but there were links to videos for dozens of these key concepts as well as videos of most of the main theorists and researchers mentioned in the course. She also included speeches related to education, motivation, and learning from prominent people such as Bruce Lee, J. K. Rowling, Steve Jobs, Arnold Schwarzenegger, and Tony Robbins. Not yet done, she included sections on course-relevant news, conferences, and Web resources. And with news from places like the New York Times, CNET,

Engadget, and so on, the list continually updates. Not surprisingly, this tremendously engaging glossary is still used in the course.

Key Instructional Considerations

Risk index: Medium
Time index: Medium
Cost index: Low to High (depending on resources used)
Learner-centered index: High
Duration of the learning activity: As needed

Activity 73. Talking Dictionaries and Language Translation

Description and Purpose of Activity. Imagine the possibilities of young or older students understanding the cultures and people of those in distant lands by hearing native speakers' voices respond to their queries. If you teach world history, linguistics, geography, foreign languages, multicultural education, or some other related topic, talking dictionaries can play a role in your instruction.

Such supplemental resources for exploring languages and cultures have exploded during the past decade. Many rare languages and extinct cultures can come to life with online glossaries, podcast shows, practice exams, real-time conversations with language partners, and other resource materials. As an example of this trend, National Geographic, Living Tongues Institute for Enduring Languages, and Swarthmore College teamed up to help preserve several unique languages as part of the Enduring Voices Project (Hotz, 2012). Among these languages is Celtic as well as the Ho language spoken by over one million people in Eastern India. A couple of other languages targeted by this project are Tuvan, which is a Turkic language used in the Republic of Tuva in south-central Siberia, and Siletz, spoken by the Native American Siletz tribes once local to northern California, Oregon, and southwest Washington.

Extensively researched, there are more than 32,000 words in these "talking dictionaries" and over 24,000 audio recordings of native speakers pronouncing different words and sentences in eight endangered languages (Giardinelli, 2012; The Canadian Press, 2012). In some cases, the talking dictionaries contain photos of different cultural objects and artifacts to assist in learning. In these sites, learners can listen to how different words are pronounced and see how they are written. The use of talking dictionaries fosters an appreciation for the diverse cultures of the world, especially those that are gradually becoming extinct.

The Enduring Voices Project is just one example of many through which languages are not only being preserved but extended. With speech-to-text translation dictionaries, mobile applications that translate written signs or conversations into different languages, and online podcast shows of hundreds of different languages, the opportunity to listen to a language is increasingly possible. Of course, in some languages, the oral traditions may be the only form of communication.

The Word Lens tool is a prime example of this fast-emerging technology for language learning and translation. It translates printed words instantly through a video camera.

As a dictionary, the Word Lens will look up words for you and then show how they are used in a context. Such devices are evolving. Search engines like Bing now come with language translation options as do user postings in Facebook. Of course, most Web users have likely used or seen Google Translate at some point.

Skills and Objectives. Includes listening skills, language fluency, the appreciation of diverse cultures, information access, learning through multimedia, self-directed learning and resource exploration, and practice and review of content. Learners can revisit these sites and practice their skills repeatedly whenever needed.

Advice and Ideas. Languages are becoming endangered or abandoned completely at an alarming rate. According to the mission statement of the Living Tongues Institute for Endangered Languages (2013), "Every two weeks the last fluent speaker of a language passes on and with him/her goes literally hundreds of generations of traditional knowledge encoded in these ancestral tongues." Embedded in these languages is an immense store of knowledge about foods, plants, animals, sustainable living, and cultural traditions (Moskowitz, 2012). Educators are among those with a keen responsibility to help value and preserve the rich human cultural diversity of minority communities.

Have your students suggest a sentence that they want translated and listen to the results as a class. Such random searching through the database can excite and better involve students in the learning process. Or you could assign your students to learn a set number of words that they must use in their writing or be able to speak in front of the class. If you want to build on that, assign your students to teams that each write a document or rehearse a speech of that culture. Another idea would be for students to research a particular endangered language and use the talking dictionary as a multimedia component for their research papers or projects.

Variations and Extensions. Consider assigning students to create a product based on their learning from a talking dictionary site. For instance, they could create a short story, poem, or podcast. With younger learners, the product might be a storybook or some other basic literacy materials. Students can also compose test questions for their peers based on their learning. Alternatively, they could write a paper about a culture or people who utilized that particular language; as part of those efforts, they might interview one or more people who still use that language.

Key Instructional Considerations

Risk index: Medium
Time index: Medium
Cost index: Low
Learner-centered index: High
Duration of the learning activity: Every week or as needed

Activity 74. Interactive Timelines

Description and Purpose of Activity. We have found interactive timelines to be among the more powerful learning aids ever developed. Learners have a guided context in which they can explore and learn. They can scroll up and down along the timeline for key historical events, unique information, and something that is familiar or intriguing to them. Increasingly, the developers of such timeline tools are embedding multimedia components. With such technology, learners can often find a video or audio clip that captures the actual event that they are reading about. As they do, they can see and hear history unfold as it really happened. When a particular interest is satisfied, they can scroll up or down to the next piece of information.

Timelines exist for all sorts of events, people, disciplines, and topic areas. Those wanting to stretch far back in time can explore the "Prehistoric Timeline" from National Geographic (see Web resources associated with this chapter). If recent technological changes are of interest, timelines that appeared in the press when Steve Jobs passed away as well as when Bill Gates retired (Mintz, 2008) are highly engaging (again see Web resources section). A simple scroll through the inventions in the Steve Jobs timeline heightens awareness of the fast pace of technological change as the user observes the personal computer in the 1970s, the Macintosh in the 1980s, the Newton in the 1990s, and the iPod, iPhone, and iPad in the 2000s. Such a journey is also a dynamic history lesson.

Educators wanting to stretch such a technology timeline further back in time are in luck. *The New York Times* published an interactive technology timeline in September 2010. This overview of "learning machines" started with horn-books or wooden paddles with lessons written on them in the 1600s, chalkboards in the 1890s, the radio in 1925, overhead projectors in 1930, educational television in 1958, Scantron-scored exams in 1972, hand-held graphing calculators in 1985, and the iPad in 2010. Those hoping to peer ahead can check out the timeline of the future of computing from *The New York Times* as well as estimate the year in which each of the inventions predicted might actually appear.

Such timelines of technology can be used to supplement course materials or lectures as a means to illustrate key points or foster learner engagement. When the event has paralleled students' own lives, it will be even more empowering. There are also timelines for US presidents where interactive content pops up as you click on a particular person or year. Similarly, the National Constitution Center in Philadelphia has a "Constitutional Timeline" encapsulating over 200 years of stories in the United States with key dates, events, issues, and people that shaped the nation as well as the Constitution. Journeys along the timeline are supplemented by images, audio clips, pop-up text, and other interactive content. Without a doubt, such interactive timeline tools are a sign of Web-based engagement possibilities to come.

Skills and Objectives. Includes interactivity, intrigue, system feedback, visual discrimination skills, data analysis, comparison and contrast, visual thinking, inquiry, self-directed learning and resource exploration, and application of what was learned. Timelines give learners a sense of wholeness or macro lens for a particular field or topic within a field.

Advice and Ideas. Spend an hour or two in a focused search on different key topics, people, concepts, or events related to your class. Search, share, and save timelines that are related to your field. If nothing appears, you might explore the website Timeline Help which has a wide array of timelines that you and your students can access for different countries (e.g., Ancient Greece, Africa, Ireland, and so on), subjects (e.g., Airplanes, Atomic Theory, Telescopes, and so on), events (e.g., the Cuban Missile Crisis, the Great Depression, and so on), people (e.g., Albert Einstein, Oprah Winfrey, Mark Twain, Eleanor Roosevelt, and so on), and technology inventions.

Alternatively, ask your students to find a timeline that relates to their papers or projects. For instance, if they are studying Martin Luther King Jr., there is an online timeline of his life from *USA Today* which was embedded in an online article the day that the MLK National Memorial was unveiled. In addition, you could ask them to make use of one or more timelines in any oral presentation assignments.

Timelines or portions of them may reappear on course quizzes and examinations, with questions related to identifying events, people, and places. Such exams could also ask students to compare and contrast the timelines of two or more people, inventions, wars, religions, or political systems. To push them deeper in a topic, person, or event, you may also ask them to identify key elements or pieces of information missing from a particular timeline. Be sure to evaluate their effectiveness with students and share the results of such activities with colleagues.

Variations and Extensions. Consider having learners create a timeline, either individually or as a group, of a particular topic, unit, product, person, time period, event, and so forth. To accomplish this, they could use a tool like Capzles, Dipity, xTimeline, Simile (MIT), or the Timeline Tool 2.0 from the University of British Columbia. Peer review of timelines created could be incorporated to enhance the quality. When done, consider presenting those timelines in a synchronous or F2F class session. A gallery of timelines created each semester that the course is taught would be a means to showcase student work as well as expand the potential audience for it.

Key Instructional Considerations

Risk index: Medium
Time index: Medium
Cost index: Low
Learner-centered index: High
Duration of the learning activity: Every week or as needed

Activity 75. Exploring Animations, Simulations, and Pop-Up Media

Description and Purpose of Activity. Much experimentation in the forms and types of interactive content has taken place since the emergence of Web-based learning. Many graphs, pictures, and diagrams now contain additional content that can be accessed by clicking on it. Such pop-up media is common in digital books and interactive timelines. In opinion polls about politicians, for instance, pop-up media often indicate how males and females voted as well as how people from different educational levels or income levels feel about an issue.

As development and storage costs have come down, there is much experimentation with animation of prior events as well as interactive forecasts of the future. In the previous activity, we noted that timeline tools are especially engaging. Now add rich animation to the mix and the types and forms of learning accelerate.

For instance, in "Visualizing Emancipation," there is an interactive timeline that looks back 150 years to slave emancipation in the United States from January 1, 1861 to January 30, 1866. With this tool, students can watch events unfold over the months and years of the Civil War. This animation sequence can be paused and reviewed at any time to reveal emancipation events, union army locations, the changing legality of slavery, and event "heatmaps" indicating areas where much news was occurring (Chen, 2012). Any event can be selected and additional information will appear. Such a timeline sheds light on where and when slaves become free during the Civil War. It reveals the complex stories of emancipation through letters, military correspondences, newspaper reports, and assorted diaries of the time. Students could be asked to compare the events and resources found here to other online Civil War records such as "The War of the Rebellion: a Compilation of the Official Records of the Union and Confederate Armies."

Animations like "Visualizing Emancipation" are just one form of media that can enhance learner engagement. We have also seen an increase in simulations and science lab activities for chemistry, physics, biology, and other scientific content areas. The University of Colorado at Boulder, for instance, has built a set of research-based simulations for middle school through college age students called the PhET. These interactive simulations are fun, engaging, and highly informative. In PhET, students test hypotheses and deepen their understanding of important scientific and mathematical phenomena. Instruments like stopwatches, voltmeters, and thermometers allow users to measure or view the results of different tests or settings. For instance, learners can see what happens in a fluid and pressure simulation when flow rate, gravity, or fluid density is manipulated. In this particular simulation, the learner can predict pressure in a variety of situations as well as how fluid motion affects the pressure and how to convert water pressure to water velocity (see Figure 11.1).

FIGURE 11.1: FLUID PRESSURE AND FLOW SIMULATION FROM THE PhET INTERACTIVE SIMULATIONS PROJECT AT THE UNIVERSITY OF COLORADO (PhET).

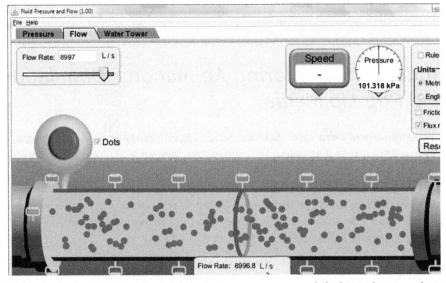

Other physics-related simulations include magnets, sound, light, radiation, electricity, and circuits. Students can explore generators, Ohm's Law, battery voltage, and semiconductors, among many other concepts. In addition to physics, there are dozens more simulations for biology, chemistry, earth science, and mathematics, each of which is available in other languages such as Chinese, Serbian, Korean, Turkish, Arabic, Spanish, and many more. It is a stockpile of math and scientific concepts vital for digital learning in the twenty-first century; especially in an age of vast concern about student abilities related to STEM. Suffice it to say, PhET is an amazing resource!

Another simulation we found exceptionally engaging is an interactive guide to toxic substances and the environment. This simulation, developed by the National Library of Medicine in Bethesda, Maryland, is called Toxic Town. Users of Toxic Town are typically in high school or college. When in the simulation, they can explore a port, town, city, farm, or the US-Mexico border community and discover different types of environmental hazards. If the user selects a port neighborhood, options appear for different port locations such as the beach, cruise ship, river, and fish farm with links to health and hazardous material information for each one. After selecting beach, for example, links will appear for information related to sun exposure, drowning, water pollution, water safety, and oil spills. The selection of office locations will bring up issues of drinking water, ergonomics, molds, secondhand smoke, and so on. In effect, Toxic Town is a fascinating review of the chemicals and substances that are encountered in a variety of environments or situations.

These are but a few examples of animations, simulations, and pop-up media that can augment and potentially transform learning. Simulations of manufacturing environments exist for business classes, school simulations for education classes, and mock courtrooms for law courses. Each is ripe for engaging learners.

Skills and Objectives. Includes empathy, visual discrimination skills, reflection, learner involvement, insight, trial and error testing, intrigue, learning through multimedia, self-directed learning and resource exploration, comparing and contrasting, visual encoding of information, and application of what was learned. Clearly, such animation and simulation tools provide rich ways to grasp complex content.

Advice and Ideas. Conduct literature reviews and online searches for animations and simulations in your discipline. Search open educational resources such as MERLOT, Connexions, Jorum, and the Open Educational Resources Commons for such media elements. Also talk to colleagues known for their creative and engaging pedagogy. Be sure to obtain the necessary copyright permission to use their materials. Given that animations and simulations can be powerful learning tools, make sure that they match your course learning goals and objectives. Also consider focusing student search and use with guiding questions and activities. When done, debrief on the activity and discuss other possible uses and activities.

Variations and Extensions. An animation, simulation, or pop-up media element could be used to start class discussion, or as a conceptual anchor for later discussion. Consider asking students to rate such resources at the end of the semester. Alternatively, students could sign up to find and present one or more forms of media during the semester. In this way, the pool of media elements continues to expand.

Key Instructional Considerations

> *Risk index: Medium*
> *Time index: Medium*
> *Cost index: Low to high (depending on availability)*
> *Learner-centered index: High*
> *Duration of the learning activity: 1–2 weeks or as needed*

Activity 76. Virtual Tools & Scientific Instruments

Description and Purpose of Activity. The Web offers innumerable new ways to manipulate objects and understand content without stepping into the real world. Many tools and objects are first touched and employed in a virtual space. It is a safe harbor for experimentation, hypothesis generation, and reflection. Such devices include drawing tools for architects, interactive spreadsheets for accountants, virtual companies for future business managers, virtual telescopes for budding astronomers, and online grade books and student portfolios for teacher trainees.

Virtual microscopes are popular in training future biologists, pathologists, and biomedical scientists. In the case of virtual microscopy, an entire microscopic slide is scanned at great detail and stored as a series of indexed, tiled images. When a student, physician, or researcher accesses the digitized slide, the indexed images are streamed and organized on the client's monitor based on the location of the client's cursor. Moving the cursor changes the field of view while a slide-bar permits change in magnification.

Unlike traditional courses in pathology and histology where microscopic glass slides can become faded or clouded by aging, smeared with dirt, or even broken, virtual samples can be reused by unlimited numbers of students without such concerns or constraints. In addition, students can change the brightness, opacity, contrast, area to be studied, and magnification (see Figure 11.2). They can also capture the screen image, write a caption, provide a comment, or insert an annotation related to what they found. Such features foster innovative ways for instructors to promote cooperative learning and the peer-to-peer sharing of information. A virtual microscope sample might contain an endoscopic biopsy, a surgical specimen, a blood smear, or even a doctor's office biopsy.

FIGURE 11.2: FEATURES OF VIRTUAL MICROSCOPE (Courtesy Of Dr. Mark Braun, Indiana University).

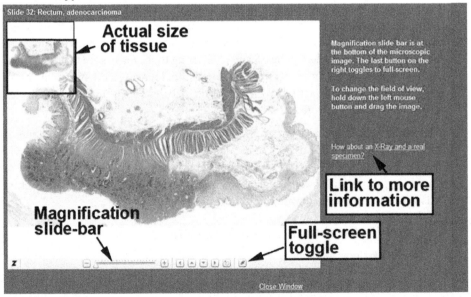

According to Dr. Mark Braun in the pathology department at Indiana University (IU) in Bloomington, Indiana, second-year IU medical students must complete all of their graded laboratory assignments and related assessments online. For the individual assignments, each student receives an e-mail message with links to virtual microscopic samples of conditions they have previously been assigned (see Figure 11.3 for a sample slide). Students are required to describe and diagnose the "unknown" microscopic sample. To assist in this process, each assessment exercise comes with a short medical history and appropriate clinical laboratory or X-ray data. As they work their way through a problem, students are required to describe the salient features of the tissue sample that supports their diagnosis.

A related group exercise reverses this process. In this case, previously designated groups of four to five medical students work collectively. Each member of the group receives the same e-mail of a link to a virtual microscopic slide. Their job is to identify the name of the organ that the biopsy came from and provide a short diagnosis. Now, instead of describing the salient microscopic features of the mystery challenger slide, each group must collectively write a plausible clinical scenario of that patient. In addition, they must devise clinical laboratory results, and possibly X-ray findings, compatible with the condition that they feel the slide represents. When done, the group collectively authors two multiple choice–style questions regarding their diagnosis and clinical scenario. Groups are given about thirty minutes to complete their scenarios and questions. Finally, all groups present their work to the class during a discussion session.

FIGURE 11.3: SAMPLE SLIDE OF CANCER CELLS WITH VIRTUAL MICROSCOPE (Courtesy of Dr. Mark Braun, Indiana University).

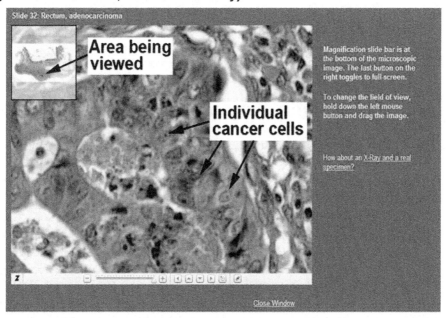

Skills and Objectives. Includes excitement and involvement in learning, discovery and inquiry learning, analysis, visual discrimination skills, data analysis, evaluation, self-directed learning, and the application of what was learned. Learners assume the role of scientist as they peer into virtual blood, algae, pollen, mites, human cells, bacteria, viruses, and various microbes.

Advice and Ideas. List the instruments, devices, tools, and artifacts used by professionals and practitioners in your discipline or related to a particular course or unit. Next, conduct a focused search for animations, demonstrations, simulations, or other media related to such devices. Explore the functionality of those discovered. Ask a couple of prior students of the course to rate or rank such media elements. Together you might author a screencasted demonstration of the tool or device if one does not exist. Prior students could also assist you in designing a set of FAQs related to the activity.

Whether you are using virtual microscopes, telescopes, stopwatches, binoculars, or cameras, you should indicate the type of analyses you are expecting, where students should record and share their results, and how they will be evaluated. You might start with a simple task to help adjust students to the virtual environment.

Variations and Extensions. Students could be assigned virtual lab partners with whom they collaboratively complete a set of assignments. Their findings could be posted in a virtual classroom space which is reviewed by two or more other teams. Results across the various teams are compared.

Our friend Professor Braun has a different approach. He has his students view an assortment of slides and then write case scenarios and a few test questions from them. He refers to his method as a reverse problem-based learning approach.

Key Instructional Considerations

Risk index: Low
Time index: Medium
Cost index: Medium
Learner-centered index: High
Duration of the learning activity: 1–2 weeks or as needed

Activity 77. Microblogging Course Discussions

Description and Purpose of Activity. Microblogging has proliferated during the past few years. With technology like Twitter, such microblogging is typically limited to 140 character posts. David Parry, an early adapter of Twitter at the University of Texas at Dallas, finds that it changes the classroom dynamics and gets students to build closer relationships with instructors as well as peers (Briggs, 2008).

Similarly, Professor Reynol Junco of Purdue University has conducted several studies revealing that such technology can engage students in very positive academic ways. In his studies, Twitter encouraged cooperative learning among students, improved contact between students and faculty, offered prompt forms of feedback, increased time on task, provided an outlet to discuss and show respect for diversity, communicated high expectations, and helped students relate course material to their lived experiences (Junco et al., 2010). Not only were students more engaged when using Twitter, but their instructors assumed a more active and participatory role.

Junco and his colleagues have used Twitter as a tool to extend class discussions about book assignments beyond F2F sessions. He and his colleagues have found rich discussions of themes as well as new friendships emerging from the short tweets. In addition to extending class discussions about assigned books, Twitter was used to remind students about course assignments and campus events. It also provided a low-stress way to ask questions, support students, organize study groups, and coordinate projects. Some instructors also use Twitter as a means to gather class opinions and to vote on different polling questions. Finally, Twitter can connect online and on-campus students by providing a vehicle to share advice, successes, and struggles while cheering each other on to other course milestones and accomplishments (Billiot, 2011).

Skills and Objectives. Include prompt feedback, peer-to-peer as well as student-instructor interaction, reflection, learner involvement, multiple levels of information processing, responsiveness, resource sharing, and community building. Provides automatic course and general information updates.

Advice and Ideas. Be clear about the activity. Junco and his colleagues, for instance, included four required Twitter assignments during the final four weeks of the semester. In three of them, students were required to post two tweets as well as two replies to other students' posts about what they had read, watched, or browsed. While this occurs, the instructor should monitor the postings and interactions as well as model such behaviors. Instructors may need to conduct a training session or provide an online guide sheet or job aid for those who are unfamiliar with microblogging. Before you do that, conduct a quick poll of student experiences with blogging as well as microblogging.

Our colleague Dr. Noeline Wright at the University of Waikato in New Zealand conducted a study with teacher education students using Twitter to post weekly reflections (Wright, 2011). Her question choices for students included:

- What am I learning now?
- What might I say about my learning right now?
- What do I need to overcome or solve?
- Where am I learning right now?
- What am I going to do next?

Twitter was used successfully during this seven-week teaching practicum to help students stay connected as a community of learners while developing into reflective practitioners.

Variations and Extensions. There are many simple extensions of using Twitter for course discussions. First, you could require students to post one online resource with each Tweet. Second, you could assign them a specific person or pair of people to follow or respond to in Twitter each week. Third, Twitter posts could provide the base or starting point for weekly podcasts produced by the students in the class. Fourth, the Twitter posts could also be used as a means to foster student questions for the instructor to respond to at a set time each week. And fifth, an assignment could be to have students link as many of the weekly Twitter posts as they can into a story, case scenario, or set of course themes.

Key Instructional Considerations

Risk index: Medium
Time index: Medium
Cost index: Low
Learner-centered index: High
Duration of the learning activity: All semester or as needed

Activity 78. Online Subject-Specific Picture Galleries

Description and Purpose of Activity. In previous chapters, we discussed how video and sound can augment or enhance learning. Selecting and rewatching a video segment can be deeply engaging. Content-specific video and audio files, however, can be complex and time-consuming to develop, and instructors may resort to pictures, graphics, charts, and other image files instead. Using images, in fact, can inspire students to delve deeper into a content area. For instance, in physics, inertia is a fundamental principle wherein an object resists changes in its state of motion. An image of a game of tug-of-war could be used to prompt a discussion of how force is exhibited by the push or pull that is exerted upon an object by way of interaction with another object. The force exhibited by participants in tug-of-war when pulling on the rope is transmitted through the rope to opposing team participants.

Not only can force be illustrated through one or more pictures of tug-of-war but other pictures can display inertia or Newton's First Law of Motion (e.g., a hovercraft), equilibrium (e.g., resting a nail or a screw head on a sheet of paper or a table), and constant speed (e.g., a hockey player skating across the ice). Searching that database of pictures, students will also find examples of Newton's Second Law of Motion related to objects accelerating when they experience an unbalanced force (e.g., a bicyclist falling down). Also contained in that portal of pictures will be those that exemplify Newton's Third law that states that for every action there is an equal and opposite reaction. This principle can be graphically illustrated by a photograph of a bug splattered on a windshield. Want more? Speed of objects, friction, acceleration, circular motion, and so on, can all be displayed through pictures of stopwatches, Ferris wheels, speedometers, radar guns, games of billiards, speed motion detectors, snowboarding, skydiving, and so forth. Fortunately, access to such resources is nearly instantaneous today.

Pictures can help the learner understand laws and principles related to light refraction, energy, static electricity, and sound waves. In fact, photos can assist students in almost any content area or discipline. In particular, they can enhance the learning of history, geography, statistics, politics, and sociology. Rich sets of pictures for cities like Salt Lake City, Chicago, Buenos Aires, Manila, Seoul, or Helsinki can help students understand how a city evolved over time. Pictures of different animals can bring to life text-related information about endangered species and the loss of habitat.

What is clear is that we are no longer limited by what the publisher has provided in textbooks, digital media, or other supplemental resources. Today, instructors have ready access to digital images from award-winning photographers and established organizations like National Geographic, the BBC, and Earthwatch. In addition to websites from established institutions and nonprofit organizations, instructors can now link any activity, assignment, or project to visual image resource-sharing sites like Flickr, Picasa, Photobucket, Pinterest, and SmugMug.

Physics, earth science, and biology class tasks might entail linkages from theory to the real world. Students might be asked to find a visual that represents a term, concept, idea, or principle. Other activities might be self-paced matching tests or quizzes or reflections on how a particular photo or illustration depicts a key term. Photos can also be repackaged into visual glossaries and chapter concept overviews.

Skills and Objectives. Include visual discrimination skills, reflection, matching, evaluation, dual coding of content, comparison and contrast, visual thinking, multimedia learning, and application of what was learned. These techniques strengthen student conceptual understanding and provide multiple cues for retrieval.

Advice and Ideas. Reflect on how you might augment or enhance your class with a photo sharing site. Spend an hour or two searching for photos and other visual elements related to your field or course. As part of this effort, be sure to search Creative Commons for freely available photos. Index or bookmark those photos that are comprehensive, eye-catching, or show promise. If the usage rights are not clearly spelled out, write to the author or designer for permission to use in your classes.

Place different pictures in a wiki and have the students work in small teams to explain the concepts that are demonstrated. You could also have them sequence pictures according to stages or phases of a theory or perspective. Another idea is to provide a series of pictures for each concept and ask students to rank the quality of each picture or find the best match. In this way, students become more engaged in the task than they would simply reading or browsing content. To foster critical thinking, they could be required to rate, rank, compare and contrast, or evaluate each image. Students might also use tools like VoiceThread to comment on a sequence of pictures that teammates could expand upon or other teams could counter and debate.

Variations and Extensions. Students could add to the database of photographs with one or more of their own. Consider establishing a discussion forum for students to comment on each other's visual connections. The top three or four such visuals can then be added to the database for the next time the course is taught.

Key Instructional Considerations

Risk index: Low
Time index: Medium
Cost index: Low
Learner-centered index: Medium
Duration of the learning activity: Anytime as needed

Activity 79. Interactive Online Exhibits (e.g., Art and Bones)

Description and Purpose of Activity. Learners are often most engaged when they can manipulate objects and artifacts that they are learning about or can experience them in different ways. In the past, those teaching art relied on books, slide images, and visits to an art museum. Today it is increasingly common to experience art and other types of museums virtually. In fact, virtual encounters with art are likely much more common today than physical experiences.

Instructors of art, literature, history, world cultures, and many other topics can explore the Google Art Project. Places to explore virtually include the National Gallery in London, the Art Gallery of New South Wales, the Museum of Modern Art (MoMA) in New York, the Hong Kong Heritage Museum, and the Tokyo National Museum. In a word, the Web is expansive.

Immersed in the Google Art Project, the user can search over 32,000 artworks in high resolution, more than 150 art museum or institute collections, and 5,400 user galleries, representing the work of thousands of artists. The browsing can take place by type of art, artist, the artwork, the museum, and the country, city, and collection (Google, 2012). Often, there are only partial views of what a particular museum holds; still, the Google Art Project is extremely rich in culture and content. As with Street View in Google Maps, the user can walk down museum hallways and approach different pieces of art for close-up views (Croxall, 2011). In fact, with zooming capabilities, the close-up views are quite stunning. Google includes details of the catalogue and viewing notes as well as links to other pieces of work by that artist. It even includes links to associated videos in YouTube if available. Finally, users can build their own collections of favorites and share those collections publicly.

The Google Art Project is not the only game in town. Such resources are also available for disciplines like archaeology and anthropology. For instance, there is an amazing virtual tour of the Smithsonian National Museum of Natural History. For those wanting to explore actual bones of animals, anthropology Professor Herbert Maschner of Idaho State University has developed a "Virtual Zooarchaeology of the Arctic Project" that includes an online, interactive, virtual museum of animal bones from the North American Arctic as well as Greenland, including fish, birds, and mammals (Monaghan, 2011). Once there, visitors will find thousands of two- and three-dimensional images to search through.

Skills and Objectives. Include interactivity, student autonomy and choice, reflection, visual discrimination skills, multimedia learning, data analysis, evaluation, comparison and contrast, visual thinking, inquiry, self-directed learning and resource exploration, and identification of key concepts. There are ample hands-on learning experiences as learners experience the artifact, product, or item.

Advice and Ideas. If you find virtual exhibits in your domain, you can embed them in many ways. First, the exhibit can be a supplement to course readings for one or more weeks. In a psychology course, for instance, students could engage in specific well-known experiments that display particular principles or concepts (e.g., figure-ground experiments in perceptual psychology). They could write reviews of the exhibit and reflect on how such principles are used in real life. In art or art history classes, virtual exhibits can bring students closer to a particular masterpiece or a less well-known part of a collection. Students can write reflection papers on their encounters with the works of one or more artists. Alternatively, prior to the virtual experience, they can read background materials on a particular artist, exhibit, or time period, reflecting on the degree to which the experience matched their incoming expectations.

Reflection papers are one form of engagement. Instructors may also consider having teams of students create a rubric for evaluating the interactive online exhibit and overall experience. Next, they should write reflections papers on the collaboration process as well as the resulting rubric.

Variations and Extensions. Consider surveying students on the user experience, including questions probing specific interactive features or content that could be added to the user experience. Alternatively, have students create surveys for users of a particular site, and then send the survey results and written report to the site development team. Such research could also be presented at conferences.

Key Instructional Considerations

Risk index: Medium
Time index: Medium
Cost index: Low
Learner-centered index: Medium
Duration of the learning activity: Anytime as needed

Activity 80. Three-Level Questioning

Description and Purpose of Activity. Since ancient Athens, engagement and involvement in learning were often made salient through different forms of questioning. During the past few decades, educational researchers have dug deeply into the types and levels of questions asked in the classroom. Whether in K–12 or higher education settings, what they discovered was that the instructional focus is too often at the knowledge level, which, as many know, is the lowest level of Bloom's famed taxonomy. Here, learners are asked to match, list, or identify something. Some educators suggest asking questions at all six levels of Bloom, namely, knowledge, comprehension, application, analysis, synthesis, and evaluation.

There are simpler ways to foster discussion than the six levels of Bloom. Arthur Costa, for instance, introduced the three-level questioning technique. At Level 1, the questions asked are at the factual level to determine what students do and do not know. This is akin to the first level of Bloom's taxonomy (i.e., knowledge). For instance, you may ask, "What do you know about this particular case or situation already?" or "What is the formula or equation for this problem?" Common knowledge level words include name, define, state, label, select, and recall.

At Level 2, the questioning shifts to interpretation and analysis, not just facts. Interpretative questions address implications of different results or data, the motives or causes of a particular historical event or recent news reports, and searching for relationships between pieces of information that are provided. Words like organize, grouping, break down, compare and contrast, infer, and sequence could be used here.

At Level 3, thinking shifts to still higher-level concerns where learners evaluate datasets and make hypotheses about a particular psychological experiment. They may also use their imaginations to design a model or framework, compose a poem or song, or make predictions about a company's performance or the entire industry sector. Commons words here include decide, summarize, evaluate, apply, assess, construct, and critique.

With such a three-level framework in hand, an instructor can attempt to foster different types of thinking in an online discussion forum or in a synchronous class chat or reflection activity. One or more questions of each type can be posted weekly. Alternatively, instructors could have a question at each of the three levels for every article, chapter, or other resource required for the week.

Skills and Objectives. Includes feedback, fostering reflection, evaluation, comprehension, concept attainment, depth of information processing, and content review. With multiple levels of questioning, there are alternative ways for learners to demonstrate their learning.

Advice and Ideas. Be clear regarding how many questions to address each week as well as the length of responses. Also provide explicit assessment criteria. Consider having three separate discussion forums each week: one for factual or declarative questions, one for interpretative types of questions, and one for application and evaluation questions. Alternatively, three or more questions could be embedded within discussion threads for each article or topic of discussion. Instructors may also consider adopting a policy of including several of these discussion forum or practice questions on course quizzes and examinations.

Experiment with other forms of questioning or make up your own system. The important factor is to push students to reflect on what they are reading, browsing, exploring, or critiquing. With the wealth of content available online today, it is vital to find ways to involve or engage your students in the content. Perhaps have them cite page numbers or mention new concepts learned each time they post. You could also have them offer linkages between concepts mentioned in two or more postings. And each time a student posts a response or answer to a particular reflection question posed by the instructor or fellow students, that person must also reply to one or more peer posts. You may also employ the "three sentence" rule detailed in Starter-Wrapper Technique (Activity #43) in Chapter Eight.

Bear in mind that incorporating Costa's ideas about levels of questioning into your fully online and blended courses will only work if you are explicit about the purpose of the activity with your students. You could attempt to foster metacognitive aspects of reading and writing by requiring short and perhaps sporadic reflection papers on their responses to the questions. Remember Claude Cookman's TAR method back in Chapter Six when discussing Just-in-Time-Teaching (Activity #25). Using the TARs approach to capture student comprehension of the content in a discussion forum prior to class can help the instructor shift the live class session toward student interests as well as misconceptions.

Variations and Extensions. One obvious variation would be to assign students to design their own sets of questions and post them to the course management system. Another extension could be to use four, five, or six levels of questions; for example, following Bloom's taxonomy, have students post questions at the following six levels: knowledge, comprehension, application, analysis, synthesis, and evaluation. At the end of the course, students could be asked to select the best questions posted from each of the six categories of Bloom. You could reuse the highest-rated questions during the following semester.

Key Instructional Considerations

Risk index: Low
Time index: Medium
Cost index: Low
Learner-centered index: Medium
Duration of the learning activity: 1–2 weeks or as needed

Final Reflections on Engagement

There is little doubt that students want to be involved and engaged in the learning process. When that happens, there are increased levels of student investment and effort. The ramifications are immense. If an instructor or entire program found ways to engage learners at higher levels than normal, retention and completion rates would certainly rise. As Richardson and Newby (2006) argue, we hope that some of the ideas we have mapped out can help professional educators design more engaging and successful online learning environments and activities.

The forms of engagement discussed in this chapter have mainly addressed the learner-content variety though we included a couple of learner-learner and learner-instructor interaction ideas as well. Our examples included the use of interactive timeline tools, exhibits, glossaries, simulations, talking dictionaries, comprehensive databases, and scientific equipment like virtual microscopes. We also described new forms of pop-up media that can engage learners as they read a digital book or browse an online portal or reference resource. In addition, with creative insights and a bit of thoughtful tinkering, engagement can be fostered by using the countless free and open picture galleries, sound clips, Twitter feeds, and animation files at our disposal today. What might have been deemed a static picture can quickly come to life when juxtaposed against difficult course concepts and thorny theoretical principles that the picture helps to clarify.

Such forms of learner-content engagement are proliferating so quickly that it is extremely difficult to keep up. Without a doubt, there will be many unique ways for learner engagement and involvement that will spring up during the coming decade in every discipline. These learner-content experiences will feel highly authentic and visually realistic. As virtual spaces increase in fidelity and take on an increasing sense of realism, there will be a reduced need for early field experiences and direct contact with the materials, resources, and tools of the practitioner. This is not to say that physical experiences will no longer be important. What we do believe, however, is that Principle #8 of the TEC-VARIETY model will become a centerpiece of most any fully online or blended course or experience. To raise completion rates and success, the recent emergence of MOOCs and other unique course delivery methods and innovations will need to incorporate activities for greater learner engagement and investment in the learning process. Electronic page turning will no longer suffice.

The ideas mapped out in this chapter can only be a starting point. It is up to you to find the content, resources, and tools that can send learner engagement soaring to new heights. As already mentioned several times, the focus of the previous chapter on learner-learner interactivity should be combined with the learner-content examples of this chapter. Additional forms of learner-content and learner-learner interactivity and engagement are discussed in the following chapter. Chapter Twelve is concerned with taking advantage of the power of tension and conflict or sense of dissonance when learners realize that they do not have all the requisite skills and knowledge or that they actually misunderstand a key term or concept. When that is case, learners are motivated to seek out additional information. Online instructors and instructional designers must find innovative ways to take advantage of such a sense of controversy, conflict, and bewilderment. Effective learning environments include collaboration and engagement, discussed in the previous two chapters, as well as some sense of conflict and competition elaborated on in the next. Just witness the success of massive multiplayer online gaming.

And so we push on to a chapter on how to foster some sense of conflict and competition. In Chapter Twelve, we will discuss Principle #9, namely, Tension as well as Challenge, Dissonance, and Controversy. Before you turn the page, we want you to reflect on the times in which you were tense or felt a state of dissonance and then sought additional information. Then list the factors that nudged you to want to learn more. What were they? How might you take advantage of such forms of dissonance in your fully online and blended courses? Read on.

CHAPTER TWELVE

PRINCIPLE #9 TENSION

(includes Challenge, Dissonance, and Controversy)

> The ultimate measure of a man is not where
> he stands in moments of comfort and conveniences,
> but where he stands at times of challenge and controversy.
>
> —Martin Luther King Jr.

As Walter Isaacson's 2011 thick biography of Steve Jobs illustrates, one individual's devotion to perfection can generate products and processes that truly change the world. Underlying that constant striving toward product perfection, however, was much human imperfection. Steve Jobs could be extremely tough, impetuous, demanding, brazen, pushy, rude, and dehumanizing. He would openly denigrate people and projects that were not producing fast enough or working out as planned. To many, he was a jerk. Writing in Wired, Ben Austen (2012) took a slightly softer stance and described him as highly devout in rejecting ideas that he did not like. From another point of view, he was passionate and intense in finding ways to design products reaching unsurpassed quality standards.

Though Jobs was clearly passionate about everything that happened at Apple, did he take the notion of tension and challenge too far? Perhaps underlying it all was a belief in challenging initial product designs so as to make them better. For instance, Isaacson's book reveals that Jobs had a taste for office environments rich with interaction, collaboration, and dialogue. In fact, Apple's future "spaceship" campus in Cupertino, California, is being designed for "serendipitous and fluid meeting spaces" (Isaacson, 2011, p. 535) among the 13,000 employees who will work there (Gross, 2012). There will also be an immense courtyard about the length of three football fields for strolls through apricot orchards to discuss pressing issues, product designs, and project schedules.

Without a doubt, Jobs was a controversial figure whose challenges often resulted in higher-quality products. Similar things might be said of many educators and their elevated student project standards. To help you better understand such perspectives and approaches, we discuss instructional challenges and competitions in many sections of this chapter; other aspects of this chapter have to do with controversy as well as cognitive tension or dissonance.

The news media and movies often portray Steve Jobs as someone who was extremely self-assured. He had an intuitive sense that he was right about particular product design features or major company decisions. Not all of us are so lucky. Have you ever had that sense of not knowing something on the way home from school or work and then looking it up online when you got home and feeling satisfied? Naturally, that seeking behavior is often even more pronounced when you are pretty sure that you know the answer already but simply cannot retrieve the needed information at that exact moment. When you encounter such tip-of-the-tongue experiences, you are dealing with internal conflict or tension between what you think you know and your mental abilities to retrieve that information.

At that point, you have entered what famed psychologist Jean Piaget (1969) referred to as a state of disequilibrium. You may also enter such a state when you misunderstand something like a mathematical or scientific concept such as how we arrive at the seasons of the year or the conditions needed for a solar eclipse.

Such states of not knowing, misunderstanding, and contradiction are essential for effective instruction. The perception of inadequate knowledge fosters curiosity and focused energy to find the needed information. Despite the amazing power of mental tension and conflict, David and Roger Johnson from the University of Minnesota point out that educators are often extremely apprehensive about instilling a climate of controversy or intellectual conflict because it can lead to undesirable outcomes such as anger, explicit hostility, feelings of distrust among students, damaged relationships, and outright rejection (Johnson & Johnson, 2009).

Johnson and Johnson point out that Piaget's theory of cognitive development was a key part of the theoretical framework for the cooperative learning technique called constructive controversy. Piaget (1926) believed that interacting with others helps students confront their own misconceptions. Interpersonal disagreements create a sense of disequilibrium within an individual's cognitive structure. And, as noted in Chapter Six on Curiosity, it is that state of disequilibrium which motivates the search for a more adequate understanding of some topic (Piaget, 1969). In effect, opportunities for peer interaction help a learner move away from an egocentric viewpoint and begin to reason from multiple perspectives. In a Piagetian framework, peer confrontation and conflict can trigger cognitive dissonance or disequilibrium, causing one or more of the group members to seek additional information to resolve the conflict (Inhelder & Piaget, 1958).

To combat such trends, the Johnson brothers developed the constructive controversy method. In constructive controversy, the learners present opposing positions or points of view along with their rationale. The challenges from others result in some type of internal conceptual conflict or uncertainty about whether one's point of view is correct. But unlike debate situations in which participants are typically not open to differing points of view, in constructive controversy, learners are motivated to search for additional information in order to reach consensus or agreement. There is an emphasis on criticizing ideas and not people as well as listening to everyone's ideas.

Across the steps or stages of constructive controversy, learners are motivated to improve their understanding. They have a strong desire to learn more about a particular topic. They want to defend their ideas and resolve differences in an intelligent manner. How is that displayed? Well, they seek out more resources, read more materials, request additional information from others, and convert open hours or free time into study time (Reeve, 1996). And in fully online and blended classes, the available resources to scan and to search are seemingly endless.

There are many factors that can have an impact on the success of such challenging learning environments. According to Reeve (1996), if there is a reward like a grade in the end, students will lean toward the easier or less challenging tasks. However, when the situation involves self-directed learning pursuits, students will choose tasks at optimal levels of challenge in order to improve their competencies and master the content. If they had to choose between something easy and something hard, self-directed learners would side with the harder task.

Educators should be aware that there are many ways to build in challenge, dissonance, conflict, and mental tension. To challenge students, an instructor might individualize assignments, offer enrichment or supplemental activities, design open-ended tasks that require the display of at least some creativity, embed opportunities for learner exploration of content, and give students some choice in their assignments (Stipek, 1998). To foster conflict or dissonance, the same instructor might call attention to unusual or exotic elements of a problem, note exceptions to general rules, point out unexpected, paradoxical, or incongruous aspects of the data or information (Brophy, 1998). It is the discomfort or cognitive dissonance from such inconsistencies that instructors can tap into to spur learners to seek additional information (Festinger, 1957).

Technologies for Principle #9: Tension

When you say the word "tension" or "controversy," is there an activity involving an online technology that springs to your head as an instructor? If you have taught several classes online, you likely have read through many discussion forums brimming with controversial issues and intense learner interactions and debates. You may have also witnessed firsthand passionate debates during interactive videoconferences among students from different parts of the world (Lee & Bonk, 2013). Your students may have taken part in interactive role plays and mock trials that involved heavy doses of tension and heated interactions. If so, they have likely been quite effective and energizing experiences.

There are many other methods available to arouse learner tension and curiosity. For instance, we have used discussion forum tools that did not allow our learners to read the contributions of their peers until they had first completed some assigned task. In addition, some of our colleagues have used argument maps or debate tools like Argunet or Cohere to foster debate and interaction. Such tools help learners externalize their reasoning processes about a topic or issue. Concept maps and mind maps, which are explained in Bonk and Zhang (2008), can serve similar purposes.

That is just a start. With some brief reflection and restructuring, the timeline, multimedia glossary, simulation, animation, virtual microscope, and other activities in Chapter Eleven could also be used for intense course challenges and debates. In fact, every chapter in this book is likely replete with tools and resources for fostering controversy, tension, and cognitive dissonance.

Ronald Cole and Teresa Crawford (2007) document how different information and communication technologies can be used for conflict resolution and peace building. Online dispute resolution tools (ODRT) can help process information, frame arguments, and ultimately resolve conflicts. Such tools can foster debate, negotiation, and arbitration. Text messaging can mobilize people for large-scale political protests and demonstrations (e.g., as we have seen in Iran, Egypt, the Philippines, and Libya) and similar social purposes. Cole and Crawford also noted how online discussion forums allowed people from Burundi to discuss the root causes of problems that they were facing and figure out ways to move forward during intense internal fighting there. As bandwidth expands, video messages can also be used to communicate personal perspectives, instead of just relying on text-based discussions.

There are many technologies for conflict resolution. Radio, e-mail, simulations and games, website portals, blogs, and instant chat can all play a role. More recently, social networking technologies like Twitter, Flickr, Ning, Facebook, and Meetup are being used to connect people for educational purposes as well as to address and lend hope for those in quite dire social, economic, or political situations. As an example, in South Korea, students voiced their displeasure with intense college entrance exams by organizing a protest through text messaging.

The tools and resources for fostering as well as resolving conflict and controversy will increase in the coming years. Educators must expose students to these resources in order to better prepare them for the real world. We are not suggesting that teachers equip their learners with tools for violence, but rather that they help students understand how to use technology to resolve conflict in a peaceful manner. Although technologies cannot create peace, they can equip people with the means to communicate more effectively and better understand a situation or point of view.

Ten Online Activities in Principle #9: Tension

As mentioned, there will not be as many new technologies to explore in this chapter as in the last few. The debates, role plays, and structured controversies of this chapter rely on text, video, digital images, and other online resources already detailed in many sections of this book. As a result, the Web resources associated with this chapter will be rather thin in comparison to others.

Instead of concerning yourself with tackling an assembly of technology tools to foster tension and cognitive dissonance, you might think about how you can structure fully online and blended courses for intense discussions, debates, and challenges using the technologies you are already comfortable with. At the same time, you should push your students out of their comfort zones. This will not always be easy to accomplish; however, staying attuned to recent news and cultural events and continuing to think about how they might be used for class discussion of critical issues will likely spark extensive learner interest in your course as well as long-lasting knowledge gains.

Activity 81. Debating Controversial Online News, Blogs, and Other Media

Description and Purpose of Activity. With the emergence of participatory online news, blogs, and video reports, there is increasing controversy reflected in the news media. Video-sharing sites like ForaTV and LinkTV are filled with videos of controversial societal issues. Hundreds of blog posts each week in the Huffington Post, CNN, and the BBC alone provide a cornucopia of political, cultural, and social news brimming with material for potential class controversies and debates. Adding to the landscape of online media content, places like Big Think offer a treasure trove of issue-based videos as well as opinion-heavy blog posts. And traditional newspapers like the *Boston Globe,* the *New York Times, Washington Post,* and the *Wall Street Journal* are now overflowing with reader opinions in op-ed blog postings and reviews as well as minimally censored reader comments to posted articles.

Such blog posts, videos, online news reports, and social media feeds often raise significant issues which have two or more perspectives. Typically, it does not take more than a few moments to find high-quality videos on YouTube, Big Think, and TED related to hotly debated topics such as global warming, stem cell research, legalized gambling, gun control, and health care reform. In this age of climate change and ecological destruction, environmentally related news stories are especially potent. For instance, when nearly 2 million gallons of dispersants were poured into the Gulf of Mexico in spring and summer of 2010 after the infamous BP gulf oil spill catastrophe, there were questions about its future impact on the quality of marine life (Fischman, 2012).

Social and political media are equally emotional, such as when thousands of people in Wisconsin protest actions by their governor, Scott Walker, concerning collective bargaining (Imam, 2012). Similarly, videos, photographs, Twitter feeds, Facebook updates, blogs, and online news reporting helped people around the world understand why Egyptian people were protesting in Tahrir Square during the Arab Spring. Such types of news reporting are now part of our daily lives. As CNN Tech reporter Jareen Imam (2012) notes, the Web is the most valuable resource today for information, communication, and news.

One place where you will find a wide range of controversial environmental concerns is from the Notes from Sea Level blog postings of our friend, noted filmmaker, adventurer, award-winning journalist, and blogger, Jon Bowermaster. His OCEANS 8 project explored the world's oceans from the seat of a sea kayak and was funded, in part, by National Geographic. Fortunately, OCEANS 8 programming can now be freely viewed online at LinkTV. Equally important, his media-rich blog postings have provided immense amounts of content on wide-ranging environmental issues for more than a decade. Notes at Sea Level, as well as Bowermaster's latest website, TakePark, set the stage for a rich collection of engaging curricular activities. Lately, he has been concerned with hydraulic fracturing (also known as "fracking") (Bowermaster, 2012a, 2012b), which is being debated in his home state of New York (Gibney, 2012). Of course, there are plenty of bloggers, writers, and videographers on the more conservative side of the spectrum who supply substantive amounts of content for opposing viewpoints, if needed.

Skills and Objectives. Includes comparison and contrast, data analysis, seeking reasoned judgments, evaluating claims, judging the credibility of sources, appreciating other points of view, forming arguments and rebuttals, logical reasoning, and backing up claims. Learners may also get involved in a social issue or cause. Involvement may lead to further study in an area.

Advice and Ideas. Make note of online media when issues related to your field are raised. In fact, you could devote entire weeks of the course to controversial issues that students can select to explore and react to. Once they have investigated such resources, students can respond to debates that the instructor has designed in an online discussion forum, private or public wiki, or course blog. Students might be assigned to particular sides of such a debate and be requested to cite from two or more online articles or blog posts with appropriate online links, to back up each major comment submitted. When done, each student or team of students could draft papers on the topic, including their reflections on the debate process.

In the case of op-ed pieces and blog posts, your students can often post personal comments and reactions at the online news site. Instructors could, in fact, require students to post their reactions, or, alternatively, record them in a personal blog or course wiki. The news writer or filmmaker might be invited to respond to student questions, concerns, and issues related to their work in a Webcast or online chat. Such experts could also comment on any related student projects or discussions. In addition, others affected by the controversial topic (e.g., those in local communities impacted by contaminated waters) might be interviewed. Students could even join protests and community forums.

Variations and Extensions. Instead of text-based debates, students on each side of a debate could be required to find two or more visuals that back up their side. Such visuals might include shared online videos, animations, simulations, photographs, or graphic designs. They must use them to support their online or F2F discussions and debates. An independent panel or pair of students could judge the quality of the visual connections.

Key Instructional Considerations

Risk index: Medium
Time index: Medium
Cost index: Low
Learner-centered index: High
Duration of the learning activity: 1–2 weeks or as needed

Activity 82. Structured Controversy

Description and Purpose of Activity. As indicated earlier, constructive forms of controversy can foster rich instructional situations where learners seek out additional knowledge. Controversies arise when there is some sort of mismatch, or conflict, in the attitudes, beliefs, and theories of individuals or groups of people about some topic or subject area. Tension can also simmer and suddenly ignite when there are differences in access to available information. Controversies will also heat up when blatant misstatements and misconceptions are deliberately or inadvertently placed in information sources. When educators find such a topic, dilemma, or issue, it can serve as a lightning rod for student quests to gather more information and then share their knowledge and opinions. Of course, with the bountiful information available on the Web today, that quest is increasingly taking place in online environments.

There is much that needs to be done to set the table for a successful structured controversy event. For instance, Johnson and Johnson (1995) argue that students must be reminded to listen to opposing points of view and make an effort to understand different positions or perspectives related to the controversy. They must also be willing to change their minds as evidence is presented. Learners should also attempt to arrive at a solution only after all evidence has been submitted and adequately analyzed. Disagreements during the process are to be directed only at the other positions, not at the person or team holding the positions (Johnson & Johnson, 2009).

There are a wealth of benefits when a structured controversy is effectively planned, including forcing students to grasp and organize content and ideas, prepare their positions, and search for new experiences or information to resolve the uncertainty or dilemma (Zainuddin & Moore, 2003). Such intellectual struggles are powerful learning tools. In addition to cognitive gains during the process, students will be actively engaged and their curiosity will be sparked.

The typical procedure for structured controversy is for students to be presented with a controversial issue or dilemma of some type. These controversies might be found in recent news such as drilling in the Arctic refuge, bombing specific locations in Yemen or Mali suspected of harboring terrorists, lifting the national debt ceiling, and expanding tax exemptions for manufacturers of electric cars and other key sources of alternative energy. Next, pairs or teams of students are assigned to research their particular advocacy position. Naturally, the instructor should provide supporting documents, resources, and references to help each pair or team conduct their research. Students from different groups will then present their positions. In fully online courses, this presentation could be either asynchronously conducted in an online discussion thread or occur synchronously in an online Web conference. Different sides of an issue are then argued and debated with main points highlighted. Any uncertainty or misstatements in the respective presentations will arouse disequilibrium and conceptual conflict (Johnson & Johnson, 1995).

After a set amount of time has elapsed, student teams will switch roles and research the other side of the issue. In the process, learners must reconceptualize and reorganize the content in unique ways. The groups of pro and con sides then meet again online to discuss the two different positions or points of view. Each team of two people representing a side could present a dilemma or issue for the other one to resolve. At some point, the pair drops their advocacy role and prepares a joint consensus report on the problem, issue, or question.

Skills and Objectives. Includes seeing multiple sides to an issue, intellectual inquiry, building intellectual arguments, synthesizing various information sources, critical analysis of a problem, rebutting another's challenges, seeking reasoned judgments, teamwork, comparison and contrast, data analysis, backing up claims, listening skills, and communication (Zainuddin & Moore, 2003). Learner perspective taking is elevated when they exchange roles or points of view.

Advice and Ideas. List some possible controversial topics in your field. To help in such endeavors, skim through recent online journals, newsletters, blogs, and reports. Choose one or more such topics and begin to draft a curriculum activity around it. Run it by colleagues or former students for suggestions and potential resources. Be sure to tie your assessments to your learning goals and expectations. Consider drafting an initial grading rubric and share that with your students.

In setting up the controversial task, organize a set of resources that adequately frame the major arguments on each side of the issue. Try to avoid any personal bias in the selection, organization, and explanation of such resources. At the same time, fully explain student roles, expected time frames and results, and how student performance will be evaluated. Learners should realize that in such a structured debate format, unlike a traditional debate situation, the ultimate goal is not to win but to achieve some form of consensus and compromise position through active listening and remaining open to alternative points of view. If the discussion and debate is taking place online, the instructor might act as a moderator who checks for understanding of the different viewpoints and clarifies points made.

To avoid situations where some team members do more work than others, require everyone to present. There should also be time assigned for teams to ask clarifying questions of other teams. Students could compose the compromise position in a wiki or a discussion forum which is posted for other teams to respond to. A final paper can be written and expanded based on such feedback.

Variations and Extensions. Experts or practitioners from the real world might be solicited to assist each team or viewpoint, possibly providing timely resources, ideas, or insights into a field or debate topic. Such assistance can serve to deepen the debate as well as apprentice students into a field of study.

Key Instructional Considerations

Risk index: Medium
Time index: Medium
Cost index: Low
Learner-centered index: High
Duration of the learning activity: 1–2 weeks or as needed

Activity 83. Structured Role Debates (e.g., Court Forums)

Description and Purpose of Activity. In Activity #32 (Chapter Seven) we discussed a virtual world role play. Later on in Activity #61 (see Chapter Ten), we discussed role play of a scholar, scientist, or innovator. Those role-play activities were highly open ended and intended to foster creative thinking and reflection. However, as shown in the preceding Activity #82, such role play can also be more structured and specifically designed to foster debate and controversy. For instance, in the Kelley Direct online MBA program at Indiana University, a special "role-play forum" was designed in 2005 for students to take on specific roles in case and scenario discussions and debates on different topics.

With this course management system tool, business law professors could create a "court forum" in which students assumed the role of plaintiffs, defendants, and judges (Liu, Lee, Bonk, Magjuka, & Liu, 2008). The court forum was a modified tool for asynchronous conferencing that was specifically tailored as a space for interaction, discussion, and debate of business law cases. Students could place their arguments in the simulated court forum. When properly structured, students encountered real-world conflicts and controversies that they might later experience in the business world. Our research indicated that instructors and students found such activities to be highly interactive (Liu et al., 2008). In some cases, instructors assumed the role of a judge who asked difficult questions of both sides after the plaintiffs and defendants (i.e., the students) had posted a summary of their arguments. Students could view what was happening on the other side of the argument but were not allowed to post to it. In the next round, a group of judges weighed in. Such judges might be experts in the field, prior students of the course, or students currently taking the course (Lee, Magjuka, Liu, & Bonk, 2006).

This technique is a method of dividing the task responsibility while structuring the forms of interaction and debate. Learners will have seen court situations in movies, dramas, and possibly in real life. The online court forum energizes learners to come up with the winning point of view. They must dig deep into the data and make logical arguments.

Another example of a structured role-play situation can be found in a course on the Introduction to Electricity Markets taught by Professor Gregory Thurnher at Tulane University's Freeman School of Business. Thurnher's students in the MBA and master of finance programs are assigned different "power broker" roles such as electric utility analyst, utility dispatchers, power traders, and independent power producers (Brannon, 2010). The simulation and role-play activity is designed to closely approximate what the students might later experience in a utility and independent power trading and dispatch desk. The goal is to expose learners to real-world experiences that challenge even the most senior trading executives and energy professionals.

Such hands-on experiences using advanced professional trading tools is a new approach to understanding energy finance. It is also quite helpful for students to land positions in energy companies, specialist securities firms, banks, and different types of trading organizations.

Skills and Objectives. Includes spontaneity, creative expression, building intellectual arguments, assuming roles or identities, interactivity, backing up claims, comparison and contrast, data analysis, evaluation of data, appreciating other points of view, and forming arguments and rebuttals. Learners begin to grasp the skills required for different occupations or societal roles.

Advice and Ideas. Carefully select the content and topic of the online debate. Some content might be prepackaged from book publishers or designed by someone in your department or program. Naturally, students will need specific details on when to start, how to interact, and how to respond to each other. Be clear on student roles including the types and forms of interaction, the expected posting or participation behaviors, and the resources students are required to master or allowed to use. Instructors might assume one or more roles so as to model expected behaviors as well as monitor student progress. Consider assigning a final reflection paper at the end of the activity. You may also hold a debriefing session on the intended purpose and final results of the activity.

Variations and Extensions. Roles could be rotated on a weekly or per-event basis. Students can also script in new roles that they have researched and assume them. And prior students of the course could be offered cameo appearances in the role play or simulation, possibly participating weekly.

Alternatively, a different person can be specifically assigned the role of devil's advocate each week. This assignment of this role should be made by the instructor via a private e-mail; as it is a secret, the other students in the course will not immediately realize why someone finds an idea, comment, or solution problematic. The devil's advocate will take positions that she does not necessarily agree with but is doing so for the sake of argument. In effect, the devil's advocate is attempting to engage others in a conversation through argumentative discussion. As such, the technique tests the quality of original arguments and identifies weaknesses.

Key Instructional Considerations

Risk index: High
Time index: Medium
Cost index: Low to High (depending on the system used)
Learner-centered index: High
Duration of the learning activity: 1–2 weeks or as needed

Activity 84. Online Study Group Challenges

Description and Purpose of Activity. As noted above, the days of F2F study groups are fading fast in favor of online environments. Classes that break into study teams can help learners stay on task with course reminders and supports. Web resources like OpenStudy allow students to sign up for groups in such domains as finance, biology, chemistry, computer science, engineering, linear algebra, writing, and health sciences. They may also be forming groups around topics from the MIT OpenCourseWare (OCW) project. In OpenStudy, learners who are struggling can get help from peers around the world.

Online study groups like OpenStudy are beginning to award medals for helping peers learn. Among these medals are achievement awards for those who are active participants in the open study dialogue. Such individuals are the ones who ask questions, answer questions, and socialize in the study group. Not surprisingly, they are also the ones who other users are "fans" of for being particularly helpful to them (Watters, 2011). The system also notes the number of days studied, people helped, and testimonials received. As a user amasses many fans, she can "level up" to become a hero and, if particularly helpful, perhaps a Super Hero. Users have ratings for their teamwork, problem-solving, and engagement skills. For each of these, they accumulate points to earn status as a Rookie, Hatchling, Neophyte, Learner, Helper, Champion, Mentor, Facilitator, Lifesaver, and Lifesaver Ambassador. Achievement medals can result both from support within a group on a particular topic as well as across the OpenStudy site as a whole. As of July 2012, there were over 100,000 students from 170 different countries and 1,600 schools in OpenStudy. That will make for many potential fans and heroes!

There are other tools that learners can use to form study groups, including Homework Help from Chegg, Grockit, and NoteMesh; the latter is a free service intended for college students that relies on wiki technology. With NoteMesh, students post lecture notes for specific courses that they have taken as well as make contributions to existing notes. Such team collaboration can foster community building and interaction among students. In contrast, with test prep tools like Grockit, a student from Houston can prepare for a college entrance exam with a student from Milwaukee, Wisconsin, Mumbai, India, or Aberdeen, Scotland (Koebler, 2011).

Skills and Objectives. Includes teamwork and support, sharing, competition, goal setting, interactivity, excitement for learning, appreciating other points of view, and the application of what was learned. Given that students are already in study groups, adding specific challenges or competitions offers possibilities for community building and identity.

Advice and Ideas. Instructors might form study group teams for a course or allow students to determine their own teams. They might also have learners form a class team in OpenStudy or NoteMesh specifically designed for online study groups. The advantage of OpenStudy is that it will accumulate points in terms of help offered within the system. Other systems like Piazza and Course Networking, mentioned in Chapter Ten, might also be used for such purposes; the particular advantage of these is that they can be used privately for a specific class or set of classes.

Learners may be challenged to answer correctly the greatest number of their peers' questions or, at least, to offer the most responses or questions attempted. Although learning analytics are still somewhat primitive, course management systems will normally track the number of postings made by each student. Study teams could also be rewarded for highest overall average test scores among members of their team. In addition, instructors could post challenge questions, puzzles, difficult cases or scenarios, and quizzes for teams to answer. Consider expanding such activities beyond an individual class to multiple sections of the same class or to classes in other locations.

Variations and Extensions. Create some type of point system for different study group competitions during the semester. Instead of one challenge dictating the winner, there can be multiple opportunities for success and recognition. To foster a sense of learner-centeredness, students could also be solicited for possible challenge questions or problems to post across online study group teams.

Key Instructional Considerations

Risk index: Medium
Time index: Medium
Cost index: Low
Learner-centered index: High
Duration of the learning activity: Every week or as needed

Activity 85. Timed Disclosures and Issue Voting

Description and Purpose of Activity. In a F2F class, the instructor can pause at any moment and collect student opinions, votes, suggestions, and nominations. Often, however, the ideas shared are public. This sharing can lead to notions of groupthink with everyone agreeing with the more domineering individuals in the course. Worse still, when this occurs, shy, introverted, and less confident students in the course feel inhibited from participating fully in a particular task and in the class as a whole. However, as Susan Cain eloquently argues in her book, *Quiet: The Power of Introverts in a World That Can't Stop Talking* (2012), oftentimes it is the more introverted individual who has the most creative or insightful solutions. Despite years of being marginalized or overlooked in schools, there are many passionate leaders, acclaimed innovators, and strong contributors to society among the introverted population.

That is a serious educational problem. Fortunately, it is one that fully online and blended learning can address. With proper structuring, online environments can help shy or introverted students to feel more comfortable participating. When online, they can step into an asynchronous discussion forum, wiki, or personal blog—places where introverts find themselves in a safe harbor to tinker and refine their thoughts and ideas. Typos and even misconceptions can be edited or corrected on a virtual napkin such as an online notepad or in a wiki. Eventually, these ideas can be shared. At that point, some Web tools and pedagogical practices can still maintain the anonymity of all student postings and suggestions.

In Activity #12, detailed in Chapter Five, we discussed course polling and voting ideas as a means to enhance student interactivity and feedback. There are many aspects of voting and voting activities that we did not address in that chapter. For instance, students could be asked their opinions on an issue and the overall survey results may not be displayed until they vote or until a certain time or date has passed. This is referred to as a timed disclosure task.

Another activity not mentioned in Chapter Five is called the value line. Instead of a simple "Yes/No" poll, the instructor might select a "value line" activity. In such an activity, students mark their values or preferences of where they stand on an issue on a scale such as from "1" (i.e., Strongly Disagree) to "10" (i.e., Strongly Agree). Students indicate the degree to which they agree or disagree with a value statement. For example, "nuclear power should be expanded" following the 2011 tsunami in Japan. Or perhaps the issue is "Gun control laws should not be changed" after the Aurora, Colorado, movie theater shooting on July 20, 2012 or the horrific Sandy Hook, Connecticut, mass murders of elementary school students and teachers in December of that same year. With a value line activity, students might be allowed to revote after hearing how everyone feels about the issue. When that happens, they must grapple with the differing points of view of others in the class. And such value lines can be privately or publicly posted online.

A few years ago, we experimented with a tool called the Q&A Forum in the Indiana University Kelley School of Business online MBA program. This tool restricted MBA students from seeing peer postings until they posted their own opinions in a discussion thread or on a virtual bulletin board. Tools like the Q&A Forum provide additional time and opportunities for students to contemplate their perspectives and articulate their ideas. As indicated, shy and introverted populations of students especially benefit from such an approach. At the same time, this feature helps all students to reflect on their learning and facilitate their own knowledge construction processes, independent of the thoughts and biases of others.

An option to this approach is to reveal participant comments, votes, and opinions at a preset time and date. With that approach, learners will not be biased by other points of view until they have had adequate time to reflect. Unlike a physical classroom which changes with each new class, the Web becomes an ideal vehicle for the collection, storage, and later revisiting and disseminating of such information.

Skills and Objectives. Includes empathy, patience, engagement, reflection, dealing with conflicting viewpoints, peer interaction, comparison and contrast, data analysis, evaluating data and situations, appreciating other points of view, and providing rationale. Fine-tuning listening skills (and patience) is also embedded in this technique.

Advice and Ideas. Determine whether the course management system or other technology tools used by your organization allow for timed disclosure or the revealing of information at a set time and date. If not, ask your technical support team how you could embed such activities. Allow ample time to design the questions, comments, and issues for your students to deliberate on. And be sure to debrief on the activity upon completion.

Variations and Extensions. The respective value line activities might be designed by the students enrolled in the course. If it is a cross-cultural activity, the value lines or issues for voting might be generated by students in other organizations or localities. Students might then rate or rank each other's issues. When done, be sure to debrief on the activity and solicit comments from all sites involved.

There could even be several rounds of timed disclosure activities embedded in a particular task that build on one another in a recursive loop. For instance, value line or polling questions for teacher educators could be related to the traits or characteristics of ideal teachers. The next round may concern rating each of these favorite teacher traits. Next, they could suggest items for new teacher rating schemes. In each round, peer suggestions would not be reviewable until that person has posted or only after a particular time and date has passed.

Key Instructional Considerations

Risk index: Medium
Time index: Medium
Cost index: Low
Learner-centered index: High
Duration of the learning activity: 1 week or as needed

Activity 86. Argument and Debate Mapping

Description and Purpose of Activity. In Activity #66 in Chapter Ten, we discussed a number of tools for concept and mind mapping. Some instructional situations, however, may be more focused on argument and debate instead of a conceptual representation of ideas. If that is the case, the instructor may require students to use argument map tools to help learners put their chain of thinking on display. Today, using such tools as Argumentum, Argunet, Cohere, Compendium, and Truthmapping, users may be asked to explicate their reasoning and list the pros and cons of different problem solutions or resolution paths as well as the evidence, relationships between variables, assumptions, opinions, questions, and solutions. With Argunet, students can search for arguments as well as share, download, and present them. In Truthmapping, users read premises for different statements and then decide whether to agree with a statement or to critique it.

Such online assistants help to organize students' thoughts and ideas. Users can locate specific ideas or aspects to a debate through private as well as public tagging systems. Tools like Cohere allow for feeds from discussion tools, blogs, and other social networking resources. Ideas posted can be tagged as data, opinions, predictions, questions, solutions, and theories. And connections between ideas might be labeled by the user as "supports," "causes," "improves on," and "reminds me of." Clearly, online debate and argument mapping tools are becoming increasingly sophisticated.

With such systems, not only is a student's thinking explicated, but relationships between two or more ideas are made salient. Also explicit is the student's overall framework or conceptual structure for thinking on a topic. With these external representations, learners can better comprehend the strength of their arguments as well as their knowledge growth over time. Such argument and debate maps can be used for student presentations, debates, reflections, and other interactions.

Skills and Objectives. Includes interactivity, the visualization of ideas, dual coding of content, logic, chains of reasoning, causal relationships, comparison and contrast, data analysis, the evaluation of data provided, appreciation of other points of view, argument formation and rebuttals, backing up claims, and self-directed learning and resource exploration. As is apparent, in such activities many dimensions of critical thinking are addressed.

Advice and Ideas. Check the functionality of different argument and debate tools. Perhaps ask departmental colleagues as well as former students of the course for their opinions and suggestions about them. As you survey the landscape of available tools and resources, think carefully about how to embed such technology in your courses. Sketch out one or two curriculum activities as well as potential assessment schemes. Instructors might score such maps for their depth and breadth, causal connections and reasoning, relationships drawn, logic, originality, accuracy, support provided, and overall structure. As a metacognitive or self-monitoring aid, students could craft a reflection paper on the concepts and processes that they mastered during the activity.

Variations and Extensions. Students can be required to write reflection papers on how their argument mapping structures are similar and different from those of other individuals or teams. Alternatively, they could be forced to combine argument or debate maps from two or more individuals, after which they would make a joint presentation.

Key Instructional Considerations

Risk index: High
Time index: Medium
Cost index: Low to High (depends on system used)
Learner-centered index: High
Duration of the learning activity: 2–3 weeks

Activity 87. Challenge-Based Videoconferencing (e.g., World Affairs Challenges)

Description and Purpose of Activity. International and global education consultant Jennifer Klein accurately points out that discussion of twenty-first-century skills became salient in schools in the late 1990s (Klein, 2010). These conversations are even more heated today. In particular, to be successful, young people need collaborative skills to work together across borders, both visible and invisible, to begin solving the immense world problems in front of them. As Klein accurately stated, global education enhances their capabilities to understand societal issues from multiple perspectives. In the process, they are developing what Merry Merryfield (2003) describes as "worldmindedness."

One curriculum innovation Klein describes is called the "World Affairs Challenge." In this approach, students are given issue-based topics of study such as poverty in the Sub-Saharan Africa, limited Internet access in Tanzania, and waterborne diseases in Cambodia. After conducting their research, students come together for a one-day tournament in Denver to present their research findings. After that, they are grouped with students from other schools to solve a different real-world issue, problem, or question. To apprentice such young people into a new field or discipline, prominent community leaders serve as guides and judges.

Such F2F sessions have many advantages. However, today with ePals, Round Square, iEARN, Soliya, and TakingITGlobal, mentioned previously, these same activities take place on the Web with tens of thousands of youth. In some cases, the use of Web conferencing and interactive videoconferencing bring K–12 as well as college students together who normally could not afford to travel (Lee & Bonk, 2013). In those online videoconferences, teams of learners can discuss and submit solutions related to pressing world problems.

Lee and Hutton (2007) discuss the many benefits of interactive video-conferencing for international education. For instance, students can hold extended, substantive, and collaborative discussions where issues are addressed in a deep and meaningful way. In effect, as Lee and Hutton note, videoconferencing can foster a greater exchange of information between learners than would otherwise be possible. When properly structured, such videoconferencing and Web conferencing events can be a platform for integrating ideas across locations while simultaneously challenging students to generate unique solutions and predictions.

At the higher education level, learners have much to offer to global videoconferences. During the past two decades, Bonk and his colleagues have used interactive videoconferencing to foster student challenges across countries including Korea, China, Finland, Malaysia, Taiwan, Peru, the United Kingdom, and the United States (Lee & Bonk, 2013). In cross-institutional projects, he has had students jointly solve case problems, make presentations, write wikibooks, and critique each other's work (Bonk et al., 2009). The videoconference becomes the platform for meeting global peers and for discussing issues, posing challenges, and sharing final products. When students know they will have to submit their work to a global audience, they are willing to expend more time and effort perfecting it.

Skills and Objectives. Includes empathy, collaboration, leadership, inquiry research skills, knowledge synthesis, extensive feedback, appreciation of multiple points of view, deeper understanding of global, political, social, and environmental systems, cross-cultural engagement, self-confidence, cognitive dissonance, peer interactivity, reflection, learner involvement, deeper levels of information processing, responsiveness, resource sharing, and community building. This activity allows for much spontaneity and creativity.

Advice and Ideas. Extensive planning will be required for any Web conference or videoconference. Be sure to prepare students for cultural differences and displays of human sensitivity including the appropriate types and ways of interacting. Special training programs or curricula may need to be developed. Provide examples of potentially problematic expressions, questions, responses, content, and so forth. Some of these suggestions and examples may come from prior experiences with video or Web conferencing.

As Bonk and his colleague Mimi Lee at the University of Houston recently detailed, there are many procedures and issues involved in cross-cultural videoconferencing (Lee & Bonk, 2013). As they note, a topic and potential time for the session should first be agreed to by all participants. Once a tentative topic, time, and date are established, the Internet Protocol (IP) of each participating site must be shared and tested. They recommend that a script or agenda should be drafted, shared, and agreed to at least a week prior to the session. At the same time, a key lesson that they have learned is the importance of some spontaneity or memorable moments during any synchronous sessions. As Lee and Bonk (2013, p. 127) note, "no session can be entirely preplanned. From our perspective, the spontaneous nature of these sessions brings forth an increased sense of authenticity to these real time interactions."

To foster cross-site interaction and democratic participation, moderators at each location can monitor learner questions. Such moderators might also intervene to restate questions, summarize discussion, or interpret what someone from a remote site has said. If experts are being brought in, it is wise to have students discuss their articles and ideas in an asynchronous forum before and after the live videoconferencing session.

Each team or group of students could be allocated a set amount of time to present their research findings and related solutions to the problem. That presentation could entail conducting a skit, holding a debate, forming an expert panel, or using interactive polling tools with the audience. Employees of local organizations with a background in global development or cross-cultural collaboration might serve as judges (Klein, 2010). Awards can be given for the most innovative problem solutions, most engaging presentations, most insightful questions, and most creative or spontaneous responses, among other areas or categories for potential recognition.

Variations and Extensions. Instead of instructor-created challenges, the challenges could be posed by a manager of a government organization, director of a nonprofit organization, or founder of a social cause. The best solutions could be posted on the sponsoring foundation or nonprofit website. Previous students of the course as well as experts in the field such as book authors, researchers, practitioners, and leaders, could serve as judges of such challenges and competitions.

Key Instructional Considerations

> *Risk index: High*
> *Time index: High*
> *Cost index: Low*
> *Learner-centered index: High*
> *Duration of the learning activity: All semester or as needed*

Activity 88. Digital Media Competitions

Description and Purpose of Activity. Competition often spurs learning excellence. The explosion of collaborative learning technologies combined with cheap online storage, has made it possible for students in fine arts, fashion design, new media, instructional technology, and telecommunications departments to engage in cross-institutional collaborations as well as intense and highly publicized competitions. Today, students in such departments can engage in online design competitions that bear significant prizes or recognitions. Internationally recognized experts can judge the products and lend timely and insightful feedback. When such a learning apprenticeship occurs, learners become energized about their field of study; in addition, new social networks and relationships are formed.

Since the late 1990s, our friend Rick Bennett in the College of Fine Arts at the University of New South Wales has experimented with many forms of digital interactions. Much of this work has centered on an innovative collaboration concept and technology that he called "Omnium." His work with Omnium has resulted in a series of online global creativity studios or classrooms (Bennett, 2011). The fully online international projects that Bennett has coordinated have focused on the creative design process within small teams of artists, graphic designers, and digital media enthusiasts interested in online studio art, photomedia, graphic design, and visual communication. Initially, Omnium project participants were mentored by international panels of professional designers, professors, and digital technicians located in such countries as the United Kingdom, South Africa, Hong Kong, Singapore, Germany, Canada, Puerto Rico, Australia, and many other parts of the world. Omnium provided the shared space for all this collaboration and meeting of the minds to happen.

As Rick Bennett has shown, we live in an age when students from geographically distant art and design studios can work together on intriguing projects with a host of tremendously creative results. Systems like Omnium can break down the various cultural, social, physical, and technical barriers that such students would have faced prior to the Web. Today, these students can log in and watch lectures, check out image galleries, participate in online discussions, share resources and files, check calendars and team notices, and submit or review work in pin-up walls of best artwork. Users' in-process work and completed products can also be commented on by peers as well as international panels of experts (Martini, Harrison, & Bennett, 2009). Projects rated the highest in competitions are posted to an online visual image gallery by Omnium personnel. With such incentives, online participants in the various Creative Waves competitions strive to have the most creative and engaging final artworks to share. Bennett's students have joined forces with students in the health sciences to create visual awareness campaigns that highlighted issues related to specific health concerns such as HIV and malaria for small rural villages in Kenya as well as issues concerning waterborne diseases and diarrhea in Uganda. Clearly, collaborative art and design with Omnium can lead to significant social action and potential change.

Skills and Objectives. Includes creativity, empathy, societal perspective taking, visual literacy skills, awareness of social issues, design, planning, idea refinement, social networking, expert and peer feedback, learning in a context of use, and collaboration and teamwork. Rewards from winning digital media competitions and other recognitions, such as having work posted to an online media gallery, last a lifetime.

Advice and Ideas. Determine the type of digital media project that is appropriate for your content area or discipline. Allowing for student input and choice in this process can ensure that the project(s) you set up will be relevant and of interest to them. In many content areas, a digital movie or online book chapter may serve as a final product that best represents student learning. Consider potential judges. Then, before you contact them, ponder the suitability of the forms of interaction and kinds of feedback that these judges can provide to help your students enhance their work and add to their understanding.

Think carefully about the design of any competition or collaboration concerning student work. Train students as well as judges about your expectations in terms of feedback, interaction, and sharing. Naturally, they should focus their feedback on product improvement without personally attacking the individual artist or team. Before you start, set up target milestones, major phases, and deadlines for the designs or products. Perhaps include simple calendar or scheduling tools to keep participants aware of key moments in project planning.

Document the results. For instance, consider collecting student questionnaires as well as qualitative feedback throughout every stage of the project. You should also conduct both formative and summative evaluations so as to assess any technology or task limitations. At the same time, there may be culturally sensitive issues that arise during the project in terms of timing, language, customs, and so on to monitor or address.

Variations and Extensions. Instead of entering one's own work, learners might nominate the work of their peers or perhaps even of experts in the field. Students could also serve as online judges in the competition.

Key Instructional Considerations

Risk index: High
Time index: High
Cost index: Low to High (depending on tools employed)
Learner-centered index: High
Duration of the learning activity: 3–4 weeks or during entire course

Activity 89. "Best of" Nominations (e.g., Quotes)

Description and Purpose of Activity. As evident throughout this book, there are countless of pages of Web content with potential educational uses. Nevertheless, it can be overwhelming for instructors to find high-quality material online. They can search open educational resources such as the OER Commons and online repositories like Connexions, MERLOT, and Jorum. Resources found at MERLOT, for instance, are often peer evaluated and rated. However, journeys into any learning portal can sometimes lead to many hours of casual browsing.

There are many options to conducting a time-consuming search through online materials. For instance, one can turn to colleagues or experts for suggestions of high-quality online resources. Alternatively, one can read emerging technology reports and forecasts such as the Horizons Report from the New Media Consortium and EDUCAUSE (Johnson, Adams Becker, Cummins, Estrada, Freeman, & Ludgate, 2013). However, your best resource may actually be the learners in your classroom. Your students, better than anyone, know what they like and what will motivate them to learn. So ask them. Learners could be charged with finding the best quotations, articles, speeches, papers, news reports, animations, simulations, blogs, or podcasts in the field. They might be assigned specific theories, terms, principles, authors, researchers, and so forth, to explore.

Learners can submit the content that they have found to a course resource library, discussion forum, or wiki. Consider holding a contest or tournament to find the very best content. These types of competitions can energize learners to conduct an extended search of available content. In the process, they will be supplementing their learning of the course material and extending far beyond it.

Skills and Objectives. Includes information search, feedback, involvement, student autonomy and choice, reflection, comparison and contrast, self-directed learning and resource exploration, content review, and identification of key concepts. This activity requires that students explore course content well beyond any assignment or instructor-led activity.

Advice and Ideas. There are many resources for students' "best of" search. If they are in need of a quotation, they might use Wikiquote, BrainyQuote, Goodreads, or a biography website to find such material. Alternatively, they might use online tools like Tricider to nominate, review, discuss, and rate the best books, ideas, or researchers in the field. Experts in the field could also help evaluate and rate the quality of the content. The "best of the best" content would be saved for use by students in future versions of the course.

In addition to social voting or ranking tools like Tricider, instructors could create a course wiki for students to nominate the top course content. If the task is to come up with the best quotes for people, topics, or issues, the headings and subheadings for each should be inserted prior to the start of the activity. Students should include their names or initials on every quotation they submit. Next to each quotation might be a link to a rating form or poll for students in the course as well as external guests to rate it. The content resources accumulating the highest votes would be considered the winners of the quotation competition. You may want to develop a course "hall of fame" for annual winners of this competition as well as for the person who originally nominated each content object. Course instructors may consider handing out gold, silver, and bronze medals as in the Olympics, or different kinds of trophies or awards.

It is vital to establish procedures for such competition submissions and judging. For submissions, instructors can conduct a review prior to posting to the Web as learners may have selected something that is inappropriate, redundant, lacking in sufficient functionality, or even no longer available. In addition, students will need to know where, when, and how to submit the content. In terms of judging, a set of quality criteria can be generated and shared with the class. For example, dimensions judged or rated may include the functionality, richness of the media employed, currency, relevance to the course, extendibility beyond course content, and uniqueness. Solicitation of external judges should take place at least a few weeks prior to the start of the activity. Such judges may even be former students of the course. Given all the steps, consider generating a learning scaffold or guide sheet for the entire activity.

Variations and Extensions. An alternative or extension here would be team collaborations to find the best video, quotation, paper, book, and the like. Such collaborations could take place across two or more courses. Of course, students in other environments, cultures, or learning situations may have access to totally different content and resources, thereby significantly extending the possible results.

Key Instructional Considerations

Risk index: Medium
Time index: Medium
Cost index: Low
Learner-centered index: High
Duration of the learning activity: Anytime as needed

Activity 90. Online Games, Puzzles, and Quizzes

Description and Purpose of Activity. Technology research firm Gartner predicts that more than 70 percent of the top 2,000 global organizations will use gamified applications for training and performance by 2014 (Snider, 2012). As shown by people who play mobile or online games, people are motivated to see their names and achievements listed on leaderboards in a mobile app. They are also motivated to pass a particularly difficult level or challenge within a game. Games offer challenges, interesting stories, feedback on performance, and tangible incentives and rewards (Lauby, 2012).

These same principles are finding their way into education in various online and mobile games (Miller, 2012). Besides being listed in leaderboards, learners could earn badges, trophies, certificates, and newsletter recognition. Quizzes, flashcards, practice questions, and other interactive online tools can test students' learning while they're playing the game. The basic premise is that learning can be fun and rewarding when packaged in a gamelike format.

As noted in Chapter Seven, most of us likely have at least one friend or family member who is addicted to social games such as Words with Friends, Farmville, CityVille, and Angry Birds. Of course, there are tens of thousands of educational games on mobile applications, especially at the K–12 level, for math, science, and English. These games can be used to prepare students for exams and quizzes. Among them are simple crossword puzzles, word searches, mazes, hangman and jeopardy games, and wheel of fortune. Many online sites like Puzzlemaker from Discovery Education as well as EclipseCrossword offer free templates to design your own game or challenge. Increasingly, educators will be embedding educational games and puzzles into their courses for learner review and challenge. Challenge games will be one way to hold students accountable in MOOCs with thousands of students as well as in more restricted traditional courses with just a dozen or two enrolled.

Skills and Objectives. Includes feedback, content review, challenge, skill evaluation, information retrieval, discrimination, insight, entertainment, and suspense. An online game show could serve as a screening or course preparation tool prior to enrolling in a class.

Advice and Ideas. Review your content for topic areas, terms, or theories that students often have difficulty mastering or that are critical to later learning in your course or in follow-up courses. Search existing open educational resources for challenge games or quiz shows in your discipline. Talk or write to colleagues for advice and suggestions.

If your search comes up empty, perhaps meet with available technology support personnel to discuss your needs. Before you do, sketch out a preliminary game design or plan. Alternatively, you could rely on basic crossword puzzlemaker tools noted in the Web resources associated with this chapter. You may find yourself creating an engaging crossword puzzle quiz for every week, unit, or chapter. Be sure to gather both formative as well as summative evaluation data on their effectiveness, and consider presenting the results at teaching- and learning-related conferences and events.

Variations and Extensions. Not only can instructors create games or use those that they find online, but they can ask learners to design a set of alternative questions or issues, or perhaps an extension of the game. Students could also be asked to design their own course challenge activity or game for others to take. The person or team building the best game design could be awarded bonus points or an option to drop a course assignment.

One of our students created a fascinating identity challenge game. When designing the game, she used technologies like Adobe Captivate, MacBook Webcam, Adobe Premiere Elements (for video editing), and several YouTube and Vimeo videos found online. In her game, the user had to identify statements, questions, or issues associated with particular people studied in the course. The game questions and people discussed followed the order of the weeks in the course. With each correct answer, the game player accumulated points. Online audio and video files from many of the experts were incorporated.

Clearly, challenge games and assignments to build challenge games are among the most powerful educational tools today. Students rehearse much of the content across the entire semester from this one exercise. In such an activity, content is meshed with technology in a highly interesting and interactive manner.

Key Instructional Considerations

Risk index: High
Time index: Medium
Cost index: Low to High (depending on tools used)
Learner-centered index: Medium
Duration of the learning activity: 1–2 weeks or as needed

Final Reflections on Tension

As shown in this chapter, a tad bit of tension or conflict can lead to intensive effort to want to know more. There are many ways to spark such flames and nudge learners into a state of uncertainty or sense of not being confident about what they currently know or believe. Such bewilderment, however, can vary in intensity from a slight sense of puzzlement to complete frustration.

Local and international news is alive with tension every day. Learners within a particular class or across the world can now debate each other about such news virtually and perhaps even brainstorm viable solutions that can add to the general discourse on a topic. Such debating, role play, and discussions of controversial issues can also foster respect and deeper insights into diverse cultures and norms. As our colleague Mimi Lee (2007) at the University of Houston points out, these types of activities motivate students and deepen their intercultural awareness. When learners begin to understand how ideas of "difference" are constructed, they simultaneously better understand themselves and others. Learners in remote or rural settings can engage with those in highly dense parts of the world. And when they do, they may discover that issues that seem controversial or critical to resolve in one region of the world have not even been encountered or discussed in another.

The ideas and activities here are a starting point. Each online and blended course should build in ample doses of challenges and controversies to wrestle with. Decades of research into collaborative and interactive learning technology has shown that virtual collaboration among team members offers unique incentives as well as supports for a successful and engaging learning environment (Bonk & King, 1998; Koschmann, 1996). Now combine such collaborative endeavors with competition across teams or classes of students to come up with the most innovative or useful solutions. When you do, the standards for success will be elevated even higher.

Take stock of the resources, content, technologies, and student backgrounds in your particular environment that might be useful in fostering tension and challenge. You or your departmental colleagues may have connections to people in other parts of the country or around the world who might want to engage in an activity such as structured controversy or a world affairs challenge. Depending on the situation, you may want your students to assume a set of particular roles or personalities when doing so. Or perhaps your learners will vote to have some sort of digital media competition. Increasingly, we will see educators taking advantage of Web technology for such international competitions and collaborations. As an example, they could pose some type of online study group challenge or competition to see which teams can offer the most support or solve the most cases or problems.

We have covered much territory related to online motivation and retention in the first twelve chapters of this book. However, we are not quite done. We have the granddaddy of motivators left to address—namely, learner goals, preferably the kind that yield some type of product. We humans, by our very nature, are goal-driven creatures. We need a vision or target to shoot for or an overriding goal to work toward. You do. I do. Your students do. For some, it becomes a personal quest for a glorious ending product. And in fully online and blended learning environments, such goals are particularly vital because they help maintain learner focus when there is no one in the immediate environment to structure and provide feedback on student learning.

In Chapter Thirteen on "Yielding Products," we excitedly address the final principle of the TEC-VARIETY framework. Some may view this as the pinnacle moment of the book. As you turn the pages, you will find ideas related to learner creation of products and associated ownership and feelings of success about them. You will notice that this tenth principle closely corresponds to the second wave of Web-based technologies, such as podcasts, wikis, and blogs. It is one area that you may continue to experiment with long after many of the technologies mentioned in other parts of this book fall out of favor and are replaced by new ones. We look forward to hearing about the types of products that your learners have designed and the unique pedagogical strategies you employed to get them there.

CHAPTER THIRTEEN

PRINCIPLE #10 YIELDING PRODUCTS

(Includes Goal Driven, Purposeful Vision, and Ownership)

> You must know for which harbor you are headed
> if you are to catch the right wind to take you there.
>
> —Seneca, Roman Stoic philosopher, statesman, dramatist, and humorist

The Final Act

It is hard to believe that we are already at the final principle of the TEC-VARIETY framework. Many courses and training programs end with the production or creation of something special by the participants. This could be a research summary report, musical performance, original poem, mobile application, or multimedia presentation. And so it is with our framework: we end on the notion of yielding products. Such products involve a sense of purpose and vision as well as ultimate ownership of what was produced. In a word, they are goal-driven. For instance, we had a goal to get to this point of the book; this goal gave us an end state toward which to work. As the nineteenth-century Scottish-born writer and historian Thomas Carlyle proclaimed, "A man without a goal is like a ship without a rudder."

Learners, whether they are in physical or virtual classes, need the same. They glance upon a set of proposed activities in a syllabus and work toward completing what is assigned. That sense of task completion is not the only reason we sought to arrive at this chapter. We realized that goal completion and yielding products serve as the basis of many popular views in education today. When you involve learners in forms of learning based on products, projects, cases, or problems, you incentivize the system. Learners are driven to complete some type of high-quality, tangible product for others to see, share, use, comment upon, or remix. That reuse and remixing of the final product abides by John Dewey's hypothesis that "arriving at one goal is the starting point to another."

As alluded to in the previous chapter, Steve Jobs had a distinct—and often controversial and combative—way of sharing a vision and passion that excited thousands of people at Apple to work toward a common goal (Isaacson, 2011). Whether it was the Macintosh, the iPod, iTunes, the iPhone, or the iPad, there was something special about the announcement of a completed product that was thinner, more colorful, more innovative, or more powerful than anything ever available before. Steve Jobs was driven to design and produce the best products on the planet. Educators can instill the same passion and zeal within their students by having them search for and find their learning goals. When learners have a chance to produce something unique and valuable for an audience beyond the class, it can inspire them to dig deep and commit extensive amounts of time and effort. Goals give direction and purpose to such efforts, particularly when times are tough or the challenges high (Ray, 2004).

As Roy Baumeister and John Tierney (2011) note in their bestselling book, *Willpower: Rediscovering the Greatest Human Strength*, an individual's success often comes from commitment and persistent striving toward stated goals. There are many types of goals, however; for instance, learners can benefit from specific daily goals (also called "proximal" goals). When they meet such goals, they can gradually build up self-confidence and enhance their self-efficacy as learners. At the same time, establishing long-term or more distal goals such as those related to potential career interests or overall success in their college program of studies can help students overcome the drudgery of some of the daily work. As many know, it is the recording of learning-related goals as well as their completion that foster feelings of personal self-control over the learning situation. Then, when significant obstacles are faced, an inner striving or willpower arises within self-directed learners; some refer to this as tenacity or grit.

Goals alone will not determine success; to achieve success, goals must be realistic and valued. Such realism and value depends on past experiences and future intentions. When learners have some prior experience or knowledge in an area, they can be pushed to accomplish a more challenging target. And, as Stanford Professor Deborah Stipek (1998) and many other psychologists have found, charting their progress and accomplishments along the way can help learners attain even higher levels of success (Stipek, 1998). So can gentle nudging and spot-on advice from instructors and outside experts. Research indicates that when learners periodically evaluate their progress toward those goals with support from an instructor or expert, they can decide whether a change in their strategic approach is needed (Pintrich & Schunk, 1996).

This research makes an important distinction between performance-related goals that often involve outdoing other learners in the class or winning approval from someone, and learning-related goals that concern individuals' mastery of a task. The motivator behind performance goals is often extrinsic in nature, whereas learning goals tend to come from inside the learner. Again, as Baumeister and Tierney (2011) explain, over the long haul, inner passion and willpower typically trump external carrots and sticks.

This differentiation between performance and learning goals is critically important to understand because individuals with performance goals who have limited self-confidence will select rather easy tasks to complete. In contrast, those with learning goals might reach for the next mountain without much hesitation. One of the intentions of the TEC-VARIETY framework is to nudge learners toward increasingly challenging but still attainable tasks. As shown by this tenth principle, when learners can design or build a product of some kind, doing so elevates the potential audience for that work. As the audience expands, typically so too do the summits that learners attempt to reach.

Technologies for Principle #10: Yielding Products

In the *Icarus Deception*, Seth Godin (2012) argues that we humans should make art. In terms of online or blended learning experiences, such art might be a short documentary video posted to YouTube, a new entry in Wikipedia, a video song parody (Korey, 2009), a unique mobile application, a chapter in a wikibook, an innovative game, or an insightful speech, perhaps in the form of a podcast. Godin laments that the recitation models that have often epitomized schooling have reduced learner opportunities to produce and ship such art.

In addition to new models of education that seek to empower learners and give them more opportunities to produce knowledge, Godin suggests that people need grit to overcome the endless critics whom they will encounter along the way toward producing their art. According to Godin, grit includes such factors as personal perseverance, hardiness, resilience, ambition, commitment, and flow. As he appropriately notes, the resistance that an individual faces is often internal as well. A learner may harbor doubts in the back of her mind that she can successfully produce something viable. As these doubts mount, the brain suffers great discomfort, leading to an inner reluctance to reach more challenging goals.

Fortunately, an emphasis on creating something unique is increasingly common in this age of the Web 2.0 and beyond. In fully online and blended learning courses, instructors can now incorporate activities that foster a type of creative renaissance. According to Sir Ken Robinson (Robinson & Aronica, 2013), it is vital to help learners find the element or situation in which they feel deeply passionate. Offering learners alternative choices in their course projects is one way to clear such a path. A modest media project today may lead to a new career interest, hobby, or budding area of expertise tomorrow. A learner might find such a passion when creating an online multimedia glossary in a wiki that future students can later augment or use. Another might discover a new interest area while creating a screencasted help system for a new software system or free learning tool used in a public library or computer lab.

Need more examples? If so, take, for instance, the simple podcast. Students could create a series of short podcast shows as a means to document and share their personal growth and development within in the course. When they are posted, peers and instructors could offer feedback or recommendations in a course discussion forum or blog. Research by Khoo and her colleagues indicates that podcasts can foster high levels of learner engagement and reflection, enhanced understanding of key course concepts, and overall personalization of learning. And in the process, learners also gain confidence with digital technologies (Forbes, 2011; Forbes, Khoo, Johnson, 2012).

In addition to podcasts, screencasts, and multimedia glossaries, some students may create infographics of emerging trends or areas of personal interest. Still others may post online books or book reviews and then engage in online discussions of them with their peers and with outsiders not enrolled in the course. As their audience expands, students will find a growing sense of purpose or meaning in their course work.

Clearly, there are numerous online activities that can yield valuable course products. Once posted or shared, they can be reused, remixed, and enhanced by present and future students (Ferlazzo, 2013). To be honest, many of the ideas presented in this chapter for yielding course products are not entirely new. In fact, most were already taking root over two decades ago when hypermedia and multimedia learning hit center stage. The opportunities for innovative course projects and products today, however, are infinitely more pervasive, accessible, and expected. With that, the resistance that Godin speaks about has started to subside.

Ten Online Activities in Principle #10: Yielding Products

The activities of this chapter push students. They force them to synthesize new learning competencies and insights into some type of unique project, scheme, venture, design, invention, or innovation. It is the doing part of this task that is infectious. Each person in a group or on a team will find a purpose from the activity's embedded goals and the potential to influence countless onlookers, lurkers, and browsers. Accordingly, these activities are not easy. They typically take much planning, deliberation, and persistence from initial design to task completion. When finished, however, students will have much to celebrate.

To be successful in this product-intensive world, learners must be able to delay gratification. They often do so by envisioning what the final product might look like and intensely working toward that imagined result. Instructors can help build those visions by providing examples of prior course success stories. They might even bring back former students to discuss their accomplishments, or they might share student testimonials that they already collected.

In the following pages, you will discover ten activities for yielding products, fostering goal setting, embedding purpose and passion, and creating ownership. They are not just the final ten activities for this book; instead, as you scan the skills and objectives associated with each one, you will come to realize that these are examples of some of the most powerful pedagogical activities that you can place in your fully online and blended learning arsenal. Of course, they are also just a start. Build on them. Reshape them. And perhaps combine them. Then share the results with your colleagues as well as with us.

Activity 91. Cartoon and Animated Movie Productions

Description and Purpose of Activity. The Web has shifted from a resource for finding information to a platform for designing new forms of creative expression. Among the more interesting tools for expressing your creativity are sites for crafting your own animated movies or cartoons. Never heard of them? Well, an abundance of animation and cartoon creation sites have recently sprung up including, GoAnimate, Devolver, Voki, Zimmer Twins, PowToon, and Bitstrips (Kessler, 2010). With some of these tools, the user can manipulate the facial expressions, body movements, and voice of an avatar or animated character. In addition to character expressions and gestures, users can customize the scenes (i.e., background images, setting, color, etc.), add dialogue, and perhaps even record audio tracks—and then lay out all those items in a timeline that is easy to navigate.

Many of these systems remain limited in terms of customization features and the real-life sense of the characters. Nevertheless, they offer opportunities for fostering creativity in the form of humor, movement, interaction, and story development. Importantly, students can be actively involved in designing a movie or cartoon, instead of passively watching one. As movie development unfolds, students begin to grasp how humans communicate and interact in complex situations. Cartoons and animated movies are ideal for depicting political debates and civics, historical events, science fiction scenarios, product marketing techniques, and job interviewing skills (Parry, 2011). Such technology can also be used in teaching English, rhetoric, and argument structures (Jones, 2012).

Skills and Objectives. Includes spontaneity, role play, visual communication, interactivity, creativity expression, originality, risk taking, and design and artistic skills. These activities also promote a sense of participatory learning as well as content review, deeper and richer understanding of course content, and logical sequencing of content. Designing an animation or cartoon movie based on course content offers a sense of freedom of expression that most traditional course activities do not allow.

Advice and Ideas. Such a task might be novel for learners. Hence, it is important to gather sample animation movies or cartoons clarifying the requirements of such an assignment. Be specific on the length, interaction structures, and multimedia components of the task as well as your grading procedures. You may want to have students draft scripts for your approval prior to creating their movies. Post your criteria and requirements to a wiki or a course management system so that students can later refer to them. Students may also create a set of criteria to vote on the best animations. For instance, there might be competitions for Most Creative Design or Animation Sequence, Best Line, Best Screenwriting, and Most Outstanding Animated Movie of the Semester.

Variations and Extensions. Students in assigned collaborative teams might be asked to extend their cartoon or animated movies with additional effects or added length. Again, there might be competitions for best team performances. Students wanting a somewhat challenging experience could try Machinima, a more time-intensive system as it requires creating a digital video in a 3D virtual world using avatars. The result, however, is a crisper cinematic production than they would have made using the other options already mentioned.

Key Instructional Considerations

Risk index: Medium
Time index: High
Cost index: Low
Learner-centered index: High
Duration of the learning activity: 1–3 weeks or as needed

Activity 92. Student Documentaries

Description and Purpose of Activity. Some course goals necessitate highly immersive final projects. Fortunately, as the costs of media production have plummeted, students have access to digital technologies that can significantly contribute to a course. Given that instructors often lack time and sufficient resources to produce elegant video footage that they can be proud of or want to reuse, new waves of low-cost production tools are quickly being embraced in K–12 schools and in higher education. In fact, we have had several students produce documentaries and digital stories of our courses in podcast and video formats. Some of these projects get highly creative with rich animations, in-depth interviews of prior students, and extensive filming as well as sophisticated editing.

Georgetown University's Center for New Designs for Learning and Scholarship (CNDLS) sponsors a number of innovative projects. One unique collaborative effort with Columbia University's Center for New Media Teaching and Learning is called Project Rebirth. This initiative involves students producing a documentary related to the traumatic events of September 11, 2001. Students, faculty members, and community members collaborate to edit the footage as well as tag and annotate it for various educational uses. Students reflect on the resulting documentary footage through their blogs as well as their multimedia digital stories. Proceeds from the documentaries are intended to help professionals and volunteer agencies involved in the recovery from such traumatic experiences. Having such authentic audiences for their coursework helps students to focus the project and adds key incentives.

Columbia University's Graduate School of Journalism trains master's students to be independent film producers and directors. Many of their works have appeared on PBS and have won awards leading to jobs at CBS Evening News, BBC Radio, and NPR. Today, however, students can be producing documentaries on any aspect of life. Such work does not have to be as salient as the tragedies surrounding life in New York after 9/11. For instance, students at Johns Hopkins Bloomberg School of Public Health have produced shows on topics ranging from food ecology to safe streets resulting from the reduction of gun violence.

Students do not have to be enrolled in acting, filmmaking, or journalism classes for the documentary task to succeed. In fact, our own students have done documentaries on the use of mobile technology during holiday travel as well as on the home schooling of one's own children. Today, rich and engaging documentaries can spring forth from nearly anywhere.

Skills and Objectives. Course objectives may include task persistence and effort, intellectual inquiry, enhanced audience awareness and empathy, data filtering and analysis, planning and logical sequencing, and teamwork. In terms of generative skills, there are possibilities for greater insight, spontaneity, creative expression, design and artistic skills, originality, risk taking, and a need to synthesize various information sources. In addition, students learn important presentation and visual communication skills. There are many stakeholders and audiences that must be considered in conducting a documentary. As such, there is increased awareness of skills needed in the real world.

Advice and Ideas. Instructors should provide clear guidelines about length, purpose, audience, grading, and other expectations. If the learners are new to video production, they will need suggestions and examples on how to film and how to conduct interviews. Find websites with documentary guidelines for planning and storyboarding the documentaries as well as for recording, editing, and distributing them. Instructors should foster a sense of experimentation with sound effects and editing, music, voiceovers, transitions, themes, and editing. Students will need tips about equipment and software availability (e.g., Camtasia, iMovie, Movie Maker, or Adobe Premiere). Much of the project might even be completed with an inexpensive smartphone.

Of course, each production team will also need to be cognizant of negotiating rights and clearances for footage taken of people or certain situations. The team should also be aware that they need not travel to the most exotic or dangerous locations to create a high-quality product (Siegchrist, 2012). Stories and advice from previous class production teams might help students grasp what is realistically possible. At some point, they must also take into account the potential longevity and shelf life of their final product.

Students could begin by watching documentaries from prior semesters or from other schools or universities that are available online. Such best-practice examples could be placed in a course portal for later review. Students may discuss these examples as well as their own project ideas in an online forum, and, once there, they could ask for advice on narrowing or researching their chosen topic.

Consider assigning students to teams of three or four members. For instance, one person might be the camera person while others could be assigned to be the musical director or sound manager, documentary director or technician, and script writer or editor. As indicated, students should be given advice on narrowing their topic as well as researching it.

When done, there should be a showing. The class, or multiple sections of a class, could hold a film festival. The learners in the class can assist the instructor(s) with determining possible awards and categories ahead of time. For instance, there might be awards for Best Screenplay (writing of the narration), Best Photography or Cinematography (e.g., image selection), Best Musical Score (for use of appropriate or engaging music), and Best Overall Direction and Production (for best overall documentary quality).

Variations and Extensions. External clients could be solicited for watching and rating student documentaries. If successful, learners will gain a deeper appreciation and respect for the discipline or their chosen field of study. The client or set of clients might be co-evaluators or judges of each team's final work.

Key Instructional Considerations

Risk index: High
Time index: High
Cost index: Low to High (depending on the technology employed)
Learner-centered index: High
Duration of the learning activity: 2–4 weeks

Activity 93. Course Video Summaries and Movie Festivals

Description and Purpose of Activity. Instead of animated movies or documentaries as in the previous two activities, here students design summary videos of key terms or ideas that they learned in the course. Short videos of five or ten minutes force students to rethink the concepts that they have learned. When done, the instructor might hold a "movie festival" week for students to showcase their final products.

Digital video production has an impact on many skills, including communication, problem solving, critical and creative thinking, and abstract thinking (Hakkarainen, 2011). Students also gain vital digital technology skills as well as an understanding of copyright, journalism, film production, and design. If they are working in a group, they also learn collaboration, group dynamics, and decision-making skills. Research from Paivi Hakkarainen (2011) from the Centre for Media Pedagogy at the University of Lapland in Finland indicates that such tasks foster learner emotional involvement and resulting course satisfaction, feelings of challenge, interest, and sense of community in the course.

When learners are assigned to summarize or recap their learning in the course in a short video of 5–10 minutes, they have to filter an enormous amount of information into a short production. They are forced to reflect on key topics, principles, constructs, and themes in the course. Once they have grappled with the complex problem of condensing all the course texts, research papers, lectures, online resources, class activities, and so on, they must design a way to depict and digitally reflect on their learning journey. Effective storyboarding takes time and insight. In addition, people must be contacted to appear in the video and proper release forms must be signed. In addition, students must make decisions about the particular concepts or ideas that will be discussed or emphasized.

Skills and Objectives. Such activities foster task ownership and effort as well as deeper and richer understanding of the course content. When conducted in teams, there is often intense resource sharing and collaboration. Creative risk-taking muscles are strengthened with insight, spontaneity, individual expression and originality, design and artistic skills, visual communication, and synthesis across various information sources. Logical skills are also enhanced with requirements for planning and logical sequencing as well as overall content review. As a course capstone event, these activities foster a sense of course community and commitment.

Advice and Ideas. As with all tasks discussed in this book, instructors should clarify the key aspects of the video summary task. For instance, what are the expectations in terms of content coverage and topics addressed, media incorporated, video length, and technology employed? If the goal is a video reflection on students' learning, the instructor should provide guiding questions or issues. Sample videos from previous semesters could be made available to showcase how prior students addressed similar issues.

We typically assign reflection papers with such video production projects. Naturally, students should be informed about the expected genre of the paper—persuasive, personal journal, descriptive, narrative, short story, monologue, expository, satire, and so on. Students should also have tactical information about the length of the paper and the number and type of references needed, if any. Learners might be asked to reflect on how such a task encourages a different form of teaching and learning. How does a participatory learning environment foster their critical thinking skills, motivation, and commitment to the course?

Former students as well as current ones can serve as judges or feedback givers. Alternatively, scores could be assigned by external judges or fellow students in the course. What might they look for? Student work could be rated or assessed on many dimensions, including insightfulness and grasp of course content, relevancy of that content, completeness or sufficiency of content coverage, design and visual effects, coherence and logical sequence of the content, and originality in both style and substance or content. Evaluators might be looking at how snappy, exciting, engaging, and compelling they find the final product. Other assessment variables might include the use of multimedia, quality storytelling, humor, emotional content, and a conversational tone. Do these last five sound familiar? They should. Dunlap and Lowenthal (2011) found that these were the dimensions displayed in the most popular TED talks. Finally, the product might be rated for depth, artistic effort, and task commitment.

In the end, students who perform well could be asked to contribute their videos to the course catalogue or gallery of sample student work. Such a gallery can be used within as well as outside the class to promote it and the institution or organization.

Variations and Extensions. Instructors might talk to others offering similar courses or course activities. There could be a joint event at the end of the course to share student movie productions. Awards and prizes can be handed out for different categories, such as Best Synthesis, Most Original Video, Best Production Quality, Most Innovative Content and Information, and Best Overall Video. Once established, such awards could carry forward to the following semesters.

Key Instructional Considerations

> Risk index: High
> Time index: High
> Cost index: Low to High (depending on the technology employed)
> Learner-centered index: High
> Duration of the learning activity: 2–4 weeks

Activity 94. Book Trailers

Description and Purpose of Activity. One culminating project involves the creation of a book trailer. Although more common in K–12 settings, such an assignment is utilized in higher education and other educational settings. A book trailer is akin to a movie trailer. Professional book trailers are used to promote a particular book as well as to encourage readership. In contrast, the creation of a book trailer in an educational environment fosters learner engagement and synthesis of the content. It is both a learning experience and a means to encourage learners within and outside the course to read the book.

Assigning students to teams for the book trailer will allow them to utilize their expertise and experience. They can take on different roles, including director, script writer, storyboarder, video editor, publicity specialist, and so on. Once a particular book is chosen, each team should begin to discuss and storyboard their book trailer project. At some point, they will need to find talented people to act in the video or provide other necessary resources. After the actors and resources are assembled, the video shooting commences, followed by the editing process. Next, special effects can be added. For instance, there might be special graphics, animations, or synchronized music. Of course, there should be a title at the start and the appropriate credits displayed at the end.

Skills and Objectives. This task fosters creative thinking including insight, spontaneity, creative expression, design and artistic skills, originality, risk taking, and visual communication. It also entails aspects of participatory learning, logical sequencing of the content, and deeper and richer understanding of course content. Given the hands-on nature of the task, information embedded in the book trailers will reside in the memories of the producers well after the course ends.

Advice and Ideas. You might start this project by showing example book trailers from such websites as The Book Life, Book Trailers for Readers, and Book Riot. It is also vital to provide learners with clear task requirements in terms of length, format, and due dates. They will also need to know what technology resources and media elements (e.g., pictures, music, and so forth) are available to help. For instance, instructors should create a list of video editing resources in addition to freely available media such as images, sound, and videos. We recommend that as part of their task learners should write reflection papers on the activity, or, alternatively, design a set of promotional material for the trailer.

Once the trailers are completed, consider different presentation formats for sharing them as well as alternative assessment and reward options. Those of higher quality might be posted to a gallery or website of course examples. Once established, that gallery of video trailers could be used in later years as promotional materials for the course. Finally, instructors could also send a link of each trailer to the author(s) of the book for their observations and comments.

Variations and Extensions. Consider holding competitions or a special book trailer night. Experts from the local community or prior students in the course might rate each trailer using a set of assessment criteria. Awards might be handed out for different categories such as Most Creative Trailer, Best Director, Best Actor, and the like. Learners might also enter into competitions to build upon or remix trailers from previous semesters. Again, students from previous semesters might be brought back to rate their work.

Key Instructional Considerations

Risk index: High
Time index: High
Cost index: Low to High (depending on the technology employed)
Learner-centered index: High
Duration of the learning activity: 2–4 weeks

Activity 95. Online Book Reviews

Description and Purpose of Activity. Perhaps someone in your class will one day write book reviews for the *New York Times, NPR,* the *LA Times,* or *Barnes and Noble.* Younger and less experienced writers, however, can now perform book review activities as part of a class or other learning experience. Book reviews force students to summarize or condense what they have read. In the process, they obtain valuable practice in writing for a more varied and extended audience than what is available from a single class. And such reviews are not just read by others around the world, but often are reused, extended, or commented on. Stated another way, a good review could enhance a student's reputation and sense of identity.

There are numerous websites for student book reviews. K–12 learners might use Scholastic's Share What You're Reading website to pen reviews and read those submitted by their global peers. They might also review books in a wiki or podcast show. Such young learners' book reviews can also be in the form of a video such as in Club Recap from 60 Second Recap. Adult learners might critique a book and post it to LibraryThing, Goodreads, Scribd, or Amazon.com. Graduate students and professionals might post their book assessments to Academia.edu or LinkedIn. They might also attempt to publish professional reviews at Kidreads, Teenreads, 20SomethingReads, or Book Reporter. If successful, such reviews could be added to their résumés. Seeing their reviews appear on one of these sites is a strong incentive to work diligently on the task.

Some might wish to push the book review envelope while keeping the reviews private within a class. Take, for instance, Professor Julie Gahimer, who teaches a course on Professionalism in Physical Therapy (PT) at the University of Indianapolis. Julie has experimented with using a tool called Animoto for multimedia book reviews. With Animoto, students can combine photos, videos, and music in their reviews. In one of her classes, each student read a different book and reviewed it with Animoto. As students added images and sound to their book reviews, the books came to life and were much more memorable. Naturally, during the process, they were asked to relate the content of their book to the PT field.

Skills and Objectives. Such a task forces learners to justify their reasoning, back up their claims, engage in comparison and contrast, and evaluate arguments and ideas. In addition, learners engage in summarization, content synthesis, content sharing, deeper and richer understanding of course content, and content review or extension. Others skills might include rebutting challenges or comments to one's book review. A learning network, and thus a community, forms and expands around the book reviews and social sharing. Within that community, students bond and often form a personal identity within the field.

Advice and Ideas. Even though students have likely done book reviews since they entered school, some guidance is nonetheless essential. Consider asking them to write about the key book themes, purpose, or impetus for the book as well as the intended audience, key points or contributions, implications, conclusions, and sources used. A book review could also discuss the author background as well as related books on the topic. Naturally, the publisher, publication date, and title of book should typically be included. Before starting, students should be told how they will be assessed on the book review project.

Depending on their age or familiarity with the field, students may be hesitant or reluctant to post a book review on display to the world. One means to reduce that tension is to store the reviews in a password-protected site. Instructors could also partner students in a class or across different classes or institutions for joint book reviews.

Variations and Extensions. Learners could be asked to comment on the online book reviews of one or more of their peers; consider offering a guide sheet or learning scaffold with examples of the types of comments expected. The person writing the review could reflect on the comments received in a short paper, blog post, or a response to a discussion forum thread.

The book reviews or comments could be posted to a social networking group forum. For instance, at Goodreads and Scribd, posted book reviews and recommendations are shared with a social network of friends. Rethink Books extends such ideas, using a mobile application that allows learners in a class to share ideas and notes taken on a book with others reading the same book. Users can highlight and then leave public notes on different books. Such notes can also be offered on specific chapters or sections within a book. Favorite parts of a book might be highlighted as students read it and then are sent out to others via their Facebook or Twitter account (Wortham, 2010). Users of Rethink Books can also comment on the notes of others. As this occurs, books spring forth to life as learners realize how active the process is.

Key Instructional Considerations

> *Risk index: Medium*
> *Time index: Medium*
> *Cost index: Low*
> *Learner-centered index: High*
> *Duration of the learning activity: 1–2 weeks*

Activity 96. Content Databases and Learning Portals

Description and Purpose of Activity. Sometimes learners are not excited by the assembly of course tasks and activities. They may not find them meaningful or authentic enough. One solution is to give them options to design their own final tasks or projects. Unique final task ideas often arise when students conduct in-depth research literature searches on one or more topics relevant to the course or when they are involved in an internship experience. When done, they may wish to share their work with present and future students of the course in the form of an interactive article database or content portal.

For example, in a course on e-learning administration or leadership, students could focus on topics such as educational data mining, learning analytics, information visualization, and social network analysis. Students can find a wealth of new articles and resources on those topics that can enhance the course. They may also review, categorize, and rate or comment on what they have found. When done, they could develop a database or learning portal for the articles, videos, podcasts, and so on that they discovered, or they could develop supplemental content for every week of the course. In later years, such resources can be pruned or expanded as needed. When done effectively, learners can feel a sense of pride that their work will find use by hundreds or even thousands of peers who take different iterations of the course, as well as countless others who stumble upon the course website or learning portal.

Skills and Objectives. Skills enhanced include design and creative expression, communication skills, knowledge filtering and synthesis, content review and analysis, and logical sequencing. Students also engage in deeper and richer understanding of course content, synthesize various information sources, sequence content, and reflect on their final product. Along the way, they become more self-directed in their learning. Such activities require students to think about multiple uses of the articles or resources, not just for their peers in the course today, but for potential learners in the coming years. Hence, this resource compilation work heightens their audience awareness skills.

Advice and Ideas. Make the final course assignment options fairly open with only the basic requirements outlined. Such an open-ended approach grants learners more freedom to explore and express themselves, allowing them to frame the key variables such as the audience, currency and richness of the content, design and delivery format, underlying technology platform or database, and opportunities for others to add to or comment on the content.

Prior course participants could be recruited as mentors, guides, or evaluators. If your students are working on a particularly ambitious project, you may consider breaking it into stages of completion. In addition, as each stage is completed, you might require a meeting with the course instructor, designated project mentors, or teaching assistants. Student databases or website portals or prototypes should be approved before extensive labor is committed. If more than one person is designing the product, part of the design team should be involved in usability testing and formative evaluation. In addition, a link to the project or website could be placed in MERLOT, Connexions, or some other knowledge repository. Finally, such work should be presented to the entire class to acknowledge and celebrate it.

Variations and Extensions. A request for articles to include in the database could be made to content experts, departmental colleagues, friends, and prior students from the course. Such an announcement may also be posted in relevant social media groups in Ning, Facebook, Twitter, and Wikispaces. Once suggestions are received, students in the course need to make decisions about what to include in the final database.

Key Instructional Considerations

> *Risk index: Medium*
> *Time index: Medium*
> *Cost index: Low to Medium*
> *Learner-centered index: High*
> *Duration of the learning activity: 2–4 weeks or as needed*

Activity 97. Oral History Interviews

Description and Purpose of Activity. As noted by the Oral History Society in the United Kingdom, history is all around us in the living memories of people we interact with every day—from our personal family to people in our local community. We just need to ask some of the interesting individuals we meet to tell us their respective stories and record them. Everyone has a story, although obviously some people are involved in more momentous historical events than others. What we read in books cannot begin to inform learners of all the emotionally compelling and noteworthy experiences connected to any single event that they are learning about.

Often the voices and accounts of those who have been marginalized—women, the disabled, certain ethnic communities, the unemployed, those in poverty, and so forth—are missing, overlooked, or hidden. Oral histories can fill in those gaps. As noted at the UC Berkeley Regional Oral History Office (ROHO) website, oral histories are a method of collecting historical information with the goal of adding to present historical records or markers. As such, they are not the final or verified account of the event(s).

Requiring your students to conduct one or more oral histories is a unique means to help them better connect with course content. Such activities are especially relevant in sociology, history, education, music, and qualitative research methodology courses.

Designing a unique oral history project can inspire both the learners involved in the production and those affected by the final result. As Dr. Joan Kang Shin from the University of Maryland Baltimore County told us, students—whether they be teenagers or older adults—want to work on meaningful projects that can make a difference in the world. In her teacher training programs for English as a Foreign Language (EFL), Dr. Shin works with teachers from all parts of the globe including Russia, Libya, Egypt, Morocco, Cuba, Saudi Arabia, Thailand, Laos, Cambodia, Vietnam, El Salvador, Guatemala, and Peru. Given that English is increasingly an international language, Dr. Shin has her teachers utilize various global resources such as Idealist.org and TakingITGlobal to design curricula to help teenage learners foster social change in different communities.

For example, as an extension of a community leadership challenge program from the US State Department, Dr. Shin's students sometimes interview elders in the community. Their resulting work becomes a database of oral histories or an online documentary of that community. As the project unfolds, students feel empowered to make a difference in their global communities while using their emerging English skills as a vehicle for doing so. When done, students draft a series of "This I Believe" statements based on the results of the project. Dr. Shin finds these projects exceedingly motivational and engaging.

Skills and Objectives. Includes the ability to sift through masses of data, authentic data analysis, decision making, leadership and communication skills, interpreting results, and grasping possible audiences. Skills also include information filtering, synthesizing various information sources, appreciating multiple points of view and diversity, extending course connections, listening skills, deeper and richer understanding of course content, and various inquiry skills. Conducting an oral history can excite and engage learners about the content in general or a special element or aspect of it from which they might expand and build their expertise.

Advice and Ideas. Although there are rich veins of interview content to sort through related to the opinions, perspectives, controversies, and decisions of the past, there may be reasons to require students to conduct their own oral interviews and perhaps even create an oral interview website. Students might interview particular people from an ever-expanding class list of possible interviewees. Alternatively, they might find one or more people whom they are interested in interviewing and send their ideas to the instructor for approval. The Oral History Society's practical advice includes asking for recommendations from friends, relatives, neighbors, and work colleagues as well as local history groups, professional and voluntary organizations, and schools and college centers.

The instructor should lay out the assessment and evaluation criteria for the oral history assignment, and solicit from students suggestions that support the purpose, audience, and tenor of the project. For instance, students should know how many media elements that they are expected to include, the expected length of the interviews, the types of questions that might be asked, the ways of conducting the interviews, and the minimum number of references or citations for their work, if any. Connections to websites and other resources on how to conduct an oral history should be provided. In addition, an assessment template or guide should be posted online and explained. Prior examples of student oral histories could be posted to a project gallery or class oral history website. Have students write reflection papers, reports, interview summaries, or other papers based on the oral histories that they have conducted. A set number of course connections could be required for each oral history created.

Variations and Extensions. As a class, students may decide to combine their respective interviews to create an oral history website for a topic. If none exists, they could be assigned to collect a set of interviews from living legends on a particular topic. Initially, they might seek out relevant online resources on the topic. Students will need guidance on how to solicit interviews, the typical length of such interviews, the types of questions to ask, the protocol for the interview procedures, and how to submit their completed projects. As a class, they will need support related to establishing the online oral history website. A set of scaffolds or guide sheets should be created to nurture their success.

Key Instructional Considerations

Risk index: High
Time index: High
Cost index: Low to High (depending on the actual technologies and resources available and used)
Learner-centered index: High
Duration of the learning activity: 2–5 weeks at the end of the term

Activity 98. Grammar Check, Peer Check

Description and Purpose of Activity. As indicated in several earlier activities in this book, writing is a form of thinking. It involves heavy doses of effortful cognition and involvement in the task. Writing is hard for many students. When done, students want their final products to be as accurate and professional as possible. Fortunately, there are online support tools for learner writing that are freely available. Tools like Ginger, Grammarly, GrammarCheck, Language Tool Style and Grammar Check, PaperRater, WritersDiet Test, and SpellCheckPlus have free versions or trial options that can be used to help students sort through various writing issues such as run-on sentences, sentence fragments, shifting tense, missing prepositions, the use of conjunctions, wordiness, passive versus active writing, comma splices, vague words, and so on. In addition to grammar, some of these devices have options to check spelling, style, and plagiarism. Most important, many of them are fairly straightforward to employ; to use these tools or systems, the user often just has to copy and paste in his paper or section of the paper, and allow the system to check for potential errors and problematic expressions (YourDictionary, 2012). Quick, consistent, and often free!

That is the micro level aspect to revising papers which can now be effectively provided by a machine or set of software code. To complement such mechanized feedback there ought to be peer reactions to what students have written. Professors Hui-Chin Yeh and Yu-Fen Yang at the National Yunlin University of Science and Technology in Taiwan have developed an online writing system called WRITeam to support peer review for structural or macro-level changes as well as grammatical or micro-level changes (Yang, 2010). The system records student writing activities in action logs to help understand student revision processes. According to their research, with peer-flagged potential changes, students are more engaged in the writing task and the quality of their papers is raised (Yang, Yeh, & Wong, 2010; Yeh & Yang, 2011).

Naturally, human feedback is highly valuable even when a system like WRITeam is not available. Papers can be shared and peer reviewed using a dropbox in a course management system like Blackboard or Moodle. This powerful combination of machine and human feedback can significantly enhance the quality of student writing. In addition, there is a focus on the micro or specific grammatical or spelling changes as well as changes that are more global or related to the macro side of the writers' revisionary practices.

Anyone who has been on a work team realizes that there are many moments in the real world when individuals must edit or revise a report. Coworkers must become savvy at incorporating others' ideas while maintaining a personal voice. At the same time, they need to know how to make suggestions for changes and corrections on reports written by others. Forcing students to use online grammar and support tools as well as to label their revisions as surface or deep will foster greater awareness of the writing process. They will better understand issues related to word usage, grammar, sentence structure, and text organization. Juxtaposing multiple drafts of papers and analyzing the potential local and global revisions can highlight these changes. It will also engage them more fully in the activity.

Skills and Objectives. Includes extensive peer feedback, gaining diverse perspectives, peer-to-peer interaction, critical analysis and reflection, attention to detail, audience awareness, and knowledge construction and negotiation. Of course, other objectives might include elevating student writing skills, resolving cognitive conflict, and internalizing new skills such as students' ability to self-monitor their own writing.

Advice and Ideas. Students may not understand the difference between surface level and global or more structural forms of revision. In addition, awareness of revisionary practices might not transfer into practice and may vary across age groups. To deal with this issue, instructors could show examples of different versions of texts that detail changes in writing development, style, and organization. Alternatively, they may consider including a series of guide sheets or writing templates on the various types of changes expected. Instructors can also experiment with using multiple rounds of review and revision. As part of these efforts, students would compare papers and label the types of revisions made. Discussion forums and chats can also be utilized to reflect on different revisionary practices and evaluate changes over time.

Variations and Extensions. Have students create a wiki of revisionary tactics and strategies at the micro and macro levels along with labels for each of them. Ensuing classes could add to the list. In addition, students from previous semesters or versions of the course might return to train current students in both macro and micro forms of revision.

Key Instructional Considerations

Risk index: Medium
Time index: Medium
Cost index: Low to high (depending on tool availability)
Learner-centered index: High
Duration of the learning activity: 2–4 weeks or as needed

Activity 99. Recording Accomplishments (e.g., I Done It)

Description and Purpose of Activity. As discussed in Activity #4 back in Chapter Four, posting course commitments can help in course retention because students' goals are on display for others to read. Tracking your progress on different goals is fast becoming accepted in business settings. Such tracking can promote persistence or willpower (Baumeister & Tierney, 2011). People today track everything from calories consumed to miles flown to training courses completed to baseball games attended each year. Some refer to technologies that enable us to track activities and various performances as "auto-analytics" (Wilson, 2012). Often workers experience significant gains in productivity as well as improvements in self-awareness and life and job satisfaction from using these technologies.

There are many auto-analytic tools available for helping individuals with their goals. For instance, IDoneThis provides a daily e-mail reminder to post what you have accomplished during the day. Using technology, your goals and accomplishments are on display privately or more publicly for colleagues or other team members to discover. Launched in 2011, IDoneThis quickly became recognized as one of the most effective productivity tools available. Timelines, word clouds, quips, and project names can focus the individual on tasks that need to be accomplished (Purdy, 2012). The daily e-mail summaries of users' goals and accomplishments can also be exported to an Excel spreadsheet for searching and for reflecting on personal goals. In effect, these are performance results that can keep a person engaged and motivated in the activity.

IDoneThis is just one such tool for goal setting. While IDoneThis costs a few dollars each month, 43 Things is a free service used by millions of people to list their goals, share their progress toward each one, and provide feedback to others with similar goals. A somewhat more robust tool is Lifetick. This innovative system includes options for tracking multiple goals and the capability to build plans for each one. With special graphs and reports, a learner can review progress over time and in each individual area. Other websites like Milestone Planner allow users to visualize how close they have come to meeting task goals or milestones, while Goalscape utilizes concentric wheels with varying sizes indicating the relative importance of different goals (Henry, 2012).

For those wanting a more simple and cost-effective way to keep track of their goals, there is Joe's Goals. This free online system is straightforward and fun. It permits the user to check off if she did or did not meet a particular goal each day of the week. Mindbloom Life Game is another free tool. In a nutshell, it is a self-improvement game in the form of a life tree that tracks things that you want to do now (e.g., eat better, perform random acts of kindness, exercise, and so on) (Henry, 2011). It includes features to collaborate with others on goals and share your progress with others. These tools and systems allow users to establish personal goals and to-do lists, monitor progress, set up step-by-step plans, and review priorities.

Skills and Objectives. Includes setting personal goals, working backward as well as planning ahead, analyzing progress, visualizing success, and forming commitments and convictions. The physical act of record keeping provides both a series of benchmarks and reflection points on the journey to success, and as such, it should enhance metacognitive monitoring skills.

Advice and Ideas. Imagine a day when such auto-analytic tools are ubiquitous in every fully online and blended course. With such embedded goal-related information and feedback, learners could become more self-directed in their learning quests. As part of this self-directedness, they could better visualize their course tasks and assignments. And they will be doing so when in line at a grocery store or while boarding a plane. In fact, mobile applications will soon be common for tracking course-related goals and accomplishments.

In the meantime, instructors can do several things to foster such goal setting. First, they could create a course accomplishments thread in a discussion forum for learners to list what they have done to date. Alternatively, they may post goals in different sections of a wiki to indicate major as well as more minor accomplishments. These could range from short-term goals related to the course to more impactful ones that cut across one's different learning experiences. Learners could also blog their course goals and accomplishments each week or as each unit passes. All three of these ideas would foster learner reflection while building a semipermanent goal accomplishment history; the blog, in particular, would be a place for personal reflection long after the course has ended.

Another idea would be to send out weekly or biweekly e-mails asking students to list their upcoming goals for the week as well as those that they have fulfilled for the preceding one. However, providing constant and genuine feedback to all learners on their accomplishments each week may prove too time-intensive for instructors. As an alternative, they could recruit mentors from the ranks of those who have completed the course in the past. Such mentors could send out individualized weekly reminders pertaining to their specific learning goals. Incorporating personalized reminders and feedback helps to humanize the process, instead of relying on system e-mails and feedback in the form of data visualizations. Both approaches—system as well as human feedback—are better than having no goal setting within a course.

Experiment with one or two of these ideas and see what works best for your course or situation. You might pilot-test free services like 43 Things, Mindbloom, or Joe's Goals and see how such goal setting affects learner performance in your classes. Be sure to review each one and see which is applicable to your age group or class topic. In addition, gather formative feedback from your learners on each idea that you have tested and ask for their suggestions on improving the activity.

Variations and Extensions. If the course-related accomplishments posted are public, the instructor could create a matching game at the end of the semester for students to figure out the person who achieved a particular accomplishment. The game could be played as a final activity to signal who was actively participating in the course. Students might have options within the game to add bonus or trick questions; possibly they could even design a learner accomplishment game or test as a team.

Another option to recording accomplishments is to detail what you have yet to do and to plan for the future. In this method, the learner would map out a plan of action for upcoming weeks, months, or years so as to continue learning once the course has ended.

Key Instructional Considerations

> Risk index: Medium
> Time index: Medium
> Cost index: Low to Medium
> Learner-centered index: High
> Duration of the learning activity: Semester long

Activity 100. Poster Sessions and Gallery Tours

Description and Purpose of Activity. One technique that we have found effective online for nearly two decades is to inform students that a key goal of the course is to post their midterm or final projects to the Web as a public resource. Our students have contributed to free wikibooks (Bonk, Lee, Kim, & Lin, 2009, 2010) as well as designed multimedia glossaries in a wiki. They have also designed summary videos, produced podcast shows, compiled interactive literature reviews, created research journals, designed interactive Webquests (Ehman, Bonk, & Yamagata-Lynch, 2005), and written and performed songs. Posting work online offers online and blended learners an audience beyond the instructor. They quickly realize that not only could their peers view their work, but so could family members, friends, future students, future employers, and countless people they will never formally meet. The stakes are elevated.

When working with professionals such as practicing teachers, it is quickly apparent that working adults want to perform at an extremely high level. The standards of working adults are often a few levels above those who recently left secondary school. Not too surprisingly, their elevated level of personal expectations often raises their course-related tensions and anxieties. However, when they can review prior student work in the form of an online gallery or poster session of prior student work, much of these tensions abate. Why? Well, they now have examples and a target to work toward.

Skills and Objectives. Includes audience awareness, goal setting, communication and presentation skills, and synthesizing across various information sources. It also fosters feedback from a range of sources, creative expression, knowledge construction, task engagement and involvement, and student autonomy and choice. There is perpetual content review and deeper understanding of key concepts. Of course, student projects, documents, and media posted to an online gallery by the course instructor can be added to the student's résumé or digital portfolio.

Advice and Ideas. Think carefully about the goals of an online gallery or poster session. Perhaps start with just a few examples of student work. Solicit feedback from a few students on the initial design. It is important not to embarrass anyone while attempting to motivate them by publicly displaying student work that they are not happy with. Be sure to ask for their permission before posting and then ask them how it looks when done. As the gallery expands over semesters or years, instructors should prune prior examples that are no longer relevant to the course or that simply are not of suitable quality.

An online gallery or archive of prior student work creates a legacy for the course. It could even be a key component of a community of learners. Previous students would feel a connection to current students through that gallery; instructors should ponder ways to take advantage of such course sentiments. At the same time, inquiries may be received from students and instructors at other institutions about the content that is being displayed. We recommend that you respond whenever possible to such inquiries as international course connections might lead to interesting tasks and activities in future versions of the course. Research might also emanate from such initial correspondences.

Variations and Extensions. Learners could engage in competitions across sections of a course or between multiple institutions for the best representation of particular concepts, theories, principles, people, or new trends. The top-rated work would be highlighted in a special website or open educational resource.

Another variation would be to invite several experts within the field to critique the student posters or galleries in private one-to-one discussions with each learner. Students could be asked to write reflection papers based on that feedback.

Key Instructional Considerations

> *Risk index: Medium*
> *Time index: High*
> *Cost index: Low to Medium*
> *Learner-centered index: High*
> *Duration of the learning activity: 1–2 weeks*

Final Reflections on Yielding Products

Production. It seems that life in the twenty-first century revolves around that word. Secondary and higher education students produce reports that are shared with real-world clients. Even very young learners today design their own online radio and television shows. Learners have the opportunity to document aspects of life in their local community or try to document something much more global in nature. The audience for such products may be current students of the course or future ones. Alternatively, onlookers could also be learners at other institutions or parts of the planet. And with article databases, creative song summaries, and gallery tours, there may be informal learners who get inspired from their casual browsing of the online course content.

That is what this chapter was all about—the yielding of products; or, as Seth Godin (2011) might say, the production and shipment of art. When tasks are effectively designed, learners have a sense of purpose or passion to complete them. There is an underlying vision or end state. With such visions, learners can create goals and accomplish them one by one. In the process, they take ownership over the task. And that is what this tenth and final principle of the TEC-VARIETY framework is all about.

Throughout this book, we have inserted numerous examples of the types of learner outputs that instructors could use to foster learner success and ownership. Given that we are in the age of the Web 2.0, we could have detailed countless more. Such course products often yield unimaginable benefits. Each offers learners a goal or milestone from which to gauge their course competencies. And each offers something tangible not only to submit to their instructor or their peers, but to take from the class and personally share with others in the months and years to come. There are also personal takeaways such as pride and identity. Of course, there is no real way of knowing just how many people might purposefully or serendipitously drop in to be inspired or find a small clue or minor insight that they can use or perhaps build upon. And so it is that knowledge, when shared with a global audience of peers, continues to evolve and find new uses.

Take one of more of the ten activities outlined here and build upon them. Share them with others. Talk to your students about how goal setting in a fully online or blended course can lead to long-term goals and perhaps even a future job or career someday. Take, for instance, the gallery tours, oral histories, posters, podcast shows, YouTube videos, book trailers, and wikibooks that students might design and share. Each one of these can become a course legacy and the start of a more permanent and evolving course community. Invite former students back, perhaps as mentors, judges, consultants, feedback partners, and tour guides for the course. Anything is now possible in this digital age. Experiment and reflect on the results.

Recapping the Ten

These are definitely exciting times to be a learner as well as someone who can assist with that learning. In these past 10 chapters, we have detailed 100 ways in which you can foster such excitement and passion for learning in this digital age. We also inserted one or more variations and extensions for each of those 100 activities. With each set of 10 activities and assorted variations, online instructors have much to choose from and chew on.

It is almost time to briefly recap the ideas we have detailed in this book. Chapter Fifteen will offer such a recap as will the ending list of resources and references in the appendices of this book. First, however, in Chapter Fourteen, we offer a bit of advice on how instructors who are less experienced or more reluctant or resistant might be supported in the use of the TEC-VARIETY framework and others like it (e.g., R2D2).

Thanks for joining us on this journey into TEC-VARIETY. We hope that you can now incorporate some of the ideas of this chapter as well as the preceding ones in your online and blended courses as well as FTF ones. Adding some TEC-VARIETY may be just what this generation of learners is looking for. If you need some support, well, then, it is time to read Chapter Fourteen.

CHAPTER FOURTEEN

SUPPORTING AND MOTIVATING INSTRUCTORS

> Motivation is the art of getting people to do what
> you want them to do because they want to do it.
>
> —Dwight D. Eisenhower

We have traversed much territory in this book. As you have discovered, there are a wide range of Web tools, resources, and potential activities to enhance and perhaps even transform online and blended learning environments. When instructors thoughtfully follow a framework like TEC-VARIETY, these activities can significantly stretch the pedagogical possibilities of most course management systems. We believe that the best solution, at the present time, is to deliberately embed interactive and engaging online teaching and learning solutions around these first- or second-generation online learning environments.

Consequently, in this book, we have laid out more than 100 strategies that you can use right away in your online teaching and learning. The vast majority of these ideas should be available regardless of the system you are afforded, the technological capabilities of your particular organization, or your personal level of educational technology knowledge and skill. Although some of our ideas and suggestions take advantage of bleeding-edge technologies, across the 100+ examples, most should be easy to implement and straight-forward to use. If you find a strategy more challenging, consider scaling the activity down to its most basic level during implementation. To situate and better understand these 100+ strategies and help you realize such goals, we organized them under the TEC-VARIETY acronym.

While the TEC-VARIETY framework may be of value to you and your colleagues, many instructors and trainers will need additional support to overcome their fears and hesitancies. We have found that with sustained strategic assistance, they too will give it a go. Of course, once you identify the items that can hinder or block effective online instruction, it is possible to design resources, training programs, and policies to address them. In the pages that follow, we discuss some of the obstacles and barriers as well as what might support and motivate instructors to engage in online learning. After that, we offer 10 strategies or ideas that we have found effective in supporting those who remain reluctant or are new to this form of instruction. What you will notice is that much is now possible in terms of support. First, however we approach the roadblocks.

Online Roadblocks and Resistance

Each year, tens of thousands of instructors working across all disciplines and in every sector of education and training are being asked to teach or collaborate with other instructors online. But a seasoned F2F instructor's first forays into Web-based instruction can be extremely daunting, especially for those lacking sufficient training or self-confidence. Murphy's Law, "If anything can go wrong, it will," often comes into play, and so do frustrations, disappointments, and bouts of anxiety over instructional events that did not proceed as planned. While we are advocates of online and blended forms of learning, we also wrote this book as a means to help elevate its quality. At the same time, we readily admit that online instructors often might face technological challenges. New software tools and features must be learned. Passwords must be remembered. And assorted advice, instructional aids, and guidelines must be developed for students.

Even when such issues are resolved, there are many other reasons for instructors to be reluctant to offer an online or blended learning course. Among the more salient reasons are lack of time, low-quality materials, lack of skills, workload, pay or financial incentives, and insufficient training opportunities. Some of the more openly hesitant instructors are concerned with potentially high withdrawal rates. Others are concerned about the cheapening of education. And still others worry about the sheer inappropriateness of online delivery formats for the types of learners that they currently teach.

That is just for starters. Four common questions or concerns that we hear relate to assessment difficulties, copyright issues, experiences with plagiarism, and difficulty finding quality content and courses. Additional factors that deter professional educators from participating in online education include fears related to losing control over the classroom, heavy doses of skepticism, prior technology frustrations, and a general lack of internal support and encouragement.

Given these issues, we have to expect heavy pockets of faculty reluctance or resistance to online learning. Many of us, in fact, have colleagues who take offense to being obliged to change to a new delivery format or who resent that significant resources are being diverted from more traditional educational formats. In the past, however, they might have been able to simply wait it out until retirement. Not anymore. In fact, for most organizations and institutions, online learning is just in the beginning stages. It will only increase in use and importance in the coming decades. There really is no way to turn back the clock so we believe it is best to find ways to thoughtfully and reflectively embrace the change and perhaps even ramp up the change process a notch or two.

Additional aspects of instructors' reluctance toward transitioning to online learning include the misconception that they must learn to teach all over again because they perceive online learning to be a new environment. This assumption can lead to instructors and trainers feeling a general lack of confidence and low self-esteem about teaching online. They may also feel intimidated and pressured into thinking it is yet another burden in their already time-strapped list of work-related responsibilities.

To make matters worse, most instructors and trainers have never experienced online learning as a student—not yet, anyway. Nor have most ever seen best practices modeled for them by those who are more experienced with online instruction. Like most educators, they teach according to how they themselves had been taught. They fear that the move to online learning will challenge some of their long-standing beliefs and assumptions about their practice.

Typically, such resistance or protest subsides significantly once instructors become more familiar and comfortable with the new technology or instructional delivery mechanism. In fact, we have found that there are six stages to the online learning resistance and adoption cycle. These six stages are detailed in the following paragraphs. In many ways, they are somewhat oversimplified here to make a point.

Before any resistance movement can take root, educators must become aware of fully online and blended learning. As shown in Table 14.1, we refer to such awareness as the first stage of the online learning adoption cycle (Stage One: Awareness of Online Learning). As awareness increases, so too does resistance as instructors realize that some of their favorite instructional ideas and activities will no longer work, or at least not the same way. In the process, tried and tested resources and approaches might have to be given up or, at the very least, significantly adjusted or modified. That is Stage Two: Resistance to Online Learning. We spent much of the first decade of Web-based instruction in these first two stages; to situate this period in time, it would span from about 1996 to 2005.

TABLE 14.1: STAGES OF THE ONLINE LEARNING ADOPTION CYCLE.

Stage One	Awareness of Online Learning
Stage Two	Resistance to Online Learning
Stage Three	Understanding the Online Learning Possibilities
Stage Four	Doing Online Learning
Stage Five	Sharing Online Learning Resources and Activities
Stage Six	Advocating Online Learning

During the next stage, greater understanding of the instructional possibilities arises (Stage Three: Understanding the Online Learning Possibilities). As instructors become more accepting of the advantages of teaching with technology, they share examples, browse resources, read books and papers, and hold intense discussions with colleagues and experts. At some point, instructors move on to Stage Four: Doing Online Learning and begin to experiment with online tools and activities in their own courses. This experimentation continues to grow and eventually evolves into complete online modules or even fully online courses. Today, many would argue that, as a society, we are fully immersed in Stages Three and Four, which involve not just understanding the possibilities of online education but actually doing something interesting and engaging to boost learner motivation and retention.

Once instructors feel comfortable with this new concept of teaching online, they begin to share their online activities and resources with their colleagues as well as with people whom they might never physically meet. We refer to this as Stage Five: Sharing Online Learning Resources and Activities. With emerging Web technologies for collaboration and social interaction, Stage Five is not only increasingly possible, but is displayed in highly salient ways with ratings of one's shared contents in MERLOT or in extended dialogue about an idea in an online instructor community. As a result, sharing your course content and ideas is a new mantra in many educational settings today. Some might post their best practices to MERLOT, Connexions, Creative Commons, or some other online repository of course materials. For many this is a bold step. They have moved outside the comfort zones of their walled classrooms to share their most sacred instructional practices in an online space. It is at this point in the process where pieces of their instructional identities are fully on display for others—including complete strangers—to browse, adopt, and comment upon.

A few do not stop there. They not only begin to share resources and course materials with others, but they also become advocates and perhaps even leading proponents for online and blended learning (Stage Six: Advocating Online Learning). Here, they might inform or train colleagues and others about online learning via online Webinars, conferences, workshops, and summer faculty summits. They might write articles for online learning magazines and newsletters. They might even pen a book or article on the topic.

During the past decade, many institutions and organizations have seen their instructors move from the resistance stage to the understanding and use stages. Recently, however, there has been the emergence of a new online learning concept called the MOOC (Johnson et al., 2013) which we first brought up back in Chapter Two and elaborated on in Chapter Eight. The idea of learning delivery via a MOOC is forcing most organizations to reflect on how to effectively offer courses to potentially thousands or tens of thousands of learners in a single course.

Not surprisingly, we have thus entered a new cycle of online learning resistance. In many cases, we are back to Stage One of awareness as people struggle to understand what a MOOC actually is as well as its benefits and potential audiences it attracts. As MOOCs find the limelight and are projected to grow exponentially, many have quickly moved to Stage Two (i.e., resistance to MOOCs, or perhaps better stated as reflection on the true benefits and challenges of MOOCs). Higher education faculty members at places like Harvard, American University, and San Jose State University are now calling MOOCs into question for various thought-provoking reasons (Berrett, 2013; Kolowich, 2013a, 2013b).

College instructors are not the only ones raising red flags about this movement toward MOOCs; many university provosts and other administrators are skeptical and worried about the pace at which MOOCs have taken hold in higher education settings during the past few years (Rivard, 2013). Clearly, instructors volunteering to teach a MOOC or thinking about doing one need innovative and consistent forms of support. The TEC-VARIETY framework as well as other online learning models and frameworks could perhaps address some of the serious retention and resource use issues revealed in the emerging research on MOOCs (Koller, Ng, Do, & Chen, 2013).

Keep in mind that there are a multitude of ways to address instructor and trainer hesitation and resistance related to online learning besides the use of our framework. In dealing with the rapid growth of online learning, various guidelines and best practices can be found in corporate training environments (Hyder, 2002) as well as in higher education. There are books on many topics in higher education including how to moderate discussion, create community, design blended learning environments, and assess learning outcomes (Garrison & Vaughan, 2008; Palloff & Pratt, 2007; Salmon, 2011, 2013). In addition, there are numerous other resources, conferences, and online forums that deal with instructor hesitancy or resistance regarding online teaching and learning environments. There are also competency checklists, certificates, and entire degree programs to help endorse or evaluate the quality of your own online instruction. Suffice it to say, if someone is seeking online learning and instruction support, it can easily be found.

Online Instructor Motivations and Perceptions

Online learning delivery mechanisms force instructors as well as learners to rethink their roles. There is often more emphasis on knowledge construction and collaboration among the online and blended learners than on the lecturing or direct instruction practices of traditional education. And there are many free and open resources to use in your online and blended courses and activities. As a result, we often see instructors taking on roles of learning counselor, concierge, and curator of content. A learning curator, for instance, finds resources and makes them available to learners enrolled in her course as well as those who happen to browse it. As with MOOCs, online and blended courses are increasingly open and available for anyone to tap into. Clearly, the long-standing role of instructor as imparter of knowledge is shifting to one of resource gatherer, learning activity coordinator, and moderator of the learning process.

Of course, there are incentives to encourage "trial runs" by those remain hesitant about taking such new roles. Researchers like Catherine Schifter (2002) have found that it is more often the intrinsic factors that are crucial to bring newcomers to online environments. Instructors might be attracted to the heightened intellectual challenges, flexibility in course delivery and scheduling, and job satisfaction. Such intrinsic factors typically take precedence over extrinsic ones like financial rewards, release time, grants, or reduced teaching load.

While extrinsic factors often can attract someone into online teaching or training, nonetheless it is ultimately internal motivational variables that sustain such interests. To verify this claim, over a decade ago, Angie Parker (2003) analyzed more than 100 articles related to the motivators and incentives associated with instructors teaching with distance education technologies. She found that both intrinsic and extrinsic factors matter. The key intrinsic motivators included self-satisfaction, flexible scheduling, and the ability to teach a wider and more diverse audience. Popular extrinsic items in her study included monetary stipends, the reduction of one's workload or release time, and the chance to learn and use emerging technologies. She rightfully concludes that many of these reasons are the same ones that attract faculty to teaching in traditional settings.

Diane Chapman (2011) from North Carolina State University conducted a more recent study of nearly 300 contingent faculty and those who were tenured or tenure track. Like Parker, Chapman also found that flexible schedules, self-satisfaction, and opportunities to use emerging learning technologies were hugely attractive for those teaching distance education courses. However, her results differed somewhat from Parker's when it came to external incentives. She found that financial incentives such as stipends for professional development, free professional development opportunities, and the potential for higher pay for continuing to teach in online courses were among the higher ranked external motivational factors. But as in the Parker study, both intrinsic and extrinsic motivators were important. And while tenured and tenure track faculty rated high-quality technical support as a key motivator, the contingent faculty were interested in participating in on-line instructor communities where they could discuss and share ideas related to teaching online courses with their virtual peers.

With the enormous growth in online learning over the past two decades, such findings related to instructor incentives and motivation online should find their way into the strategic planning documents of many an organization or institution.

Overcoming Reluctance and Resistance

Despite numerous recent online learning inroads, scores of educators and administrators remain hesitant, reluctant, and perhaps even exceedingly resistant to attempt fully online and blended learning. We have nevertheless observed that the accelerating demand for online learning, significantly reduced budgets, and the emergence of hundreds of free or relatively inexpensive Web technologies have actually turned much of the resistance into at least lukewarm acceptance. At the same time, many still need convincing and many more require support for their acceptance of online instruction assignments.

The following items are 10 ways to assist those who are either new to online or blended learning or who remain somewhat hesitant or reluctant to embrace the Web for their online courses, programs, and events. Keep in mind, however, that there are actually dozens of additional instructor support ideas, some of which are embedded in the sub-points.

1.   **Incremental Change:** Change is always complex and difficult. Shifts to on-line teaching and learning are no different. We recommend that those who might be nervous or more hesitant start with small steps or minor course adaptations. Perhaps a training program could begin by having these indi-viduals find online resources that they can later use. During training, they could select from an assortment of low-cost, low-risk, low-time strategies. In fact, the previous 10 chapters of this book describe more than 100 strategies by their degree of risk, amount of time required, and potential cost. One or two well-placed low-risk, low-time, low-cost strategies may be the requisite fuel needed to ignite many a wild online learning flame. At the end of such

a training or orientation program, participants should indicate where they presently are on a risk continuum or meter as well as where they would like to be in a few years.

2. **Shared Success Stories and Best Practices:** Another option is to show instructors and trainers examples of what actually works. Thousands of online learning examples and models can be found in books, newsletters, technical reports, e-mail messages, DVDs, and Web portals. Consider having these stories developed by peers and colleagues whom others respect and trust, instead of by vendors or external consultants. Best practices and success stories are decidedly beneficial. And such sharing can take place using social networking software and online community building tools.

3. **Training and Development:** We have found that starting with a simple technology tool or resource that can be mastered and applied is more important than explaining the underlying instructional approach, philosophy, or pedagogy. Of course, such discussion can be conducted once the trainee is excited after tentatively trying it out and actually witnessing some of the immediate benefits. Providing incentives for the completion of the training is also important (e.g., a stipend, certificate, laptop, tablet, and so on).

More than a decade ago, Varvel, Lindeman, and Stovall (2003) found that a structured faculty development program offered by the Illinois Online Network (ION) enhanced both instructor self-confidence and participant satisfaction with teaching online. The ION program, in fact, led to a "Master Online Teacher Certificate" which certified faculty, staff, and administrators who demonstrated sufficient knowledge in online teaching and learning (e.g., methods of assessment, roles of online instructors as well as students, learning activities in online courses, technologies for delivery, and the like). With the continued rise in online teaching and learning, such programs are proliferating. Ask your organization to consider creating one.

4. **Just-in-Time Support:** Support staff could be on call when needed for 1:1 help and advice. Technical support personnel and trainers should not dictate a single approach or instructional philosophy, but rather should listen to client needs and respond accordingly. Allow online instructors to select the training topics that they are interested in, rather than preselecting the topic(s) for them. Bonk has found that training instructors in the technologies that they had access to was far superior to training them in software that he just happened to like or use himself.

This is no minor issue. In fact, current trends and practices in online instructor training and support have embraced situated online professional development (PD). Such approaches target specific online instructor needs rather than sending instructors and instructional design staff to attend one-off workshops and institutes. As a result, we are increasingly seeing online personnel benefit from support that is authentic, situated, and targeted to their teaching needs.

Just-in-time support strategies offer exactly that. They allow an instructor to identify what he needs in terms of external and internal assistance. Once identified, the appropriate support resources and activities are systematically supplied to help him integrate Web-based technologies and associated resources in a thoughtful manner. Equally important, interactive pedagogical practices are demonstrated or made available for later online review. When combined, such technology and pedagogy training and support elevate the overall teaching and learning environment that the instructor is attempting to design. In fact, the second author's work with novice online instructors found value in systematic cycles of just-in-time support via an approach called the negotiated intervention. This internal support method helped bring about longer lasting understanding and development in practice (Khoo, & Cowie, 2011).

Dynamic forms of feedback that arise during the negotiated intervention are powerful because they are highly responsive to the instructor's needs and concerns. Such just-in-time approaches may also allow instructors to experience for themselves what their novice students might be experiencing. And these approaches offer hands-on practice to address the issues faced. At the same time, just-in-time 1:1 support can also make use of a combination of F2F instructional assistance and online tutorial-based support which can be completed in a self-paced manner at the instructor's convenience.

5. **An Atmosphere of Sharing:** Fostering change in terms of technology integration and use will only come when there is an atmosphere of change. Such an atmosphere can definitely build up over time. For instance, the final 5–10 minutes of a department or program meeting might be saved for a live presentation of an emerging technology or discussion of ideas related to how instructors are using Web technology. We also see this sharing occurring at the school and university level with annual innovative use of technology in teaching events or awards. Many universities also sponsor brown bag lunches during which a visiting scholar, local expert, or faculty member will present some interesting technology or online activity. Colloquia institutes, video-conferences, Webinars, and other events can also be employed to cultivate this change in atmosphere. Again, social networking tools like LinkedIn or Twitter can foster such sharing as might the learning management system that an organization is presently using. Ideally, the result will be a community of practice made up of those interested in online learning.

6. **Awards and Incentives:** As indicated, training programs may include incentives such as stipends, travel funds, awards, and technology. For example, those who are innovative might be the first in line for hardware or software upgrades and replacements. We have seen such programs work. The School of Education at Indiana University, for instance, has been innovative in sponsoring iPad and laptop programs through which enlisted faculty members receive an iPad or a laptop computer for their instructional use after completing a designated number of hours of technology-related training. Those who already are technology leaders can also receive such technology awards if they provide a set number of hours of training to others in the program.

    Other incentives could include assistance in writing grants for specific technology or for designing innovative pedagogy with technology, or for money for associated conference travel with such innovations. There could be competitions for interactivity in online course development, outstanding course awards, and annual events for innovation in online instruction. Organizations such as Brandon Hall Research, the United States Distance Learning Association (USDLA), and the eLearning Guild promote or directly provide various types of online and distance learning awards or recognitions.

The ultimate goal of these recognitions, of course, is the design of high-quality online learning courses and resources. These types of efforts are vital because part of creating a community of online educators is to support success and then to celebrate such success when it occurs.

7. **Modeling:** We have found that modeling the use of online learning by your colleagues and supervisors is highly valuable. In effect, when your friends and organizational leaders are adopting it, so can you. And when the corporate CEO or university president generates a podcast show or presents her state of the university address via videostreaming, people throughout the organization tend to take notice. Modeling also creates opportunities for discussion and interaction to occur around the topic or content area being shown, resulting in a sense of community among those who are interested in or already attempting the new ideas.

8. **Mentoring and Coaching:** While technology-oriented training increasingly relies on technology-based tutorials and online professional support communities, opportunities for 1:1 advice and consultation are bound to have long-lasting impact. When new instructors, designers, or trainers enter into an online environment or situation, it is vital to provide some form of cognitive apprenticeship. For instance, someone savvy with technology or knowledgeable about online teaching and learning could be asked to support one or more novice instructors or designers. We both have been involved in mentoring programs in the past and have found them to be genuinely successful from a technological standpoint as well as from the viewpoint of developing a sense of community. In such situations, instructors and staff members experienced with various educational technologies serve as mentors for more novice and junior members. And they often receive modest stipends for such efforts.

9. **External Supports:** Most of the preceding ideas relate to internal forms of support within an organization or institution. Naturally, given the expansiveness of the Web, some external supports can be provided, such as access to online teaching examples, certificate programs for online instruction and online administration, and even master's degrees. In addition, an organization or institution could subscribe to an online newsletter for its online instructors. Other organizations and communities such as EDUCAUSE Learning Initiative offer interesting conference events and discussions related to instructional practices with emerging learning technologies. For those in the K–12 world, the George Lucas Educational Foundation (GLEF) has produced numerous high-quality examples of innovative teaching approaches with and without technology. Taking advantage of the wide array of online support for teaching online is simple and extremely inexpensive. In fact, any organization or institution can now create a Web portal with extensive links to such sites.

10. **Frameworks and Models:** We believe that one of the more significant ways to overcome the resistance movement is to use models, overviews, and other frameworks during training. Frameworks offer a means to reflect on what works and what is not working. They provide a macro lens to any online teaching and learning situation. And they can help to categorize or make sense of the never-ending mounds of information or data that instructors must deal with each day. In effect, frameworks reduce the apprehensions and angst that educators and administrators might feel related to teaching and learning in online environments.

The TEC-VARIETY framework that forms the basis of this book and the R2D2 model (Bonk & Zhang, 2008) detailed in the first chapter are two pedagogically focused examples of how to support faculty with a simple structure or mnemonic. Other online learning models and frameworks outline the various levels of Web integration and the types of assessments possible. Such instructional aids also help in developing and coordinating virtual teams, understanding the forms of online interaction, and training novice online instructors in the forms of instructional assistance and scaffolding that they might initially rely upon (Bonk & Dennen, 2007). With tools such as TEC-VARIETY and R2D2 at the ready, normally hesitant or resistant instructors can, in a relatively brief amount of time, become models and advocates of online education in modest or more substantive ways.

There are many other possible forms of online instructor training and support. Popular extrinsic incentives include release time, royalties, extra pay, summer stipends, travel funds, and technology upgrades. In terms of training and technology support, there could be online training and community support groups, small-group workshops and discussions, help desks, corporate-university-school partnerships, needs analyses, interactive Web-based training, online tutorials, and online databases of exemplar projects. Services such as Lynda.com, for instance, offer online tutorials for many types of technologies.

Training from online video will increase rapidly in the coming decade. In 2010, Bonk created a series of 27 videos related to teaching online nicknamed the "Video Primers in an Online Repository for e-Teaching and Learning" or V-PORTAL. To foster their use, these videos were each limited to a maximum of 10 minutes in length. The video primer topics included reducing plagiarism, providing feedback, managing an online class, finding quality supplemental materials, and wiki uses and applications.

These 27 video primers are now free to the world to use, remix, download, and share (see http://www.youtube.com/TravelinEdMan). As a result, the V-PORTAL is finding use in K–12 schools, higher education, military training, and other places.

Anyone involved in organizational change will readily admit that change is typically systemic in nature. Consequently, we recommend that you consider how all ten categories of ideas listed in this chapter can support instructor training and development and perhaps even help in efforts to transform your entire organization or institution.

Given the masses of technologies and pedagogical possibilities associated with such technologies, there is a growing need for frameworks that help online educators begin to grasp new and emerging learning possibilities. Frameworks, models, advice, and other guidance can boost the confidence of novice users in online and blended environments. With such support, they can feel more secure in their understanding of how online learning can work and how they can make use of it to serve and extend their teaching goals and adventures.

We now move to the closing chapter of the TEC-VARIETY book. There you will discover a conceptual recap of our journey in this book as well as a summary table of 100+ activities for motivation and retention online described in the previous 10 chapters. This table is intended to help you rethink your online learning approaches and strategies. We hope that as you browse through it you will rediscover and rethink the pedagogical possibilities for your online learning courses and programs.

CHAPTER FIFTEEN

RECAPPING TEC-VARIETY

> Twenty years from now you will be more disappointed
> by the things you didn't do than by the ones you did.
> So throw off the bowlines. Sail away from the safe harbor.
> Catch the trade winds in your sails. Explore. Dream.
>
> —Mark Twain

This book has been a journey. This journey integrated psychological theory and research on motivation with educational practice. Linking theory to practice was intentional. After opening with a couple of chapters summarizing the theory and research related to online learning retention and motivation from different psychological perspectives, Chapters Four through Thirteen detailed more than 100 activities that you can use on their own or in combination to motivate your fully online and blended students.

Not enough? Keep in mind that each strategy has one or more variations. Of course, as mentioned in Chapter One, there are another 100+ ideas in the book *Empowering Online Learning* based on the R2D2 model (Bonk & Zhang, 2008). In addition to the hundreds of pedagogical ideas found in these two books, you now have access to two models or frameworks—R2D2 and TEC-VARIETY—to guide your use of these activities. Not all of these will work in every setting, but of course you only need a few powerful ideas to get started. As you experiment with some of these activities, you will find that many will work just as effectively in F2F settings as they do in online ones.

All 100 activities described in this book can be found in Table 15.1. As you scan this table, you will notice that it includes a quick overview of the degree of risk, time, cost, and learner-centeredness of each activity as well as our best estimates as to its duration. In effect, Table 15.1 and Table 1.1 are snapshots of the entire book. Also keep in mind that Table 3.1 details the particular learning theory or approach that coincides with different motivational principles as discussed in this book. It is conceivable that you will use the tables more than any other feature of this book.

TABLE 15.1: SUMMARY OF 100+ ACTIVITIES FOR TEC-VARIETY WITH KEY INSTRUCTIONAL CONSIDERATIONS.

Principle		Learning Activity	Risk	Time	Cost	Learner Centeredness	Duration of Activity
T ONE/CLIMATE	1.	Personal Introductions	Low	Medium	Low	High	1–2 weeks
	2.	Video Introductions	Medium	Medium to High	Medium	Low to Medium	1–2 weeks
	3.	Goals and Expectations	Medium	Low	Low	High	1 week
	4.	Personal Commitments	Medium	Low	Low	High	1 week
	5.	Eight Nouns	Low	Medium	Low	High	1–2 weeks
	6.	Two Truths and One Lie	Low to medium	Low	Low	High	1 week
	7.	Accomplishment Hunts	Low	Medium	Low	High	1–2 weeks
	8.	Course Fan Pages	Medium	Medium	Low	High	1–2 weeks (or possibly ongoing)
	9.	Favorite Websites	Low	Medium	Low	High	1 to 2 weeks
	10.	Online Cafés	Low to medium	Medium	Low	High	Weekly or as needed
E NCOURAGEMENT	11.	Critical Friends	Low to Medium	Medium to High	Low	High	Throughout the course or as needed
	12.	Student Polling and Voting	Medium	Medium	Low to High	High	As needed
	13.	Online Suggestion Box	Medium	Low	Low	High	Throughout the course or as needed
	14.	Minute and Muddiest Point Papers	Medium	Medium to High	Low	High	As needed

Principle	Learning Activity		Risk	Time	Cost	Learner Centeredness	Duration of Activity
	15.	Comments and Annotations	Medium	Medium	Low	High	As needed, depending on assignment
	16.	Screencasted Supports and Directions	Low	Medium to High	Low to High	Medium	As needed
	17.	Embedded Reviews and System Scored Practice Tests	Low	Medium to High	Low	Medium	As needed
	18.	Asynchronous Expert Feedback and Mentoring	Medium	Medium	Low to Medium	High	Weekly or as needed
	19.	Synchronous and Mobile Mentoring	Medium to High	Medium	Low to High	High	Weekly or as needed
	20.	Learner-Self Interaction and Self Feedback Forms	Low	Medium	Low	High	As needed
CURIOSITY	21.	Online Events in the News	Medium	Medium	Low	High	Throughout the course or as needed
	22.	Live Science, Creative Expression, or Artistic Invention	Medium	Medium	Low	Medium	1–2 weeks
	23.	Live Scientific Discovery or Invention	Medium	Medium	Medium	Medium	1–2 weeks
	24.	Just-in-Time Syllabus	High	High	Low	High	Throughout the course or as needed

Principle		Learning Activity	Risk	Time	Cost	Learner Centeredness	Duration of Activity
	25.	Just-in-Time Teaching	High	High	Low	High	Throughout the course or as needed
	26.	What's My Line Guest Games	Low to Medium	Low to Medium	Low	Medium	As needed
	27.	A Day in the Life of a Scientist, Scholar, or Celebrity	Medium	Medium	Low	High	1–3 weeks
	28.	Cultural or Contextual Blogs and Resources	Medium	Medium to High	Low to High	Medium	As needed
	29.	Extreme Learning	High	Medium to High	Low to Medium	Medium	1–4 weeks
	30.	Quests and Probes on the Web	Medium	Medium	Low	High	As needed
VARIETY	31.	Online Séance or Roundtable	High	Medium	Low	High	1–2 weeks
	32.	Virtual World Role Plays	High	Medium to High	Low	High	2–4 weeks
	33.	Mobile and Social Networking Content Games and Apps	Medium to High	Medium to High	Low	High	2–4 weeks or as needed
	34.	Educational Music Videos	High	High	Low to High	Medium	As needed

Principle	Learning Activity	Risk	Time	Cost	Learner Centeredness	Duration of Activity
	35. Database Problems and Search Competitions	Low to Medium	Low	Low	Medium	As needed
	36. Task and Activity Randomizer	Medium	Low to Medium	Low	Medium	As needed
	37. Time-Constrained Presentations	Medium	Medium	Low	High	As needed
	38. Virtual Community Brainstorming	Medium	Low to Medium	Low	High	As needed
	39. Extreme Teaching and Online Mentoring	High	Medium to High	Low to Medium	High	As needed
	40. Exploring Dynamic Web Content	Medium	Medium	Low	High	1 week or as needed
AUTONOMY	41. Cool Resource Provider	Medium	Medium	Low	High	Throughout the course or as needed
	42. Technology Tool Demonstrator	Medium	Medium	Low	High	Throughout the course or as needed
	43. Starter-Wrapper Technique	Medium	High	Low	High	Throughout the course or as needed
	44. Shotgun Questioning	Medium	High	Low	High	Weekly or as needed
	45. Hot Seat Questioning	Medium	High	Low	High	Weekly or as needed
	46. Open Exploration Weeks	Medium	Medium	Low	High	1 or 2 weeks as needed

Principle		Learning Activity	Risk	Time	Cost	Learner Centeredness	Duration of Activity
	47.	Open Educational Resources Explorations	Medium	Medium	Low	High	1 to 2 weeks or as needed
	48.	Pick and Choose Options	Medium	High	Low	High	As needed
	49.	Open Syllabus Course Portal with Options	High	High	Low	High	Every week
	50.	Open Teaching and MOOCs	High	High	Low to High	High	Every week
R<small>ELEVANCE</small>	51.	Multimedia Case Vignettes and Decision Making	Medium	Medium to High	Medium to High	Medium	1–4 weeks or throughout the course as needed
	52.	Job Connection and Strategic Planning Papers	Low	Medium to High	Low	High	1–2 or 4–5 weeks
	53.	Wiki Editing Projects (including Wikipedia)	Medium	High	Low	High	Throughout the course or as needed
	54.	Language Learning Conversations and Mentoring	Medium	High	Low	High	Weekly or as needed
	55.	Online Current News Feeds and Streaming Data	Medium	Medium	Low	High	Throughout the course or as needed

Principle		Learning Activity	Risk	Time	Cost	Learner Centeredness	Duration of Activity
	56.	Cross-Cultural Web Conferencing and Interactions	Medium to High	Medium	Low to High	High	1 week or session as needed
	57.	Instructor Online Video Demonstrations	Medium	Low to Medium	Low	Medium	Anytime as needed
	58.	Video Study Guides, Tutorials, and Microlectures	Low	Medium	Low	Medium	Anytime as needed
	59.	Pubcasts and Researcher Interviews	Medium	Medium to High	Low to High	Medium to High	1–2 weeks
	60.	Oral History or Situational Research	High	High	Low to High	High	3–5 weeks at the end of the term
INTERACTIVITY	61.	Scholar, Scientist, or Innovator Role Play	High	Medium	Low	High	1–2 weeks
	62.	Interactive Learner Questioning and Discussion	Medium	High	Low	High	Every week
	63.	Jigsaw the Online Content	Medium	High	Low	High	2–4 weeks or as needed
	64.	Flipping the Class	High	High	Medium	High	Every week or as needed
	65.	Product Brainstorming and Co-Creation	High	High	Low to High	High	2–5 weeks at/near the end of the course

Principle	Learning Activity	Risk	Time	Cost	Learner Centeredness	Duration of Activity
	66. Collaborative Mind Mapping and Idea Visualization	Medium	High	Low	High	2–4 weeks
	67. Collaborative Video Annotations	High	Medium	Low	High	Anytime as needed
	68. Video Discussion and Questioning	Medium	Medium	Low	Medium	Anytime as needed
	69. Word Cloud Interactions	Low	Low	Low	Medium	1–2 weeks
	70. Backchannel Conference and Course Participation	High	High	Low	High	3–5 weeks at the end of the semester
ENGAGEMENT	71. Interactive Maps and Databases	Low	Medium	Low	Medium	1–2 weeks
	72. Interactive Multimedia Glossaries	Medium	Medium	Low to High	High	As needed
	73. Talking Dictionaries and Language Translation	Medium	Medium	Low	High	Every week or as needed
	74. Interactive Timelines	Medium	Medium	Low	High	Every week or as needed
	75. Exploring Animations, Simulations, and Pop-Up Media	Medium	Medium	Low to high	High	1–2 weeks or as needed

Principle		Learning Activity	Risk	Time	Cost	Learner Centeredness	Duration of Activity
	76.	Virtual Tools and Scientific Instruments	Low	Medium	Medium	High	1–2 weeks or as needed
	77.	Microblogging Course Discussions	Medium	Medium	Low	High	All semester or as needed
	78.	Online Subject-Specific Picture Galleries	Low	Medium	Low	Medium	Anytime as needed
	79.	Interactive Online Exhibits (e.g., Art and Bones)	Medium	Medium	Low	Medium	Anytime as needed
	80.	Three Level Questioning	Low	Medium	Low	Medium	1–2 weeks or as needed
	81.	Debating Controversial Online News, Blogs, and Other Media	Medium	Medium	Low	High	1–2 weeks or as needed
Tension	82.	Structured Controversy	Medium	Medium	Low	High	1–2 weeks or as needed
	83.	Structured Role Debates (e.g., Court Forums)	High	Medium	Low to High	High	1–2 weeks or as needed
	84.	Online Study Group Challenges	Medium	Medium	Low	High	Every week or as needed
	85.	Timed Disclosures and Issue Voting	Medium	Medium	Low	High	1 week or as needed

Principle		Learning Activity	Risk	Time	Cost	Learner Centeredness	Duration of Activity
	86.	Argument and Debate Mapping	High	Medium	Low to High	High	2–3 weeks
	87.	Challenge-Based Videoconferencing (e.g., World Affairs Challenges)	High	High	Low	High	All semester or as needed
	88.	Digital Media Competitions	High	High	Low to High	High	3–4 weeks or during entire course
	89.	"Best of" Nominations (e.g., Quotes)	Medium	Medium	Low	High	Anytime as needed
	90.	Online Games, Puzzles, and Quizzes	High	Medium	Low to High	Medium	1–2 weeks or as needed
Y IELDING PRODUCTS	91.	Cartoon and Animated Movie Productions	Medium	High	Low	High	1–3 weeks or as needed
	92.	Student Documentaries	High	High	Low to High	High	2–4 weeks
	93.	Course Video Summaries and Movie Festivals	High	High	Low to High	High	2–4 weeks
	94.	Book Trailers	High	High	Low to High	High	2–4 weeks
	95.	Online Book Reviews	Medium	Medium	Low	High	1–2 weeks

Principle	Learning Activity	Risk	Time	Cost	Learner Centeredness	Duration of Activity
96.	Content Databases and Learning Portals	Medium	Medium	Low to Medium	High	2–4 weeks or as needed
97.	Oral History Interviews	High	High	Low to High	High	2–5 weeks at the end of the term
98.	Grammar Check, Peer Check	Medium	Medium	Low to high	High	2–4 weeks or as needed
99.	Recording Accomplishments (e.g., I Done It)	Medium	Medium	Low to Medium	High	Semester long
100.	Poster Sessions and Gallery Tours	Medium	High	Low to Medium	High	1–2 weeks

In addition to the 100+ activities and the two key summary tables in this book, you can use the handy acronym—TEC-VARIETY—to reflect on the motivational elements of your online classes (see the following reminder list of motivational principles). You can now build on this structure as well as many of the ideas we describe in this book and modify them as needed. We fully expect that you will generate a few interesting ones of your own. As you do, please share your respective inventions with others and with us. You should also reflect on how you are using the principles embedded in the TEC-VARIETY framework in all your instructional situations, whether you are in a F2F classroom setting, videoconference, fully online class, or some blended learning combination of these. TEC-VARIETY should work, albeit in different ways, in any instructional environment or learning situation.

1. Tone/Climate: Psychological Safety, Comfort, Sense of Belonging

2. Encouragement: Feedback, Responsiveness, Praise, Supports

3. Curiosity: Surprise, Intrigue, Unknowns

4. Variety: Novelty, Fun, Fantasy

5. Autonomy: Choice, Control, Flexibility, Opportunities

6. Relevance: Meaningful, Authentic, Interesting

7. Interactivity: Collaborative, Team-Based, Community

8. Engagement: Effort, Involvement, Investment

9. Tension: Challenge, Dissonance, Controversy

10. Yielding Products: Goal Driven, Purposeful Vision, Ownership

We hope that by now you realize that there are many benefits of TEC-VARIETY. First, it will prompt you to reflect on your instructional practices. It is a lens through which to contemplate what is and is not working. The framework is a simple yet powerful tool to guide you when designing and delivering online activities, courses, or programs. It can also play a role in the evaluation of an online course or set of course contents within an entire program. For example, do you extensively embed tone and feedback activities while too often ignoring or failing to think about issues of curiosity, autonomy, and relevance? TEC-VARIETY can serve as a means to address such matters. It can also help instructors integrate several types of motivational principles into one decidedly powerful and engaging activity.

TEC-VARIETY does not just provide a means to reflect on your teaching approaches; it can also help initiate discussions and debates about effective instruction. Such discussions can take place within and between departments as well as at online learning workshops, conferences, summits, and institutes. Whether the key ideas within it are universal in nature is still to be determined. We do know that all of us want pedagogical ideas that work. What teacher or trainer does not want to be known as effective?

The TEC-VARIETY framework can also help educators and managers consider what role some particularly lauded new technology tool or resource could play in online teaching and learning. Decision makers can more thoughtfully evaluate how a particular technology may address areas of motivational deficiency in an online course or program. Best practice ideas and activities could be posted for each of the 10 key principles of the framework.

Those are but a few areas where the TEC-VARIETY framework can empower the online instructor and hopefully elevate the entire learning environment. Keep in mind, however, that there are many things that TEC-VARIETY is not. First of all, it is not a psychological or educational theory. Instead, it is a somewhat eclectic way to view online instruction, though with a bias toward learner-centered practices. When you combine and implement various principles of the framework, your efforts should foster a noticeable positive impact on learner motivation and retention. TEC-VARIETY is a compilation of some of the most well-researched and instructionally effective motivational principles. And the examples in this book are among the best instructional ideas and practices we could find. Of course, the related pedagogical ideas and activities continue to evolve with the available learning technologies and distance learning delivery methods.

Second, as noted in Chapter One, TEC-VARIETY is not an instructional design model. Despite this caveat, there may be ways in which to utilize our framework in your practice as an instructional designer or teacher deep in the trenches of online teaching and learning. Most instructional design models are prescriptive and were designed for twentieth-century classrooms. Such models assume that teachers do something to learners. They typically help in the transportation of students from Point A to Point B. Unfortunately, in the age of the participatory Web or Web 2.0, there actually are few, if any, instructional design models that continue to work as well as they did just a couple of decades ago. Learners today need to engage in content that is dynamic and ever-evolving. Any Point B that can be targeted is soon outdated before the learner has a chance to apply it. Prescriptive models rarely work anymore. As a result, we do not offer any prescriptions about how you should apply or think about the TEC-VARIETY framework; rather, we offer only examples of activities and a few associated caveats and guidelines.

Third, TEC-VARIETY is not THE method. It is definitely not the only game in town. It addresses learner motivation. There are additional approaches and perspectives for online teaching and learning that address assessment, quality, copyright, plagiarism, and so on. With a focused search or two, you will find numerous models, frameworks, and methods that should be considered when designing fully online and blended learning. TEC-VARIETY is just one. It can help in strategic visioning for a new online initiative, program, or course, but it should not be the vision. Stated another way, TEC-VARIETY can inform and guide your planning as well as your resulting practices but it should not be the only tool or framework on which you rely.

Fourth, we realize that our 10-part framework does not address every aspect of motivation. What is missing may vary according to the course, grade level, and degree of familiarity with fully online and blended learning. With adult learners, there could be more emphasis on establishing an overall sense of purpose or mission for an activity or an entire class. In a way, issues of purpose and mission are embedded in all 10 principles, but you will find these especially in the final principle of TEC-VARIETY related to yielding products, goal setting, and having a purposeful vision. Be sure to establish your learning purpose and mission at the start of each fully online or blended course experience.

Those are some of the benefits and limitations of the framework as we see them at the present time. We also recommend that you be cognizant of the fact that any activity or approach you select for teaching online will undoubtedly address more than one aspect of TEC-VARIETY. In general, the first two components of the framework, tone or climate and feedback are required in most every properly designed online task and activity.

If we look at a course project activity like an animated movie or a shared online video production demonstrating a student's learning in a class (see Activities #91 and #93), many aspects of TEC-VARIETY will be on display. The most obvious is goal setting or yielding projects. Moreover, instructors must create a proper tone or climate, provide ample feedback, establish episodes of learner interaction and engagement and, perhaps, some degree of competition or challenge between individuals or groups. Suffice it to say, this one activity directly connects with many of the motivational principles discussed in this book.

Now assume the instructor has asked that these tasks be produced in pairs or teams. Reflect on the components of the TEC-VARIETY framework that might be employed. As indicated, such activities would contain a learner-centered tone or climate, instead of some type of teacher-made quiz or examination (i.e., Principle #1). They would also embed learner encouragement and feedback on the final product as well as drafts along the way (Principle #2). And there would be ample learner exploration and curiosity about the possible ingredients and components of the project (Principle #3), a potentially quite novel and fun task (Principle #4), learner autonomy and choice in what to produce (Principle #5), a product that one finds interesting and valuable (Principle #6), team member negotiations and contributions (Principle #7), seemingly endless hours of time and effort filled with many moments of learner engagement and involvement in the learning process (Principle #8), some debate about what ultimately to include and exclude (Principle #9), and the final video or animation presentation itself (Principle #10). There is no one motivational principle that is central to the success of such projects; each component plays a role.

Perhaps the best strategies or activities are those that touch upon the majority of principles found in the TEC-VARIETY framework. Look at the list of 100. See which ones offer motivationally powerful possibilities for your courses, audiences, and contexts.

If we were to create a chapter or two filled with comprehensive examples like the one preceding, it would seem silly to segment motivation into 10 separate principles or components. Still, the 10 chief components of TEC-VARIETY serve as a viable instructional template for building, enhancing, and sharing online and blended activities, courses, and programs. If you agree with that basic premise, our framework can be quite useful.

Considerations

Despite the wide range of applicability, you must proceed with a simultaneous sense of optimism and caution each time attempting something new in the online or blended classroom. There are issues of technology familiarity, timeliness, cognitive complexity, content adaptability, quality, assessment, and plagiarism to deal with. In addition, each task you select must be appropriate for your learners and content area. Do not just choose something that we have described simply because it sounds cool. Granted, we do encourage risk taking and experimentation with new technologies and instructional approaches, but be careful not to go overboard. Thoughtful integration of one or two ideas based on TEC-VARIETY will serve you better than randomly selecting 10 ideas meant to target each of the principles of the framework.

You should also keep in mind that no single online class is the same. An activity that was the defining moment of your teaching career in the previous semester may meet with heavy doses of resistance or even drastically flounder the next time you offer it. Every teaching or training event is different on some level. Each cohort of learners arrives with varied online learning experiences and expectations. Consequently, you will need to continue reflecting on your methods and discussing them with your colleagues and your students.

You know your instructional context best. Select tasks that are the most appropriate for your learners and particular subject matter area. As instructors, we can only nurture the conditions that give rise to successful online learning by making the best pedagogical decisions possible. The activities suggested in the preceding chapters are intended to support these efforts. Undoubtedly, many readers of this book will craft much more sophisticated and novel activities and then mesh several of these together in ways we never contemplated.

There are also issues of professional courtesy and copyright related to each activity detailed in this book. If you are relying on materials discovered online based on links provided in this book or listed elsewhere, many would consider it common courtesy to let the author(s) of that content or Web resource know of your intentions to use it in your online classes. Many organizations and institutions actually require you to ask for permission to use anything you find online—especially corporations, governmental agencies, military organizations, and nonprofit foundations. Such informal contacting of the content designer or owner might result in new partnerships, colleagues, and perhaps even updated or expanded materials. Contacting the original designers of the online resources or materials may result in useful insights into how to use them most effectively. Most people are thrilled to hear that someone is pondering using their resources. Your request might fuel their passions to create and share more such content.

Using TEC-VARIETY in the Web of Learning

In the coming decades, educators will continue to witness the rapid expansion of online and blended learning. This monumental rise will take place across all educational sectors, though it might be most pronounced at the ends of the educational spectrum with teenagers and even younger children as well as much older learners including centenarians. In terms of younger populations, as noted in the first two chapters, online learning is exploding at the K–12 level (Project Tomorrow and Blackboard, 2009, 2011; Watson et al., 2010). It is also well established in community colleges and universities (Allen & Seaman, 2010a, 2014; Carter, 2011). For adults in the workplace, online learning offers an exhilarating sense of hope to complete college degrees as well as obtain timely professional development needed to maintain a job. At the same time, it also allows those in retirement communities to find new hobbies as well as give back to society in the form of online mentoring and tutoring.

The Web of Learning will invite all such online learning participants and players. There will be endless learning paths, educational resources, and technology choices. As this occurs, educational opportunities will be increasingly ubiquitous and wrapped around your every move. Education will simply be part of what it means to be human. It may be decades in the making, but at some point, educational historians will look back as well as ahead and accurately point out that we are card-carrying members of the "Learning Century."

Renew your passport. Each new day, the Web will offer enticing invitations to learning resources that you might want to visit. There will be interactive time lines to meander around, engrossing digital books to read and share, massively open online classes to sign up for, collaborative spaces in which to meet others and share insights about what you are learning, and open educational resources to browse through and put to use. Much is possible, especially with frameworks such as TEC-VARIETY to guide the way. As with R2D2, TEC-VARIETY can benefit teachers, trainers, instructional designers, and learning managers as they navigate within this ever-expanding Web of Learning. As they come to grasp the power of TEC-VARIETY, they can perhaps design higher-quality and more motivating online learning experiences.

We hope that TEC-VARIETY and any spin-off perspectives and models can make a difference in the world of education and training. We believe that when used thoughtfully and strategically, our framework can enhance student motivation thereby resulting in greater levels of performance, satisfaction, retention, and an overall zest for learning. As indicated early on in this book, the people to whom we have presented this framework have welcomed it as practical and easy to understand. We sincerely hope you will too. Perhaps you will be adding some TEC-VARIETY to your online and blended courses. And maybe a few of you will even internalize TEC-VARIETY as a personal mantra for your own life. Whatever happens, we certainly look forward to hearing from you. Please share your applications, modifications, and extensions of the framework and activities. Thank you.

WEB LINKS, EXAMPLES, AND RESOURCES

Chapter Three: Online Motivation from Four Perspectives

Adaptive Learning Systems:

>*Knewton: http://www.knewton.com*

Chapter Four: Principle #1 Tone/Climate

Course Management Systems

>*Blackboard: http://www.blackboard.com*
>*Desire2Learn: http://www.desire2learn.com*
>*Moodle: http://moodle.org*
>*Sakai: http://sakaiproject.org*

Online Collaboration and Webconferencing Tools

>*Google Docs: https://docs.google.com*
>*Ning: http://www.ning.com*

Referenceware and Word Portals

>*Moms Who Think: http://www.momswhothink.com*
>*List of adjectives: http://www.momswhothink.com/reading/list-of-adjectives.html*

List of nouns: http://www.momswhothink.com/reading/list-of-nouns.html
List of verbs: http://www.momswhothink.com/reading/list-of-verbs.html

Shared Online Video Resources

Shared Online Video Resources, Portals, and Pedagogical Activities: http://www.trainingshare. com/resources/Summary_of_Ways_to_Use_Shared_Online_Video.php
YouTube: http://www.youtube.com
YouTube EDU: http://www.youtube.com/education?b=400

Social Networking and Web 2.0 Tools

Facebook: http://www.facebook.com/login/setashome.php?ref=home
Google+: https://plus.google.com/up/start/?sw=1&type=st
LinkedIn: http://www.linkedin.com
Twitter: http://twitter.com

Wiki Tools

PBworks: http://pbworks.com
PBworks in Education: http://pbworks.com/content/edu+overview
Wikis in Education (from WikiFoundry): http://wikisineducation.wikifoundry.com/
Wikispaces: http://www.wikispaces.com

Chapter Five: Principle #2 Encouragement/Feedback

Interactive Whiteboards

Promethean: http://www.prometheanworld.com/server.php?show=nav.15
Smart: http://smarttech.com

Lecture Capture Systems

Echo360: http://echo360.com
Mediasite: http://www.sonicfoundry.com/mediasite
Tegrity: http://www.tegrity.com

Multimedia Development Tools

Adobe Captivate: http://www.adobe.com/products/captivate.html
Adobe Dreamweaver: http://www.adobe.com/products/dreamweaver.html
Adobe Flash Professional: http://www.adobe.com/products/flash.html
Adobe Photoshop: http://www.adobe.com/products/photoshop.html
Articulate Storyline: http://www.articulate.com/products/storyline-overview.php
CamStudio: http://camstudio.org
Camtasia: http://www.techsmith.com/camtasia

Open Educational Resources and OpenCourseWare

Connexions: http://cnx.org
Curriki: http://www.curriki.org
HippoCampus: http://www.hippocampus.org
Jorum: http://www.jorum.ac.uk
MERLOT: http://www.merlot.org/merlot/index.htm
National Repository of Online Courses: http://www.montereyinstitute.org/nroc/
OpenCourseWare (MIT): http://ocw.mit.edu/index.htm
Open Educational Resources Commons: http://www.oercommons.org/
World Lecture Hall: http://wlh.webhost.utexas.edu

Online Collaboration and Videoconferencing Tools

Google Docs: https://docs.google.com
Google Hangouts: http://www.google.com
Skype (now Microsoft): http://www.skype.com/intl/en-us/welcomeback

Online Tutoring and Mentoring

Tutor.com: http://www.tutor.com

Screencasting Tools

GoView: http://goview.com
Jing: http://www.techsmith.com/jing/free
Overstream: http://www.overstream.net
Screencast-o-Matic: http://www.screencast-o-matic.com
Screenr: http://www.screenr.com

Self-Testing Systems

Assessing Blood Pressure: http://www.csuchico.edu/atep/bp/bp.html
ePrep: http://www.eprep.com
Free Rice: http://freerice.com
Khan Academy: http://www.khanacademy.org
Khan Academy (Overview) (December 14, 2009):
    http://www.youtube.com/watch?v=p6l8-1kHUsA&feature=related
Khan Academy: About: http://www.khanacademy.org/about
CNN: Google Award to the Khan Academy (September 24, 2010):
    http://www.youtube.com/watch?v=QGxgAHer3Ow&feature=channel
Khan Academy on the Gates Notes (October 21, 2010):
    http://www.youtube.com/watch?v=UuMTSU9DcqQ&feature=relmfu
Livemocha: http://www.livemocha.com
Mixxer: http://www.language-exchanges.org
Virtual Nerd: http://www.virtualnerd.com
Vocab Sushi: http://www.vocabsushi.com

Social Networking Tools and Systems

Facebook: http://www.facebook.com
Flickr: http://www.flickr.com
Twitter: http://twitter.com

Survey and Polling Tools and Systems

BlogPoll: http://www.blogpoll.com
Micropoll: http://www.micropoll.com
Mister Poll: http://www.misterpoll.com
Pollcode: http://pollcode.com
Polldaddy: http://polldaddy.com
Poll Everywhere: http://www.polleverywhere.com
Poll Host: http://www.pollhost.com
SurveyMonkey: http://www.surveymonkey.com
SurveyShare: http://www.surveyshare.com
Zoomerang: http://www.zoomerang.com

Synchronous Conferencing Systems

Adobe Connect: http://www.adobe.com/products/adobeconnect.html
Elluminate (now part of Blackboard): http://www.elluminate.com
Go2Meeting: http://www.gotomeeting.com/fec
Skype (now Microsoft): http://www.skype.com/intl/en-us/welcomeback
WebEx (from Cisco): http://www.webex.com

Training Programs and Systems

Cisco Networking Academy: http://www.cisco.com/web/learning/netacad/index.html
Java Developer Tutorials and Online Training (Oracle):
http://www.oracle.com/technetwork/java/index-jsp-135888.html

Wearable Computing

Google Glass: http://www.google.com/glass/start

Chapter Six: Principle #3
Curiosity

Adventure Learning Resources

Chasing Seals: http://chasingseals.com
Earthducation: http://lt.umn.edu/earthducation
Geothentic: http://lt.umn.edu/geothentic
GoNorth!: http://www.polarhusky.com
Ice Stories: http://icestories.exploratorium.edu/dispatches
Jason Project: http://www.jason.org/public/whatis/start.aspx
Journey North: http://www.learner.org/jnorth
Last Ocean Project: http://lastocean-project.org
North of 60: http://n60.co/about.html
Polar Husky: http://www.polarhusky.com

Biography and Other Resource Portals

Amazon: http://www.amazon.com
Biography.com: http://www.biography.com
Biography.com Search: http://www.biography.com/search
Biography Online: http://www.biographyonline.net
Encyclopedia of World Biography: http://biography.yourdictionary.com
FamousPeople.co.uk: http://famouspeople.co.uk
FamousPeople.com: http://famouspeople.com
Google Books: http://books.google.com
Google Images: http://images.google.com
Google Scholar: http://scholar.google.com
Flickr: http://www.flickr.com
Picasa: http://picasa.google.com/intl/en
Turning the Pages from the British Library: http://www.bl.uk/onlinegallery/ttp/ttpbooks.html
Wikisource: http://wikisource.org/wiki/Main_Page
Wikipedia: http://www.wikipedia.org
Wikiquote: http://www.wikiquote.org

Cultural Resources

Come and See Africa blog: http://comeandseeafrica.blogspot.com
Come and See Africa International: http://comeandseeafrica.org

Famous Scientists, Celebrities, and Inventors

Brian J. Ford on "Plagiarism at Cambridge University, February 12, 2011:
http://www.youtube.com/user/tellymonitor?blend=21&ob=5#p/u/0/1IIRk8yHHhc
Brian J. Ford Homepage: http://www.brianjford.com
Lemelson—MIT Inventor of the Week: http://web.mit.edu/invent/iow/bushnell.html

The Nolan Bushnell Atari Interview (9 of 9) (March 14, 2007):
> http://www.youtube.com/watch?v=vOAeIPA_OTE&feature=related

Nolan Bushnell—Interview Part 1 (from 1982):
> http://www.youtube.com/watch?v=h93eLDhHqY8

Twitter (Brian J. Ford): http://twitter.com/#!/brianjford
Twitter (Nolan Bushnell): http://twitter.com/#!/nolanbushnell
Tellymonitor (Brian J. Ford videos): http://www.youtube.com/user/tellymonitor?feature=watch
Wikipedia (Brian J. Ford): http://en.wikipedia.org/wiki/index.html?curid=7003520
Wikipedia (Nolan Bushnell): http://en.wikipedia.org/wiki/Nolan_Bushnell
Wikipedia (Robert Ballard): http://en.wikipedia.org/wiki/Robert_Ballard

Interactive Timelines

Archaeology's Interactive Dig: http://www.archaeology.org/interactive
Historic Jamestown: http://historicjamestowne.org/learn/interactive_exercises.php
Path to Protest: http://www.guardian.co.uk/world/interactive/2011/mar/22/middle-east-protest-interactive-timeline
Prehistoric Timeline (National Geographic):
> http://science.nationalgeographic.com/science/prehistoric-world/prehistoric-time-line.html

Language Learning Resources

BBC Learning English: http://www.bbc.co.uk/worldservice/learningenglish
Babbel: http://www.babbel.com
English Central: http://www.englishcentral.com
Infinite Family: http://www.infinitefamily.org
LiveMocha: http://www.livemocha.com

Lesson Examples

Just-in-Time Syllabus: http://ecedweb.unomaha.edu/jits.htm
Just-in-Time Teaching: http://jittdl.physics.iupui.edu/jitt
Just-in-Time Teaching (Carleton College): http://serc.carleton.edu/introgeo/justintime
Just-in-Time Teaching Digital Library: http://jittdl.physics.iupui.edu/sign_on

Live and Immediate Science

The Brain Observatory: http://thebrainobservatory.ucsd.edu/hm_live.php
The Link: http://www.revealingthelink.com
Nautilus Live: http://www.nautiluslive.com
Ocean Explorer: http://oceanexplorer.noaa.gov/welcome.html
Ocean Explorer Media:
> http://oceanexplorer.noaa.gov/okeanos/explorations/10index/background/info/info.html

Online News

BBC News: http://www.bbc.co.uk/news
CNN News International: http://edition.cnn.com
Google News: http://news.google.com
MSNBC Headline News: http://www.msnbc.msn.com
Yahoo! News: http://news.yahoo.com

Online Referenceware

Dictionary.com: http://dictionary.com
Encyclopedia Britannica: http://www.britannica.com
Gale Encyclopedia of Children's Health: Infancy Through Adolescence:
> http://childrenshealth.yourdictionary.com
Merriam Webster's: http://www.merriam-webster.com
Roget's Thesaurus: http://thesaurus.com/Roget-Alpha-Index.html
Thesaurus.com: http://thesaurus.com
YourDictionary.com: http://www.yourdictionary.com

Visual Thesaurus: http://www.visualthesaurus.com
Webster's New World Dictionary: http://www.yourdictionary.com/dictionary-definitions
Wikipedia: http://www.wikipedia.org

Podcast and Webcast Shows

Insights in Nursing: Interviews on Careers and Trends in Nursing:
    http://insightsinnursing.com/category/insights-podcast
The Nursing Show: For nurses, by nurses: http://www.nursingshow.com
The Street: Wall Street Confidential:
    http://www.thestreet.com/podcasts/wall-street-confidential.html
Wall Street Journal Podcasts: http://online.wsj.com/public/page/audio.html

Shared Online Video

Academic Earth: http://academicearth.org
BBC News Video: http://www.bbc.co.uk/news/video_and_audio
CNN Video: http://www.cnn.com/video
CurrentTV: http://current.com
Discovery News Video: http://news.discovery.com/videos
Earthwatch on YouTube:
    http://www.earthwatch.org/newsandevents/documentaries/volunteer_videos
Google Videos: http://video.google.com
National Geographic Videos: http://video.nationalgeographic.com/video
The Royal Channel: http://www.youtube.com/user/TheRoyalChannel
Take Two: The Student's Point of View: http://www.take2videos.org
TED: http://www.ted.com
YouTube: http://www.youtube.com

Chapter Seven: Principle #4 Variety

Collaboration Tools

Flipgrid: http://flipgrid.com/info
PiratePad: http://piratepad.net
MeetingWords: http://meetingwords.com

Educational Music Videos

History for Music Lovers Channel (History Teachers Channel):
    http://www.youtube.com/user/historyteachers
The Trojan War ("Tainted Love" by Soft Cell):
    http://www.youtube.com/user/historyteachers?blend=6&ob=5#p/a/u/1/CiQ4j-D5o4o
Zheng Lab—Bad Project (Lady Gaga parody):
    http://www.youtube.com/watch?v=Fl4L4M8m4d0&feature=related

Information Databases

Kentuckiana Digital Library: Oral History Collection:
    http://kdl.kyvl.org/cgi/b/bib/bib-idx?c=oralhistbib;cc=oralhistbib;page=simple
WikiQuote: http://www.wikiquote.org
Worldmapper: http://www.worldmapper.org
Wolfram Alpha: http://www.wolframalpha.com

Language Learning Resources

LiveMocha: http://www.livemocha.com
The Mixxer: http://www.language-exchanges.org
Voxopop: http://www.voxopop.com

Microblogging

Edmodo: http://www.edmodo.com
GroupTweet: http://www.grouptweet.com
identi.ca: http://identi.ca
Plurk: http://www.plurk.com/t/English
Twitter: http://twitter.com

Massive Multiplayer Online Games

Grand Theft Auto: http://www.rockstargames.com/gta
Halo: http://halo.xbox.com/en-us
World of Warcraft: http://us.battle.net/wow/en

Mobile and Social Networking Games

CityVille (in Facebook, from Zynga):
    http://www.facebook.com/apps/application.php?id=291549705119
FarmVille (Zynga): http://www.farmville.com
FarmVille (in Facebook, from Zynga): http://www.facebook.com/FarmVille
FrontierVille (in Facebook, from Zynga): http://www.facebook.com/frontierville
Mafia Wars (from Zynga): http://mafiawars.zynga.com/fbconnect
Math Drill (Instant Interactive): http://www.instantinteractive.com
Miss Spell's Class (Dictionary.com): http://dictionary.reference.com/fun/missspell
Zynga: http://www.zynga.com and http://www.zynga.com/games

Online News Aggregators

Digg: http://digg.com
Drudge Report: http://drudgereport.com
Fark: http://www.fark.com
Reddit: http://www.reddit.com
Slashdot: http://slashdot.org

Online Timers

Cash Clock: http://www.online-stopwatch.com/full-screen-cash-clock
Countdown Timer: http://www.online-stopwatch.com/countdown-timer
Custom Counter: http://www.online-stopwatch.com/custom-stopwatch
Sivasailam "Thiagi" Thiagarajan (Workshops by Thiagi): http://www.thiagi.com/about-thiagi.html
Stopwatch Bomb: http://www.online-stopwatch.com/bomb-countdown
Stopwatch Counter: http://www.online-stopwatch.com/bomb-countdown/full-screen

Open Educational Resources

Creative Commons: http://creativecommons.org
Curriki: http://www.curriki.org
MERLOT: http://www.merlot.org/merlot/index.htm

Podcast and Webcast Shows

EdTech Talk: http://edtechtalk.com

Random Number Generator

Custom Random Number Generator:
    http://www.mathgoodies.com/calculators/random_no_custom.html
GraphPad Software (Random Number Generator):
    http://www.graphpad.com/quickcalcs/randomn1.cfm

Random.org (Coin Flipper): http://www.random.org/coins
Random.org (Dice): http://www.random.org/dice
Random.org (List Randomizer): http://www.random.org/lists
Random.org (Playing Card Shuffler): http://www.random.org/playing-cards
Random.org (Random Clock Time Generator): http://www.random.org/clock-times/Random.org
(Random Sequence Generator): http://www.random.org/sequences
Random Integer Generator: http://www.random.org/integers
Research Randomizer: http://www.randomizer.org/form.htm
Stat Trek (Random Number Generator): http://stattrek.com/tables/random.aspx

Second Life Videos

Castro Salvado: http://www.youtube.com/watch?v=D4uBhZN9Oos
No Country for Old Castro: http://www.youtube.com/watch?v=ocQMf1kPo98&feature=related
The Role Play Experiment (UT Dallas):
http://www.youtube.com/watch?v=zy1sfO7nEOI&feature=related

Web-Based Content Games

Bean Counter Free Accounting and Bookkeeping Tutorials: http://www.dwmbeancounter.com
Biz/Ed Virtual Worlds: http://www.bized.co.uk/virtual/index.htm
iCivics: http://www.icivics.org
Point of Dispensing Game: http://thepodgame.com

Chapter Eight: Principle #5 Autonomy

Animation Movie Makers with 3D Characters

GoAnimate: http://goanimate.com
Xtranormal: http://www.xtranormal.com

Learning and Cognition Theory Videos

Albert Bandura: 2007 Everett Rogers Colloquium (YouTube, December 11, 2007, 1:33:07):
http://www.youtube.com/watch?v=xjIbKaSXM3A&feature=related
Bandura's Social Cognitive Theory: An Introduction from Davidson Films (YouTube, Filmed 2003, 2006, 3:56): http://www.youtube.com/watch?v=OMBIwjEoyj4
B. F. Skinner Modelagram (YouTube, September 22, 2006, 4:46):
http://www.youtube.com/watch?v=mm5FGrQEyBY&feature=related
Classical Conditioning—Ivan Pavlov (YouTube, June 22, 2007, 3:55):
http://www.youtube.com/watch?v=hhqumfpxuzI&feature=related
John Watson—Little Albert (YouTube, October 11, 2008, 2:36):
http://www.youtube.com/watch?v=Xt0ucxOrPQE&feature=related
Operant Conditioning (YouTube, March 20, 2007, 3:55):
http://www.youtube.com/watch?v=I_ctJqjlrHA&feature=related
P540 Learning and Cognition in Education (Curt Bonk):
http://www.trainingshare.com/resources/youtube_videos.php
Thorndike—Law of Effect (YouTube, October 11, 2008, 2:22):
http://www.youtube.com/watch?v=Vk6H7Ukp6To&feature=related

Montessori Schools

Google Founders Talk Montessori (Barbara Walters TV special):
http://www.youtube.com/watch?v=0C_DQxpX-Kw&feature=player_embedded#at=70

Sergey Brin and Larry Page on Google (TED talk, February 2004; posted May 2007):
    http://www.ted.com/talks/sergey_brin_and_larry_page_on_google.html

Open Educational Resources (sample Web exploration activity)

1. *C-Span: http://www.c-spanvideo.org/videoLibrary*
2. *Complete Works of Charles Darwin Online: http://darwin-online.org.uk*
3. *The Complete Works of William Shakespeare: http://shakespeare.mit.edu*
4. *Edgar Allan Poe Society of Baltimore: http://www.eapoe.org*
5. *Einstein Archives Online: http://www.alberteinstein.info*
6. *EveryStockPhoto.com: http://everystockphoto.com*
7. *Federal Resources for Educational Excellent project: http://free.ed.gov*
8. *Global Text Project: http://globaltext.org*
9. *Google Art Project: http://www.google.com/culturalinstitute/project/art-project*
10. *Jane Austen: http://www.janeausten.org*
11. *The Jane Goodall Institute: http://www.janegoodall.org*
12. *NASA Learning Technology site: http://learn.arc.nasa.gov*
13. *OER Commons: http://oercommons.org*
14. *OpenCourseWare Consortium: http://www.ocwconsortium.org*
15. *Public Library of Science (PLOS): http://www.plos.org*
16. *Scitable (from Nature): http://www.nature.com/scitable*
17. *Stanford Encyclopedia of Philosophy: http://plato.stanford.edu*
18. *Timeless Hemingway: http://www.timeleshemingway.com*
19. *Trailblazing (350 years of Royal Society Publishing): http://trailblazing.royalsociety.org*
20. *WikiEducator: http://www.wikieducator.org/Main_Page*

Open Syllabi, Open Teaching, and Massive Open Online Courses (MOOC)

Dave's Educational Blog (Dave Comier): http://davecormier.com/edblog
David Wiley: http://davidwiley.org
David Wiley (Open Content):
    http://opencontent.org/wiki/index.php?title=David_Wiley#Winter_2010
Instructional Ideas and Technology Tools for Online Success:
    http://events.blackboard.com/open
Online Learning Today...and Tomorrow (eduMOOC): http://sites.google.com/site/edumooc
Google Groups discussion for eduMOOC: http://groups.google.com/group/edumooc?hl=en
Wiki for eduMOOC: http://edumooc.wikispaces.com
Ray Schroeder: http://sites.google.com/site/rayschroeder
Stephen Downes: http://www.downes.ca
The World Is Open with Web Technology (Spring 2013, Instructor: Curt Bonk):
    http://php.indiana.edu/~cjbonk/Syllabus_R685_Spring_of_2013.htm
What is a MOOC? from David Cormier (YouTube):
    http://www.youtube.com/watch?v=eW3gMGqcZQc

Photomedia

Everystockphoto.com: http://www.everystockphoto.com
Panoramio: http://www.panoramio.com

Self-Determination Theory

Edward Deci: http://www.psych.rochester.edu/faculty/deci
Richard M. Ryan: http://www.psych.rochester.edu/faculty/ryan
Self-Determination Theory (SDT): http://www.psych.rochester.edu/SDT
Self-Determination Theory (SDT) Publications:
    http://www.psych.rochester.edu/SDT/publications_browse.php

Synchronous Conferencing Tools

AnyMeeting: http://www.anymeeting.com

Chapter Nine: Principle #6
Relevance

Open Educational Resources, Open Content, and OpenCourseWare

Biotechnology Learning Hub: http://www.biotechlearn.org.nz
BookRix: http://www.bookrix.com
CliffNotes: http://www.cliffsnotes.com
Connexions: http://cnx.org
Curriki: http://www.curriki.org
HippoCampus: http://www.hippocampus.org
The Journal of Visualized Experiments (JoVE): http://www.jove.com
Khan Academy: http://www.khanacademy.org
Mark Braun's Pathology Slides and Laboratory Units:
*   http://medsci.indiana.edu/c602web/602/c602web/toc.htm*
MERLOT: http://www.merlot.org/merlot/index.htm
Open CourseWare Consortium: http://www.ocwconsortium.org
Public Library of Science (PLoS): http://www.plos.org
Science Learning Hub: http://www.sciencelearn.org.nz

Global Education and Collaboration

ePals: http://www.epals.com
The Flat Classrooms Project: http://www.flatclassroomproject.org
iEARN: http://www.iearn.org
RoundSquare: http://www.roundsquare.org
Seeds of Empowerment: http://seedsofempowerment.org
Soliya: http://www.soliya.net
TakingITGlobal: http://www.tigweb.org/tiged/?npc
World Class—World Vision Canada: http://www.ourworldclass.ca

Live News Feeds and Streaming and Other Online News Sources

BBC News: http://www.bbc.co.uk/news
CNN Live: http://live.cnn.com
CNN News International: http://edition.cnn.com
Discovery News: http://news.discovery.com
Explo.TV: http://www.exploratorium.edu/tv/index.php
ESPN.com: http://espn.go.com
Fox News (Foxstream Live): http://www.foxnews.com/foxstream
Google News: http://news.google.com
Livestream: http://new.livestream.com
MSNBC Headline News: http://www.msnbc.msn.com
Ustream: http://www.ustream.tv
Yahoo! News: http://news.yahoo.com

Online Language Learning Resources and Systems

About.com (from the New York Times)
a. ESL: http://esl.about.com
b. French: http://french.about.com
c. German: http://german.about.com
d. Italian: http://italian.about.com
e. Japanese: http://japanese.about.com
f. Mandarin: http://mandarin.about.com
g. Spanish: http://spanish.about.com

BBC Languages: http://www.bbc.co.uk/languages
Babbel: http://www.babbel.com
ChinesePod: http://chinesepod.com
Coffee Break Spanish: http://radiolingua.com/shows/spanish/coffee-break-spanish
Duolingo: https://www.duolingo.com
English Central: http://www.englishcentral.com
iTalkie: http://www.italki.com
Japanese Online http://japanese-online.com
Korean Online http://learn-korean.net
Livemocha: http://www.livemocha.com
LoMasTV (online Spanish immersion TV): http://lomastv.com
Mango Languages: http://www.mangolanguages.com
The Mixxer (uses Skype): http://www.language-exchanges.org
Palabea: http://www.palabea.com
PalTalk: http://www.paltalk.com
Rosetta Stone: http://www.rosettastone.com
Voxopop: http://www.voxopop.com

Oral History Websites

Archives of American Art from the Smithsonian Institution: http://www.aaa.si.edu
Archives of American Art: Oral History Interviews (the Smithsonian):
http://www.aaa.si.edu/collections/interviews
Best of History Websites: Oral History (EdTech Teacher Resource):
http://www.besthistorysites.net/index.php/oral-history
Born in Slavery: Slave Narratives from the Federal Writer's Project, 1936–1938:
http://lcweb2.loc.gov/ammem/snhtml/snhome.html
Densho: The Japanese American Legacy Project: http://www.densho.org
The Gulf War: An Oral History (from PBS Frontline):
http://www.pbs.org/wgbh/pages/frontline/gulf/oral
History Matters: U.S. Survey Course on the Web (George Mason University):
http://historymatters.gmu.edu
Regional Oral History Office (ROHO) (UC Berkeley): http://bancroft.berkeley.edu/ROHO/
Oral History Association: http://www.oralhistory.org
Oral History Association Wiki: http://www.oralhistory.org/wiki/index.php/Main_Page
Oral History Online (GMU): http://historymatters.gmu.edu/mse/oral/online.html#exemp
Oral History Society: http://www.oralhistory.org.uk
Rutgers Oral Histories Online: http://oralhistory.rutgers.edu
Southern Oral History Program (University of North Carolina at Chapel Hill): http://sohp.org
United States Holocaust Memorial Museum: http://www.ushmm.org

Shared Online Video Websites

60 Second Recap: http://www.60secondrecap.com
Academic Earth: http://www.academicearth.org
BBC News: Video and Audio: http://www.bbc.co.uk/news/video_and_audio
Big Think: http://bigthink.com
ClubRecap at 60 Second Recap: http://www.60secondrecap.com/club-recap
CNN Video: http://www.cnn.com/video
Earthwatch: http://www.earthwatch.org/newsandevents/documentaries/volunteer_videos/
Grovo: http://www.grovo.com
Khan Academy: http://www.khanacademy.org
Learning Theory Videos: http://mypage.iu.edu/~cjbonk/youtube_videos.htm
LearnZillion: http://www.learnzillion.com
LinkTV: http://www.linktv.org
Lynda.com: http://www.lynda.com
MedTube: http://medtube.net

MIT World: http://video.mit.edu
SchoolTube: http://www.schooltube.com
SciVee: http://www.scivee.tv
SciVee: "Early participation in prenatal food supplementation program ameliorates the nega-
tive association of food insecurity with quality of maternal-infant interaction" from Amy Frith of
Ithaca College: http://www.scivee.tv/node/48125
Share My Lesson: http://www.sharemylesson.com
Sophia: http://www.sophia.org
TED: http://www.ted.com
TED Ed: http://education.ted.com and http://www.youtube.com/user/TEDEducation
TubeChop: http://www.tubechop.com
TVLesson: http://www.tvlesson.com
WatchKnowLearn: http://watchknowlearn.org
YouTube: http://www.youtube.com/index
YouTube EDU: http://www.youtube.com/education?b=400

Wiki Tools and Resources

PBworks: http://pbworks.com
Wikispaces: http://www.wikispaces.com
Wikibooks (from the Wikimedia Foundation): http://www.wikibooks.org
Wikipedia Education Program:
    http://outreach.wikimedia.org/wiki/Wikipedia_Education_Program

Chapter Ten: Principle #7 Interactivity

Cooperative Learning Resources

Cooperative Learning Institute: http://www.co-operation.org
Jigsaw: http://www.jigsaw.org

Document Collaboration and Co-Creation Tools

Google Documents: http://docs.google.com
Hotseat: https://www.purdue.edu/hotseat
MeetingWords: http://meetingwords.com
PBworks: http://pbworks.com
PiratePad: http://piratepad.net
Wikis in Education (from WikiFoundry): http://wikisineducation.wikifoundry.com
Wikispaces: http://www.wikispaces.com

Female Entrepreneurs Web Sites

ForbesWoman: http://www.forbes.com/forbeswoman
Women 2.0: http://women2.com

Interactive Questioning Tools

Canvas (from Instructure): http://www.instructure.com
Course Networking: http://coursenetworking.com and http://www.thecn.com
Seeds of Empowerment (SMILE): http://www.seedsofempowerment.org/wp/projects/smile/
Stanford Inquiry Mobile Learning Environment (SMILE):
    http://suseit.stanford.edu/research/project/smile
Piazza: https://piazza.com/
Piazza Blog: http://blog.piazza.com/

Lecture Capture and Recording Tools

Adobe Connect: http://www.adobe.com/products/adobeconnect.html
Camtasia: http://www.techsmith.com/camtasia.html
Echo360: http://echo360.com
Elluminate (Blackboard Collaborate): http://www.elluminate.com
MediaSite: http://www.sonicfoundry.com/mediasite

Mindmapping and Collaboration Tools

The Brain: http://www.thebrain.com
Bubbl.us: https://bubbl.us
Comapping: http://comapping.com
Creately: http://creately.com
Gliffy: http://www.gliffy.com/examples
Loomio: https://www.loomio.org
MindMeister: http://www.mindmeister.com/features
Mindomo: http://www.mindomo.com
Popplet: http://popplet.com
Webspiration: http://www.mywebspiration.com

Video Interaction and Discussion Tools

Flipgrid: http://flipgrid.com/info
Google+ Hangouts: https://plus.google.com
Grocket: https://grockit.com
Grocket Answers: https://grockit.com/answers
TED Ed: http://ed.ted.com
Vialogues: https://vialogues.com
Watch2gether: http://watch2gether.com

Word Cloud Tools:

ABCya: http://www.abcya.com
TagCrowd: http://tagcrowd.com
Tagul: http://tagul.com
Tagxedo: http://www.tagxedo.com
ToCloud: http://www.tocloud.com
Worditout: http://worditout.com
Wordle: http://www.wordle.net
WordSift: http://wordsift.com

Social Media and Networking Tools:

Course Networking: http://coursenetworking.com
Facebook: https://www.facebook.com
Google+ Hangouts: http://www.google.com/+/learnmore/hangouts
Ning: http://www.ning.com
Piazza: https://piazza.com
Popplet: http://popplet.com
Twitter: https://twitter.com

Video Annotation Tools

Bubbleply: http://www.bubbleply.com/index.htm
Viddler: http://www.viddler.com
VideoANT: http://ant.umn.edu
VoiceThread: http://voicethread.com
YouTube Annotations: http://www.youtube.com/t/annotations_about

Video Demonstrations of Various Tools and Activities

Interactive Shell Game (video annotation example):
http://www.youtube.com/watch?v=SzEvcS01Cl0

Chapter Eleven: Principle #8 Engagement

Interactive Maps

Adults with College Degrees in the United States by County:
http://chronicle.com/article/Adults-With-College-Degrees-in/125995
CNN Electoral Map: http://www.cnn.com/election/2012/ecalculator#?battleground
Climate Source (USDA Plant Hardiness Zone Maps):
http://www.climatesource.com/PHZM/gis_data.html
Freshman Migration Patterns: http://joshmkeller.com/work/migration.html
Graduation Rates from College: http://joshmkeller.com/work/graduation.html
Huffington Post Election Dashboard: http://elections.huffingtonpost.com/2012/results
Josh Keller (interactive graphics), Chronicle of Higher Education: http://joshmkeller.com
USDA GIS Data Downloads:
http://planthardiness.ars.usda.gov/PHZMWeb/DownloadsPublic.aspx

Interactive Multimedia Glossaries

Essential Genetics: A Genomics Perspective:
http://www.jbpub.com/genetics/essentials4e/interactive_glossary.cfm
Glossary of Computer and Internet Terms for Older Adults:
http://nihseniorhealth.gov/toolkit/toolkitfiles/pdf/Glossary.pdf
Harcourt Multimedia Math Glossary:
http://www.harcourtschool.com/glossary/math_advantage/glossary1.html
Instructional Design (formerly theory into practice):
http://www.instructionaldesign.org/index.html
Learning Planet (Shutterfly): http://learningplanet.shutterfly.com
Learning Theories: http://www.instructionaldesign.org/theories/index.html

Multimedia Feedback Tools

Vocaroo: http://vocaroo.com
VoiceThread: http://voicethread.com

Online Timeline Examples

The American Presidents Interactive Timeline:
http://www.americanpresidentsseries.com/timeline2.htm
Arab Spring (i.e., The Path to Protest): An Interactive Timeline of Middle East Protests
(The Guardian): http://www.guardian.co.uk/world/interactive/2011/mar/22/middle-east-
protest-interactive-timeline
Centuries of Citizenship: A Constitutional Timeline (National Constitution Center):
http://constitutioncenter.org/timeline/index.html and the National Constitution Timeline:
http://constitutioncenter.org/timeline/flash/cw.html
Gates Through the Years (USA Today): http://www.usatoday.com/tech/techinvestor/
corporatenews/2008-06-27-gates-microsoft-goodbye_N.htm
The Learning Machines (The New York Times): http://www.nytimes.com/
interactive/2010/09/19/magazine/classroom-technology.html

Martin Luther King Jr. National Memorial Timeline (USA Today):
    http://www.usatoday.com/news/destinations/story/2011-08-25/Martin-Luther-King-Jr-
    Memorial-in-Washington-A-closer-look/50136470/1?csp=34news
Predicting the Future of Computing (The New York Times):
    http://www.nytimes.com/interactive/2011/12/06/science/20111206-technology-timeline.html
Prehistoric Timeline (National Geographic Society):
    http://science.nationalgeographic.com/science/prehistoric-world/prehistoric-time-line
Steve Jobs Career Timeline (CNN):
    http://www.cnn.com/2011/TECH/innovation/10/05/steve.jobs.timeline/index.html
Steven P. Jobs: His Life, His Companies, His Products (The New York Times):
    http://www.nytimes.com/interactive/2011/10/05/business/20111005jobs-life-timeline.html
Visualizing Emancipation: http://dsl.richmond.edu/emancipation
The War of the Rebellion: A Compilation of Official Records of the Union and Confederate
Armies: http://ebooks.library.cornell.edu/m/moawar/waro.html

Online Timeline Tools

Capzles (social storytelling/online timeline): http://www.capzles.com
Dipity: http://www.dipity.com
Simile (MIT): http://www.simile-widgets.org/timeline
Timeline Tool 2.0 (University of British Columbia):
    http://www.learningtools.arts.ubc.ca/timeline.htm
xTimeline: http://www.xtimeline.com/index.aspx

Photo Sharing Services

Flickr: http://www.flickr.com
Flickr Creative Commons: http://www.flickr.com/creativecommons
Photobucket: http://photobucket.com
Picasa: http://picasa.google.com
Pinterest: http://pinterest.com
SmugMug: http://www.smugmug.com
Shutterfly: http://www.shutterfly.com

Simulations

PhET Interactive Simulations (University of Colorado at Boulder): http://phet.colorado.edu
PhET Interactive Simulations Program Information:
    http://outreach.colorado.edu/programs/details/id/161
Tox Town (National Library of Medicine): http://toxtown.nlm.nih.gov/index.php

Subject-Specific Photo Galleries

Kinematics: http://www.flickr.com/photos/physicsclassroom/galleries/72157625424161192
Library of Congress' Photo Stream: http://www.flickr.com/photos/library_of_congress
National Geographic World Wide: http://www.flickr.com/groups/893835@N20
Newton's Laws: http://www.flickr.com/photos/physicsclassroom/galleries/72157625278916478
The Physics Classroom Photo Gallery: http://www.physicsclassroom.com/gallery
Projectile Motion:
    http://www.flickr.com/photos/physicsclassroom/galleries/72157625381723822
Salt Lake City Utah Historical Photos:
    http://www.flickr.com/photos/locosteve/galleries/72157624716507836
Work and Energy:
    http://www.flickr.com/photos/physicsclassroom/galleries/72157625199307955

Talking Dictionaries and Language Translation

Center for Turkic and Iranian Lexicography and Dialectology:
    http://www.indiana.edu/~ctild/InteractiveAudioPrimer/BeingAGuest
Comparative Celtic Lexicon: http://celtic.swarthmore.edu

Going Silent: Areas with several languages near extinction (map):
   http://online.wsj.com/article/SB10001424052970204880404577228982976760026.
   html#articleTabs%3Dinteractive
Ho Talking Dictionary: http://ho.swarthmore.edu
Living Tongues Institute for Enduring Languages: http://www.livingtongues.org
National Geographic Talking Dictionaries:
   http://travel.nationalgeographic.com/travel/enduring-voices/talking-dictionaries
Siletz Talking Dictionary: http://siletz.swarthmore.edu
Swathmore Talking Dictionaries: http://talkingdictionary.swarthmore.edu
Tuvan Talking Dictionary: http://tuvan.swarthmore.edu
Word Lens: http://www.youtube.com/watch?v=h2OfQdYrHRs

Thinking and Questioning

Art Costa Centre for Thinking: http://www.artcostacentre.com
Bloom's Taxonomy of Learning Domains: http://www.nwlink.com/~donclark/hrd/bloom.html

Virtual Online Exhibits

Google Art Project: http://www.googleartproject.com/artists
Smithsonian National Museum of Natural History: http://www.mnh.si.edu/panoramas
Virtual Zooarcheology of the Arctic Project: http://vzap.iri.isu.edu/ViewPage.aspx?id=230
Virtual Zooarcheology of the Arctic Project, Dynamic Imaging Engine:
   http://bones.iri.isu.edu/Default.aspx

Virtual Tools, Instruments, and Artifacts

Kbears Virtual Microscope: http://www.kbears.com/sciences/microscope.html
Sample virtual microscopic slide:
   http://medsci.indiana.edu/c602web/602/c602web/virtual/path_32.html
SkyView (the Internet's Virtual Telescope): http://www.virtualtelescope.eu
University of Delaware Virtual Microscope:
   http://www.udel.edu/biology/ketcham/microscope/scope.html
Virtual Lab: Blood Pressure:
   http://www.mhhe.com/biosci/genbio/virtual_labs/BL_08/BL_08.html
Virtual slides including some for iPad (Mark Braun, Indiana University):
   http://medsci.indiana.edu/c602web/602/c602web/index.htm
The Virtual Microscope (UIUC): http://virtual.itg.uiuc.edu
The Virtual Telescope Project: http://www.virtualtelescope.eu
Web-based Virtual Microscopy: http://www.webmicroscope.net

Chapter Twelve: Principle #9 Tension

Argument Maps

Argumentum: http://arg.umentum.com
Argunet: http://www.argunet.org
Cohere: http://cohere.open.ac.uk/#screencast
Compendium: http://compendium.open.ac.uk/institute
Truthmapping: http://www.truthmapping.com

Online News Blogs:

BBC Blog Network: http://www.bbc.co.uk/blogs
Big Think Blogs: http://bigthink.com/blogs

CNN Blogs: http://www.cnn.com/exchange/blogs
CurrentTV Blog: http://current.com/blog
Huffington Post: http://www.huffingtonpost.com
The New York Times Blogs: http://www.nytimes.com/interactive/blogs/directory.html
Notes from Sea Level (Jon Bowermaster): http://www.jonbowermaster.com
Wall Street Journal Blogs: http://www.nytimes.com/interactive/blogs/directory.html
Washington Post Blogs and Columns: http://www.washingtonpost.com/blogs

Collaboration Tools

Omnium (Online Collaborative Communities): http://www.omnium.net.au

Debate Tools

bCisive Online: http://bcisiveonline.com
Debategraph: http://debategraph.org/home#61932_5__1

Crossword Puzzles

Crossword Puzzles: http://www.crossword-puzzles.co.uk
Crossword Puzzle Maker: http://www.armoredpenguin.com/crossword
EclipseCrossword: http://www.eclipsecrossword.com
Puzzlemaker (from Discovery Education):
http://www.discoveryeducation.com/free-puzzlemaker/?CFID=456773&CFTOKEN=55784387

Mobile Games

Words with Friends: http://www.wordswithfriends.com

Quote Portals

BrainyQuotes: http://www.brainyquote.com
Goodreads Quotes: http://www.goodreads.com/quotes
Wikiquote: http://en.wikiquote.org/wiki/Main_Page

Social Brainstorming and Voting Tools

Tricider: https://tricider.com

Virtual Study Groups and Interactive Questioning Tools

Course Networking: http://coursenetworking.com and http://www.thecn.com
Grocket: https://grockit.com
Homework Help (Chegg): http://www.chegg.com/homework-help
OpenStudy: http://openstudy.com
Piazza: https://piazza.com
Wikidot: http://www.wikidot.com

Chapter Thirteen: Principle #10 Yielding Products

Book Trailer Resources

The Book Life: http://www.thebooklife.com/2012/01/upcoming-2012-ya-book-trailers.html
BookSurge Video Book Trailer Samples:
http://www.booksurge.com/content/Video_Book_Trailer_Samples.htm
Book Trailer Assignment: https://sites.google.com/a/colonial.net/cchsmsfleming/sophomore-english/independent-reading-presentation

Book Trailers for Readers:
   http://www.booktrailersforreaders.com/How+to+make+a+book+trailer
Book Riot: http://bookriot.com/category/book-trailer
Creative Commons Images: http://search.creativcommons.org
How to Create a Viral Book Trailer: http://www.fourhourworkweek.com/blog/2013/04/10/how-to-
   create-a-viral-book-trailer-or-get-1000000-views-for-almost-anything
Play Free Music: http://freeplaymusic.com
Royalty Free Music: http://incompetech.com/music/royalty-free
Stupeflix (make videos): http://studio.stupeflix.com/en
WavSource.com: http://www.wavsource.com/sfx/sfx.htm

Global Projects

English Access Microscholarship Program:
   http://exchanges.state.gov/englishteaching/eam.html
Idealist: http://www.idealist.org
TakingITGlobal: http://www.tigweb.org

Grammar and Spell Checkers

Ginger: http://www.gingersoftware.com/grammarcheck
Grammarly: http://www.grammarly.com
GrammerCheck.net: http://www.grammarcheck.net
Language Tool Style and Grammar Checker: http://www.languagetool.org
PaperRater: http://www.paperrater.com
SpellCheckPlus: http://spellcheckplus.com
WritersDiet Test: http://www.writersdiet.com/WT.php
Your Dictionary: http://grammar.yourdictionary.com/style-and-usage/free-online-grammar.html

Goal Tracking Tools

43 Things: http://www.43things.com
Goalscape: http://www.goalscape.com
IDoneThis: https://idonethis.com
Joe's Goals: http://www.joesgoals.com
Lifetick: http://lifetick.com
Milestone Planner: http://milestoneplanner.com
Mindbloom Life Game: https://www.mindbloom.com

Movie Animations and Cartoons

Bitstrips: http://www.bitstrips.com/landing
Digital Films: http://www.digitalfilms.com
Dvolver: http://www.dvolver.com
GoAnimate: http://goanimate.com
Machinima: http://www.machinima.com
PowToon: http://www.powtoon.com
Voki: http://www.voki.com
Zimmer Twins: http://www.zimmertwins.com

Online Book Reviews and Social Books

20SomethingReads: http://www.20somethingreads.com
Academia.edu: http://www.academia.edu
Amazon.com: http://www.amazon.com
Barnes and Noble Review: http://bnreview.barnesandnoble.com
Book Reporter: http://www.bookreporter.com
Club Recap (from 60 Second Recap): http://www.60secondrecap.com/club-recap
Goodreads: http://www.goodreads.com
Kidreads: http://www.kidsreads.com

LibraryThing: http://www.librarything.com
Rethink Books: http://rethinkbooks.com
Scholastic Share What You're Reading: http://teacher.scholastic.com/activities/swyar
Scribd: http://www.scribd.com
Teenreads: http://www.teenreads.com

Video Documentary Software

Adobe Premiere: http://www.adobe.com/products/premiere.html
Animoto: http://animoto.com
Camtasia: http://www.techsmith.com/camtasia.html
iMovie: http://www.apple.com/ilife/imovie
Movie Maker: http://windows.microsoft.com/en-US/windows-live/movie-maker-get-started

Video Documentary Projects

BFED: Baltimore Food Ecology Documentary: http://www.jhsph.edu/research/centers-and-institutes/johns-hopkins-center-for-a-livable-future/news_events/multimedia/BFED.html
Columbia University's Center for New Media Teaching and Learning: http://ccnmtl.columbia.edu
Columbia University Graduate School of Journalism: http://www.journalism.columbia.edu/page/90-the-documentary-project/90
Georgetown University's Center for New Designs for Learning and Scholarship (CNDLS): https://cndls.georgetown.edu/#panel-1
Johns Hopkins Bloomberg School of Public Health: Safe Streets: http://www.jhsph.edu/research/centers-and-institutes/center-for-prevention-of-youth-violence/field_reports/Safe_Streets.html
Project Rebirth: http://www.projectrebirth.org
Project Rebirth Educational Initiative: https://cndls.georgetown.edu/project-rebirth

Chapter Fourteen: Supporting and Motivating Online Instructors

E-Learning Training and Support Resources

Brandon Hall Research: http://www.brandon-hall.com
EDUCAUSE Learning Initiative: http://www.educause.edu/eli
Edutopia (from the George Lucas Educational Foundation): http://www.edutopia.org
eLearning Guild: http://www.elearningguild.com
V-PORTAL (Video Primers in an Online Repository of eTeaching and Learning: http://www.youtube.com/TravelinEdMan (see also, the Indiana University School of Education Instructional Consulting Office: http://www.indiana.edu/~icy/media/de_series.html)
United States Distance Learning Association (USDLA): http://www.usdla.org
Online tutorial support: http://www.lynda.com

REFERENCES

Abilene Christian University (2008, February 25). *ACU first university in nation to provide iPhone or iPod touch to all incoming freshmen.* ACU Press Release. Retrieved from http://www.acu.edu/news/2008/080225_iphone.html

Allen, I. E., & Seaman, J. (2004). *Entering the mainstream: The quality and extent of online education in the United States, 2003 and 2004.* Needham, MA: Sloan-C. Retrieved from http://sloanconsortium.org/sites/default/files/entering_mainstream_1.pdf

Allen, I. E., & Seaman, J. (2007). *Online nation: Five years of growth in online learning.* Needham, MA: Sloan-C. Retrieved from http://sloanconsortium.org/publications/survey/pdf/online_nation.pdf

Allen, I. E., & Seaman, J. (2010a, January). *Learning on demand: Online education in the United States, 2009.* Retrieved from http://sloanconsortium.org/publications/survey/pdf/learningondemand.pdf (summary is here: http://sloanconsortium.org/publications/survey/learning_on_demand_sr2010)

Allen, I. E., & Seaman, J. (2010b, November). *Class differences: Online education in the United States, 2010.* The Sloan Consortium. Retrieved from http://sloanconsortium.org/sites/default/files/class_differences.pdf

Allen, I. E., & Seaman, J. (2014). *Grade change: Tracking online education in the United States.* Babson Park, MA: Babson Survey Research Group and Quahog Research Group. Retrieved from http://www.onlinelearningsurvey.com/reports/gradechange.pdf

Ambient Insight (2011, July 28). *Global self-paced eLearning market research.* Monroe: WA: Ambient Insight Research. Retrieved from http://www.ambientinsight.com/Reports/eLearning.aspx

Ambient Insight (2012, July). *The North America market for self-paced eLearning products and services: 2011-2016 Forecast and Analysis.* Retrieved from http://www.ambientinsight.com/Resources/Documents/AmbientInsight-2011-2016-NorthAmerica-SelfPaced-eLearning-Market-Abstract.pdf

Ambient Insight (2013, January). *The worldwide market for self-paced elearning products and services: 2011-2016 Forecast and Analysis.* Retrieved from http://www.ambientinsight.com/Resources/Documents/AmbientInsight-2011-2016-Worldwide-Self-paced-eLearning-Market-Premium-Overview.pdf

Ames, C. (1992). Classrooms: Goals, structures, and student motivation. *Journal of Educational Psychology, 84*(3), 261–271.

Ames, C. A. (1990). Motivation: What teachers need to know. *Teachers College Record, 91*(3), 410–421. Retrieved from http://web.uncg.edu/soe/bf_course669/docs_session_6/motivtion-whatteachersneedtoknow.pdf

Ames, C., & Ames, R. (Eds.). (1989). *Research on motivation in education* (Vol. 3): Goals and cognitions. Orlando, FL: Academic Press.

Anderberg, K. (2010). Basic accounting games. *eHow*. Retrieved from http://www.ehow.com/list_6830614_basic-accounting-games.html

Anderson, M. D. (2001). Individual characteristics and Web-based courses. In C. R. Wolfe (Ed.), *Learning and teaching on the World Wide Web* (pp. 45–72). San Diego: Academic Press.

Andrew, G. R. (2009, August 9). 8 free poll tools for your Website. *Social Times*. Retrieved from http://socialtimes.com/8-free-poll-tools-for-your-website_b5913

Aragon, S. R., & Johnson, E. S. (2008). Factors influencing completion and noncompletion of community college online courses. *The American Journal of Distance Education, 22*(3), 146–158. doi:10.1080/08923640802239962

Arbaugh, J. B. (2000). Virtual classroom characteristics and student satisfaction with Internet-based MBA courses. *Journal of Management Education, 24*(1), 32–54. doi:10.1177/105256290002400104

Arbaugh, J. B. (2001). How instructor immediacy behaviors affect student satisfaction and learning in web-based courses. *Business Communication Quarterly, 64*(4), 42–54.

Arrington, M. (2011, July 6). Facebook video chat v. Google Hangouts: It's no contest. *TechCrunch*. Retrieved from http://techcrunch.com/2011/07/06/facebook-video-chat-google-hangouts/

Associated Press (2010, August). Robotic sub films new species off of Indonesia. *CBC News*. Retrieved from http://www.cbc.ca/news/technology/story/2010/08/26/indonesia-okeanos-explorer-new-species.html

Atkinson, J. W. (1964). *An introduction to motivation.* Princeton, NJ: Van Nostrand.

Atkinson, T. (2008, May/June). Second Life for educators: Inside Linden Lab. *TechTrends, 52*(3), 16–18.

Aungst, T. (2013, March 11). How Google Glass could revolutionize medicine. *iMedicalApps*. Retrieved from http://www.imedicalapps.com/2013/03/google-glass-medicine/

Austen, B. (2012, August). The story of Steve Jobs: An inspiration or a cautionary tale? *Wired, 20*(8), 72–79. Retrieved from http://www.wired.com/business/2012/07/ff_stevejobs/all/

Ausubel, D. P. (1978). In defense of advance organizers: A reply to the critics. *Review of Educational Research, 48*(2), 251–257.

Baig, E. (2011, July 7). Pros, cons of Facebook's new video chat. *USA Today*. Retrieved from http://www.usatoday.com/tech/columnist/edwardbaig/2011-07-06-facebook-video-chat_n.htm

Bajaj, V. (2011, July 4). Beneath a temple in southern India, a treasure trove of staggering riches. *New York Times*. Retrieved from http://www.nytimes.com/2011/07/05/world/asia/05india.html

Bandura, A. (1986). *Social foundations of thought and action: A social-cognitive theory.* Englewood Cliffs, NJ: Prentice Hall.

Bandura, A. (1986). *Social foundations of thoughts and actions.* Englewood Cliffs, NJ: Prentice-Hall.

Bandura, A. (1989). Human agency in social cognitive theory. *American Psychologist, 44*(9), 1175–1184.

Bandura, A. (1997). *Self-efficacy: The exercise of control.* New York: W. H. Freeman.

Barab, S. A., & Roth, W.-M. (2006). Curriculum-based ecosystems: Supporting knowing from an ecological perspective. *Educational Researcher, 35*(5), 3–13. doi:10.3102/0013189x035005003

Bates, A. W. (1991). Third generation distance education: The challenge of new technology. *Research in Distance Education, 3*(2), 10–15.

Bates, T. A. W. (1995). *Technology, open learning and distance education.* New York: Routledge.

Baumeister, R. F., & Tierney, J. (2011). *Willpower: Rediscovering the greatest human strengths.* New York: Penguin.

Bennett, R. (2011). *Global classrooms, rural benefits: Creative outreach through computing in education.* Paper and keynote presentation at the 2nd Global Learn: Global Conference on Learning and Technology, Association for the Advancement of Computing in Education (AACE), Melbourne, Australia.

Berge, Z. L., & Huang, Y. P. (2004). A model for sustainable student retention: A holistic perspective on the student dropout problem with special attention to e-Learning. *DEOSNEWS, 13*(5). Retrieved from http://www.ed.psu.edu/acsde/deos/deosnews/deosnews13_5.pdf

Berger, D. (2011, January 18). South African teens get virtual mentoring from all over the world. *CNN.* Retrieved from http://www.cnn.com/2011/LIVING/01/13/cnnheroes.stokes/index.html

Bergmann, J., & Sams, A. (2012, May 21). How to implement the 'flipped classroom.' *eSchool News.* Retrieved from http://www.eschoolnews.com/2012/05/21/how-to-implement-the-flipped-classroom/

Berrett, D. (2012, February 19). How 'flipping' the classroom can improve traditional lecture. *The Chronicle of Higher Education.* Retrieved http://chronicle.com/article/How-Flipping-the-Classroom/130857/

Berrett, D. (2013, May 10). Debate over MOOCs reaches Harvard. *The Chronicle of Higher Education.* Retrieved from http://chronicle.com/article/Debate-Over-MOOCs-Reaches/139179/?cid=at&utm_source=at&utm_medium=en

Billiot, T. (2011, September 29). In one online class, Twitter brings students together. *The Chronicle of Higher Education.* Retrieved from http://chronicle.com/article/article-content/129120/

Black, R. (2008, April 28). Colossal squid comes out of ice. *BBC News.* Retrieved from http://news.bbc.co.uk/2/hi/7367774.stm

Blight, G., & Pulham, S. (2011). Arab spring: An interactive timeline of Middle East protests. *The Guardian.* Retrieved from http://www.guardian.co.uk/world/interactive/2011/mar/22/middle-east-protest-interactive-timeline

Blumenfeld, P. C., Soloway, E., Marx, R. W., Krajcik, J. S., Guzdial, M., & Palincsar, A. (1991). Motivating project-based learning: Sustaining the doing, supporting the learning. *Educational Psychologist, 26*(3–4), 369–398.

Bonk, C. J. (2002a, January). Executive summary of "Online teaching in an online world." *United States Distance Learning Association (USDLA) Journal, 16*(1). Retrieved from http://209.151.89.205/usdla.org/public_html/cms/html/journal/JAN02_Issue/article02.html (Note: Full report available at: http://www.publicationshare.com/docs/faculty_survey_report.pdf)

Bonk, C. J. (2002b, March). Executive summary of "Online training in an online world." *United States Distance Learning Association (USDLA) Journal, 16*(3). Retrieved from http://209.151.89.205/usdla.org/public_html/cms/html/journal/MAR02_Issue/article02.html (Note: Full report available at: http://www.publicationshare.com/docs/corp_survey.pdf)

Bonk, C. J. (2009a, November 23). Benefits and audiences of online learning in K–12 environments. *Inside the School.* Madison, WI: Magna Publications. Retrieved from http://publicationshare.com/Benefits-and-Audiences-of-Online-Learning-in-K-12-Environments-Inside-the-School.htm

Bonk, C. J. (2009b, October 19). The wide open learning world: Sea, land, and ice views. *Association for Learning Technology (ALT) Online Newsletter,* Issue 17. Retrieved from http://archive.alt.ac.uk/newsletter.alt.ac.uk/newsletter.alt.ac.uk/1h7kpy8fa5s.html

Bonk, C. J. (2009c). *The world is open: How Web technology is revolutionizing education.* San Francisco: Jossey-Bass.

Bonk, C. J. (2011, July 28). EduMOOC on the loose: An interview with Ray Schroeder. *TravelinEdMan blog.* Retrieved from http://travelinedman.blogspot.com/

Bonk, C. J. (2011). YouTube anchors and enders: The use of shared online video content as a macrocontext for learning. *Asia-Pacific Collaborative Education Journal, 7*(1). Retrieved from http://apcj.alcob.org/?mid=Issue&category=5&document_srl=826

Bonk, C. J. (2012, February). Plenary Talk: *Technology-enhanced teaching: From tinkering to tottering to totally extreme learning.* Proceedings of the 1st International Conference on Open and Distance Learning, Manila, the Philippines. Available: http://trainingshare.com/pdfs/Curt_Bonk_Extreme_Learning_Philippines_Conference--Citation.pdf

Bonk, C. J. (2013, February 22). Want some MOOC with your TV dinner? *The EvoLLLution.* Part I retrieved from http://www.evolllution.com/featured/want-some-mooc-with-your-tv-dinner-part-1/; Part 2 retrieved from http://www.evolllution.com/media_resources/want-some-mooc-with-your-tv-dinner-part-2/

Bonk, C. J., & Cunningham, D. J. (1998). Searching for learner-centered, constructivist, and sociocultural components of collaborative educational learning tools. In C. J. Bonk & K. S. King (Eds.), *Electronic collaborators: Learner-centered technologies for literacy, apprenticeship, and discourse* (Chapter 2, pp. 25–50). Mahwah, NJ: Erlbaum.

Bonk, C. J., & Dennen, V. (2007). Frameworks for design and instruction. In M. G. Moore (Ed.), *Handbook of distance education* (2nd ed.) (pp. 233–246). Mahwah, NJ: Erlbaum.

Bonk, C. J., & King, K. S. (Eds.). (1998). *Electronic collaborators: Learner-centered technologies for literacy, apprenticeship, and discourse.* Mahwah, NJ: Erlbaum.

Bonk, C. J., & Zhang, K. (2006). Introducing the R2D2 model: Online learning for the diverse learners of this world. *Distance Education, 27*(2), 249–264.

Bonk, C. J., & Zhang, K. (2008). *Empowering online learning: 100+ activities for reading, reflecting, displaying, and doing.* San Francisco: Jossey-Bass.

Bonk, C. J., Appelman, R., & Hay, K. E. (1996). Electronic conferencing tools for student apprenticeship and perspective taking. *Educational Technology, 36*(5), 8–18.

Bonk, C. J., Daytner, K., Daytner, G., Dennen, V., & Malikowski, S. (2001). Using Web-based cases to enhance, extend, and transform pre-service teacher training: Two years in review. *Computers in the Schools, 18*(1), 189–211.

Bonk, C. J., Ehman, L., Hixon, E., & Yamagata-Lynch, L. (2002). The pedagogical TICKIT: Teacher Institute for Curriculum Knowledge about the Integration of Technology. *Journal of Technology and Teacher Education, 10*(2), 205–233.

Bonk, C. J., Fischler, R. B., & Graham, C. R. (2000). Getting smarter on the Smartweb. In D. G. Brown, (Ed.), *Teaching with technology: Seventy-five professors from eight universities tell their stories* (pp. 200–205). Boston: Anker.

Bonk, C. J., Kim, K. J., & Lee, S. H. (2004). Pedagogical and motivational techniques in corporate e-learning. In S. Reddy (Ed.). *E-Learning and technology: New opportunities in training and development* (pp. 93–112). ICFAI Books: Hyderabad, India.

Bonk, C. J., Kim, K. J., & Lee, S. H. (2004). Pedagogical and motivational techniques in corporate e-learning. In S. Reddy (Ed.), *E-Learning and technology: New opportunities in training and development* (pp. 93-112). Hyderabad, India: ICFAI Books.

Bonk, C. J., Lee, M. M., Kim, N., & Lin, M.-F. (2009, December). The tensions of transformation in three cross-institutional wikibook projects. *The Internet and Higher Education, 12*(3–4), 126–135.

Bonk, C. J., Lee, M. M., Kim, N., & Lin, M.-F. (2010). Wikibook transformations and disruptions: Looking back twenty years to today. In H. H. Yang, & S. C-Y. Yuen (Eds.), *Collective intelligence and e-learning 2.0: Implications of Web-based communities and networking* (pp. 127–146). Hershey, PA: Information Science Reference.

Bonk, C. J., Medury, P. V., & Reynolds, T. H. (1994). Cooperative hypermedia: The marriage of collaborative writing and mediated environments. *Computers in the Schools, 10*(1/2), 79–124.

Bonk, C. J., Olson, T., Wisher, R. A., & Orvis, K. L. (2002). *Reflections on blended learning: The Armor Captains Career Course.* (Research Note #2002-13). Alexandria, VA: US Army Research Institute for the Behavioral and Social Sciences.

Bowermaster, J. (2012a, May 30). 5 ways fracking is making you sick. *Notes from Sea Level.* Retrieved from http://jonbowermaster.com/blog/2012/05/5-ways-fracking-is-making-you-sick/

Bowermaster, J. (2012b, May 30). New study says fracking chemicals will poison aquifers. *Notes from Sea Level.* Retrieved from http://jonbowermaster.com/blog/2012/05/new-study-says-fracking-chemicals-will-poison-aquifers/

Brannon, K. (2010, March 9). Students learn smart grid power trading. *Tulane University Press Release.* Retrieved from http://tulane.edu/news/releases/pr_0304b2010.cfm

Bransford, J. D., Brown, A. L., & Cocking R. R. (2000). *How people learn: Brain, mind, experience and schooling* (Vol. Expanded). Washington, DC: National Academy Press.

Briggs, L. L. (2008, March 5). Micro blogging with Twitter. *Campus Technology.* Retrieved from http://campustechnology.com/articles/2008/03/micro-blogging-with-twitter.aspx

Brophy, J. (1998). *Motivating students to learn.* Boston: McGraw-Hill.

Brophy, J. (2010). *Motivating students to learn* (3rd ed.). New York: Routledge.

Brown, D. (2002, January). Interactive teaching. *Syllabus, 15*(6), p. 23.

Brown, J. S. (2006, December 1). *Relearning learning—Applying the long tail to learning.* Presentation at MIT iCampus, Available from MITWorld. Retrieved from http://video.mit.edu/watch/relearning-learning-applying-the-long-tail-to-learning-9174/

Brown, J. S., & Adler, R. P. (2008, January/February). Minds on fire: Open education, the long tail, and learning 2.0. *EDUCAUSE Review, 43*(1), 16–32. Retrieved from http://www.educause.edu/ero/article/minds-fire-open-education-long-tail-and-learning-20

Brown, J. S., & Duguid, P. (2000). *The social life of information.* Boston: Harvard Business School.

Brown, J., Collins, A., & Duguid, P. (1989). Situated cognition and the culture of learning. *Educational Researcher, 18*(1), 32–42.

Buckner, E., & Kim, P. (2012). Mobile innovations, executive functions, and educational development in conflict zones: A case study from Palestine. *Educational Technology Research & Development, 60*(1), 175–192.

Buckner, E., & Kim, P. (2013). Integrating technology and pedagogy for inquiry based learning: The Stanford Mobile Inquiry-based Learning Environment (SMILE). UNESCO.

Butler, K. (2003). *How to keep online students motivated.* Australian Flexible Learning Community. Retrieved from https://nationalvetcontent.edu.au/alfresco/d/d/workspace/SpacesStore/b55fdd65-ce9b-45a7-9270-75e1752658f9/14_06/content/espace/facilitator/qa/motivated.htm

Byrne, R. (2010, July 28). VideoAnt—Discuss and annotate videos. *Free Technology for Teachers.* Retrieved from http://www.freetech4teachers.com/2010/07/video-ant-discuss-and-annotate-videos.html

Byrne, R. (2011, May 14). Popplet—Collaborative mind maps and sticky notes. *Free Technology for Teachers.* Retrieved from http://www.freetech4teachers.com/2011/03/popplet-collaborative-mind-maps-and.html

Byrne, R. (2012a, April 27). A thought or two about TED Ed. *Free Technology for Teachers.* Retrieved http://www.freetech4teachers.com/2012/04/thought-or-two-about-ted-ed.html

Byrne, R. (2012b, March 19). Three ways to watch videos and discuss them in real time online. *Free Technology for Teachers.* Retrieved from http://www.freetech4teachers.com/2012/03/three-ways-to-watch-videos-discuss-them.html

Byrne, R. (2012c, June 25). Vialogues—Form discussion around videos. *Free Technology for Teachers.* Retrieved from http://www.freetech4teachers.com/2012/06/vialogues-form-discussions-around.html

Cain, S. (2012). *Quiet: The power of introverts in a world that can't stop talking.* New York: Crown.

Campbell, J. O. (1997). Evaluating ALN: What works, who's learning. *ALN Magazine, 1*(2).

Canadian Press (2012, February 17). Newly unveiled talking dictionaries aim to document, preserve endangered languages. *Winnipeg Free Press.* Retrieved from http://www.winnipegfreepress.com/arts-and-life/entertainment/books/newly-unveiled-talking-dictionaries-aim-to-document-preserve-endangered-languages-139527703.html

Carr, S. (2000, February 11). As distance education comes of age, the challenge is keeping the students. *The Chronicle of Higher Education.* Retrieved from http://chronicle.com/article/As-Distance-Education-Comes-of/14334

Carter, D. (2011, January 28). *Report predicts online learning explosion by 2015.* Retrieved from http://www.ecampusnews.com/top-news/report-predicts-online-learning-explosion-by-2015/

CBS News. (2011, May 1). Osama bin Laden is dead. *CBS News.* Retrieved from http://www.cbsnews.com/stories/2011/05/01/national/main20058777.shtml

Cellilo, J. (n.d.). Motivation in on-line classes. *On course workshop.* Retrieved from http://www.oncourseworkshop.com/Motivation015.htm

Chafkin, M. (2009, April 1). Nolan Bushnell is back in the game. *Inc.* Retrieved from http://www.inc.com/magazine/20090401/the-gamer.html

Chang, A. (2012, January 6). Pooja Sankar raises $6M for her EduTech startup Piazza to help college Students with their coursework. *Forbes Woman.* Retrieved from http://www.forbes.com/sites/women2/2012/01/06/pooja-sankar-raises-6m-for-her-edutech-startup-piazza-to-help-college-students-with-their-coursework/

Chapman, D. D. (2011). Contingent and tenured/tenure track faculty: Motivations and incentives to teach distance education courses. *Online Journal of Distance Learning Administration, 16*(3). Retrieved from http://www.westga.edu/~distance/ojdla/fall143/chapman143.html

Chen, A. (2012, June 12). Interactive map traces slaves' path to emancipation. *The Chronicle of Higher Education*. Retrieved from http://chronicle.com/blogs/wiredcampus/interactive-map-traces-slaves-path-to-emancipation/36729

Chen, D. P., Gonyea, R. M., & Kuh, G. D. (2008). Learning at a distance: Engaged or not? *Innovate: Journal of Online Learning, 4*(3), 1–8.

Chickering, A. W., & Gamson, Z. F. (1987). Seven principles for good practice in undergraduate education. *AAHE Bulletin, 39*(7), 3–7. Retrieved from http://teaching.uncc.edu/sites/teaching.uncc.edu/files/media/files/file/InstructionalMethods/SevenPrinciples.pdf

Chronicle of Higher Education (2009, December 2). Human brain is being dissected in a live Webcast. *Tweed, Chronicle of Higher Education*. Retrieved from http://chronicle.com/blogs/tweed/human-brain-is-being-dissected-in-a-live-webcast/9053

Chronicle of Higher Education (2010, August 29). Opening up learning to all. *Chronicle of Higher Education*. Retrieved from http://chronicle.com/article/Opening-Up-Learning-to-All/124169/

Chronicle of Higher Education (2012, June 11). Building different MOOC's for different pedagogical needs. *The Chronicle of Higher Education* (Interviewer: Jeffrey R. Young). Retrieved from http://chronicle.com/article/article-content/132127/

Clem, F. A. (2005). *Culture and motivation in online learning environments*. (Doctoral dissertation, San Diego State University and the University of San Diego). Retrieved from http://eric.ed.gov/?id=ED485100

CNN (2010, May 25). BP will continue live video feed during "top kill" attempt. *CNN*. Retrieved from http://articles.cnn.com/2010-05-25/us/gulf.oil.spill_1_london-based-oil-giant-bp-rig?_s=PM:US

CNN (2011). Map: Impact of Japan tsunami and earthquake. *CNN*. Retrieved from http://www.cnn.com/SPECIALS/2011/japan.quake/map/

Cocea, M. (2007). *Assessment of motivation in online learning environments* (Unpublished master's thesis). National College of Ireland, Dublin. Retrieved from http://trap.ncirl.ie/352/1/Mihaela_Cocea.pdf

Cocea, M., & Weibelzahl, S. (2006). Motivation—included or excluded from e-learning. *Cognition and Exploratory Learning in Digital Age, CELDA 2006 Proceedings*, Barcelona, Spain (pp. 435–437). Retrieved from http://www.easy-hub.org/stephan/cocea-celda06.pdf

Cognition and Technology Group at Vanderbilt (1990). Anchored instruction and its relationship to situated cognition. *Educational Researcher, 19*(6), 2–10.

Cognition and Technology Group at Vanderbilt (1991). Technology and the design of generative learning environments. *Educational Technology, 31*(5), 34–40.

Cole, R., & Crawford, T. (2007, June). Building peace through information and communications technologies. *Idealware*. Retrieved from http://idealware.org/articles/building-peace-through-information-and-communications-technologies

Collins, A., Brown, J. S., & Newman, S. (1989). Cognitive apprenticeship: Teaching the craft of reading, writing, and mathematics. In L. B. Resnick (Ed.), *Knowing, learning, and instruction: Essays in honor of Robert Glaser* (pp. 453–494). Hillsdale, NJ: Erlbaum.

Collins, J. (2011, March 10), CliffNotes goes digital. *Marketplace Tech*. Retrieved from http://www.marketplace.org/topics/tech/cliffsnotes-goes-digital

Conklin, M. S. (2007). *101 uses for Second Life in the college classroom*. Elon, NC: Elon University. Retrieved from http://www.computing.surrey.ac.uk/2L/glshandout.pdf

Conrad, R.-M., & Donaldson, J. A. (2004). *Engaging the online learner: Activities and resources for creation instruction*. San Francisco: Jossey-Bass.

Cookman, C. (2009). Using JiTT to foster active learning in a humanities course. In Simkins, S. & Maier, M. (Eds.), *Just-in-Time Teaching* (pp. 163–178), Sterling, VA: Stylus. Retrieved from http://journalism.indiana.edu/webspace/ccookman/crtcltnkng/pdfs/jitt_bkcptr.pdf

Coppola, N. W., Hiltz, S. R., & Rotter, N. G. (2004). Building trust in virtual teams. *IEEE Transactions on Professional Communication, 47*(2), 95–104. doi:10.1109/TPC.2004.828203

Croxall, B. (2011, February 8). Getting started with the Google Art Project. *The Chronicle of Higher Education*. Retrieved from http://chronicle.com/blogs/profhacker/getting-started-with-google-art-project/30496

Cummings, J. A., Bonk, C. J., & Jacobs, F. R. (2002). Twenty-first century college syllabi: Options for online communication and interactivity. *The Internet and Higher Education, 5*(1), 1–19.

Deci, E. L., & Ryan, R. M. (1985). *Intrinsic motivation and self-determination in human behavior*. New York: Plenum Press.

Deci, E. L., & Ryan, R. M. (2008). Facilitating optimal motivation and psychological well-being across life's domains. *Canadian Psychology, 49*, 14–23. Retrieved from http://www.psych.rochester.edu/SDT/documents/2000_DeciRyan_PIWhatWhy.pdf

Deci, E. L., Vallerand, R. J., Pelletier, L. G., & Ryan, R. M. (1991). Motivation and education: The self-determination perspective. *Educational Psychologist, 26*(3), 325–346. doi:10.1207/s15326985ep2603&4_6

Dennen, V. P. (2001). *The design and facilitation of asynchronous discussion activities in Web-based courses*. Unpublished doctoral dissertation, Indiana University, Bloomington, Indiana, USA.

Dennen, V., & Bonk, C. J. (2007). We'll leave the light on for you: Keeping learners motivated in online courses. In B. H. Khan (Ed.), *Flexible learning in an information society* (pp. 64–76). Hershey, PA: The Idea Group.

Dennen, V., & Bonk, C. J. (2008). We'll leave a light on for you: Keeping learners motivated in online courses. In L. Tomei (Ed.), *Online and distance learning: Concepts, methodologies, tools, and applications* (pp. 704–714). Hershey, PA: Information Science Reference.

Dennis, A., Bichelmeyer, B., Henry, D., Cakir, H., Korkmaz, A., Watson, C., & Brunnage, J. (2006). The Cisco Networking Academy: A model for the study of student success in a blended learning environment. In C. J. Bonk & C. R. Graham (Eds.), *Handbook of blended learning: Global perspectives, local designs* (pp. 550–567). San Francisco: Pfeiffer.

Doering, A. (2006). Adventure learning: transformative hybrid online education. *Distance Education, 27*(2), 197–215.

Doering, A., & Veletsianos, G. (2008). Hybrid online education: Identifying integration models using adventure learning. *Journal of Research on Technology in Education, 41*(1), 23–41.

Driscoll, M. (2005). *Psychology of learning for instruction* (3rd ed.). New York: Allyn & Bacon.

Duffy, T. M., & Jonassen, D. H. (1992). *Constructivism and the technology of instruction: A conversation.* Hillsdale, NJ: Erlbaum.

Dunlap, J. C., & Lowenthal, P. R. (2011, October 18). Situational qualities exhibited by exceptional presenters. *ECAR Research Bulletin.* Boulder, CO: EDUCAUSE Center for Applied Research.

Dweck, C. S. (1986). Motivational processes affecting learning. *American Psychologist, 41,* 1040–1048.

Dybwad, B. (2009a, November 3). Purdue University adds Twitter and Facebook to class participation. *Mashable.* Retrieved from http://mashable.com/2009/11/03/hotseat/

Dybwad, B. (2009b, October 23). University makes Twitter a required class for journalism students. *Mashable.* Retrieved from http://mashable.com/2009/10/23/twitter-class/

Egbert, J. (2005). *CALL essentials: Principles and practice in CALL classrooms.* Alexandria, VA: TESOL Publications.

Ehman, L., H., Bonk, C. J., & Yamagata-Lynch, L. (2005). A model of teacher professional development to support technology integration. *AACE Journal, 13*(3), 251–270.

Ertmer, P. A., & Newby, T. J. (1993). Behaviorism, cognitivism, constructivism: Comparing critical features from an instructional design perspective. *Performance Improvement Quarterly, 6*(4), 50–72.

Ertmer, P. A., Richardson, J. C., Belland, B., Camin, D., Connooly, P., Coulthard, G., Lei, K., & Mong, C. (2007). Using peer feedback to enhance the quality of student online postings: An exploratory study. *Journal of Computer-Mediates Communication, 12*(2). Retrieved from http://jcmc.indiana.edu/vol12/issue2/ertmer.html

eSchool News Staff (2011, May 27). Five ways readers are using iPads in the classroom. *eSchool News.* Retrieved from http://www.eschoolnews.com/2011/05/27/five-ways-readers-are-using-ipads-in-the-classroom/

FarmVille (2011). *Wikipedia.* Retrieved from http://en.wikipedia.org/wiki/FarmVille

Ferenstein, G. (2011, February 16). How Bill Gates' favorite teacher wants to disrupt education. *Fast Company.* Retrieved from http://www.fastcompany.com/1728471/change-generation-bill-gates-favorite-teacher-wants-to-disrupt-education

Ferlazzo, L. (2013). *Self-driven learning: Teaching strategies for student motivation.* Larchmont, NY: Eye on Education.

Festinger, L. (1957). *A theory of cognitive dissonance.* Stanford, CA: Stanford University Press.

Fini, A. (2009). The technological dimension of a massive open online course: The case of the CCK08 course tools. *International Review of Research in Open and Distance Learning. 10*(5), 1–26. Retrieved from http://www.irrodl.org/index.php/irrodl/article/view/643/1402

Fischer, G. (2003, May). *Learning paradigms of the 21st century: New mindsets, new cultures, and new media for learning.* Paper presented at the Waikato Management School, University of Waikato, Hamilton, New Zealand.

Fischman, J. (2011, May 8). The rise of teaching machines. *The Chronicle of Higher Education.* Retrieved from http://chronicle.com/article/The-Rise-of-Teaching-Machines/127389/

Fischman, J. (2012, July 3). Taking apart an oil slick. *The Chronicle of Higher Education.* Retrieved from http://chronicle.com/blogs/percolator/taking-apart-an-oil-slick/29891

Flood, J. (2002). Read all about it: Online learning facing 80% attrition rates. *Turkish Online Journal of Distance Education, 3*(2). Retrieved from http://tojde.anadolu.edu.tr/tojde6/articles/jim2.htm

Forbes, D. (2011). Beyond lecture capture: Student generated podcasts in teacher education. *Waikato Journal of Education, 16*(1), 51–63.

Forbes, D., Khoo, E., & Johnson, M. (2012). "It gave me a much more personal connection": Student-generated podcasting and assessment in teacher education. In M. Brown, M. Hartnett & T. Stewart (Eds.), *Future challenges, Sustainable challenges. Proceedings ASCILITE Wellington 2012,* (pp. 326–330). Retrieved from http://researchcommons.waikato.ac.nz/handle/10289/8407

Ford, B. J. (2010, April 24). The secret power of the single cell. *New Scientist, 206*(2757), 26–27. Retrieved from http://www.brianjford.com/a-10-NSc-single_cell.pdf

Foreman, K. (2010, July 24). Graduating class of 2010. *Come and See Africa (CASA).* Retrieved from http://comeandseeafrica.blogspot.com/2010/07/graduating-class-of-2010.html

Fountain, H. (2009, September 17). Fossil find challenges theories on T. Rex. *New York Times.* Retrieved from http://www.nytimes.com/2009/09/18/science/18dinosaur.html

Frankola, K. (2001, August). Training e-trainers. *Learning Circuits,* Retrieved from http://www.trainingshare.com/temp/Training_E-Trainers.pdf

Frankola, K. (2001). Why online learners drop out. *Workforce, 80*(10), 52–61.

Franzen, J. L., Gingerich, P. D., Habersetzer, J., Hurum, J.H., von Koenigswald, W., et al. (2009). Complete primate skeleton from the Middle Eocene of Messel in Germany: Morphology and paleobiology, *PLoS ONE, 4*(5). Retrieved from http://www.plosone.org/article/info%3Adoi%2F10.1371%2Fjournal.pone.0005723

Ganzel, R. (2001). Associated learning. *Online Learning, 5*(5), 36–38. Retrieved from http://www.resultsdirect.com/Files/PDFs/Associated_learning.pdf

Garrison, D. R., & Vaughan, N. D. (2008). *Blended learning in higher education: Framework, principles, and guidelines.* San Francisco: Jossey-Bass.

Giardinelli, A. (2012, March 21). Watch: Linguist K. David Harrison launches talking dictionaries for endangered languages. *Swarthmore College News and Events.* Retrieved from http://www.swarthmore.edu/watch-linguist-k-david-harrison-describes-efforts-to-help-endangered-languages-survive.xml

Gibney, A. (2012, July 5). Songs against drilling. *New York Times.* Retrieved from http://www.nytimes.com/2012/07/06/opinion/songs-against-drilling.html?_r=1

Glasser, W. (1998). *Choice theory. A new psychology of personal freedom.* New York: HarperCollins.

Godin, S. (2011). *Linchpin: Are you indisposable?* New York: Portfolio/Penguin.

Godin, S. (2012). *The Icarus deception.* New York: Portfolio/Penguin.

Goldsmith, M., Kaye, B., & Shelton, K. (2000). *Learning journeys: Top management experts share hard-earned lessons on becoming mentors and leaders.* Palo Alto, CA: Davies-Black.

Goodreads.com (2013). *Quotes about examinations.* Retrieved from http://www.goodreads.com/quotes/tag?utf8=%E2%9C%93&id=examinations

Google (2012, April 3). Google goes global with expanded project. *Google Press Release.* Retrieved from https://sites.google.com/a/pressatgoogle.com/art-project/press-release

Gorman, M. (2010, February 28). Welcome back Wordle . . . plus 7 other free word cloud generators. *21st Century Educational Technology and Learning.* Retrieved from http://21centuryedtech.wordpress.com/2010/02/28/waiting-for-wordle-free-word-cloud-options-to-use-now/

Grabinger, R. S., & Dunlap, J. C. (1995). Rich environments for active learning: A definition. *ALT-J, 3*(2), 5–34.

Gross, D. (2012, May 22). Apple's new "spaceship" campus: What will the neighbors say? *CNN Tech.* Retrieved from http://www.cnn.com/2012/05/22/tech/innovation/new-apple-campus/index.html?hpt=hp_bn11

Guertin, L. (no date). *Just-in-Time Teaching (JiTT) warmup activity: Groundwater and archaeology.* Starting Point: Teaching Entry Level Geoscience, Carleton College Science Education Resource Center. Retrieved from http://serc.carleton.edu/introgeo/justintime/examples/groundarch.html

Gunawardena, C. N., & Zittle, F. J. (1997). Social presence as a predictor of satisfaction within a computer-mediated conferencing environment. *American Journal of Distance Education, 11*(3), 8–26.

Hakkarainen, P. (2011). Promoting meaningful learning through video production-supported PBL. *The Interdisciplinary Journal of Problem-Based Learning, 5*(1). Retrieved from http://docs.lib.purdue.edu/cgi/viewcontent.cgi?article=1217&context=ijpbl

Hammad (2012, January 10). 5 online tools to create tag clouds. *Make Tech Easier.* Retrieved July 4, 2012, from http://maketecheasier.com/5-online-tools-to-create-tag-clouds/2012/01/10

Hampton, K. N., & Goulet, L. S., Rainie, L., & Purcell, K. (2011, June 16). *Social Networking Sites and Our Lives, Pew Internet and American Life Project.* Retrieved from http://www.pewinternet.org/2011/06/16/social-networking-sites-and-our-lives/

Hane, P. J. (2007, August 27). PLoS and partners offer video communications with SciVee. *Information Today.* Retrieved from http://newsbreaks.infotoday.com/nbReader.asp?ArticleId=37308

Haq, H. (2011, July 6). In South Korea, all textbooks will be e-books by 2015. *Christian Science Monitor.* Retrieved from http://www.csmonitor.com/Books/chapter-and-verse/2011/0706/In-South-Korea-all-textbooks-will-be-e-books-by-2015

Hara, N., & Kling, R. (2000). Students' distress with a Web-based distance education course. *Information, Communication & Society, 3*(4), 557–579. doi: 10.1080/13691180010002297

Hara, N., Bonk, C. J., & Angeli, C., (2000). Content analyses of on-line discussion in an applied educational psychology course. *Instructional Science, 28*(2), 115–152.

Harris, M. E. (2012, March 19). Revisiting Japan: A year after the tsunami. *KoreAm.* Retrieved from http://iamkoream.com/march-issue-revisiting-japan-a-year-after-the-tsunami/

Hartnett, M., Bhattacharya, M., & Dron, J. (2007). *Diversity in online learners: Searching for differences that may matter.* Advanced Learning Technologies, 2007. ICALT 2007. Seventh IEEE International Conference on Advanced Learning Technologies (ICALT 2007) (pp. 899–900). IEEE Computer Society. Retrieved from http://www.computer.org/csdl/proceedings/icalt/2007/2916/00/29160899.pdf

Hartnett, M., St. George, A., & Dron, J. (2011). Being together: Factors that unintentionally undermine motivation in co-located online learning environments. *Journal of Open, Flexible and Distance Learning, 15*(1), 1–16.

Hattie, J., & Timperley, H. (2000). The power of feedback. *Review of Educational Research, 77*(1), 81–102.

Henry, A. (2011, September 28). Mindbloom is a game that rewards you for living a rich, full life. *Lifehacker*. Retrieved from http://lifehacker.com/5844586/ mindbloom-is-a-game-that-rewards-you-for-living-a-rich-full-life

Henry, A. (2012, January 8). Hive five: Five best goal tracking services. *Lifehacker*. Retrieved from http://lifehacker.com/5873909/five-best-goal-tracking-services

Herbert, M. (2006). Staying the course: A study in online student satisfaction and retention. *Online Journal of Distance Learning Administration, 9*(4). Retrieved from http://fsweb.bainbridge.edu/qep/Files/TeachingRes/Staying%20the%20Course.pdf

Herrington, J., Oliver, R., & Reeves, T. C. (2003). Patterns of engagement in authentic online learning environments. *Australian Journal of Educational Technology, 19*(1), 59–71.

Herrington, J., Reeves, T. C., & Oliver, R. (2006). Authentic tasks online: A synergy among learner, task, and technology. *Distance Education, 27*(2), 233–247. doi:10.1080/01587910600789639

Herrington, J., Reeves, T. C., & Oliver, R. (2010). *A guide to authentic e-learning*. New York: Routledge.

Hidi, S. (1990). Interest and its contribution as a mental resource in learning. *Review of Educational Research, 60*(4), 549–571.

Hillman, D., Willis, D., & Gunawardena, C. (1994). Learner-interface interaction in distance education: An extension of contemporary models and strategies for practitioners. *American Journal of Distance Education, 8*(2), 30–42.

Hiltz, S. R., & Goldman, R. (2005). *Learning together online: Research on asynchronous learning networks*. Mahwah, NJ: Erlbaum.

Hoch, M. (2010, August 2). New estimate puts oil leak at 205 million gallons. *PBS Newshour*. Retrieved from http://www.pbs.org/newshour/rundown/2010/08/ new-estimate-puts-oil-leak-at-49-million-barrels.html

Hodgson, B. (1993). *Key terms and issues in open and distance learning*. London: Kogan Page.

Hotz, R. L. (2012, February 18). Talking the talk, for posterity oral online dictionaries help preserve languages, cultures muted by modernity. *The Wall Street Journal*. Retrieved from http://online.wsj.com/article/SB100014240529702048804045772 28982976760026.html#articleTabs%3Darticle

Howard, C. D. (2011, November). *Video annotated teaching observations: Analyses of asynchronous collaborative viewing*. Paper presented at the annual conference of the Association of Educational Communications and Technology, Jacksonville, FL.

Howard, C. D. (2012, April). *The impact of modeling and staggered participation in video-annotated pre-service teacher discussions*. Paper presented at the annual conference of the American Educational Research Association, Vancouver, BC, Canada.

Howard, C. D., & Myers, R. D. (2010) Creating video-annotated discussions: An asynchronous alternative. *International Journal of Designs for Learning, 1*(1) multimedia. Retrieved from http://scholarworks.iu.edu/journals/index.php/ijdl/ article/view/853/912

Huffington Post (2011, June 24). Ancient Mayan tomb's secrets revealed with tiny camera In Mexico (video). *The Huffington Post*. Retrieved from http://www. huffingtonpost.com/2011/06/24/ancient-mayan-tomb-secrets-mexico-revealed- tiny-camera-_n_884030.html

Hutchins, H. M. (2003). Instructional immediacy and the seven principles: Strategies for facilitating online courses. *Online Journal of Distance Learning Administration, 6*(3). Retrieved from http://www.westga.edu/~distance/ojdla/fall63/hutchins63.html

Hyder, K. (2002). Teach in your pajamas: Becoming a synchronous e-trainer. *The E-Learning Developer's Journal*. Retrieved from http://www.elearningguild.com/pdf/2/112502MGT-H.pdf

Imam, J. (2012, July 27). From families to revolutions: Life "because of the Internet." *CNN Tech*. Retrieved from http://www.cnn.com/2012/07/27/tech/ireport-because-of-the-internet/index.html

Ingram, A. L. (2005). Engagement in online learning communities. In J. Bourne and J. C. Moore (Eds.), *Elements of quality online education: Engaging communities,* Volume 6 in the Sloan-C Series. Needham, MA: Sloan Consortium. Retrieved from http://kentstate.academia.edu/AlbertIngram/Papers/582901/Engagement_in_online_learning_communities

Inhelder, B., & Piaget, J. (1958). *The growth of logical thinking: From childhood to adolescence*. New York: Basic Books.

Isaacson, W. (2011). *Steve Jobs*. New York: Simon & Schuster.

Jaggars, S. S., & Xu, D. (2010). *Online learning in the Virginia community college system*. New York: Columbia University, Teachers College, Community College Research Center. Retrieved from http://ccrc.tc.columbia.edu/media/k2/attachments/online-learning-virginia.pdf

Jarvenpaa, S. L., & Leidner, D. E. (1998). Communication and trust in global virtual teams. *Journal of Computer-Mediated Communication, 3*(4), 1–21. Retrieved from http://onlinelibrary.wiley.com/doi/10.1111/j.1083-6101.1998.tb00080.x/full

Jaschik, S. (2011, July 19). Online and incomplete. *Inside Higher Ed*. Retrieved from http://www.insidehighered.com/news/2011/07/19/study_finds_higher_dropout_rates_for_community_college_students_who_take_online_courses

Johnson, D. W., & Johnson, R. T. (1995). Structuring academic controversy. In S. Sharan (Ed.) *Handbook of cooperative learning methods*. Westport, CT: Greenwood Press.

Johnson, D. W., & Johnson, R. T. (2009). Energizing learning: The instructional power of conflict. *Educational Researcher, 38*(1), 37–51. Retrieved from http://edr.sagepub.com/content/38/1/37.full.pdf+html

Johnson, L., Adams Becker, S., Cummins, M., Estrada, V., Freeman, A., & Ludgate, H. (2013). *NMC Horizon Report: 2013 Higher Education Edition*. Austin, Texas: The New Media Consortium. Retrieved from http://www.nmc.org/pdf/2013-horizon-report-HE.pdf

Johnson, M. (2010, June 11). Seeing is believing: Using video annotation tools to teach and learn. *Teacher with Technology Idea Exchange*. Retrieved from http://ttix.org/archives/2010-sessions/seeing-is-believing-effectively-using-video-annotations-tools-to-teach-and-learn/

Jonassen, D. H. (1994). Thinking technology: Toward a constructivist design model. *Educational Technology, 34*(4), 34–37.

Jones, J. B. (2012, April 4). Using Xtranormal against straw men. *Chronicle of Higher Education*. Retrieved from http://chronicle.com/blogs/profhacker/using-xtranormal-against-straw-men/39348

Jukes, I., McCain, T., & Crockett, L. (2010). *Understanding the digital generation: Teaching and learning in the new digital landscape*. Vancouver, BC: 21st Century Fluency Project.

Jun, J. (2005). Understanding E-dropout? *International Journal on E-Learning, 4*(2), 229–240.

Junco, R., Heibergert, G., & Loken, E. (2010). The effect of Twitter on college student engagement and grades. *Journal of Computer Assisted Learning, 27*(2), 119–132. Retrieved from http://onlinelibrary.wiley.com/doi/10.1111/j.1365-2729.2010.00387.x/pdf

Kaplan, D. A. (2010, August 10). Bill Gates' favorite teacher. *CNN Money.* Retrieved from http://money.cnn.com/2010/08/23/technology/sal_khan_academy.fortune/index.htm

Kawachi, P. (2002). How to initiate intrinsic motivation in the on-line student. In V. Phillips, B. Elwert, L. Hitch, & C. Yager (Eds.), *Motivating & retaining adult learners online—virtual university gazette* (pp. 46–61). Vermont: GetEducated.com.

Keller, J. (1983). Motivational design in instruction. In C. Reigeluth (Ed.), *Instructional-design theories and models: An overview of their current status* (pp. 383–434). Hillsdale, NJ: Erlbaum.

Keller, J. M. (1987). The systematic process of motivational design. *Performance and Instruction, 26(9),* 1–8.

Keller, J. M. (1999). Using the ARCS motivational process in computer-based instruction and distance education. *New Directions for Teaching and Learning, 1999*(78), 37–47.

Keller, J. M. (2010). *Motivational design for learning and performance: The ARCS model approach.* New York: Springer.

Keller, J., & Suzuki, K. (2004). Learner motivation and E-learning design: A multi-nationally validated process. *Journal of Educational Media, 29*(3), 229–239 doi:10.1080/1358165042000283084

Kelsey, K. D., & D'souza, A. (2004). Student motivation for learning at a distance: Does interaction matter? *Online Journal of Distance Learning Administration, 7*(2). Retrieved from http://www.westga.edu/~distance/ojdla/summer72/kelsey72.html

Kember, D. (1989). A longitudinal-process model of drop-out from distance education. *The Journal of Higher Education, 60*(3), 278–301.

Kember, D., Ho, A., & Hong, C. (2008). The importance of establishing relevance in motivating student learning. *Active Learning in Higher Education, 9*(3), 249–263. doi:10.1177/1469787408095849

Kessler, S. (2010, October 7). Six free sites for creating your own animations. *Mashable.* Retrieved from http://mashable.com/2010/10/27/create-animations-online/

Khoo, E., & Cowie, B. (2011). A framework for developing and implementing an online learning community. *Journal of Open, Flexible and Distance Learning, 15*(1), 47–59. Retrieved from http://journals.akoaotearoa.ac.nz/index.php/JOFDL/article/viewFile/12/15

Khoo, E. & Forret, M. (2011). Evaluating an online learning community: Intellectual, social and emotional development and transformations. *Waikato Journal of Education, 16*(1), 123–142.

Khoo, E. G. L. (2005). Extricating the Web of learning: The case for learning communities. In C.-K. Looi, D. Jonassen, & M. Ikeda (Eds.), *Proceedings of the 13th International Conference on Computers in Education (ICCE2005)* (Towards Sustainable and Scalable Educational Innovations Informed by the Learning Sciences, Volume 133, Frontiers in Artificial Intelligence and Applications, pp. 736–739). Amsterdam, The Netherlands: IOS Press.

Khoo, E. G. L. (2010). *Developing an online learning community: A strategy for improving lecturer and student learning experiences.* Unpublished doctoral dissertation, University of Waikato, Hamilton, New Zealand. Retrieved from http://researchcommons.waikato.ac.nz/handle/10289/3961

Khoo, E., & Cowie, B. (2011). Cycles of negotiation and reflection: A negotiated intervention approach to promote online teacher development and transformations. *Educational Action Research Journal, 19*(3), 345–361.

Khoo, E., & Forret, M. (2011). Evaluating an online learning community: Intellectual, social and emotional development and transformations. *Waikato Journal of Education, 16*(1), 123–142.

Khoo, E., Forret, M., & Cowie, B. (2010). Lecturer-student views on successful online learning environments. *Waikato Journal of Education, 15*(3), 17–34.

Kim, K.-J. (2009). Motivational challenges of adult learners in self-directed e-learning. *Journal of Interactive Learning Research, 20*(3), 317–335.

Kim, K.-J., & Bonk, C. J. (2006). The future of online teaching and learning in higher education: The survey says . . . . *Educause Quarterly, 29*(4), 22–30. Retrieved from http://www.educause.edu/ero/article/future-online-teaching-and-learning-higher-education-survey-says%E2%80%A6

Kim, K.-J., & Frick, T. W. (2011). Changes in student motivation during online learning. *Journal of Educational Computing Research, 44*(1), 1–23.

Kim, P., Higashi, T., Gonzales, I., Carillo, L., Gàrate, A., & Lee, B. (2011). Socioeconomic strata, mobile technology, and education: A comparative analysis. *Educational Technology Research & Development, 59*(4), 465–486.

Klein, J. (2010, Winter). The World Affairs Challenge. *ICOSA Magazine.* Retrieved from http://www.theicosamagazine.com/the-world-affairs-challenge

Klein, J. (2012). Taking your schoolhouse global: The role of professional development in shifting school culture. *NSSSA Leader, 26*(1), 16–18, 27–29. Retrieved from https://www.box.com/s/da5fbb22f8a5fe9b620c

Koebler, J. (2011, May 27). America's most popular online teacher. *U.S. News and World Report.* Retrieved from http://www.usnews.com/mobile/blogs/high-school-notes/2011/5/27/americas-most-popular-online-teacher.html

Koebler, J. (2011, October 17). Teens take studying online. *U.S. News and World Report: High School Notes.* Retrieved from http://www.usnews.com/education/blogs/high-school-notes/2011/10/17/teens-take-studying-online

Koike, H., Ishikawa, T., Akama, K., Chiba, M., & Miura, K. (2005). Developing an e-learning system which enhances students' academic motivation. *Proceedings of the 33rd annual ACM SIGUCCS fall conference* (pp. 147–150). doi:10.1145/1099435.1099468

Koller, D., Ng, A., Do, C., & Chen, Z. (2013, June 3). Retention and intention in massive open online courses: In depth. *EDUCAUSE Review Online.* Retrieved from http://www.educause.edu/ero/article/retention-and-intention-massive-open-online-courses-depth-0

Kolowich, S. (2010, September 7). Editing, enhancing Wikipedia becomes project at colleges. *USA Today.* Retrieved from http://www.usatoday.com/news/education/2010-09-07-IHE-wikipedia-college-project08_ST_N.htm

Kolowich, S. (2013a, May 9). As MOOC debate simmers at San Jose State, American U. calls a halt. *The Chronicle of Higher Education.* Retrieved from http://chronicle.com/article/As-MOOC-Debate-Simmers-at-San/139147/

Kolowich, S. (2013b, May 6). Faculty backlash grows against online partnerships. *The Chronicle of Higher Education*. Retrieved from http://chronicle.com/article/Faculty-Backlash-Grows-Against/139049/

Kolowich, S. (2014, January 15). Doubts about MOOCs continue to climb, survey finds. *The Chronicle of Higher Education*. Retrieved from http://chronicle.com/article/Doubts-About-MOOCs-Continue-to/144007/

Kop, R., Fournier, H., & Mak, J. S. F. (2011, November). A pedagogy of abundance or a pedagogy to support human beings? Participant support on massive open online courses. *International Review of Research on Open and Distance Learning (IRRODL), 12*(7). Retrieved from http://www.irrodl.org/index.php/irrodl/article/view/1041/2025

Korey, A. (2009, April 26). Historyteachers videos in the classroom: Interview with Amy Burvall. *Art Trav History*. Retrieved from http://www.arttrav.com/conversations/historyteachers-videos-classroom/

Koschmann, T. (Ed.). (1996). *CSCL: Theory and practice of an emerging paradigm*. Mahwah, NJ: Erlbaum.

Kuh, G. D. (2003). What we're learning about student engagement from NSSE. *Change, 35*(2), 24–32.

Kuh, G. D. (2009a). The National Survey of Student Engagement: Conceptual and empirical foundations. In R. Gonyea and G. Kuh (Eds.), *Using student engagement data in institutional research, New Directions for Institutional Research*, No. 141. San Francisco: Jossey-Bass.

Kuh, G. D. (2009b). What student affairs professionals need to know about student engagement. *Journal of College Student Development, 50*(6), 683–706.

Kuh, G. D., Cruce, T. M., Shoup, R., Kinzie, J., & Gonyea, R. M. (2008). Unmasking the effects of student engagement on first-year college grades and persistence. *The Journal of Higher Education, 79*(5), 540–563.

Kulp, R. (1999). *Effective collaboration in corporate distributed learning: Ten best practices for curriculum owners, developers and instructors*. Chicago: IBM Learning Services.

Lambert, N., & McCombs, B. L. (Eds.). (1998). *How students learn: Reforming schools through learner-centered education*. Washington, DC: American Psychological Association.

Lapadat, J. C. (2002). Written interaction: A key component in online learning. *Journal of Computer-Mediated Communication, 7*(4). Retrieved from http://onlinelibrary.wiley.com/doi/10.1111/j.1083-6101.2002.tb00158.x/full

Lauby, S. (2012, June 15). The evolution of gamification in the workplace. *Mashable*. Retrieved from http://mashable.com/2012/06/15/gamification-business-evolution/

Lave, J., & Wenger, E. (1991). *Situated learning: Legitimate peripheral participation*. New York: Cambridge University Press.

Lee, M. (2007). "Making it relevant": A rural teacher's integration of an international studies program. *Intercultural Education, 18*(2), 147–159.

Lee, M. M. (2010). "We are so over pharaohs and pyramids!" *Re*-presenting the *othered* lives. *International Journal of Qualitative Studies in Education, 23*(6), 737–754.

Lee, M. M., & Bonk, C. J. (2013). Through the words of experts: Cases of expanded classrooms using conferencing technology. *Language Perspectives and Facts, 31*, 107–137.

Lee, M., & Hutton, D. (2007, August). Using interactive videoconferencing technology for global awareness: The case of ISIS. *International Journal of Instructional Technology and Distance Learning, 4*(8). Retrieved from: http://www.itdl.org/Journal/Aug_07/article01.htm

Lee, S. H., Magjuka, R. J., Liu, X., & Bonk, C. J. (2006). Interactive technologies for effective collaborative learning. *International Journal of Instructional Technology and Distance Learning. 3*(6), 17–32. Retrieved from http://www.itdl.org/Journal/Jun_06/article02.htm

Lee, Y., Choi, J., & Kim, T. (2012). Discriminating factors between completers of and dropouts from online learning courses. *British Journal of Educational Technology, 44*(2), 328–337. Retrieved from http://dx.doi.org/10.1111/j.1467-8535.2012.01306.x. doi: 10.1111/j.1467-8535.2012.01306.x

Lepper, M. R., & Hodell, M. (1989). Intrinsic motivation in the classroom. *Research on motivation in education, 3,* 73–105.

Liang, M. Y., & Bonk, C. J. (2009). Interaction in blended EFL learning: Principles and practices. *International Journal of Instructional Technology & Distance Learning, 6*(1), 3–15. Retrieved from http://www.itdl.org/journal/jan_09/article01.htm

Lindsay, J., & Davis, V. A. (2013). *Flattening classrooms, engaging minds: Move to Global collaboration one step at a time.* Boston: Pearson.

Liu, X., Lee, S. H., Bonk, C. J., Magjuka, R. J., & Liu, S. (2008). Technology use in an online MBA program: Issues, trends and opportunities. In Kidd, T. & Song, H. (Eds.), *Handbook of Research on Instructional Systems and Technology* (pp. 614–630). Hershey, PA: Information Science Reference.

Living Tongues Institute for Endangered Languages (2013). *Mission statement.* Retrieved from http://www.livingtongues.org/

Lloyd, J. (2012, January 26). New USDA climate zone map reflects northward warming trends. *USA Today.* Retrieved from http://www.usatoday.com/news/nation/environment/story/2012-01-26/USDA-climate-zone-map/52787142/1

Longview Foundation (2008). *Teacher preparation for the global age: The imperative for change.* Longview Foundation for World Affairs and International Understanding, Silver Spring, MD. Retrieved from http://www.longviewfdn.org/files/44.pdf

Maddrell, J. (2008, June 25). The effect of backchannel Interactions on cognitive load. *Scribd.* Retrieved from http://www.scribd.com/doc/3727549/Backchannel-Research-Paper-Jennifer-Maddrell

Maehr, M. L. (1984). Meaning and motivation: Toward a theory of personal involvement. In R. Ames & C. Ames (Eds.), *Research on motivation in education: Student motivation* (pp. 115–143). Orlando: Academic Press.

Makice, K. (2012, April 13). Flipping the classroom requires more than video. *Wired/Geek Dad Blog.* Retrieved from http://www.wired.com/geekdad/2012/04/flipping-the-classroom/

Malone, T. W. (1981). Toward a theory of intrinsically motivating instruction. *Cognitive Science, 4,* 333–369.

Markoff, J. (2011, August 15). Virtual and artificial, but 58,000 want course. *New York Times.* Retrieved from http://www.nytimes.com/2011/08/16/science/16stanford.html?_r=1

Martini, N., Harrison, J., & Bennett, R. (2009). Creating waves across geographical and disciplinary divides through online creative collaboration. In A. T. Ragusa (Ed.), *Interaction in communication technologies & virtual learning environments, human factors* (pp. 9–25.). Hershey, PA: IGI Global.

Maslow, A. H. (1987). *Motivation and personality* (3rd ed.). New York: Harper and Row.

Massive Open Online Course (2011). *Wikipedia.* Retrieved from http://en.wikipedia. org/wiki/Massive_open_online_course

Mayer, R. E. (2001). *Multimedia learning.* New York: Cambridge University Press.

Mayer, R. E. (2003). Theories of learning and their application to technology. In H. F. O'Neil & R. S. Perez (Eds.). *Technology applications in education: A learning view* (pp. 127–157). Mahwah, NJ: Erlbaum.

McCombs, B. L., & Pope, J. E. (1994). *Motivating hard to reach students.* Washington, DC: American Psychological Association.

Mello, R. (2002). 100 pounds of potatoes in a 25-pound sack: Stress, frustration, and learning in the virtual classroom. *Teaching with Technology Today, 8*(9). Retrieved from http://www.wisconsin.edu/ttt/articles/mello.htm

Merrill, D. M. (2002). First principles of instruction. *Educational Technology Research and Development, 50*(3), 43–59.

Merryfield, M. M. (2003). Like a veil: Cross-cultural experiential learning online. *Contemporary Issues in Technology and Teacher Education* [Online serial], *3*(2). Retrieved from http://www.citejournal.org/vol3/iss2/socialstudies/article1.cfm

Merryfield, M. M. (2007). The Web and teachers' decision-making in global education. *Theory and Research in Social Education, 35*(2), 256–276.

Merryfield, M. M. (2008). The challenge of globalization: Preparing teachers for a global age. *Teacher Education & Practice, 21*(4), 434–437.

Merryfield, M. M., & Kasai, M. (2009). How are teachers responding to globalization? In Walter Parker (Ed.), *Social Studies Today: Research and Practice* (pp. 165–173). New York: Routledge.

Meskill, C. (2005). Triadic scaffolds: Tools for teaching English language learners with computers. *Language Learning and Technology, 8*(4), 46–59.

Meyerson, D., Weick, K. E., & Kramer, R. M. (1996). Swift trust and temporary groups. In M. Kramer & T.R. Tyler (Eds.), *Trust in organizations: Frontiers of theory and research* (pp. 166–195). Thousand Oaks, CA: Sage.

Miller, A. (2012, January13). Gamification vs. game based learning in education. *Gamification Company Blog.* Retrieved from http://gamification.co/2012/01/13/gamification-vs-game-based-learning-in-education/

Miller, C., Veletsianos, G., & Doering, A. (2008). Curriculum at forty below: A phenomenological inquiry of an educator/explorer's experience with adventure learning in the Arctic. *Distance Education, 29*(3), 253–267.

Miller, L. M., Chang, C.-I., Wang, S., Beier, M. E., & Klisch, Y. (2011). Learning and motivational impacts of a multimedia science game. *Computers & Education, 57*(1), 1425–1433. doi:10.1016/j.compedu.2011.01.016

Minenko, A. (2012). How MOODLE "ladders," flipped classroom and "change up" created value-added redesign in a medical school. In A. H. Duin, E. A. Nater, & F. X. Anklesaria (Eds.), *Cultivating change in the academy: 50+ stories from the digital frontlines at the University of Minnesota in 2012.* Retrieved from http://conservancy.umn.edu/handle/125273

Mintz, J. (2008, June 29). Gates bids farewell to fulltime work at Microsoft with tears. *USA Today.* Retrieved from http://www.usatoday.com/tech/techinvestor/corporatenews/2008-06-27-gates-microsoft-goodbye_N.htm

MIT (2011). *Sloan School of Management, generating business value from information technology.* MIT OpenCourseWare. Retrieved from http://ocw.mit.edu/courses/sloan-school-of-management/15-571-generating-business-value-from-information-technology-spring-2009/

Monaghan, P. (2011, July 10). Anthropologist puts an Idaho museum's many bones within virtual reach. *Chronicle of Higher Education*. Retrieved from http://chronicle.com/article/Anthropologist-Puts-Idaho/128170/

Montessori, M. (1912). *The Montessori method*. Translated by Anne Everett George. New York: Frederick A. Stokes. Retrieved from http://digital.library.upenn.edu/women/montessori/method/method.html

Moore, M. G. (1989). Three types of interaction. *American Journal of Distance Education, 3*(2), 1–7. Retrieved from http://www.ajde.com/Contents/vol3_2.htm#editorial

Moore, M. G., & Kearsley, G. (1996). *Distance education: A systems view*. Boston: Wadsworth.

Moran, M., Seaman, J., & Tinti-Kane, H. (2011, April). *Teaching, learning, and sharing: How today's higher education faculty use social media*. Pearson Learning Solutions and Babson Survey Research Group. Retrieved from http://www.pearsonlearningsolutions.com/educators/pearson-social-media-survey-2011-bw.pdf

Moreno, R., & Mayer, R. (1999). Cognitive principles of multimedia learning: The role of modality and contiguity. *Journal of Educational Psychology, 91*, 358–368.

Moreno, R., & Mayer, R. (2007). Interactive multimodal learning environments. *Educational Psychology Review, 19*(3), 309–326.

Moskowitz, C. (2012, February 18). Talking dictionaries document endangered languages. *MSNBC*. Retrieved from http://www.msnbc.msn.com/id/46437964/ns/technology_and_science-science/t/talking-dictionaries-document-endangered-languages/

Mukherjee, D. (2011, March 18). Screencast—get it & flaunt it. *Technology personalized*. Retrieved from http://techpp.com/2011/03/18/screencasting-tools/

Murday, K., Ushida, E., & Chenoweth, N. A. (2008). Learners' and teachers' perspectives on language online. *Computer Assisted Language Learning, 21*(2), 125–142.

National Geographic News (2009, May 19). "Missing Link" found: New fossil links humans, lemurs? *National Geographic News*. Retrieved from http://news.nationalgeographic.com/news/2009/05/090519-missing-link-found.html

National Survey of Student Engagement (2006). *Engaged learning: Fostering success for all learners. Annual Report 2006*. Bloomington: Indiana University Center for Postsecondary Research.

Novak, G. M. (2000). Just-in-time teaching: Blending active learning with Web technology. In D. G. Brown (Ed.), *Teaching with technology: Seventy-five professors from eight universities tell their stories* (pp. 59–62). Boston: Anker.

O'Shea, P, M., Baker, P. B., Allen, D. W., Curry-Corcoran, D. E., & Allen, D. B. (2007). New levels of student participatory learning: A wikitext for the introductory course in education. *Journal of Interactive Online Learning, 6*(3). Retrieved from http://www.ncolr.org/jiol/issues/pdf/6.3.5.pdf

Paivio, A. (1986). *Mental representations: A dual coding approach*. New York: Oxford University Press.

Paivio, A. (1991). Dual coding theory: Retrospect and current status. *Canadian Journal of Psychology, 45*, 255–287.

Palloff, R. M., & Pratt, K. (2007). *Building online learning communities: Effective strategies for the virtual classroom*. San Francisco: Jossey Bass.

Pan, G., Sen, S., Starett, D., Bonk, C. J., Rodgers, M., Tikoo, M., & Powell, D. (2012). Instructor-made videos as a learner scaffolding tool: A case study. *Journal of Online Learning and Teaching, 8*(4), 298–311. Retrieved from http://jolt.merlot.org/vol8no4/pan_1212.htm

Papert, S. (1980). *Mindstorms: Children, computers, and powerful ideas*. New York: Basic Books (Harper-Collins).

Papert, S. (1993). *The children's machine: Rethinking school in the age of the computer*. New York: Basic Books.

Park, J. H. (2007). *Factors related to learner dropout in online learning. Online Submission* (p. 8). Presented at the Paper presented at the International Research Conference in The Americas of the Academy of Human Resource Development (Indianapolis, IN, Feb. 28–Mar. 4, 2007). Retrieved from http://eric.ed.gov/PDFS/ED504556.pdf

Park. H., & Baek, Y. (2010). Empirical evidence and practical cases for using virtual worlds in educational contexts. In H. H. Yang, & S. C-Y. Yuen (Eds.), *Collective intelligence and e-learning 2.0: Implications of Web-based communities and networking* (pp. 228–247). Hershey, PA: Information Science Reference.

Parker, A. (2003). Motivation and incentives for distance faculty. *Online Journal of Distance Learning Administration, 6*(3). Retrieved from http://www.westga.edu/~distance/ojdla/fall63/parker63.htm

Parry, D. (2008). Twitter for academic. *Academhack*. Retrieved from http://academhack.outsidethetext.com/home/2008/twitter-for-academia/

Parry, M. (2010, September). Preventing online dropouts: Does anything work? *The Chronicle of Higher Education*. Retrieved from http://chronicle.com/blogAuthor/Wired-Campus/5/Marc-Parry/89/

Parry, M. (2011, January 11). So you think an English professor's life is just a cartoon. *Chronicle of Higher Education*. Retrieved from http://chronicle.com/article/So-You-Think-an-English/125954/

Parry, M. (2011, July 21). U. of Illinois at Springfield offers new "Massive Open Online Course." *Chronicle of Higher Education*. Retrieved from http://chronicle.com/blogs/wiredcampus/u-of-illinois-at-springfield-offers-new-massive-open-online-course/31853

Pea, R. D. (1996). Seeing what we build together: Distributed multimedia learning environments for transformative communications. In T. Koschmann (Ed.), *CSCL: Theory and practice of an emerging paradigm* (pp. 171–186). Mahwah, NJ: Erlbaum.

Pea, R. D., Kurland, D., & Hawkins, J. (1985). Logo and the development of thinking skills. In Chen, M., and Paisley, W. (Eds.), *Children and microcomputers*. Beverly Hills, CA: Sage.

Perkins, D (1992). *Smart schools: From training memories to educating minds*. New York: The Free Press.

Peters, L. (2009). *Global education: Using technology to bring the world to your students*. Washington, D.C.: International Society for Technology in Education.

Phipps, R. A., & Merisotis, J. P. (2000, April 28). *Quality on the line: Benchmarks for success in Internet-based distance education*. Washington, DC: The Institute for Higher Education Policy. Retrieved from http://www.ihep.org/assets/files/publications/m-r/QualityOnTheLine.pdf

Piaget, J. (1926). *The language and thought of the child*. New York: Harcourt Brace.

Piaget, J. (1963). *The origins of intelligence in children*. New York: Norton.

Piaget, J. (1969). *Psychology of intelligence*. New York: Littlefield, Adams.

Picciano, A. G., & Seaman, J. (2008). *K–12 online learning: A 2008 follow-up of the survey of US school district administrators*. Retrieved from http://sloanconsortium.org/sites/default/files/k-12_online_learning_2008.pdf

Pink, D. H. (2009). *Drive: The surprising truth about what motivates us.* New York: Riverhead Books.

Pintrich, P. R., & DeGroot, E. (1990). Motivational and self-regulated learning components of classroom academic performance. *Journal of Educational Psychology, 82,* 33–40.

Pintrich, P. R., & Schunk, D. H. (1996). *Motivation in education: Theory, research, and applications.* Englewood Cliffs, NJ: Merrill.

Pogue, D. (2011, October 11). New iPhone conceals sheer magic. *New York Times.* Retrieved from http://www.nytimes.com/2011/10/12/technology/personaltech/iphone-4s-conceals-sheer-magic-pogue.html?pagewanted=all

Poulos, K. (2013, February 22). Google Glass—what would you do with it? *In Crowd Blog.* Retrieved from http://www.incrowdnow.com/2013/02/google-glass-what-would-you-do-with-it/

Project Tomorrow and Blackboard Inc. (2009, June 30). *Learning in the 21st century: 2009 trends update.* Retrieved from http://www.tomorrow.org/speakup/learning21Report_2009_Update.html

Project Tomorrow and Blackboard Inc. (2011, June 28). *Learning in the 21st century: 2011 trends update.* Retrieved from http://www.blackboard.com/Markets/K-12/Learn-for-K12/Leadership-Views/Education-in-the-21st-Century.aspx (Note: must register for report)

Purdy, K. (2012, April 18). Track thyself: Quantify your life for productivity, fun. *Fast Company,* Retrieved from http://www.fastcompany.com/1833871/track-thyself-quantify-your-life-productivity-fun

Qasem, A. (2012, April 2). Using Piazza to encourage interaction. *Chronicle of Higher Education.* Retrieved from http://chronicle.com/blogs/profhacker/using-piazza-to-encourage-interaction/39317?sid=wc&utm_source=wc&utm_medium=en

Raffini, J. P. (1996). *150 ways to increase intrinsic motivation in the classroom.* Boston: Allyn & Bacon.

Raman, S., Shackelford, J., & Sosin, K. (2002, January 5). *Just-in-Time Syllabus.* Poster session at the American Economic Association Poster Session: Teaching techniques that promote active learning, Atlanta, Georgia.

Randerson, J. (2009, May 19). Fossil Ida: Extraordinary find is "missing link" in human evolution. *The Guardian.* Retrieved from http://www.guardian.co.uk/science/2009/may/19/ida-fossil-missing-link

Rasmussen, K. L., Nichols, J. C., & Ferguson, F. (2006). It's a new world: Multiculturalism in a virtual environment. *Distance Education, 27*(2), 265–278.

Ray, M. (2004). *The highest goal: The secret that sustains you in every moment.* San Francisco: Berrett-Koehler.

Reeve, J. M. (1996). *Motivating others: Nurturing inner motivational resources.* Needham Heights, MA: Allyn & Bacon.

Reeves, T. C. (2006). How do you know they are learning? The importance of alignment in higher education. *International Journal of Learning Technology, 2*(4), 294–309.

Reinhardt, W., Ebner, M., Behan, G., & Costa, C. (2009). How people are using Twitter during conferences. In Hornung-Prähauser, V., Luckmann, M. (Eds.), *Creativity and innovation competencies on Web. Proceeding of 5.* EduMedia Conference, 145–156, Salzburg.

Reiss, S. (2004). Multifaceted nature of intrinsic motivation: The theory of 16 basic desires. *Review of Cognitive Psychology, 8*(3), 179–193.

Richardson, J. C., & Newby, T. (2006). The role of students' cognitive engagement in online learning. *The American Journal of Distance Education, 20*(1), 23–37.

Riel, M. (1993). Global education through learning circles. In L. Harasim, (Ed.), *Global networks* (pp. 221–236), Cambridge, MA: MIT Press.

Riel, M. (1996). Cross-classroom collaboration: communication and education. In T. Koschmann (Ed.), *CSCL: Theory and practice of an emerging paradigm* (pp. 187–207). Mahwah, NJ: Erlbaum.

Rivard, R. (2013, June 19). MOOC-skeptical provosts. *Inside Higher Education.* Retrieved from http://www.insidehighered.com/news/2013/06/19/big-10-provosts-question-partnerships-ed-tech-companies

Rivard, R. (2013, May 8). Measuring the MOOC dropout rate. *Inside Higher Education.* Retrieved from http://www.insidehighered.com/news/2013/03/08/researchers-explore-who-taking-moocs-and-why-so-many-drop-out

Robinson, K., & Aronica, L. (2013). *Finding your element: How to discover your talents and passions and transform your life.* New York: Viking.

Rogers, C. R. (1969). *Freedom to learn: A view of what education might become.* Columbus, OH: Charles Merrill.

Rogers, C. R. (1983). *Freedom to learn for the 80s.* Columbus, OH: Charles E. Merrill.

Rogoff, B. (1990). *Apprenticeship in thinking: Cognitive development in social context.* New York: Oxford University Press.

Rogoff, B. (2003). *The cultural nature of human development.* Oxford, UK: Oxford University Press.

Rourke, L., Andersen, T., Garrison, D. R., & Archer, W. (1999). Assessing social presence in asynchronous text-based computer conferencing. *Journal of Distance Education, 14*(2), 50–71. Retrieved from http://www.jofde.ca/index.php/jde/article/viewArticle/153/341

Rovai, A. P. (2003). In search of higher persistence rates in distance education online programs. *The Internet and Higher Education, 6*(1), 1–16.

Rowe, A. (2009, July 12). Top ten scientific music videos (Weird Science). *Wired.* Retrieved http://www.wired.com/wiredscience/2009/07/sciencemusic/

Ryan, R. M., & Deci, E. L. (2000). Self-determination theory and the facilitation of intrinsic motivation, social development, and well-being. *American Psychologist, 55*, 68–78. Retrieved from http://www.psych.rochester.edu/SDT/documents/2006_RyanDeci_Self-RegulationProblemofHumanAutonomy.pdf

Salmon, G. (2011). *E-moderating: The key to teaching and learning online* (3rd ed.). New York and London: Routledge.

Salmon, G. (2013). *e-Tivities: The key to active online learning* (2nd ed). New York: Routledge.

Salomon, G. (1993). No distribution without individuals' cognition: A dynamic interactional view. In G. Salomon (Ed.), *Distributed cognitions: Psychological and educational considerations* (pp. 111–138). Cambridge, UK: Cambridge University Press.

Sams, A., & Bennett, B. (2012, May 31). The truth about flipped learning. *eSchool News.* Retrieved from http://www.eschoolnews.com/2012/05/31/the-truth-about-flipped-learning/

Sankar, P. (2011, September 27). Former Facebook engineer launches EduTech startup Piazza. *Women 2.0.* Retrieved from http://women2.com/former-facebook-engineer-launches-edutech-startup-piazza/

Savery, J. R., & Duffy, T. M. (1995). Problem-based learning: An instructional model and its constructivist framework. In B. Wilson (Ed.), *Constructivist learning environments: Case studies in instructional design* (pp. 135–148), Englewood Cliffs, NJ: Educational Technology Publications.

Savignon, S. J., & Roithmeier, W. (2004). Computer-mediated communication: Texts and strategies. *CALICO Journal, 21*(2), 265–290.

Schifter, C. (2002). Perception differences about participating in distance education. *Online Journal of Distance Learning Administration, 5*(1), 1–14. Retrieved from http://www.westga.edu/%7Edistance/ojdla/spring51/schifter51.html

Schrage, M. (1990). *Share minds: The technologies of collaboration.* New York: Random House.

Schroeder, S. (2010, December 24). "CityVille" is now bigger than "Farmville." *Mashable.* Retrieved from http://mashable.com/2010/12/24/cityville-bigger-farmville/

Schrum, L. M. (1991). *Telecommunications: Working to enhance global understanding and world peace.* Paper presented at the American Educational Research Association annual convention, Chicago, IL.

Schunk, D. H. (2008). *Learning theories: An educational perspective.* Upper Saddle River, NJ: Pearson Merrill Prentice Hall.

Schunk, D. H., Pintrich, P. R., & Meece, J. L. (2008). *Motivation in education: Theory, research, and applications* (3rd ed.). Upper Saddle River, NJ: Pearson Merrill Prentice Hall.

Scott, T., Cole, M., & Engel, M. (1992). Computers and education: A cultural constructivist perspective. *Review of Research in Education, 18,* 191–251.

Selman, R. L. (1980). *The growth of interpersonal understanding: Developmental and clinical analysis.* New York: Academic Press.

Seol, S. (2012). *SMILE (Stanford Mobile Inquiry-based Learning Environment).* Seeds of Empowerment. Palo Alto, CA.

Shahid, A. (2011, March 11). Tsunami, earthquake rock Japan: A look at world's most powerful earthquakes and tsunamis. *New York Daily News.* Retrieved from http://articles.nydailynews.com/2011-03-11/news/28699750_1_86-magnitude-quake-tsunami-earthquake-hits

Sheffield, B. (2008, July 7). Nolan Bushnell: What the game industry misses. *Gamasutra.* Retrieved from http://www.gamasutra.com/view/feature/3717/nolan_bushnell_what_the_game_.php

Shieh, D. (2009). These lectures are gone in 60 seconds. *The Chronicle of Higher Education.* Retrieved from http://chronicle.com/article/These-Lectures-Are-Gone-in-60/19924

Shontell, A. (2012, February 5). 14 incredible women to watch in Silicon Valley. *Business Insider.* Retrieved from http://www.businessinsider.com/14-incredible-women-to-watch-in-silicon-valley-2012-2?op=1

Shroff, R. H., Vogel, D. R., Coombes, J., & Lee, F. (2007). Student e-learning intrinsic motivation: A qualitative analysis. *Communications of the Association for Information Systems, 19*(1), 241–260.

Siegchrist, G. (2012). How to make a documentary. *About.com.* Retrieved from http://desktopvideo.about.com/od/homevideoprojects/ht/How-To-Produce-A-Documentary.htm

Simpson, O. (2004). The impact on retention of interventions to support distance learning students. *Open Learning, 19*(1), 79–95.

Singer, J., Marx, R. W., Krajcik, J., & Chambers, J. C. (2000). Constructing extended inquiry projects: Curriculum materials for science education reform. *Educational Psychologist, 35*(3), 165–178.

Singh, S., Singh, A., & Singh, K. (2012). Motivation levels among traditional and open learning undergraduate students in India. *The International Review of Research in Open and Distance Learning, 13*(3), 19–40.

Skinner, B. F. (1938). *The behavior of organisms: An experimental analysis*. Englewood Cliffs, NJ: Prentice-Hall.

Smith, A. (2010, July 7). Mobile access 2010. *Pew Internet & American Life Project*. Retrieved from http://www.pewinternet.org/~/media//Files/Reports/2010/PIP_Mobile_Access_2010.pdf

Smith, D. (2011). Gaddafi threatens attacks in Europe. *The Guardian*. Retrieved from http://www.guardian.co.uk/world/2011/jul/08/gaddafi-threat-to-attack-europe

Snider, M. (2012, July 30). Businesses use game principles in marketing. *USA Today*. Retrieved from http://www.usatoday.com/money/smallbusiness/story/2012-07-29/efficient-small-business-using-game-technology/56545082/1

Song, S. H., & Keller, J. M. (2001). Effectiveness of motivationally adaptive computer-assisted instruction on the dynamic aspects of motivation. *Educational Technology Research and Development, 49*(2), 5–22.

Soo, K. S., & Bonk, C. J. (1998, June). *Interaction: What does it mean in online distance education*. Paper presented at Ed-Media & Ed-Telecom 98, Freiberg, Germany. (ERIC Document Reproduction Service No ED 428724)

Stansbury, M. (2012, June 26). ISTE 2012: Educators seek the brass ring of student engagement. *eSchool News*. Retrieved from http://www.eschoolnews.com/2012/06/26/iste-2012-educators-seek-the-brass-ring-of-student-engagement/

Stipek, D. J. (1998). *Motivation to learn: From theory to practice* (3rd ed.). Boston: Allyn & Bacon.

Strauss, V. (2010, December 30). Learning the French Revolution with Lady Gaga: Teachers sing history lessons. *The Washington Post*. Retrieved from http://voices.washingtonpost.com/answer-sheet/arts-education/learning-the-french-revolution.html

Sugar, W. A., & Bonk, C. J. (1998). Student role play in the World Forum: Analyses of an Arctic learning apprenticeship. In C. J. Bonk, & K. S. King (Eds.), *Electronic collaborators: Learner-centered technologies for literacy, apprenticeship, and discourse* (pp. 131–155). Mahwah, NJ: Erlbaum.

Svinicki, M. D. (1999). New directions in learning and motivation. *New Directions for Teaching and Learning, 1999*(80), 5–27. doi:10.1002/tl.8001

Swan, K. (2001). Virtual interaction: Design factors affecting student satisfaction and perceived learning in asynchronous online courses. *Distance Education, 22*(2), 306–331.

Swartz, J. (2011, July 7). Facebook says membership has grown to 750 million. *USA Today*. Retrieved from http://www.usatoday.com/tech/news/2011-07-06-facebook-skype-growth_n.htm

Swartz, J. (2012, June 4). How women are changing the tech world. *USA Today*. Retrieved from http://www.usatoday.com/tech/news/story/2012-06-04/female-tech-executives/55382536/1

Teng, L. Y.-W. (2008, May). Students' backgrounds and behaviors in a Web-assisted learning environment. *International Journal of Instructional Technology and Distance Learning, 5*(5). Retrieved from http://itdl.org/journal/may_08/article02.htm

Thomas, D., & Brown, J. S. (2011). *A new culture of learning: Cultivating the imagination for a world of constant change.* CreateSpace Independent Publishing Platform (Amazon).

Tinto, V. (1975). Dropout from higher education: A theoretical synthesis of recent research. *Review of Educational Research, 45*(1), 89–125.

Toporski, N., & Foley, T. (2004). Design principles for online instruction: A new kind of classroom. *Turkish Online Journal of Distance Education, 5*(1). Retrieved from http://tojde.anadolu.edu.tr/tojde13/articles/toporski.html

Tudge, C. (2009). *The link: Uncovering our earliest ancestor.* New York: Little, Brown.

Tutor.com (2011, April 7). Tutor.com To Go™ releases the first education app that connects students to an expert tutor. *Tutor.com.* Retrieved from http://www.tutor.com/press/press-releases-2011/20110406

Tyler-Smith, K. (2006). Early attrition among first time eLearners: A review of factors that contribute to drop-out, withdrawal and non-completion rates of adult learners undertaking eLearning programmes. *Journal of Online Learning and Teaching, 2*(2). Retrieved from http://jolt.merlot.org/vol2no2/tyler-smith.htm

Usher, A., & Kober, N. (2012, May 22). *What nontraditional approaches can motivate unenthusiastic students?* Background paper 6 in Student Motivation—An overlooked piece of school reform. Center on Education Policy. The George Washington University, Washington, DC.

Varvel, V. Jr., Lindeman, M., & Stovall, I. (2003, July). The Illinois Online Network is making the virtual classroom a reality: Study of an exemplary faculty development program. *Journal of Asynchronous Learning Networks, 7*(2). Retrieved from http://sloanconsortium.org/jaln/v7n2/illinois-online-network-making-virtual-classroom-reality-study-exemplary-faculty-developme

Veletsianos, G., & Klanthous, I. (2009). A review of adventure learning. *International Review of Research in Open and Distance Learning, 10*(6), 84–105. Retrieved from http://www.irrodl.org/index.php/irrodl/article/view/755/1435

Vygotsky, L. S. (1978). *Mind in society.* Cambridge, MA: Harvard University Press.

Wang, Q., Woo, H. L., Quek, C. L., Yang, Y., & Liu, M. (2011). Using the Facebook group as a learning management system: An exploratory study. *British Journal of Educational Technology* [Early view online version]. doi:10.1111/j.1467-8535.2011.01195.x

Wang, S.-L., & Wu, P.-Y. (2007). Examining the role of feedback on self-efficacy and performance in Web-based environment. In *Second International Conference on Innovative Computing, Information and Control (ICICIC 2007)* (p.161). Los Alamitos, CA: IEEE Computer Society. Retrieved from http://doi.ieeecomputersociety.org/10.1109/ICICIC.2007.296

Warlick, D. (2009, December 9). 10 observations about backchannel. *2¢ Worth.* Retrieved from http://davidwarlick.com/2cents/?p=2088

Watson, G. (2000). PHYS345 electricity and electronics for engineers. In D. G. Brown (Ed.), *Teaching with technology: Seventy-five professors from eight universities tell their stories* (pp. 63–66). Boston: Anker.

Watson, J. B. (1930). *Behaviorism* (revised ed.). Chicago: University of Chicago Press, p. 82.

Watson, J. F. (2007, April). *A national primer on K–12 online learning.* NACOL. Retrieved from http://www.ncsl.org/print/educ/08AMNationalPrimer.pdf

Watson, J., Murin. A., Vashaw, L., Gemin, B., & Rapp, C., and colleagues at Evergreen Education Group (2010, November). *Keeping pace with K–12 online learning: An annual review of policy and practice*. Retrieved from http://www.kpk12.com/cms/wp-content/uploads/KeepingPaceK12_2010.pdf

Watters, A. (2011, April 27). Can gamification boost independent learning? *KQED MindShift Blog*. Retrieved from http://blogs.kqed.org/mindshift/2011/04/can-gamification-boost-independent-learning/

Webb, N. M., & Palincsar, A. S. (1996). Group processes in the classroom. In D. C. Berliner & R. C. Calfee (Eds.). *Handbook of educational psychology* (pp. 841–873). New York: Macmillan Library Reference.

Weiner, B. (1980). *Human motivation*. New York: Holt, Rinehart & Winston.

Wenger, E. (1998). *Communities of practice: Learning, meaning, and identity*. Cambridge: Cambridge University Press.

Wenger, M. S., & Ferguson, C. (2006). A learning ecology model for blended learning from Sun Microsystems. In C. J. Bonk & C. R. Graham (Eds.). *Handbook of blended learning: Global perspectives, local designs* (pp. 76-91). San Francisco: Pfeiffer.

Wikipedia Education Program. (2012). *Wikipedia*. Retrieved from http://outreach.wikimedia.org/wiki/Wikipedia_Education_Program

Williams, S. B. (1992). Putting case-based instruction into context: Examples from legal and medical education. *The Journal of the Learning Sciences, 2*(4), 367–427.

Willis, B. (1993). *Distance education: A practical guide*. Englewood Cliffs, NJ: Educational Technology Publications.

Wilson, H. J. (2012, April 2). Employees, measure yourselves. *Wall Street Journal*. Retrieved from http://online.wsj.com/article/SB10001424052970204520204577249691204802060.html

Winkler, K. (2011, October 18). Grocket Answers—Crowdsourced Q&A sites around YouTube and Vimeo videos. *Big Think*. Retrieved from http://bigthink.com/disrupt-education/grockit-answers-crowdsourced-qa-sites-around-youtube-and-vimeo-videos

wiseGEEK (n.d.). What does the "hot seat" mean? Retrieved from http://www.wisegeek.com/what-does-the-hot-seat-mean.htm

Wlodkowski, R. J. (1999). Motivation and diversity: A framework for teaching. *New Directions for Teaching and Learning, 1999*(78), 5–16. doi:10.1002/tl.7801

Wolcott, L. L. & Burnham, B. R. (1991). *Tapping into motivation: What adult learners find motivating about distance education*. In Proceedings of the 7th Annual Conference of Distance Teaching and Learning (pp. 220–227), Madison, WI.

Wolverton, B. (2011, July 7). New tool could help researchers make better use of oral histories. *Chronicle of Higher Education*. Retrieved from http://chronicle.com/blogs/players/new-tool-could-help-researchers-make-better-use-of-oral-histories/28855?sid=at&utm_source=at&utm_medium=en

Wortham, J. (2010, November 11). Social books hopes to make e-reading communal. *New York Times Blog*. Retrieved from http://bits.blogs.nytimes.com/2010/11/11/social-books-hopes-to-make-e-reading-communal/

Wright, N. (2011). Tweeting to reflect on teaching practicum experiences. *Waikato Journal of Education, 16*(1), 65–75. Retrieved from http://edlinked.soe.waikato.ac.nz/research/journal/view.php?article=true&id=708&p=8

Xie, K., & Ke, F. (2010). The role of students' motivation in peer-moderated asynchronous online discussions. *British Journal of Educational Technology, 42*(6), 916–930. doi:10.1111/j.1467-8535.2010.01140.x

Xie, K., DeBacker, T. K., & Ferguson, C. (2006). Extending the traditional classroom through online discussion: The role of student motivation. *Journal of Educational Computing Research, 34*(1), 68–78.

Xu, D., & Jaggars, S. S. (2011). *Online and hybrid course enrollment and performance in Washington State Community and technical colleges* (No. CCRC Working Paper No. 31). Columbia University, New York.

Yang, Y.-F. (2010). Cognitive conflicts and resolutions in online text revisions: Three profiles. *Educational Technology & Society, 13*(4), 202–214.

Yang, Y.-F., Yeh, H.-C., & Wong, W.-K. (2010). The influence of social interaction on meaning construction in a virtual community. *British Journal of Educational Technology, 41*(2), 287–306.

Yeh, H.-C., & Yang, Y.-F. (2011). Prospective teachers' insights towards scaffolding students' writing processes through teacher-student role reversal in an online system. *Educational Technology Research and Development, 59*(3), 351–368.

Young, J. (2011, January 2). Top smartphone apps to improve teaching, research, and your life. *Chronicle of Higher Education.* Retrieved from http://chronicle.com/article/College-20-6-Top-Smartphone/125764/

Young, J. R. (2008, September 25). When professors print their own diplomas, who needs universities? *Chronicle of Higher Education.* Retrieved from http://chronicle.com/article/When-Professors-Print-Their/1185/

Young, J. R. (2012, April 12). Students endlessly e-mail professors for help. A new service hopes to organize the answers. *Chronicle of Higher Education.* Retrieved from http://chronicle.com/article/Students-Endlessly-E-Mail/131390/

Young, L. (2011). Massive earthquake hits Japan. *Boston.com.* Retrieved from http://www.boston.com/bigpicture/2011/03/massive_earthquake_hits_japan.html

Young, S., & Bruce, M. A. (2011). Classroom community and student engagement in online courses. *Journal of Online Learning and Teaching, 7*(2). Retrieved from http://jolt.merlot.org/vol7no2/young_0611.htm

YouTube Video Blog (2008, June 4). *New beta feature: Video annotations.* Retrieved from http://youtube-global.blogspot.com/2008/06/new-beta-feature-video-annotations.html

Zainuddin, H., & Moore, R. A. (2003, June). Enhancing critical thinking with structured controversial dialogues. *The Internet TESL Journal, 9*(6). Retrieved from http://iteslj.org/Techniques/Zainuddin-Controversial.html

INDEX